D1440720

Surrogate Suburbs

To Nora,
with my very best wishes,

[signature]

Surrogate Suburbs

BLACK UPWARD MOBILITY

AND NEIGHBORHOOD CHANGE

IN CLEVELAND, 1900–1980

Todd M. Michney

THE UNIVERSITY OF NORTH CAROLINA PRESS

Chapel Hill

This book was published with the
assistance of the Anniversary Fund of
the University of North Carolina Press.

Designed by Rich Hendel
Set in Utopia, TheSerif, and Serifa types
by Tseng Information Systems, Inc.
Manufactured in the United States of America

The University of North Carolina Press has been a
member of the Green Press Initiative since 2003.

Cover illustration: Glenville's Kempton Avenue in 1956.
(Courtesy of the *Cleveland Press* Collection,
Cleveland State University Library)

Library of Congress Cataloging-in-Publication Data
Names: Michney, Todd M., author.
Title: Surrogate suburbs : black upward mobility and neighborhood
change in Cleveland, 1900–1980 / Todd M. Michney.
Description: Chapel Hill : The University of North Carolina Press, [2017] |
Includes bibliographical references and index.
Identifiers: LCCN 2016043313| ISBN 9781469631936 (cloth : alk. paper) |
ISBN 9781469631943 (pbk : alk. paper) | ISBN 9781469631950 (ebook)
Subjects: LCSH: Middle class African Americans—Housing—Ohio—Cleveland—History—
20th century. | Middle class African Americans—Ohio—Cleveland—History—20th century. |
Middle class African Americans—Ohio—Cleveland—Social conditions—20th century. |
Social mobility—Ohio—Cleveland—History—20th century. | Neighborhoods—Social aspects—
Ohio—Cleveland—History—20th century. | African American neighborhoods—Ohio—
Cleveland—History—20th century.
Classification: LCC E185.93.O2 M53 2017 | DDC 305.896/0730771320904—dc23
LC record available at https://lccn.loc.gov/2016043313

For Dad and Nihad

Contents

Maps, Tables, and Figures

Acknowledgments

Writing about one's hometown is simultaneously a joy, a burden, and a responsibility—or so it seems to me, having spent more than a decade's worth of time and energy on this project. Cleveland profoundly shaped my worldview and intellectual development before I ever aspired to professional training as a historian, in spite of my suburban upbringing—from the childhood field trips spent accompanying my father, a Cleveland public schoolteacher in some of the East Side neighborhoods I would ultimately study, to my solo explorations of downtown as a restless teenager, to my exhilarating undergraduate days at Case Western Reserve University. Long before I ever encountered them as concepts for scholarly study, I had opportunities to ponder racial, ethnic, and religious identities: in biannual visits with family friends in Glenville, during several years spent in a racially integrated Catholic grade school in Shaker Heights, and in the Orange City School District, which includes Woodmere, a substantially African American suburb. I am grateful for all my Cleveland experiences that, over time, helped me to better understand historic demographic shifts and patterns of upward mobility in the city and metropolitan area as a whole.

Along the way I have piled up immense intellectual debts and have been humbled by the generosity and encouragement of mentors, colleagues, friends, and family. First and foremost, I would like to express my gratitude to the staff at the University of North Carolina Press, and especially to editor Brandon Proia, who believed in this project from the very beginning and offered invaluable support throughout the entire process. Thank you also to Jad Adkins for handling practical matters and to Dorothea Anderson for outstanding copyediting, as well as to Jay Mazzocchi, Susan Garrett, and Kim Bryant for additional technical assistance. Extra special thanks to the anonymous reviewers who gave such generous and thoughtful suggestions on revisions. I also relished the opportunity, in preparing the final manuscript, to collaborate with an extraordinarily talented cartographer, Nat Case, on the accompanying maps; not only did he produce final drafts that far exceeded my expectations, but I got to hone my GIS skills in the process.

I am very fortunate to have had supportive mentors who encouraged my intellectual inquiries from undergraduate through graduate study and beyond.

I owe special debts to three in particular: John J. Grabowski at Case Western Reserve University and Rudolph Vecoli and David Roediger at the University of Minnesota. John first introduced me to the wonders of archival research in an undergraduate seminar and later supervised me when I worked as a manuscript processor at the Western Reserve Historical Society; he also was the first to suggest I consider pursuing a graduate degree in history. Rudy oversaw my training as I commenced graduate study in American immigration history and read numerous chapter drafts as my dissertation adviser; I particularly miss his directness and attention to detail, not to mention his twinkling gaze. Dave profoundly influenced my scholarly trajectory by expanding my knowledge of African American history and focusing my attention squarely on race, and after Rudy's untimely passing in 2008, Dave graciously mentored me through my early career. I have benefited from his sound advice on numerous occasions and am constantly amazed not just by his capacious mind, but also by his example as the very paragon of a mentor and colleague. Other particularly important teachers and mentors were Catherine Kelly, Kenneth Ledford, Erika Lee, Miriam Levin, Lary May, Jeani O'Brien, Richard Rudolph, and Angela Woollacott.

I have been blessed with supportive and engaging colleagues who helped me along the way in numerous capacities, from reading drafts and sharing valuable resources, to providing camaraderie and emotional support. At the University of Toledo, I would like to thank Ovamir Anjum, Charles Beatty-Medina, Diane Britton, Jon Elhai, Barbara Floyd, Kristin Geaman, Chelsea Griffis, Cynthia Ingham, Georgios Katsanos, Peter Linebaugh, Bob McCullough, Kim Nielsen, Bill O'Neal, Roberto Padilla, Ami Pflugrad-Jackisch, and Arjun Sabharwal. At Tulane, special thanks go to Rosanne Adderley, Jim Boyden, Emily Clark, Brian DeMare, Laura Kelley, Jana Lipman, Liz McMahon, Marline Otte, Larry Powell, Sam Ramer, Kaya Sahin, Randy Sparks, Sasha Turner, Patrick Wing, and Justin Wolfe. Most recently, at Georgia Tech, I would like to thank Dan Amsterdam, Ron Bayor, Laura Bier, Jennifer Clark, Amy D'Unger, Douglas Flamming, Steve Hodges, Anna Kim, Thomas Lodato, Gregory Nobles, Dean Jacqueline Royster, Taylor Shelton, Steve Usselman, and Naomi Williams.

For reading previous drafts of the manuscript or individual chapters, I owe special thanks to Thomas Guglielmo, Richard Harris, Andrew Kahrl, Beryl Satter, Mark Souther, and, most of all, Andrew Wiese. Without a doubt, Andy's intense and sometimes challenging critiques made this a far better book. I also benefited enormously from participation in the 2010–11 Distinguished Faculty/Graduate Seminar on New Metropolitan Studies and the Long Civil Rights Movement, organized by Angela Dillard and Matt Lassiter at the University of Michigan, where I enjoyed lively conversations with numerous participants, especially Heidi Ardizzone, Stephen Berry, Matthew Countryman, Danielle McGuire, Karen Miller, Khalil Muhammad, Kevin Mumford, Sherie

Randolph, Heather Ann Thompson, and Kidada Williams. Other academic colleagues who have shown interest in my work and offered encouragement over the past two decades include Matt Basso, Lee Bernstein, Al Broussard, Paul Buhle, John Bukowczyk, Margot Canaday, Gregory Conerly, Catherine Conner, Nathan Connolly, Elizabeth Faue, Robert Frame, David Freund, Kevin Gaines, Tim Gilfoyle, Paul Gilmore, Colin Gordon, Jennifer Guglielmo, David Hammack, Joel Helfrich, Jeff Helgeson, Deborah Henry, Rebecca Hill, Dave Hochfelder, Kwame Holmes, Bradford Hunt, Alison Isenberg, Kenneth Jackson, Alphine Jefferson, Ann Keating, Lisa Keller, Daniel Kerr, Lionel Kimble, Ania Kirchmann, Tracy K'Meyer, Nancy Kwak, Daniel LaChance, Michael Lansing, Matt Lasner, Bernard Maegi, Matt Martin, Rachel Barrett Martin, Joyce Mastboom, Glenn McNair, Zane Miller, Matt Mulcahy, Yuichiro Onishi, Dominic Pacyga, Adam Pagán, Larry Peskin, Kimberley Phillips, Wendy Plotkin, Wendell Pritchett, Peter Rutkoff, Mike Ryan, Tom Sabatini, Andrew Simpson, Mark Soderstrom, José Sola, David Stradling, Joel Tarr, Henry Louis Taylor, Mark Tebeau, Joe Trotter Jr., Sylvia Hood Washington, Jay Wendelberger, Regennia Williams, and Rhonda Y. Williams.

Archivists, librarians, and other students of Cleveland history have assisted me tremendously in pursuing research on this project and helping to promote my work. At the Western Reserve Historical Society, special thanks are due to Jane Avner, Sam Black, Ben Blake, Margaret Burzynski-Bays, Vicki Catozza, George Cooper, Pamela Dorazio Dean, Nishani Frazier, Sean Martin, Michael McCormick, Kermit Pike, Chuck Piotrowski, Ann Sindelar, and Cathy Yandek. At Cleveland State University's Special Collections, I am indebted to Bill Barrow and Lynn Bycko. At Case Western Reserve University's Special Collections, my thanks go to Mary Burns and Susie Hanson, and at its Freedman Center for Digital Scholarship, to Ann Holstein (whose GIS skills helped me out of binds aplenty). At the Cleveland City Council Archives, I relied on the expertise of Martin Hauserman. At the Cleveland Diocesan Archives, I thank Christine Krosel. At Cleveland Public Library, Elaine Herroon, Karen Martines, Brian Meggitt, and Rekiat Olayiwola offered inestimable help. I greatly enjoyed writing a historical retrospective as the lead op-ed for a 2008 series on the Mount Pleasant neighborhood that appeared in the *Plain Dealer*; special thanks to Sandra Livingston, Phillip Morris, and Bob Paynter for giving me that opportunity. Clark Dougan, Raymond Jirran, and Edward Miggins have shown a constant interest in the project, with Ed passing me crucial materials otherwise unavailable at several points. Finally, the Cleveland Restoration Society's recent efforts to have the Bussey Homes Subdivision designated a historic landmark, a project headed up by Kathleen Crowther and Michael Fleenor, provided me with a much-needed boost toward the end of the project, not to mention a welcome opportunity for collaboration.

Extra special thanks go to all of my interviewees, who allowed me to ask them about, and trusted me to record, their personal experiences. Individuals who went above and beyond the call were: Eugene Brudno, Adeline Davis, Joseph DeLuca, Jean Dorgham, Ezra Giterman, Stanley Lasky, Collins Munns, Seymour Press, the late Councilwoman Odelia Robinson, Joseph Russo, Harold Ticktin, Dr. Gerald and Roleen Waxman, and Donna Whyte. Community members whose advice was particularly useful, but who were not specifically interviewed for the study, include Judge Jean Murrell Capers, Richard M. Peery, and the late Jean Y. Tussey.

I could not have completed this book without the support of friends and family, or the guidance provided by additional life mentors outside of academia. Among my Cleveland friends, I cannot thank Charles Peirce enough for hosting me at his house while conducting research in town, only the latest help he has offered me in a friendship extending back over a quarter century. Many thanks to Dave Bortz for treating me to inspiring dinners, and for the supplementary wage work that helped make ends meet. For physical and spiritual training, I cannot begin to express my profound gratitude to Jisui Craig Horton, Sifu Aaron Arden, Craig Kiessling, Allen Carroll, and Imam Shamsuddin Waheed. For delightful fellowship over the past year I would also like to thank my friends Nathan Delaney, Greg Zinman, Lauren Klein, Yanni Loukissas, Kate Diedrick, Jake Selwood, Ann Claycombe, Nassim Jafarinaimi, Azad Naeemi, Javier Garcia, Dawn Peterson, Mark Liebert, Narin Hassan, Max Brzezinski, Sarah Harlan, Troyce Docherty, and Jack Carson.

A source of strength for me has always been my family, whose encouragement and assistance enabled me to pursue this life path and career. I thank my mother, Patricia, and my late father, Michael, for supporting my educational and career choices emotionally and financially, and for taking a keen interest in this project. I am forever thankful to my late grandmother, Agnes, for allowing me to set up in her basement and write, and for the time we shared during those years. Special thanks to my brother, Jay, and his partner, Nancy, for accommodating me on research trips to Washington, D.C., and for all the fun and delicious dinners together. Thanks to my sister, Michelle, and her partner, John, for hosting me on their amazing farm, where I got the chance to tend to different projects and take joy from other sorts of digging besides just in the archives. Most of all, I would like to express my sincere and profound thanks to my dear life partner, Nihad, for your brilliant insights on and peerless copyediting of the manuscript, not to mention your companionship and unwavering supportiveness on a daily basis. What a pleasure it has been to have merged our family circles; I so appreciate the encouragement this project has received from my new relatives, Dr. Faheem and Mariam Farooq, Nabil and Mariam Hyder Farooq, and dear Mumma Jaan, whom we miss so much.

Surrogate Suburbs

Introduction

"SECOND GHETTO" OR SURROGATE SUBURB?

BLACK MOBILITY IN THE TWENTIETH-CENTURY OUTER CITY

You can squeeze 'em in the ghetto,
An' with written covenant,
Make 'em live in teeming hovels
Where they pay excessive rent.
You can threaten banks an' bankers
An' make money hard to get,
But there'll always be some fishes
Who escape the jim-crow net.

So in free an' liberal Cleveland
Where the bigots hide their hand
There has been a constant movement
To the East Side "promised land"
'Cause the lure of ready money
An' the yen to make a buck
Is what trips the race-containers
Who are simply out of luck.

Sure the banks refuse you money,
An' the neighbors start to yell,
An' the bigots stir their stooges
Into raisin' lots of hell.
But the movin' finger's writin'
An' the words are plain as day,
An' the courts have spoken plainly
That jim-crow is dead to stay.

An' us Negroes on the sidelines
Have to give a silent cheer,
To the Negro who is willing,
To become a pioneer
On the road that leads away from
Rotten houses in the ghetto
An' who're deaf to racial discord
Of the bigots liberetto [sic].[1]

1

Penned in mid-1953 by Charles H. Loeb, the managing editor of Cleveland's main black newspaper, this "Editorial in Rhyme" expressed confidence that housing opportunities for African Americans were improving, even as it underlined the unacceptable living conditions still faced by many. In writing these verses for the *Call & Post*, Loeb alluded to recent U.S. Supreme Court rulings that had begun to address decades of legally sanctioned residential segregation: *Shelley v. Kraemer*, the 1948 landmark decision that invalidated deed restrictions against racial minorities, as well as *Barrows v. Jackson*, which had reaffirmed *Shelley* just one month earlier. Such progress notwithstanding, Loeb simultaneously emphasized the economic underpinnings of the "ghetto," where an artificial housing shortage ensured that many African Americans had little choice but to pay exorbitant prices for overcrowded and dilapidated housing. But on the general direction of the black freedom struggle, Loeb was an optimist. He had reported on civil rights gains as a World War II correspondent for the Negro Newspapers Publishing Association, and in a 1947 book he had chronicled the successes of the Future Outlook League—a militant local pressure group to which he belonged—dedicating it "to the new generation of American Negroes, who are no longer content with second-class citizenship, and who intend to do something about it." In another rhymed editorial from earlier in 1953, Loeb had exhorted readers, "Don't be a dope an' give up hope / When vic'try's close at hand / I can remember when the world / Was rougher on the colored man," and then gone on to enumerate some of the Jim Crow indignities he had witnessed prior to his relocation north during the Great Depression.[2]

Loeb satirized Cleveland's supposed exemplary race relations record while evincing a shrewd understanding both of racially inflected housing market dynamics and an increasingly visible shift in the geographic setting for black upward mobility. In fact, the opening poem took its inspiration from a move by the first African American couple into Lee-Harvard, a still partially undeveloped neighborhood in the city's southeastern corner with new ranches and colonials resembling those on the nearby suburban streets of posh Shaker Heights. This event did not transpire without controversy, but with the city providing adequate police protection to the couple, Wendell and Genevieve Stewart, and after two weeks of mediation presided over by the mayor himself, Cleveland successfully preempted the violent retaliation that white residents not uncommonly mounted in response to black residential expansion in other cities—hence Loeb's sarcastic yet accurate characterization of "free an' liberal Cleveland / Where the bigots hide their hand."

That the Stewarts deserved praise for standing up to white prejudice and taking on the role of "pioneers"—a term commonly applied at the time to the initial African American families crossing residential color barriers[3]—may seem obvious. But Loeb tactfully declined to mention that the couple was motivated to leave their previous neighborhood, Glenville, because an influx of less-affluent African Americans and subsequent overcrowding was fostering what they regarded as increasingly untenable living conditions there. Thus the Stewarts' move away from an erstwhile black middle-class stronghold to all-white Lee-Harvard could be celebrated as unambiguous progress, as a collective step "On the road that leads away from / Rotten houses in the ghetto," only if it served to expand black Clevelanders' housing opportunities on the whole. Indirectly, such moves did hold that potential, of which Loeb was certainly aware. At the time, whites typically fled neighborhoods as African American buyers gained a foothold—an increasingly common outcome considering the interplay between rising black middle-class incomes and white suburbanization after World War II. Despite generally having to pay more (hence Loeb's reference to "the lure of ready money / An' the yen to make a buck"), such moves by pioneering families like the Stewarts did sometimes unlock entire new areas for African American occupancy. Indeed, this is exactly what happened as Lee-Harvard, like Glenville before it, transitioned to become almost entirely black in little more than a decade. Strikingly, increasing numbers of aspiring African American families repeated this cycle of outward movement in search of an improved quality of life as they began departing Lee-Harvard for several nearby suburbs in the mid-1970s.

This underlying context for Loeb's editorial forms the subject of *Surrogate Suburbs*, which recovers the numerous ways in which African Americans dynamically and creatively engaged with space at the urban periphery, thereby transforming it into a critically important locus of black middle-class social, economic, and political life over the course of the Great Migration era. From the turn of the twentieth century, until its final decades when the tide of Southern migration reversed and black suburbanization began in earnest, outer-city "places" increasingly supplanted older, central city neighborhoods as the context and focus for African American individual and collective aspiration, for economic and social mobility, for class and status formation, and for politics, protest, and reform. In short, the outer city can tell us a great deal about the meaning of life for African Americans over much of the twentieth century, and it needs further consideration as a counterpoint to inner-city "ghettoes"[4] and the reigning scholarly tendency to generalize life in those settings as constituting the quintessential black urban experience. As my subtitle suggests, the meanings of neighborhood "change" must be broadened to consider the lives and choices of more African American "outer-city" dwellers. While demographic turnover frequently correlated with decline in the minds of both white and upwardly mobile black observers, I refer to "changing neighborhoods" as a strategy of outward geographic mobility historically used not just by middle-class blacks but by members of numerous racial and ethnic groups in search of better living conditions.[5] In another and even more profound sense, however, "changing neighborhoods" for African Americans has meant attempting to improve and transform their living environments in order to maintain an acceptable quality of life.[6] While both of these senses of the verb "to change" demonstrate African American agency and a dynamic engagement with urban space, they also suggest converse approaches: either to stay put and confront the existing conditions, or else to move on.

Recent scholarship on race and inequality in U.S. cities has underlined the numerous constraints African Americans faced in the housing market, from federal policy that institutionalized inequity in mortgage lending, to the violent resistance of white homeowners, to the mass population displacements caused by urban redevelopment.[7] Such works have uncovered the roots of white working-class "illiberalism" that divided the New Deal constituency long before the tumultuous 1960s and also thoroughly debunked popular explanations implying that black residents themselves bear the blame for post–World War II urban decline. But notwithstanding its many valuable insights, this scholarship often has downplayed black agency—sometimes even tending toward portraying African Americans as hapless victims of structural forces beyond their control.[8] To the extent that class differences among African Americans have been treated in these works, blacks with comparatively more resources have not uncommonly been faulted for wanting to move to areas of the city with newer, better housing. While fully acknowledging and continuing to investigate the inequities that even better-off African Americans endured, the present study extends the conversation with its prioritization of personal agency and dignity, demonstrating how African Americans went about living and striving in spite of serious and continuous discriminatory barriers. Instead of a government-abetted "second ghetto," I follow upwardly mobile blacks in reimagining as "surrogate suburbs" the newer, outlying city neighborhoods to which they moved in pursuit of their aspirations.[9] By documenting the patience, persistence, pragmatism, and frequent success such upwardly mobile residents had in improving their life circumstances, I offer a less pessimistic perspective on the postwar city, a potential counterweight to renditions emphasizing urban decline and black victimization. And, by carrying the story past 1965 during a period when localized class relations between African American residents took on greater and largely unacknowledged significance, my work resists the implication that white departure was the most salient development in the history of postwar U.S. cities.

The present work builds upon studies of African American urban communities emphasizing agency and creative forms of resistance,[10] while extending the insights of this scholarship in several important ways. By turning our focus to upwardly mobile families of middling economic status—families headed by postal workers, tradesmen, and chauffeurs, as well as professionals—unexamined strategies and successes of a nascent black middle class emerge.

Notably, these outlying black families succeeded in getting financing in the pre–New Deal mortgage market, even borrowing from nearby whites in some cases. African Americans were always present in small numbers at the edges of cities—including in suburbs, a phenomenon most extensively explored by historian Andrew Wiese. However, the outer city held far more significance for upwardly mobile African Americans prior to the onset of mass black suburbanization starting in the 1960s. First, the numbers gaining access to outlying city neighborhoods up to that point were more substantial. Second, early African American suburbanization was generally a working-class survival strategy marked by rudimentary living conditions, so blacks moving there were motivated primarily by reasons other than status.[11]

Cleveland is an important yet relatively understudied locale for such an inquiry. In 1920, it was the nation's fifth-largest city and a primary producer of steel and automobiles, alongside Chicago, Detroit, and many smaller industrial centers of the Great Lakes region. When Cleveland's population peaked in 1950 at nearly 915,000 residents, it had a growing black population of more than 147,000, the tenth largest in the country and not far behind that of Los Angeles, which ranked eighth at the time. African Americans living in Cleveland that year outnumbered those in Memphis, Birmingham, Atlanta, Newark, Norfolk, Oakland, San Francisco, Miami, Boston, and Milwaukee—all of whose communities have received more scholarly attention. But despite upswings in production associated with World War II and the Korean War that bolstered a continuing influx of black Southerners, Cleveland entered a slow but steady economic decline in the postwar decades. Capital flight by industries seeking lower labor costs increasingly subsumed the city along with the rest of the formerly robust region into what became known as the "Rust Belt." By 1980, population loss had dropped Cleveland from the ten largest American cities, its rank falling precipitously to eighteenth.[12] African Americans fared disproportionately worse amid deindustrialization, and while those with middle-class jobs were less directly affected, a contracting local economy both impeded the overall potential for black upward mobility and had neighborhood-level ramifications.

The general pattern of black residential expansion in Cleveland resembled that in many Northern cities, including Chicago and Detroit. In the early twentieth century, relatively small numbers of African Americans successfully established footholds in outlying neighborhoods like Cleveland's Mount Pleasant, Glenville, Lee-Seville, and West Park, typically settling in compact enclaves.[13] Their life experiences and opportunities correspondingly diverged from those of the vast majority of black Clevelanders, who were confined to a large, increasingly overcrowded, single contiguous residential district extending dozens of blocks to the east of downtown, known as Cedar-Central (after its main thoroughfares). To the extent that their relatively well-off inhabitants could build or acquire newer and better-quality housing, outlying black settlements held the potential, at least, to visibly refute the stereotypes that increasingly linked African Americans with the decline of inner-city neighborhoods. While definitely the exception at the outset of the period under study, the experiences of African Americans living in the "outer city" became more and more mainstream in the decades after World War II, when the existing boundaries of black settlement burst and dramatically expanded—a process driven in large part by white departures to suburbs from which African Americans were largely excluded for decades. A complicated dynamic somewhat simplistically rendered as the result of "white flight," this postwar expansion of African American living space included both incremental growth at the edges of existing black settlements and the rapid demographic turnover of entire formerly white neighborhoods like Lee-Harvard.

In the first decades of the twentieth century, a racially segregated, "dual" housing market emerged that constrained black housing options, which in turn fostered overcrowding and the deterioration of housing stock—a trajectory that became a virtual self-fulfilling prophecy in most African American neighborhoods. In an effort to maintain an acceptable quality of life, upwardly mobile blacks frequently felt compelled to move beyond established areas. While sociologist William Julius Wilson famously asserted in *The Truly Disadvantaged* (1987) that 1960s civil rights reforms enabled middle-class blacks to spatially disassociate themselves from their less-fortunate brethren, scholars going back to W. E. B. Du Bois in *The Philadelphia Negro* (1899) have noted the phenomenon of geographic class stratification in African American communities, even if this amounted to nothing more than the well-to-do clustering together at the edges of settlements of poorer black residents. Clearly, black middle-class aspirations have historically depended on constantly expanding housing options. Though invested in the expansion of civil rights protections, most upwardly mobile African Americans nevertheless adapted to the racially structured housing market by accepting incremental gains. At the same time, middle-class blacks had fewer means available to maintain geographic distance, and so this separation often proved temporary with African American neighborhoods exhibiting a greater admixture of socioeconomic levels than white ones.[14]

In accomplishing residential mobility at a time when the force of segregation was reshaping entire metropolitan areas, African Americans like those examined in this study utilized a variety of strategies over time, although their motivations for moving remained remarkably consistent. In the earliest decades, they purchased land before race-based restrictions could be inserted into deeds, and in many cases built their own houses. Prior to the Great Depression, they borrowed from a handful of black-owned institutions and sought out profit-minded whites willing to issue them mortgages. After World War II, they tapped African American contractors and a small but growing number of white-owned construction firms willing to service the black housing market. Increasingly, they depended upon African American and white real estate brokers to expand the available housing options, even when this entailed aggressive and controversial sales tactics (blockbusting) and despite having to pay a premium. Over the entire period of this study, upwardly mobile African American Clevelanders moved to areas populated by Southern and Eastern Europeans, and especially Jews, who did not typically respond with violent resistance. In addition, they bolstered their economic security and cemented middle-class status by engaging multiple family members, including wives, in work for wages. Practically without exception, African Americans of middling status moved to the urban periphery to escape (or preempt) worsening living conditions in older neighborhoods. To them, outward geographic mobility meant better opportunities, more pleasant surroundings, more space, and newer and better schools and shopping facilities, as well as more prestigious housing and prosperous neighbors that made for "showcase" communities.[15]

In the economic, social, and political life of the city's black middling classes, outer-city spaces and places—as well as the people they encountered there—played a variety of roles and distinctly shaped their identities. African Americans living on the urban periphery were initially outnumbered by whites and so faced greater difficulty negotiating through formal political channels for access to public facilities—such as swimming pools—than did their counterparts living in Cedar-Central. Therefore, they were even more likely to demand fair treatment and protection from city officials by emphasizing their rights as citizens, homeowners, and taxpayers. While some black observers in the earliest decades expressed resentment at city officials' seeming favoritism toward Southern and Eastern European "foreigners" who had made earlier inroads into local Democratic Party politics, others formed strategic alliances with whites from these same ethnic groups in protesting racial discrimination, whether under Communist Party auspices or through membership in liberal intergroup relations organizations. Many more participated actively in block clubs and neighborhood councils with white residents similarly interested in maintaining "high standards" of property upkeep and personal comportment. Some black homeowners on the urban periphery even joined forces with whites living nearby to oppose postwar plans for public housing, although this alliance, in Cleveland as elsewhere, proved to be a brief and pragmatic one. But for the most part, upwardly mobile African Americans' feelings on racial integration ranged from ambivalence to indifference, as they and their white neighbors typically maintained a formal social distance. As their outlying neighborhoods became increasingly African American into the postwar decades, middle-class blacks continued to develop their already rich organizational life and worried that the increasing numbers of less-prosperous "newcomers" arriving from the inner city or the American South might be unable or unwilling to maintain lifestyles resembling theirs. Setting forth self-congratulatory explanations for their own comparative success, many proved more likely to criticize their new neighbors' property stewardship and parenting skills than to interpret neighborhood living conditions in the larger structural context of a contracting local economy.

In effect, outer-city neighborhoods for much of the twentieth century served upwardly mobile blacks as "surrogate suburbs"—places offering newer, better-quality housing and amenities compared to the inner city, where the African American masses had long been residentially confined. As certain bona fide suburbs like Shaker Heights, East Cleveland, and Warrensville Heights (among others) became increasingly accessible to the black middle class, the outer city began to lose its luster. African Americans of middling means who were increasingly able to move to the urban periphery—particularly in the decades following World War II—recognized the limits of their own agency in the face of institutionalized racial discrimination and structural inequality, but surely did not consider their new neighborhoods as the "second ghetto" theorized by historians following Arnold Hirsch. While this historiography has been valuable for its many insights into the larger macroeconomic and policy contexts fostering racial inequality, we should listen to the very different, neighborhood-level assessments of black agency made by upwardly mobile African Americans themselves, who were often more successful than the existing literature has implied.

■

Expanding the available housing options for African Americans often meant moving into solidly white neighborhoods, with the attendant potential for racial conflict. Accordingly, historians examining the growth of black settlement have emphasized the collective, violent retaliation whites not uncommonly visited upon African Americans who dared to cross the color line, in an attempt to halt (or at least delay) racial residential transition. Such violence was particularly intense in Chicago, Detroit, Philadelphia, Los Angeles, Kansas City, Dallas, and Atlanta—not to mention Birmingham, where the ferocity of white resistance earned that city the nickname "Bombingham." White resistance was especially rife over two particular intervals: in the years immediately following World War I and in the early 1950s, with Arnold Hirsch terming the latter period in Chicago an "era of hidden violence."[16] But on this question, too, Cleveland points toward a somewhat different model for understanding race-based demographic change in twentieth-century U.S. cities. Considering Cleveland's reputation through the 1950s of supposed racial liberalism, the question of violent resistance deserves particular scrutiny.[17] While Clevelanders' tolerance was certainly exaggerated by the city's political and business leadership as well as its social service establishment, the city did not experience anything remotely approaching the sustained and highly organized violence mounted by white residents in cities like Chicago and Detroit. While isolated incidents (mostly of vandalism) did indeed accompany the process of neighborhood demographic transition in Cleveland, none of these escalated into the "massive resistance" against residential integration that some scholars imply was practically as fierce toward residential integration in the urban North as to dismantling Jim Crow segregation in the South.[18]

Peripheral neighborhoods resembling the ones I study have been previously described as "undefended"[19] in terms of how whites responded to demographic change, but this descriptor does not capture the complex dynamics at play, nor how these outlying black middle-class expansion areas fit into larger patterns of race relations on the metropolitan level. Whites reacted to black residential expansion on Cleveland's urban periphery in a variety of ways over the course of the twentieth century, but in two distinct phases. In the earliest decades, the most common white response was indifference, although some whites did extend formal neighborly relations to blacks in these areas. However, when African Americans tried to use nearby public recreational facilities like swimming pools, whites commonly resorted to collective intimidation and violence. Early cross-racial encounters took these forms because outlying black residential enclaves were small and comparatively insular, and also because African Americans were settling on the still-developing urban periphery simultaneously with (or sometimes even before) white arrivals. Deed restrictions proved impractical in many of these vicinities, in part because Southern and Eastern Europeans living here were also considered "undesirable" by the mainstream real estate industry into the 1930s. This situation enabled African Americans both to acquire property and to gradually expand their existing settlements, which in turn convinced whites in the surrounding areas to more readily relinquish housing amid the slack Depression-era market. From World War II into the 1960s, as the presence of African Americans increased dramatically in these neighborhoods, a new set of white responses emerged. These included collaboration with black neighbors in organized efforts to "stabilize" communities and promote intergroup tolerance; the implementation of zoning changes to cordon off established African American settlements; scattered incidents of low-level violence, including property vandalism and fistfights among teenagers; expressions of resentment and withdrawal from participation in community life; and, most commonly, suburban flight. Thus, while neighborhood demographic transition in Cleveland was certainly characterized by tension, the process unfolded in a considerably less violent manner than in better-studied Chicago and Detroit.

A number of factors help explain Cleveland's divergence from patterns seen in these nearby cities. First, in striking contrast to Chicago and Detroit,

Cleveland's civic and business leadership proved proactive and remarkably evenhanded in mediating race-based controversies, perhaps surprising considering assessments of the first several postwar mayors as mere "caretaker" figures presiding over a parochial, ward-based political process in a city where business elites often held considerable decision-making power.[20] Even before Cleveland established its Community Relations Board in early 1945—following the example of numerous other U.S. cities but the first to do so by means of an ordinance passed by city council—its mayors had a fairly good record of providing police protection for African American residents who dared to move into white neighborhoods or who sought access to public recreational facilities, in part due to pressure from local black leaders, activists, and journalists. The Community Relations Board repeatedly proved its efficacy in mediating racial conflicts, the most serious of which was the aforementioned 1953 Wendell and Genevieve Stewart case in which Mayor Thomas Burke personally intervened. This hands-on approach stands in stark contrast both to Detroit, where conservative Republican mayor Albert Cobo hamstrung the Mayor's Interracial Committee in 1954 as a favor to exclusionary homeowners' associations, and Chicago, where the Commission on Human Relations abandoned its former activist approach and acceded to white homeowner prejudice in the 1950s. Cleveland's civic-business leadership approach produced far less contentious outcomes and served to burnish Cleveland's national reputation at the time for comparatively placid race relations.[21] Even as racial tensions subsequently mounted and ultimately broke out in the form of a 1966 riot in the city's Hough neighborhood, business leaders made the bold choice to support Carl B. Stokes in his successful 1967 campaign to become the first black mayor of a major American city. In order to facilitate more rapid and effective responses to incidents of racial tension, Cleveland's political and business leaders also worked closely with the local social service establishment and human relations groups, which over the years had institutionalized and coordinated their organizational infrastructure to a much greater extent than in other cities.[22]

Second, ethnic and religious factors among white residents in Cleveland's outer-city neighborhoods contributed to a less fractious pattern of demographic transition. Whereas many scholars have found uniformly negative white responses and argued that opposition to black incursion served to unite whites of different backgrounds—indeed, to solidify the category of "white" identity itself[23]—in Cleveland, ethnic and religious divisions shaped divergent responses and decisions. Whites of different backgrounds reacted more or less disconcertedly, some departing sooner and others later, with patterns hardly resembling unanimity. When interviewed by journalists and other contemporary researchers, some white residents (especially Jews and Protestants) claimed they had anticipated eventual demographic transition, and so were relatively unfazed. Others were cognizant of socioeconomic distinctions among blacks, which helped moderate their anxieties and extend the timing of their plans to move, even if this ultimately proved insufficient to convince them to stay. Even homeowners' associations, often described as powerful gatekeepers inhibiting African American access and which typically included whites of diverse ethnic origins, proved largely ineffectual in Cleveland. In fact, whenever organized white homeowners did attempt to thwart black entry, city officials and the local social service establishment—along with African American and white resident activists—successfully countermobilized to offer alternatives in the form of interracial "community councils," or else intervened to steer antiblockbusting efforts in nonracist directions. To be sure, racial tensions clearly accompanied the process of neighborhood demographic transition in Cleveland, with racialized anxieties sometimes finding expression in both politics and policy (for example, in battles over zoning and land development plans). However, these complex dynamics suggest we should pay more attention to such neighborhoods, instead of essentially footnoting them as "undefended."[24] Indeed, Cleveland's preponderance of neighborhoods where racial transition proceeded relatively smoothly should halt any notion that a prevailing, violent white solidarity was the norm.

The significance of Cleveland's historic Jewish neighborhoods as potential areas for African American residential expansion cannot be underestimated. As of 1920, Cleveland's Jewish population was the fourth largest in the country and was approximately twice the size of much-larger Detroit's; at an estimated 100,000, some 13 percent of the city total, Cleveland's proportion of Jewish population was second only to New York City's at the time.[25] Numerous observers have noted that Jews did not violently resist black influx, in contrast to ethnic Roman Catholics whose more permanent, less "portable" religious edifices (to mention one factor) made them more prone to territoriality.[26] My study adds considerably to our knowledge of black-Jewish relations, a history that has been investigated with regard to the leadership and decades-long collaboration between both groups on civil rights issues, but that could certainly benefit from closer scrutiny at the neighborhood level.[27] Thorny topics receive detailed attention herein, including the presence of Jewish-owned businesses in African American neighborhoods, the role of black domestic workers in Jewish homes, black-Jewish collaboration in Communist Party activism, mutual prejudices between the two groups, and the scapegoating of Jewish residents by other whites for their decisions to relocate. Furthermore, this study confirms that Jews were generally more willing than other white ethnics to participate in community-based efforts to improve race relations, a commitment which sometimes outlasted their own departure for the suburbs.[28]

As the white presence in these outer-city neighborhoods diminished into the mid-1960s, the predominant focus for tension increasingly shifted from interracial to *intra*racial and became specifically class-based. To understand the potential for social friction along these lines, a necessary first step is to briefly outline the complications surrounding African Americans' historic understandings of the category "middle class." Prior to the passage of the 1964 Civil Rights Act, the class structure of black communities differed significantly from that in the white-dominated society at large. African Americans were almost completely shut out of white-collar work and were hindered from practicing skilled trades, apart from whatever employment black-owned businesses and communities generated. In cities, including Cleveland, a small number found positions in government service, notably at the Post Office. African American proprietors, as well as professionals like doctors and lawyers, typically earned less than their white counterparts because their clientele was poorer. Jobs that lacked overall societal prestige, such as waiters, chauffeurs, and doormen, were considered high status because these positions offered far better pay than the unskilled labor to which most black men were relegated, entailed direct responsibility and a degree of personal autonomy, and necessarily involved close contact with wealthy and powerful whites. Self-employment, even of a marginal sort, enabled some individuals to circumvent the racially discriminatory job market; for example, owning a truck could make one a small-scale, hauling entrepreneur. Income-pooling also characterized African American households early on, because most black women worked for wages; earnings contributed by wives not only boosted economic security but also worked as a potential lever of upward mobility. Thus families where the wife held a "respectable" position like schoolteacher were often deemed middle-class even if the husband worked at a menial job.[29] In considering these factors, I have borrowed Burton J. Bledstein's descriptor "middling" to describe the class position of the black families studied here—thereby hoping to encompass the most flexible range of comparatively remunerative work available to some African Americans while recognizing that black class formation cannot be reduced simply to occupational structure, with the additional complication that what constituted "middle class" was simultaneously evolving in the society as a whole.[30]

Homeownership was an increasingly significant marker of middle-class status in the early twentieth century, and a crucial goal for African Americans of middling status—even though its growing importance was in part premised on their formal exclusion from the newest, more heavily capitalized housing developments springing up in outer-city neighborhoods and suburbs during the 1910s and 1920s. Middle-class interest in housing as a long-term "investment" took shape in the context of government campaigns promoting new, modern housing; novel financing methods (notably mortgage bonds) that enabled pricier, larger-scale developments with houses preconnected to electrical and sewer grids; proliferating building code regulations aimed at curbing improvised, self-built housing; and a professionalizing real estate industry that sought to standardize assessment practices across markets, in no small part by defining African Americans (regardless of class) as a "detrimental" influence on housing prices and long-term neighborhood stability.[31] But the reality was even more complicated. While Margaret Garb, in her study of Chicago in the decades leading up to World War I, does mention that "property rights in housing, even in a racially segregated block, had become a mark of status for the black middle classes" by the turn of the century, for the most part her findings underscore that not just middle-class whites, but even working-class immigrant homeowners increasingly internalized the "dramatic shift in the social function of property rights in housing" described above.[32]

Amid solidifying antiblack assumptions with regard to property acquisition—and to a considerable degree as a result of such sentiments—African American homeowners pursuing upward mobility faced a fundamental predicament in the Great Migration era: the increasingly segregated, overcrowded, and deteriorating living conditions that accompanied the influx of Southern migrants into inner-city districts like Chicago's Black Belt, providing a powerful incentive to relocate to the urban periphery insofar as this was possible. Mapping the locations of Cleveland's 1,521 homeowning black households in 1930 (nearly 9 percent of the total) makes their situation immediately obvious, both confirming the enormity of racial segregation and highlighting those places where it was breached (Map I.1). Clearly, the vast majority of black homeowners remained concentrated in Cedar-Central,[33] the eighty-block district containing nearly 90 percent of the city's African American population in that census year, particularly in its eastern reaches beyond East 79th Street. The houses here were newer, many built around the turn of the century by the prior Czech immigrant residents, although even in this portion of the neighborhood less than one-quarter of all black families owned their homes. In the Depression decade that followed, Cedar-Central's ghettoization continued as Southern migrants kept arriving, as homes were further and further subdivided to accommodate more tenants, and as the city's initial redevelopment projects in the district's western portion displaced poorer residents eastward. In 1939, Home Owners Loan Corporation evaluators noted "a concerted effort" by the section's "better class colored" to relocate to Glenville, where small numbers of African Americans had successfully purchased during the previous two decades.[34] Thus, even as they themselves were targeted by the new real estate regime, African American homebuyers were not immune to its logic; the future aspirations of upwardly mobile black Clevelanders lay in the city's outer wards, where they would encounter working-class Southern and Eastern European settlements as well as modern subdivisions with race-based deed restrictions, at a time when the meaning and potential of homeownership was changing for everyone. That African Americans sought to act like any

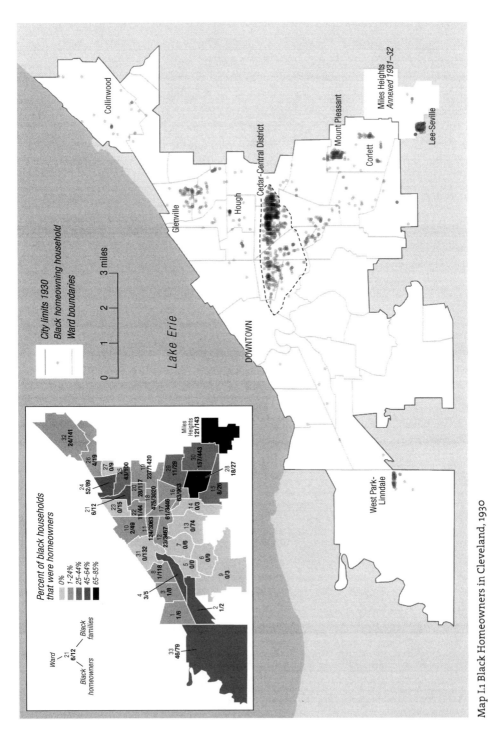

Map I.1 Black Homeowners in Cleveland, 1930

Sources: U.S. Manuscript Census, 1930; *Cleveland City Directory, 1930* (Cleveland City Directory Co., 1930); Property Deeds, Cuyahoga County Recorders Office, Cleveland, Ohio.

other property owners despite the discrimination directed against them is further illustrated by the fact that many of those who left behind neighborhoods like Cedar-Central retained their former homes as "investment property."[35]

Two concepts offer deep insights into the historic worldviews and lived experience of African American middle-class homeowners in neighborhoods resembling the ones examined here: Earl Lewis's "home sphere" and the politics of "respectability" as discussed by Victoria Wolcott, among others[36]—although this book makes clear that these concepts continued to have relevance for much longer than scholars have allowed. For Lewis, the "home sphere" held special significance for black Southerners facing political and economic setbacks under Jim Crow and essentially represented an introspective turn to concentrate energies on improving the material living conditions in African American neighborhoods over which blacks had more control. However, he concludes, simmering discontent during the Great Depression and subsequent gains during World War II led to a reawakening of black interest in formal politics and labor union activism, ultimately shifting attention away from the home sphere. As discussed by Wolcott, respectability was the basis of a long-standing though eventually discredited agenda whereby prosperous African Americans—and especially women—from the national leadership down to the neighborhood level attempted to "uplift" the black masses by promoting behavior consistent with norms of white middle-class propriety, a strategy through which they simultaneously hoped to garner increased respect within the wider society. With a timing neatly paralleling Lewis's study, Wolcott traces the decline of this emphasis to the 1930s and 1940s, a result of black working-class resentment at attempts to police their behavior, the fact that the strategy ultimately failed to earn African Americans much more respect from whites, moves by upwardly mobile black families to outlying neighborhoods where they were more exposed to white racism than to their less-fortunate brethren, and, finally, the rise of a more confrontational, "masculinist" black protest politics from the New Deal into World War II.

My research makes clear that a black middle-class emphasis on respectability extended well into the postwar decades, at least on the local, neighborhood level, and that the "home sphere" continued as a locus for reform efforts. Most important, even after escaping inner-city neighborhoods like Cedar-Central, the dynamics of racialized housing markets ensured that middle-class blacks as early as the 1950s were confronted with the reality of less-affluent African Americans moving to the periphery. In the outlying neighborhoods of Cleveland, middle-class African Americans developed innovative new organizational forms and means of defining what constituted proper behavior; furthermore, women continued to play particularly important roles here.[37] Having limited suburban options before the 1980s, black middle-class residents formulated an amazingly broad and consistent reform agenda aimed at preserving acceptable living conditions. By extending Lewis's concept of the home sphere, we can trace the long arc of this reform agenda and accompanying worldview and connect the various efforts to mobilize neighborhoods around quality-of-life issues that subsequent scholars have so far discussed only in piecemeal fashion, or else have imagined to be a far more recent development.[38] Place-based reform across Cleveland's outlying black middle-class neighborhoods encompassed housing upkeep, business revitalization, traffic safety, trash removal, and efforts to reduce liquor availability, juvenile delinquency, vice, crime, and more. On some such matters, reform-minded residents chalked up notable successes; on others, the underlying structural factors proved too immense to be overcome. Sometimes these efforts involved moralizing or exhibited an explicit class bias; at other times the approaches were more pragmatic and the analysis of underlying causes astute. Upwardly mobile middle-class blacks did not always recognize that less well-off newcomers to their neighborhoods were often motivated by similar concerns with livability. But in the end, their various attempts to take charge of their lives and communities contributed to the long-term viability of these neighborhoods and the city as a whole. Even today, well past the point where certain suburbs opened wide to African American homebuyers, these areas retain a core, though generally elderly, middle-class and homeowning component.

The structure of the book is as follows. Chapter 1 uncovers how middling black families initially gained access to the outlying neighborhoods of Glenville and Mount Pleasant, with descriptions of their communities' socioeconomic structures and their residents' lifestyles and interactions with nearby whites. A final section assesses their ability to successfully maintain a toehold at the periphery despite the economic setbacks of the Great Depression. Chapter 2 follows these same two neighborhoods from World War II into the early postwar years, examining wartime racial tensions, the organization of community councils seeking to mobilize residents along interracial lines, and the departure of many Jewish residents and institutions up to about 1950. Despite the tense racial climate, Glenville and Mount Pleasant avoided overt racial conflicts to emerge as black middle-class strongholds. Chapter 3 shifts even further to the periphery to probe the origins of the Lee-Seville enclave, before investigating several land development battles that materialized between and among black and white residents, as more upwardly mobile African American families moved to the vicinity in the two decades after World War II. The topics of black builders and developers are covered, as well as the emergence by the late 1950s of white developers willing to build for African Americans, along with how African Americans managed to gain access to the quasi-suburban Lee-Harvard neighborhood. Chapter 4 compares the various patterns of racial residential transition and the race relations accompanying the process, in Glenville and the various neighborhoods of Southeast Cleveland, finding variations mostly traceable to the white residents' ethnic and class composition as well as the built environment. Chapter 5 considers the structural factors and life dilemmas upwardly mobile black Clevelanders faced even after achieving geographic mobility, and investigates the dynamic whereby less-affluent African American families steadily moved into new, outlying black middle-class neighborhoods. It also investigates the intraracial, cross-class frictions that ensued around issues of property upkeep, personal comportment, child rearing, and leisure-time practices. Finally, chapter 6 looks at the ambitious, nearly all-encompassing reform agenda that middle-class activist residents of these various neighborhoods went on to mount, in an attempt to maintain what they considered an acceptable quality of life.

1 : : :
The Roots of Upward Mobility

OUTLYING BLACK SETTLEMENT BEFORE 1940

Fully one-third of the approximately 350 African American families living in Cleveland's outlying Mount Pleasant neighborhood owned their own homes in 1930, a reminder that some black Southerners who came to Northern cities during the Great Migration acquired land and homes fairly quickly. The challenging nature of property record research, however, has impeded sustained historical inquiry. In fact, only three of the property-owning Mount Pleasant households listed in that year's census are readily traceable in the public record.[1] Fortunately, these three families were fairly typical; details of their lives mirror the experiences of African Americans on the urban periphery, at a remove from the dense and increasingly segregated inner-city districts solidifying at this time. All three couples were Southern-born, as were 70 percent of all black Mount Pleasant spouses in 1930. All three husbands occupied upper-working-class positions, thereby providing a scaffold for economic security and upward mobility unavailable to most black families at the time. Two of the three wives also worked for wages, further bolstering their families' economic security, as did approximately one-fifth of black Mount Pleasant wives in 1930. All three couples obtained mortgage financing to build their new homes, as did virtually all African American homeowners in this outlying enclave. In addition, one bought additional vacant lots and rental properties elsewhere, also not unusual for middling black families prior to the onset of the Great Depression.

William G. Slaughter, born around 1872, was the first to arrive in Mount Pleasant, getting a building permit in September 1916 for his two-story house at 3303 East 130th Street worth $2,200. The downtown Citizens House Building Co. contracted to build the house, as it did for other black owners in the neighborhood. Slaughter's first listing in the 1916 city directory was as an "auto operator" (chauffeur) for a presumably white household in the still-posh Hough neighborhood. Over the next three years, his occupation was listed variously as "houseman," "butler," and, as of 1920, "chef" in a private home. The census additionally reveals that his wife, Gladys, worked as a maid, that they had no children, and that they were both born in Virginia. Slaughter worked as a chef for the next several years, but in 1924 he was listed as a porter. In 1926, he tried his hand at insurance, before returning to work as a chef for two more years. In 1928, he first entered carpentry, and he was classed as a carpenter in the 1930 census; Gladys by then worked as a cook for a private family.[2] Slaughter's work history reveals both versatility and also suggests something of a restless personality, while his experience typifies the overall striving for economic security by upwardly mobile black families of this era.

Clarence Scott, born around 1890, arrived next, filing a building permit in January 1917 to construct his two-story wooden house at 3255 East 128th Street, valued at an estimated $1,600. His name first appears in the 1918 city directory, as a teamster. Scott was listed variously as a teamster, a driver, and a carpenter for the next five years. The 1920 census reveals further that like many black Mount Pleasant residents, he was a garbage worker for the city; his wife, Mattie, was listed as having no occupation, and both of them were born in South Carolina, as were the oldest two of their four children. In 1925, Scott entered cement work, and he appeared in the 1930 census as a cement contractor. Although their household now included eight children, Mattie still did not work for wages.[3] Like Slaughter, Scott sought entry into the more remunerative building trades, in his case leaving a strenuous and dirty occupation, sanitation work, in which African Americans nevertheless had a relatively secure foothold. Scott was economically successful enough to support his large family on a single income, even acquiring additional properties.

Last to arrive was Luther P. Smith, born around 1882, filing a building permit in May 1923 for his two-family house at 3234 East 130th Street. A carpenter by trade, Smith listed himself as both architect and contractor for the property worth an estimated $5,000. Smith listed his home address as 10622 Arthur Avenue, another house he had purchased that same year in the eastern reaches of the Cedar-Central district, home to some 90 percent of Cleveland's black population in 1930. In November 1923, Smith also applied for a permit to build a "garage and lumber shed" on his Mount Pleasant lot, where his house must not yet have been finished because he still listed Arthur Avenue as his address. Smith may have arrived in Cleveland as early as 1916, when a laborer with his name first appeared in the city directory living at 3646 Central Avenue, in the heart of the city's largest black settlement. According to the 1920 census, Smith was working as a carpenter, living as a roomer with his wife, Margaret (who had no occupation), at 10919 Cedar Avenue in the vast black residential district's far eastern end; both of them were native Georgians. By 1925, Smith was listed as both a carpenter and a contractor. As of 1930, census records showed that Margaret worked as a caretaker in a fraternity house.[4]

The property transactions made by these three households illuminate important dimensions of their lives and suggest a nascent black middle-class experience heretofore little explored by historians. As was typical in the pre-

New Deal mortgage market, these owners were repeat borrowers, taking out a total of fourteen mortgages before 1930 on the three Mount Pleasant houses mentioned above. The Slaughters had the fewest, at three. In April 1915, they signed a note for $300 with Blanche M. Mach—the previous white, Protestant owner and wife of a local lawyer—to acquire the lot. Interest on the loan was 6 percent, and the Slaughters paid it off by February 1916. That August, prior to initiating construction, the couple borrowed $2,620 at 6 percent, from the Citizens Home Building Co., the general contractor; they paid it off in February 1924. But that January, they took out yet another mortgage for $1,400 with the Cleveland Trust Co., the city's largest bank, also at 6 percent; this one would not be paid off until 1937.[5] As for the Scotts, they took out five mortgage loans, starting in November 1917 before construction began, for $800 at 6 percent with Broadway Savings & Trust. They must have used part of this money to pay off the remainder of their original land contract of July 1916, with the Walton Realty Co., which had subdivided the allotment containing the Mount Pleasant black enclave; this is borne out by the fact that Clarence Scott acquired official title to the land the very next day. The couple then had a succession of loans with the Union Trust Co., all at 6 percent interest: in March 1924 for another $800; in March 1925 for $1,500; in January 1927 for $1,700; and in January 1930 for another $1,700. In each case, they paid off the loan in one to four years.[6]

But the Smiths proved most ambitious of the three couples in their real estate acquisitions and related transactions. Willing to carry more debt, they took out five mortgages, starting with two loans at 7 percent from the black-owned Empire Savings & Loan Co.—in June and September 1923, for $5,500 and $7,000, respectively. Although the couple paid off the first in August 1923, they were still paying on the second in June 1925, when they borrowed $1,200 more at 7 percent from an M. F. Clark whose identity cannot be established. Perhaps they took out this supplementary loan because they needed cash, Smith having purchased an adjoining lot at a public auction (sheriff's sale) the previous month, which he would hold onto for three years before reselling. The Smiths still owed Empire $6,784 and were on the verge of paying off Clark when they took out a fourth loan, in April 1926, for $2,500 at 7 percent interest. This one was from a Sam Cohen, whose common Jewish name makes it impossible to positively ascertain his identity; this the Smiths paid off by early 1929. The couple took out yet another loan with Empire in July 1927, for $1,000 at 7 percent.[7] As mentioned, Smith had purchased on Arthur Avenue while in the process of building in Mount Pleasant, and in 1926, he acquired title to a property on Cedar Avenue as security for another loan. As of 1935, Smith owned at least one rental property in Cedar-Central, at 2315 East 59th Street. After turning over management of this building to the black-owned J. E. Branham Realty Co., Smith literally came to blows with his manager the following year, following a bounced check and the revelation that Branham had withheld some of the rent monies collected.[8]

Prior to World War II, Mount Pleasant was Cleveland's fastest-growing out-lying cluster of black settlement, though it contained only about 5 percent of the city's African American population in 1930 (dwarfed as it was by the vast residential district running along Cedar and Central Avenues). However, it was not in inner-city neighborhoods like Cedar-Central—which historians for years followed convention in referring to as "ghettoes"[9]—that the future and aspira-tions of Cleveland's upwardly mobile, black middling classes lay, but rather in a handful of settlements on the urban periphery like Mount Pleasant. Not only did these clusters offer life opportunities unavailable in Cedar-Central; they powerfully affected the direction of subsequent black population expansion. During and after World War II, Mount Pleasant in the southeast and Glenville in the northeast would emerge as black middle-class strongholds where fami-lies achieved homeownership at levels far surpassing the black average. But the groundwork for this accomplishment began decades earlier, reaching back to the turn of the century.

Making Communities

Mount Pleasant in 1900 was little more than a "tiny country business center" six miles southeast of downtown Cleveland's Public Square, on the streetcar line following Kinsman Road to the town of Chagrin Falls and be-yond. Contained within the village of Newburgh, the area was not annexed to Cleveland until 1913, by which time developers had begun to lay streets and subdivide farmland and orchards into city lots. Homes on side streets and the entire area east of the future East 140th Street were not built up until the 1920s, largely with two-family "mortgage lifters" that allowed owner-occupants to rent one suite and defray mortgage payments. Like many of Cleveland's out-lying neighborhoods, Mount Pleasant saw rapid population gains between 1910 and 1930, in marked contrast to older districts with declining populations. In 1923, when the Cleveland Public Library first opened a "station" at 3335 East 118th Street, staff described the area's ethnic composition as "almost entirely Jewish, [with] some Hungarians, Italians, and a few Negroes." In the 1920s, Mount Pleasant became the second-largest Jewish settlement in Cleveland, after Glenville, with approximately 22,000 Jews by 1927; Italians were the next-largest population group in the area. Newcomers from both these groups ar-rived in Mount Pleasant from older neighborhoods closer to downtown that were being consolidated into increasingly black Cedar-Central. Jewish disper-sal from their community centered around Woodland Avenue and East 55th Street began during World War I, while some Italians arrived in Mount Pleas-ant even earlier from the "Big Italy" Sicilian settlement on the southern edge of downtown.[10] Thus both Jews and Italians had previous contact with African Americans upon coming to Mount Pleasant, a fact worth noting, though of ambiguous significance when considering subsequent patterns of race relations.

African Americans established an early presence in Mount Pleasant. According to a 1930 newspaper article, black settlement dated to 1893, when an insolvent white contractor paid his workforce by giving them "title to a number of lots in the section north of Kinsman and in the neighborhood of E. 126th to E. 130th Streets." While this story cannot be verified, the location is accurate. As of 1900, only one African American family had erected a house in the area, but by 1907 black real estate promoter Welcome T. Blue was advertising forty-by-fifty-foot lots there for as low as $200, encouraging potential buyers to "Get Away from the Crowded, Smoky City. Own Your Own Home. Raise Garden Fruit. Chickens, Hogs, Cows." Blue's ad claimed both that "100 Afro-Americans Own Choice Lots There" and "100 Afro-American Families Live There To-Day."[11] The latter, at least, was a blatant exaggeration, for the 1910 census documented only twenty-four black families living in the settlement, nineteen of them owners. And judging by the rate at which African American families acquired their deeds, the process of land acquisition remained slow before 1915. While one mortgage banker's recollection that "only tents for [black] war workers from the deep South" stood on the land by World War I is clearly overstated, it nonetheless suggests that the early community had an improvised feel. Mount Pleasant's black enclave grew to include 124 households by 1920, with at least 67 homeowners (54 percent of the total).[12]

Newcomers were drawn by Mount Pleasant's rustic feel, and families' abilities to supplement food through subsistence production, a characteristic pattern of early working-class suburbanization that was particularly important for African Americans.[13] Semirural features characterized portions of the area well into the 1920s. As one black woman whose aunt moved there recalled, Mount Pleasant was "considered the country" because "only Kinsman Road was paved," the "rest of the streets . . . [being] more or less country black top roads." Railroad man James Susong, who bought in 1923, similarly recalled "pastures and large vacant lots separating the few houses which stood on the unpaved streets." With its low population density of just thirty-three persons per acre as of 1930, Mount Pleasant had more open space than any existing black settlement except for the extreme outliers of West Park and Miles Heights (later known as Lee-Seville). In contrast, the older sections of Cedar-Central housed sixty-three persons per acre.[14]

Other sources confirm the pattern of informal and sporadic construction in early black Mount Pleasant. Contemporary fire insurance atlases reveal that many lots in the enclave remained vacant while families saved money to build their houses; at the same time, the widely differing frontages, designs, and various outbuildings testify to the widespread practice of "self-building," as noted in similar outlying areas. Confirming this pattern, assessors for the government's Home Owners Loan Corporation (HOLC) in a 1939 survey of Mount Pleasant noted a "heavy percentage of 'Jerry-Type' construction throughout," leading them to disparage the black, Jewish, and Italian occupants and give the neighborhood the lowest grade, a "D" rating.[15] Despite a fragmentary public record, the identifiable building permits taken out by thirty-three black Mount Pleasant property owners from 1913 to 1929 suggest specific strategies and timelines. At least two built their own homes, including carpenter Luther P. Smith and ironworker Marion LeGrand, and at least three others employed black tradesmen or contractors. Although three black owners started construction almost immediately after acquiring title, the median interval between acquisition and commencement was four months. One owner, slate roofer Emmett Meade, took over ten years to initiate construction after acquiring title in July 1908, despite soon thereafter founding a prosperous roofing business. It took at least four other lot owners between two and five years to start building.[16]

By 1930, 349 African American families lived in a compact cluster of twenty-seven contiguous Mount Pleasant blocks, centered roughly at East 128th Street and Luke Avenue. Mapping individual addresses (Map 1.1) reveals a solid black inner core as well as settlement on both sides of Imperial Avenue to the north, with a sprinkling of black residents in the surrounding areas, notably south of the enclave where more than a dozen families lived interspersed among white neighbors. According to a former resident raised there in the 1930s and 1940s, the settlement was "almost like a little town." In addition, a second, farther outlying cluster of seventy African American families took shape some ten blocks to the southeast, along East 142nd, East 143rd, and East 144th Streets. Black families did not begin buying here, in what was referred to as "Kinsman Heights," until the 1920s—and while some property owners purchased vacant lots, others bought existing homes. By 1939, HOLC assessors fretted that "colored encroachment" threatened nearby property values. By 1940, the original black Mount Pleasant enclave had grown to 697 families living on forty-nine contiguous blocks, while Kinsman Heights included an additional 209 households.[17]

By 1930, Mount Pleasant featured a cross section of the city's black middling classes in the Great Migration era. Of the 349 households in the main enclave, nearly three-quarters of the heads were born in the South, with Georgia sending the most, followed by Virginia and Alabama. Of their 318 spouses, seven out of ten were Southern-born, with fully one-quarter coming from Georgia. Of the Northern-born adults, Ohio was by far the most common birth state. While some were undoubtedly native Clevelanders, other Ohioans arrived from smaller cities and towns, some prior to World War I.[18] Household composition and tenure indicate considerable economic stability in the Mount Pleasant enclave, with many households engaged in commonplace strategies

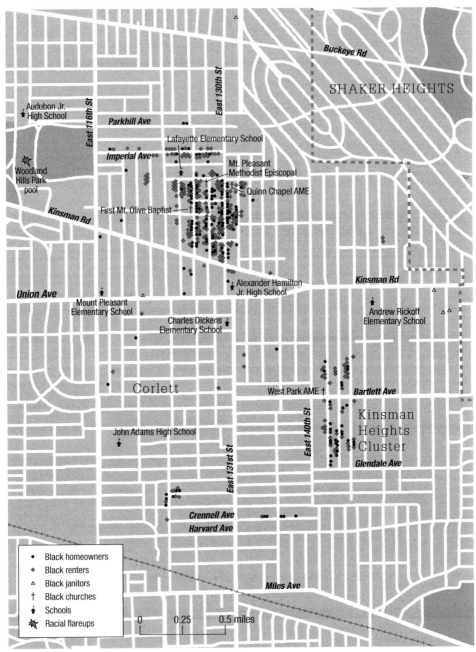

Map 1.1 African American Households in Mount Pleasant, 1930

Note: "Black janitors" lived in otherwise all-white apartment buildings.

Sources: U.S. Manuscript Census, 1930; *Cleveland City Directory, 1930* (Cleveland City Directory Co., 1930); Property Deeds, Cuyahoga County Recorders Office, Cleveland, Ohio.

Table 1.1. Occupational Structure for Employed Mount Pleasant Black Household Heads, 1930

	Male Heads (N=322)		Black Males City	Female Heads (N=19)		Black Females City
Professional	2.5%	(8)	2.7%	0		2.7%
Manager	0.3%	(1)	2.0%	0		1.1%
Clerical	8.7%	(28)	2.5%	0		1.6%
Sales	2.2%	(7)	1.5%	0		1.0%
Craftwork	15.8%	(51)	10.0%	5.3%	(1)	>0.1%
Operator	28.0%	(90)	15.9%	0		13.1%
Service	18.9%	(61)	21.6%	94.7%	(18)	78.1%
Nonhousehold:		54			3	
Household:		7			15	
Laborer	24.0%	(76)	39.9%	0		0.9%
Indeterminable			4.1%			1.5%

Sources: 1930 Manuscript Census; Cleveland City Directory, 1930 (Cleveland: Cleveland City Directory Co.); U.S. Bureau of the Census, *Fifteenth Census of the United States—Population*, vol. 4: *Occupations, by States* (Washington, D.C., 1932), 1285–88.

Notes: Private chauffeurs classed as operators to permit citywide comparison; porters in industrial settings grouped as laborers. The eight remaining heads were retired or unemployed. Nearly half of the indeterminable jobs fell under "other occupations" in the mechanical and manufacturing industries, many of which were probably unskilled work like janitors.

to cement family security. In the enclave, 25 percent housed extended families, while 14 percent kept nonrelated boarders—much lower than in the city as a whole, where fully 31 percent of African American households kept boarders in 1930.[19] Renters predominated in the Mount Pleasant black enclave, at 67 percent, compared to 33 percent who owned their houses. But since much of the housing stock in Mount Pleasant was two-family, the percentage of homeownership is considerable, exceeding the overall homeownership rate of 28 percent in the census tract as a whole.[20]

The community's occupational structure reveals a mixture of socioeconomic levels, but with considerable stability and potential for upward movement (Table 1.1).[21] Professionals made up a small portion at 3 percent, including three ministers, two lawyers, two physicians, and a dentist. Both doctors, Stanley Brown and Emerald B. Spencer, worked at Lakeside Hospital—Western Reserve University's main teaching unit and the only hospital in the city hiring black physicians at the time. Only one individual worked as a manager, illustrating the force of racial discrimination at higher levels of business leadership. Clerical workers represented 9 percent of the total, more than three times the black city average. Most worked for the U.S. Post Office—ten as clerks, seven as letter carriers, and one as a dispatcher—while two more were railroad mail clerks. These were high-status jobs, as discrimination effectively excluded African Americans from most office employment outside black-owned businesses.[22] Only 2 percent of enclave residents worked in sales, including two insurance agents, an auto salesman, a huckster, and three realty brokers. The fact that one of the latter three, Dwight Williams, quickly moved on to become assistant superintendent at the city garbage plant suggests that for him, like for many other African Americans, selling real estate was not a mainstay but rather a side pursuit.

Of the main enclave's male heads, 16 percent worked in the crafts or in the skilled trades, including eight auto mechanics, six plasterers, six molders, five carpenters, three bricklayers, and two stationary engineers. There were four foremen, two each in industrial settings and on county road crews. One female household head, a dressmaker, also did craftwork. The presence of building tradesmen is particularly striking, considering that many white-dominated labor unions barred African Americans, or denied them entry to apprenticeship programs. Some blacks began craftwork careers as helpers in the "trowel trades," experiencing less discrimination in Cleveland's bricklayer and plasterer union locals.[23] Most black craftsmen likely received their training in the South, where, ironically, segregation created more opportunities; however, two of the building tradesmen were Ohio-born, and at least one, Virginian Emmett Meade, learned the roofing trade soon after his arrival in 1903.[24] Nearly one-third of the male heads held jobs as operatives (factory workers), the second-most-common job category. Twenty were chauffeurs, also classed by the Census Bureau as operatives, though all but two drove for private families. Thirty-three of the operatives, or nearly half, were truck drivers—at least one of whom was an independent hauler. In fact, one of Cleveland's most successful black truckers, moving company owner Frank J. Hawkins, soon relocated to Mount Pleasant as well.[25]

Thus Mount Pleasant black men registered higher percentages of relatively secure and remunerative employment than among the city's African American population as a whole, by a margin of approximately 5 percent each in the clerical and craft categories, and by over 10 percent among operatives. However, other Mount Pleasant black residents held more marginal jobs. Laborers made up one-quarter of the total, but this compares favorably to the 40 percent of Cleveland's black men who held menial positions in 1930.[26] Dozens of Mount Pleasant men toiled in the steel industry and in construction, and a smaller number in sanitation and street repair.[27] Finally, a considerable number of household heads, about one-fifth, worked in service occupations, including, among the men, thirteen porters, eleven janitors, six footmen, and four waiters. As for the female household heads, nearly all were domestics who did cleaning, laundry, or cooking for private families in areas like Shaker

Heights, an affluent suburb to the immediate east. It bears reemphasizing that the force of discrimination distorted employment hierarchies in black communities, as certain categories of service work took on relatively higher status than in the broader society. Jobs were ranked according to their proximity to wealth and power, to levels of personal responsibility, and to the wearing of a uniform. Waiters, attendants, and chauffeurs—men's work, notably—were well-paid positions compared to laborers and operatives. Service occupations could also facilitate mobility through networks, information, and patronage. For example, enclave resident Bassel Parham, a doorman at the downtown Halle Brothers Co., was willed an undisclosed sum of money by a white woman and regular customer who requested that Parham attend her funeral in his uniform.[28]

Some black Mount Pleasant households bolstered their economic security by ensuring that multiple family members took jobs, a defining characteristic of upwardly mobile African American families in the postwar era. However, just 17 percent of the wives worked for wages in 1930, another indication of considerable economic security. In those double-income families, 47 percent of the spouses were domestics, while the rest worked in service sector jobs at commercial laundries, in food preparation, or as elevator operators. Social worker Bessie Trigg, whose husband was a lawyer, was exceptional as the sole professional working spouse. Not surprising, of the eighteen employed female household heads, fifteen worked as domestic servants.[29] Households with additional working family members (not boarders) were also common, especially among extended families with grown children.

Interestingly, the smaller Kinsman Heights cluster in 1930 featured a more substantial homeownership rate (43 percent) and an occupational structure with more higher-level positions, yet these seventy families struggled harder to live there. A much larger proportion of households there consisted of extended families, 41 percent, with a slightly higher proportion of boarders, at 16 percent. While no professionals or managers were present, an even higher 13 percent of the household heads held clerical positions—again, mostly at the Post Office. Most striking, nearly twice as many as in the main enclave, 27 percent, worked in craft positions, while significantly more heads held jobs as operatives, 39 percent. However, only 10 percent did service work, and just 11 percent were laborers. There was but a single female-headed household, a widow who worked as a housekeeper. A slightly higher overall percentage of spouses held paid employment, at 20 percent, a far greater proportion of them as domestics (77 percent). Not surprising, house values here averaged $7,053, compared to $6,123 for homes in the main Mount Pleasant enclave. In a further illustration of the mobility sometimes facilitated by service work, two Kinsman Heights sisters shared the story of their grandfather, a Jamaican immigrant who became the chauffeur to John D. Rockefeller's personal physician. When he moved into a house at East 142nd Street and Glendale Avenue in 1928, his employer, the physician, acted as "benefactor" to enable the purchase, actually making the down payment on the house.[30]

Glenville, in the northeast section of the city, was the other major black middle-class stronghold to emerge in Cleveland at this time. Prior to its annexation in 1905, this village served as a truck farming area supplying produce to the city, with its business center at the intersection of Saint Clair Avenue and Doan Street (later East 105th Street). It subsequently became a resort hub with the notable presence of the Glenville fairgrounds and racetrack, and by the turn of the century it had evolved into a streetcar suburb. By 1909, developers were promoting several subdivisions of sumptuous single-family homes, with more built after 1912 on the site of the former racetrack.[31] Glenville's amenities attracted the first wave of upwardly mobile immigrants and their children, and by the mid-1920s, the neighborhood had the city's largest concentration of Jews (at 32,000), who were "slightly better off economically" than their coreligionists in Mount Pleasant, as noted by Cleveland's premier Jewish social service agency, the Council Educational Alliance (CEA). HOLC, for its part, stated that the neighborhood had been "very desirable" until 1920, when "a wholesale shift of population occurred," from owners of "American stock" to Eastern European Jews from East 55th Street.[32] As early as 1937, observers noted the eastward migration of more affluent Jewish residents, into the neighborhood's newer section beyond Lakeview Road, nicknamed "Superior Thru" after the streetcar line. But Glenville was, like Mount Pleasant, also home to other ethnic and religious groups. Three Roman Catholic parishes served the vicinity by 1914, with parishioners of primarily German and Irish descent.[33]

African Americans also lived in Glenville from early on, but in far smaller numbers than in Mount Pleasant. Here, too, the initial settlement pattern took the form of an enclave, comprising two blocks in the vicinity of Beulah Avenue and East 123rd Street. According to HOLC evaluators in the 1930s, this "concentrated" pocket was "caused by one promoter who built homes for sale to colored." By 1910, five black families (twenty-eight individuals)—all headed by plasterers from Kentucky and Georgia—lived on East 120th Street in this section. Their numbers subsequently increased, and then the size of this small pocket remained stable from 1920 to 1940, at around 200 individuals.[34] Elsewhere in Glenville and in marked contrast to Mount Pleasant, black settlement prior to World War II was diffuse (see Map 1.2). As early as 1925, a report on black population dynamics noted that "the professional class of Negroes" was moving to the area. Approximately two dozen black Glenville families purchased their properties in the World War I era, with the earliest arrivals including elite barber George A. Myers, as well as Roddy K. Moon, founder and original president of Cleveland's NAACP branch, who was a meat inspector with the U.S. Department of Agriculture (and a real estate broker).[35]

Class Picture, Columbia Elementary School, 1910s. Small numbers of African Americans made their way into Cleveland's outlying Glenville neighborhood early in the Great Migration era. (Courtesy of the Western Reserve Historical Society, Cleveland, Ohio)

Cleveland's largest banks initially issued mortgages to African Americans in this overwhelmingly white area, and not only to elites—like J. Walter Wills, the city's most prominent black mortician, who bought on Grantwood Avenue in 1916—but also to borrowers like chauffeur Ernest W. Ingram, who purchased a home on Morison Avenue the previous year. In fact, the *Call & Post* later divulged that exclusionary lending in Glenville only became the rule in the late 1920s, with Cleveland Trust's refusal of a mortgage to black real estate dealer R. H. Riffe.[36] Early liberality in lending contrasts with the situation by 1940, when the exclusionary HOLC asked the Post Office to tally up how many African American families were living in Glenville. Of the 273 total, Kempton Avenue had the largest number, with sixteen families, and while others housed around a dozen each, most streets in the neighborhood had only a handful of black residents by that point.[37]

Census data from 1930 underlines the higher economic status of black residents in the wider neighborhood compared to those in the original Glenville enclave. Of 111 households in the neighborhood proper, not counting janitors in all-white apartment buildings, the first striking difference is that far fewer— slightly less than 60 percent of heads and spouses—were Southern-born. And, two-thirds of those who were came from the Upper South, especially Virginia and Tennessee. In contrast, of the forty-five households in the original Glenville black cluster, 80 percent of the heads were Southern-born and, as in the

Map 1.2 African American Households in Glenville, 1930

Note: "Black janitors" lived in otherwise all-white apartment buildings.

Sources: U.S. Manuscript Census, 1930; *Cleveland City Directory, 1930*; Property Deeds, Cuyahoga County Recorders Office, Cleveland, Ohio.

Table 1.2. Occupational Structure for Employed Glenville Black Household Heads, 1930

	Male Heads (N=103)		Black Males City	Female Heads (N=4)		Black Females City
Professional	27.2%	(28)	2.7%	0		2.7%
Manager	6.8%	(7)	2.0%	0		1.1%
Clerical	16.5%	(17)	2.5%	0		1.6%
Sales	2.9%	(3)	1.5%	0		1.0%
Craftwork	13.6%	(14)	10.0%	25.0%	(1)	>0.1%
Operator	12.6%	(13)	15.9%	0		13.1%
Service	17.5%	(18)	21.6%	75.0%	(3)	78.1%
Nonhousehold:		18			2	
Household:		0			1	
Laborer	2.9%	(3)	39.9%	0		0.9%
Indeterminable			4.1%			1.5%

Sources: 1930 Manuscript Census; Cleveland City Directory, 1930 (Cleveland: Cleveland City Directory Co.); U.S. Bureau of the Census, *Fifteenth Census of the United States—Population*, vol. 4: *Occupations, by States* (Washington, D.C., 1932), 1285–88.
Notes: Occupations classed as in Table 1.2. The remaining heads were retired or unemployed.

case of Mount Pleasant, hailed from the more rural Lower South (disproportionately Georgia). In Glenville proper, 74 percent of black households owned their homes, compared to 29 percent in the enclave. Home values averaged $8,575 in Glenville proper, and twenty were worth over $10,000—far more than in Mount Pleasant or Kinsman Heights. In the original Glenville enclave, values averaged $3,900. Three of the African American families in Glenville proper actually had black live-in servants, although 35 percent of households included extended families and boarders in Glenville, twice the rate in Mount Pleasant. Thus even some wealthy families bolstered economic security by keeping boarders, or accepted the responsibility of housing their relatives. But even with dramatically lower levels of homeownership in the original Glenville enclave, extended families and boarders were less prevalent, at 27 and just 7 percent, respectively.[38]

The occupational structure further underlines the high- and upper-middle-class status of black families in Glenville proper as of 1930 (Table 1.2). Professionals comprised the largest group among household heads, at 27 percent, ten times the proportion for black men in the city as a whole. Among these were five dentists and seven physicians, all with offices in Cedar-Central; they included Eugene Gregg, a former city councilman who had lobbied for an African American branch of the City Hospital, as well as Estes J. Gunn, a prime mover in the eventual establishment of the black-run Forest City Hospital. Six attorneys also made their homes in Glenville, including assistant police prosecutor Selmo C. Glenn and two notable black politicians: civil rights champion Harry E. Davis, who had served as an Ohio state representative from 1920 to 1928 and then as the first black member of the city's Civil Service Commission; and the older Republican Party stalwart John P. Green, whose term in the Ohio Senate from 1891 to 1893 made him the highest-serving black public official in the state to that point. Two ministers lived there, too, including the Reverend Russell Brown, pastor of the prestigious Mount Zion Congregational Church and a sitting city councilman as of 1929.[39]

Glenville's black white-collar residents further reflected the neighborhood's elite status. While the proportion of managers, proprietors, and officials among household heads was small at 7 percent, it was still more than three times the rate among the city's overall African American population. Herbert S. Chauncey, Cleveland's most dynamic African American businessman, lived in the neighborhood in 1930 but died suddenly later that year. Founder of the Empire Savings & Loan Co. in 1919, the Peoples Realty Co. in 1920, and the Crusaders Mutual Insurance Society in 1927 (a venture co-led by pharmacist George P. Craig, another black Glenville resident), Chauncey had also recently become the first black appointee to the City Planning Commission. Other resident business owners included grocer Henry Parham; Harold A. Hunt, who owned a news agency; and mortician Elmer F. Boyd, owner of the city's second-largest black funeral home. Federal meat inspector Roddy K. Moon also lived in Glenville, as did city sewer inspector Seth Nickens, a former resident of the West Park enclave and active in the Republican Club there.[40]

Clerical workers, at 17 percent of African American household heads in Glenville proper, were present at double the rate in Mount Pleasant, and over six times that among black Clevelanders overall. More than half were postal workers, notably Alonzo L. Glenn, who served as president of the National Alliance of Postal Employees, founded in 1913 to respond to the mass firing of black railroad clerks under Woodrow Wilson. The rest were messengers, except for Daniel Fairfax, a clerk in the city's Heat and Water Division, and Herbert Douglass, an assistant at the Cleveland Medical Library Association. A slightly lower percentage of residents (14 percent) worked in the crafts compared to Mount Pleasant. Half were building tradesmen; prominent among them was Charles W. Brown, an electrician trained at the Milwaukee School of Engineering who had been instrumental in organizing NAACP branches in Minneapolis and Charleston before coming to Cleveland in 1920. He was later elected the first black committeeman from Glenville. There was one foreman among the heads: Robert Hodges, at the Cleveland Hardware Co., a company remarkable for its fair treatment of African Americans. Of the 13 percent who were operatives (less than half the percentage in Mount Pleasant), three-quarters were either chauffeurs or truck drivers. Service workers, at 18 percent, included six porters, two barbers, and two of the three employed female household heads, who worked as hairdressers. In stark contrast to the city as a whole, laborers composed an insignificant 3 percent of these black Glenville household heads in 1930.[41]

Women's work likely carried a different significance for prosperous Glenville families—who were already upper- or securely middle-class—than for Mount Pleasant residents where wives' income often provided the economic boost to claim middle-class status. The number of black female-headed households in Glenville proper was small, at just seven, making up 7 percent of the total; all these women were widowed, and only four were employed. As for dual-income households, the proportion was 23 percent, but some of these wives likely worked for very different reasons than their Mount Pleasant counterparts. To be sure, four of the twenty-four Glenville working wives (17 percent) toiled as domestics for private families. Several others did service-related work outside the household setting: "janitress" of an apartment building, cook or bookkeeper for a restaurant. One was a dressmaker, another worked as a manicurist for a barbershop, and three others owned or managed beauty parlors.[42] Two others, Annie Parham and Ela Auther, co-owned or managed their husbands' grocery and real estate office, respectively. But in the greatest contrast to Mount Pleasant, nearly half of working Glenville wives were trained professionals: eight schoolteachers, a college social worker, and a nurse. Five of these had husbands who were also professionals—two of them managers—so these women likely worked for personal fulfillment over economic necessity. Regardless of class position, however, black income pooling was a platform for upward mobility across all the outlying city neighborhoods studied here.

Not surprising, the 1930 occupational structure in Glenville's original black enclave was different, more working class than middle class. As noted earlier, nearly a third of the families here were homeowners. But of thirty-seven employed male household heads, there were just four in the highest-level occupational categories, in each case making up 5 percent of the total: two ministers and two managers (a grocer and a dry cleaner). There were also two male heads in the crafts, and nine working as operatives (mostly chauffeurs and truckers) and at service occupations, representing 24 percent each. Finally, thirteen (35 percent) were unskilled laborers, approaching the city average. Six of the spouses (16 percent) also worked, all in domestic service with the exception of a manicurist. The six employed female household heads included a caterer, a dressmaker, and a telephone clerk; the remaining three worked as domestics.

The process of institution-building in Cleveland's outlying African American neighborhoods related more to settlement patterns than economic resources. In the pre–World War II period, black residents of Mount Pleasant proved more successful than their Glenville counterparts in founding churches, for example, due to the larger size and density of their community and the availability of vacant land. By the late 1930s, there were three in the main enclave: First Mount Olive Baptist, Quinn Chapel AME, and Mount Pleasant Methodist Episcopal. Paralleling the neighborhood's tradition of gradual, self-built housing, one former resident recalled the basement-only congregation of the latter, which collected tithes for years to build the upper floors. In addition, the outlying Kinsman Heights cluster had its own church, West Park AME. By contrast, black Glenville residents continued to worship outside the neighborhood, at some of the most prestigious African American churches in the city, all in Cedar-Central: Saint John's AME, Saint James AME, and Mount Zion Congregational. Besides the smaller and more dispersed population, black churches also faced white opposition in Glenville. According to HOLC, by the late 1930s, as a response to African American influx, "institutions have now mutually agreed not to sell to colored."[43]

Cleveland's black outer-city neighborhoods also spawned a rich, secular organizational life that fostered socializing and charitable giving while showcasing residents' achievements. A quick glance at the *Call & Post* gives some sense of the extent and types of activities residents engaged in. A 1934 issue, for example, announced a play at the Royal 20 Club in Mount Pleasant, the engagement of a "Happy Go Lucky Club" member's daughter, and a meeting of the Glenville Civic and Political Club in a private home, where the speaker delivered a talk on "Civic Betterment." A 1937 Mount Pleasant column listed the activities of the Joy Crafters Club, Morocco Bridge Club, Jolly Fortnighters Club, and Kinsman Heights Tennis Club, revealing the diversity and significance of social life in the area. A particularly notable local organization was the Mount Pleasant Mothers Civic Club (MPMCC), founded in 1927. By 1941, the MPMCC was reportedly sponsoring "a great deal of welfare work." When its members decided to "retire" in 1958, they donated the MPMCC's treasury of $5,000 to a bevy of black charities and churches and were praised as an organization that not only "gave teas . . . [and] made quilts," but also "incorporated and bought real estate, selling each time at a profit." Other organizations were more reflective. By the late 1930s, the Glenville Garden Club held annual flower shows to showcase members' horticultural skills and aesthetic sensibilities, and residents additionally founded the Forest City Garden Club in 1939.[44]

Playwright Adrienne Kennedy, who grew up in Mount Pleasant during the late 1930s and in Glenville after her family relocated in 1943, described the middle-class, political and social commitments of her parents' associates in this way: "They . . . read *Crisis* magazine and the *Pittsburgh Courier* . . . were members of the NAACP and the Urban League, were members of the Alpha[s], Kappas, the AKAS, the Deltas and Sigmas. . . . They worked a lifetime at their jobs as teachers, social workers, civic workers, doctors and lawyers. . . . They organized social clubs for their children, pushed them to do well in school, encouraged them to enter professions. They were devoted to the 'Negro Cause.' They worked hard, very hard, to maintain all of this."[45] While not all black Mount Pleasant or Glenville residents had yet made the transition to white-collar work like Kennedy's parents, this description captures the essence of what early African American life at the urban periphery was intended to foster: social and geographic mobility, fellowship among peers, and the cementing of the next generation's success, all of which were perceived as fully compatible—indeed, synonymous—with a commitment to the progress of the race as a whole.

Relating in Neighborhoods

Patterns of encounters between African Americans and whites in Cleveland's outer-city neighborhoods pose significant challenges to prevailing conceptions about race and urban space in the early decades of the twentieth century. Scholars cite Chicago as the classic case, tracing the rise of white antagonism during the Great Migration through a variety of forms, from discriminatory treatment in workplaces and public accommodations, to the real estate industry's equation of African American residency with property depreciation, to the violence of white vigilantism against black homebuyers.[46] But a thorough examination of white responses to African American influx in Mount Pleasant and Glenville must also consider the particular demographics of these areas, consisting mainly of immigrant and second-generation Southern and Eastern Europeans. Historians have shown a keen interest in these comparatively recent arrivals to America and their assimilation into white racial identities, noting that movement to outlying city districts—a general expression of upward mobility—was often accompanied by a solidifying consciousness of "whiteness" and a growing unwillingness to live near African Americans.[47] It is this general framework that informed Kenneth Kusmer's interpretation of the sporadic racial clashes over black access to public swimming facilities in Mount Pleasant from the late 1920s through the 1930s: "The [Southern and Eastern European] inhabitants of these areas had acquired a modest level of middle-class respectability, as is evidenced by the moderate or high incidence of home ownership in the census tracts in question. It seems likely that these ethnic communities were prone to what social scientists have called 'status anxieties.' . . . They naturally resisted the encroachment of a racial group that American society had designated as inferior."[48] Kusmer's assessment is often cited to support the premise that interactions between Southern and Eastern Europeans and African Americans were typically antagonistic.

While affirming that outlying neighborhoods indeed held significant status implications for Southern and Eastern Europeans as well as African Americans, and building on the work of scholars like Kusmer and Victoria Wolcott in their investigation of public recreational facilities, including swimming pools, as important sites of black civil rights struggles, my analysis demonstrates that cross-racial encounters at Cleveland's urban periphery were both subtler and thornier. In neither Mount Pleasant nor Glenville did white residents mount any sustained, violent resistance to black residential influx; to the contrary, some actually extended mortgage loans to African Americans, enabling them to buy in the immediate vicinity. Interracial contact in both Mount Pleasant and Glenville was initially minimized, in the former by the black enclave's insularity, and in the latter by the relatively small African American population before 1940. The few cross-racial interactions that did occur were typically benign, albeit highly formalized as neighborly and work relations. Even recurrent white antagonism (including violence) toward African Americans seeking access to neighborhood swimming facilities cannot be simply categorized in the realm of black victimization but must be carefully considered as the spark for an assertive, interracial civil rights campaign led by local black organizations and the Communist Party.

In Mount Pleasant, several factors explain the unchallenged presence of black homeowners. As outlined, the earliest families established a foothold soon after the turn of the century, with some buying lots and building houses before large numbers of Jews and Italians arrived from older downtown neighborhoods.[49] Second, African American influx during the 1920s, while substantial, was limited to just a handful of streets—a pattern true not only of the main historic enclave, but also in the new Kinsman Heights cluster. Once the Great Depression hit, the relative lack of alternative accommodations and a slack housing market deterred rapid demographic turnover. Southern and Eastern Europeans may not yet even have fully internalized knee-jerk presumptions linking black neighbors with lower property values. One Hungarian immigrant, for example, bought a brand-new, two-family house on East 132nd Street in the late 1920s, close to the main black Mount Pleasant enclave and notwithstanding that there were already African American families living on adjoining Imperial Avenue. Because he also owned a house on Parkhill Avenue three blocks north, the family moved back and forth between the two properties, "depending on where we could get tenants," his son explained. While racial boundaries were closely monitored, the nearby presence of African Americans had not dissuaded his purchase, and three black families subsequently moved onto Parkhill without any hasty departure of the white residents. Along similar lines, a Jewish woman who grew up in Mount Pleasant in the 1930s claimed whites "didn't mind a few" black neighbors, provided they were "nice, quiet people," while an African American informant stated that the small number of blacks living in Kinsman Heights was "not considered controversial" in her grandfather's day.[50]

In perhaps greatest contrast to prevailing images of white resistance, some

Table 1.3. Mortgaging by Black Mount Pleasant and Glenville Homebuyers, 1914–1930

	Total	Glenville (proper)	Mount Pleasant (orig. enclave)	Kinsman Hts.	Glenville (orig. enclave)
Mortgagors (borrowers)	105	37	46	10	12
Mortgages	188	57	97	14	20
From:					
Individuals	80	49.1%	35.1%	64.3%	45.0%
Banks	63	36.8%	34.0%	14.3%	35.0%
S&L Cos.	24	3.5%	17.5%	21.4%	10.0%
Mort. Cos.	10	8.8%	3.1%	—	10.0%
Constr. Cos.	8	—	8.2%	—	—
Others	3	1.8%	2.1%	—	—

Sources: 1920 Manuscript Census, Enumeration Districts 339, 340, 465, 467, 468, 471, 473, 477, 479, 619, and 621; 1930 Manuscript Census, Enumeration Districts 438–441, 443, 444, 446, 447, 449, 451, 452, 458, 460, 759, 761, 798, 803, and 812; Cuyahoga County Mortgage Records, Cuyahoga County Recorders Office.

whites in both Mount Pleasant and Glenville actually facilitated black residential influx by lending money to African Americans. For black buyers whose mortgages can be readily traced in the public record, the shape of the local lending regime in the period prior to 1930 is illuminating (Table 1.3). Besides the considerable access to loans from mainstream banks[51]—with the exception of borrowers in Kinsman Heights—the most significant source of financing came from private individuals, which was typical in the pre–New Deal era.[52] Approaching half of the total mortgages issued to black Glenville and Mount Pleasant residents, loans from individuals ran at a standard 6 or 7 percent interest and averaged $1,462—but ranged from as low as $200 to as high as $6,300, with a median loan amount of $1,200. Of the approximately fifty identifiable mortgagees (lenders), one-fifth were in law, construction, real estate, insurance, banking, or sales. But of the remainder, thirteen were whites from the immediate vicinity. Perhaps most strikingly, painter Mike Circelle and his wife, Lucy, lent $900 to steel mill laborer Casper W. Rumple in 1926, who bought the house next door on East 143rd Street in Kinsman Heights. Although the Circelles did move one block east by 1928, their willingness not only to lend, but also to remain in the vicinity, again implies a disjuncture regarding the racialized understandings of property values solidifying at the time. In some instances, sellers extended loans to buyers, as in the 1927 case of Henry C. Kadow to Herbert Douglass for 10923 Massie Avenue in Glenville; in the case in 1929 of Joseph and Mary Royce to dentist Jessie Bridgeman for 9503 Kempton Avenue in Glenville; and in the case of Bertha and Harry Zevenbergen in

1919 to Edward Jones for 12616 Imperial Avenue in Mount Pleasant. While these loans facilitated white departures, the mundane nature of such transactions contrasts sharply with the dwindling of finance streams for black borrowers in subsequent decades, as well as the controversy surrounding such transfers.[53]

Other loans were made on the basis of business relationships or face-to-face acquaintance. Thus wagonmaker and horseshoer Mathias Wintrichs, whose shop on Kinsman Road was just south of the main black Mount Pleasant enclave, lent to two different African American buyers in 1915 and 1916; and meanwhile, Sophia Caplin, the wife of a dentist in Cedar-Central, lent to postal clerk Charles H. Turner to buy on Greenlawn Avenue in Glenville in 1917. Mortician Elmer F. Boyd got financing in 1928 from George H. Lybarger, a Glenville dentist, while electrician Charles W. Brown borrowed in 1929 from John A. Mitermiler, a pharmacist and owner of the Glenville Drug Co. In 1928, boiler tender Speight Daniels got financing to buy on East 120th Street in the original Glenville enclave from photographer Peter Di Leone, who did business in nearby Little Italy. In 1923, Mount Pleasant resident William Jones obtained $6,000 in financing through his employer, the Davis Laundry & Cleaning Co. A handful of lenders were black themselves. Salem and Mary Miller lent $1,600 to dentist Arthur Scott to buy on Greenlawn Avenue in Glenville in 1916. In 1919, bricklayer Arthur M. Segoins lent $674 to chauffeur Walter Seawright to facilitate his purchase across the street on East 130th Street, in the main black Mount Pleasant enclave. Clara E. Christopher, wife of dentist Nina K. Christopher, lent $2,000 to Selmo Glenn for his purchase on Empire Avenue in 1925. And in 1930, Amelia L. Rucker, a physician's widow, lent $3,500 to Rev. Russell S. Brown of the Mount Zion Congregational Church—most likely her own pastor—to buy on South Boulevard in Glenville. In sum, black borrowers proved versatile in tapping their business and social networks for potential sources of financing, on both sides of the color line.[54]

While some white Mount Pleasant residents certainly opposed black influx, the insular shape of the African American settlement there, even into the 1940s, left at least some whites unaware or unperturbed. For example, a Jewish man who grew up on East 142nd Street knew that black families lived nearby; dozens already resided on the street in the two long blocks south of Kinsman Road. Curiously, however, he did not think of East 128th Street between Kinsman and Imperial Avenue—the heart of the historic enclave—as a "black neighborhood." A woman whose family rented an apartment in the 1930s and 1940s at 13106 Kinsman, immediately south of the enclave, remembered seeing black youths at the corner drugstore but mistakenly thought that few if any lived nearby. Yet another man whose family had rented throughout the area remembered African American students at Alexander Hamilton Junior High—just two blocks south of the historic enclave—but professed to have no idea where they lived. In fact, he assumed that blacks could not have lived in the neighborhood, due to discrimination or income. Other whites may have been less oblivious to the neighborhood's growing black presence, however, especially with regard to the secondary Kinsman Heights cluster. Starting in the mid-1930s, some whites began advertising in the local black press their willingness to relinquish their properties there, using terms like "sacrifice sale" and offering "special price" deals with principal, interest, and taxes bundled together. By 1937, the *Call & Post* was characterizing the situation in Kinsman Heights as "tense," following a "series of attacks" by presumably white "neighborhood residents" on the children of Verdie and Robert Thomas, and ultimately on Mrs. Thomas herself when she attempted to intervene.[55]

Thus Cleveland was not completely spared from racial violence—but incidents were few and far between compared to cities like Chicago and Detroit. In the city's most serious race-related clash over housing in the pre–World War II period, Dr. Charles Garvin did encounter organized, collective white opposition in 1925 upon initiating construction of his house on Wade Park Avenue near East 108th Street, at Glenville's extreme southeastern fringe. White neighbors circulated a crudely racist handbill upon learning that Garvin owned the property; after construction, they twice set off dynamite bombs and then drew up a racially restrictive covenant to preclude subsequent black purchases. However (as was the case in many such after-the-fact efforts), not all nearby white residents would sign. City Safety Director Edwin D. Barry also provided round-the-clock police protection for the first two years of Garvin's residency.[56] In Glenville proper, black doctor James Merida had his house splashed with paint and windows broken when he moved onto Parmalee Avenue in 1927; white residents then proceeded to form a "neighborhood improvement association," which unsuccessfully sought to prevent further African American purchases. Uncharacteristically, this group apparently had a Jewish secretary, which Harry C. Smith, editor of the *Cleveland Gazette* and a longtime civil rights champion, derided, asking: "And what kind of Jew is it, please, that will link up with the Ku Klux Klan or its fundamental sentiment or tenet? We know of many Jewish people in this community who will never endorse Mr. Eisler's course in the Merida matter." In 1938, when a group of Jewish residents filed suit to enforce a restrictive agreement following a black purchase in a section off East Boulevard, the Jewish Community Council sat down with NAACP representatives and the suit was soon withdrawn.[57]

Whites were rarely openly hostile, however. One Jewish interviewee whose family moved onto Kempton Avenue in 1918 noted that two black families had already lived on the street and claimed that there were always "very good relations between all concerned." The first African American purchase on Columbia Avenue, around 1931, was said to have generated a "great deal of resentment at the time, particularly toward the Irish family that sold, but no unpleasantness." By 1939, HOLC was noting with disapproval that in Glenville proper,

"Jewish occupants in this area have not been unwilling to sell to colored." As for the original Glenville black enclave, an African American family interviewed in 1956 claimed there were "never any racial incidents . . . [in this area] where some Negro families have resided for many years." Even Dr. Garvin later reported that some whites had "welcomed" his family to the neighborhood, and while he qualified this by saying that "no social relations existed" with his white neighbors, he clearly meant "socializing." One had brought him a book on English gardens, and another who bought next door told Garvin he "had gotten the house much cheaper than he expected 'because of racial prejudice against you,'" and was said by Garvin to be "quite friendly." Another white neighbor once prevailed on him to make a house call, knowing Garvin to be the closest physician in the vicinity.[58]

Similar anecdotes emerge from Mount Pleasant. Despite the compact and insular form of black settlement, some Jewish and Italian residents had extended contact with African Americans, and while these relations were even less intimate than those between Jews and Italians, they were similarly benign and had distinct parallels.[59] First of all, as in the case of sporadic fights between Jews and Italians, black and white interviewees alike hesitated to attribute such clashes to deep-seated racial antagonism. An African American woman whose family rented various quarters in and around the main black enclave recalled there were still "quite a few" white residents, and that she played with white children growing up; even so, she characterized race relations as "not real good," with "some confusion," as her brother was beaten up several times by Italian boys on Imperial Avenue, who nevertheless let him be, once he fought back. On the flip side, an Italian man raised on East 123rd Street between Imperial and Kinsman recalled being chased home from school by three black kids. After he turned and fought them one by one, they not only desisted but subsequently became his chums. He also claimed that the African Americans on his street had been "good neighbors and friends," with one black family living right next door. A black man whose family moved to Kinsman Heights in 1943 said he hung around with Italian, Slovenian, and Polish boys. While he said the whites he knew had never used the epithet "nigger," he recalled that "black" was considered a fighting word and that he had three or four fistfights growing up, mainly to ensure he got "respect."[60]

At least among the neighborhood's younger residents, cross-racial interactions indicate considerable familiarity. The earlier-mentioned Hungarian former resident who grew up just north of the main black enclave recalled placid intergroup relations at Lafayette Elementary School, where he estimated African Americans made up 20 percent of the enrollment. He and his friends "thought nothing" of walking through the black residential enclave to a movie theater on Kinsman Avenue, and he recalled sometimes playing in the "empty fields" (vacant lots) with black kids—a few of whom actually spoke a smattering of Hungarian, like some of the black streetcar conductors and mail-men working in the area. The reminiscences of an African American former resident, who also grew up in the 1930s on nearby Imperial Avenue at East 125th Street, provide a complementary perspective. Here at the edge of the main enclave, he recalled that black families like his "got along quite well" with their Italian, Polish, and Hungarian neighbors. When there were fights, boys from practically every ethnic group sought their help, except for the Italians—as the majority, they had no need for it, he claimed. Jewish boys recruited them for their sandlot baseball teams, while Hungarians took them home for din-ner—where they learned some words he still remembered, like *fekete*, mean-ing "black."[61]

While not all black residents had experiences approaching complete ac-ceptance, evidence indicates that when African Americans and white children lived in close proximity, they commonly played together. Playwright Adrienne Kennedy—who described Mount Pleasant as "our immigrant and Negro neigh-borhood with its small frame houses or brick double houses with small square yards"—wrote of how the Italian man next door "built a beautiful tiny grape arbor in his front yard. Twice he let his niece, Angie, and me sit inside the arbor on a bench. We ate purple grapes." Of another friend she wrote, "[Her] family spoke Italian at home," inspiring Kennedy's "love of that beautiful language." Another black woman whose family moved several blocks outside the Mount Pleasant black enclave, to East 119th Street around 1941, said she soon grew close to the Hungarian, Italian, German, and "Czechoslovak" (probably Slo-vak) children on the street; they all played together and visited each other's houses. A number of white interviewees likewise remembered their African American playmates, from a Jewish man with an African American best friend in elementary school, to another who took violin lessons with a black neighbor, practicing at one another's homes.[62]

While intimate in certain ways, some residents' recollections also suggest cross-racial social distancing. For example, while the earlier-mentioned black former Kinsman Heights resident recalled playing sports and spending time with white youths of various ethnic backgrounds, he could not recall entering his companions' houses, only sitting on their porches. Also, while he fondly re-membered his black friends' birthday parties, he was not sure whether white children even had these—more likely, they did not invite him. And in some situations, contact between black and white children may have been circum-stantial, although such interactions could nonetheless be intimate. For ex-ample, a Jewish woman recalled playing with the grandchildren of her apart-ment building's African American custodian when she was a child, while yet another Jewish former resident recounted that the black custodian, Mr. Hud-son (a foreman at Republic Steel), sometimes brought his family over to visit on Sundays.[63]

Relations between adult black residents and their Southern and Eastern European neighbors were more attenuated in these neighborhoods than those between their children. An African American woman whose family had rented in Mount Pleasant's historic black enclave said black and white neighbors occasionally borrowed foodstuffs from each other, but there had not been much "house hopping" (visiting). Similarly, a black man whose family moved to Mount Pleasant in 1941 thought that "most [people] didn't get beyond back fence talking." Incidentally, he noted that his parents' views on race were formed in the South, where they had learned not to expect much from whites, although he mentioned they felt "more positive and less distrustful" toward Jews. In Glenville, a black man whose family bought on Columbia Avenue in 1940 recalled that "a Jewish family next door watched silently as we moved in," but, "pleased at the improvement[s] [we made, they] soon extended neighborly relations." Individual black families differed in terms of the level of cross-racial contact they desired and experienced varying degrees of acceptance. One Italian woman for a time attended church with her black neighbor in Mount Pleasant, and one Glenville black family routinely played pinochle at the home of a white neighbor, even though said neighbor tended to "inveigh against Negroes as a race." At the other end of the scale were black and white families who lived in close proximity but did not interact. For example, an interviewee of Italian-Jewish parentage felt that African Americans and whites in the neighborhood had "kept to themselves"—an impression that likely stemmed from his own living situation, a rare case of white and black tenants renting units in the same house, in this case on East 142nd Street.[64]

Black and white residents also had business relations and worked together in closer proximity than previous studies have acknowledged. For example, a Jewish man whose parents owned a bakery in Mount Pleasant recalled them employing African Americans as porters and janitors; when making family trips to Syracuse for Passover, they would hire a black employee to drive them. In a particularly striking example, a black Tennessee migrant got a job at a Glenville kosher poultry market in 1940, eventually learning Yiddish and taking over the business in 1965.[65] African Americans also patronized ethnic-owned food stores in the neighborhood. One black resident recalled that "everyone" shopped at the Jewish-owned grocery store on the corner of East 121st Street and Kinsman, while another claimed all local ethnic merchants extended credit without regard to race. Another black former resident had similarly vivid memories of various white-owned businesses and their offerings: the Artino grocery store on East 125th Street and Abell, Spumoni's ice cream, Zeiger's delicatessen and its corned-beef sandwiches, cannoli, which her brother loved, and pumpernickel bread. She recalled black-owned businesses, too, including a barbershop, a fish market, a barbeque restaurant, a bar, and a pool hall. And just as some Italian boys had, her brother found work on Friday evenings as a *shabbos goy* at one of the nearby synagogues. In 1930, one synagogue in the area, N'vai Zedek at 11901 Union Avenue, had a live-in black custodian.[66]

Many of the above-mentioned work relationships between African Americans and Jews carried an important status implication, as domestic service was typically black labor. Many Jewish interviewees recalled hiring domestic help for one day a week if they could afford it, and other evidence suggests that Jews were more likely than Italians or other white ethnics to do so.[67] Several reasons explain this likelihood; first of all, Jews had a tradition of hiring assistance, which had originated in Sabbath observance, as in the *shabbos goyim* mentioned earlier. Jewish women also more commonly assisted in managing family businesses, which left less time for household chores and child rearing, as offered by the man whose parents owned a bakery and hired black domestic help. The most straightforward explanation, however, is that Jews as a group were relatively better off economically, being on an upwardly mobile track since World War I. Naturally, there were status implications associated with this "luxury," as a Jewish man explained: "Too often they [domestics] were referred to as 'My *schvartze* [black] cleaning lady'—partly descriptive, partly condescending." As the 1930 census indicates, a considerable percentage of black Mount Pleasant women who worked for wages were employed at domestic labor, although it is impossible to determine exactly where; it is also uncertain whether white families who hired black domestic help looked in the neighborhood or outside of it. It is clear that some African Americans found this work degrading, as one former resident recalled it being a point of family pride that his mother never had to do it; another man's mother hid this supplemental work from his father. But Mount Pleasant Jewish families also hired domestics of Eastern European ancestry as well as African Americans, especially during the Depression, which further complicates any racialized implications associated with this work.[68]

As mentioned by Kenneth Kusmer, one setting where cross-racial interactions in Cleveland's outer-city neighborhoods were anything but benign was at the available public swimming facilities, which exposed African Americans to white ire and, not infrequently, violent retaliation. Such incidents were typical outside the Jim Crow South and arose largely from white fears of cross-gender socialization, spectatorship, and physical contact with African Americans. Victoria Wolcott has demonstrated that the quest for equal access to pools and other public recreational outlets was central to the Northern black freedom struggle by the 1940s. But in Cleveland as in Los Angeles, this push began even earlier as the issue was tied to Depression-era left-wing politics.[69] A closer look at the local record of African American protest yields several valuable insights into the issue of swimming pool access. One concerns the role of city officials in protecting black civil rights—both the limitations that African Americans ran up against in seeking protection as well as the com-

Bathers at Woodland Hills Park Pool, 1931. Whites sought to prevent African Americans from using swimming facilities in Cleveland's outlying neighborhoods like Mount Pleasant, where a pocket of black settlement was located only blocks from Woodland Hills Park. (Courtesy of the Cleveland Public Library/Photograph Collection)

paratively amenable reception they received, which distinguish Cleveland's record from that of other Northern cities. Another serves to further clarify the nature of black relations with Southern and Eastern Europeans, which the previous discussion has revealed was not wholly antagonistic, as previously assumed, even with regard to housing access.

The potential for racial violence over swimming accessibility emerged early on in these outlying city neighborhoods. In Mount Pleasant, violence flared almost immediately after Woodland Hills Park pool opened in the summer of 1927, less than ten blocks from the main black enclave. On the evening of July 26, a melee broke out between five African American youths visiting the pool and a white mob that *Cleveland Gazette* editor Harry C. Smith claimed amounted to 300. One of the black youths suffered a fractured skull, and a white youth was stabbed. Lower-level harassment and intimidation broke out at Woodland Hills the following July, when two white youths created "a general disorder at the pool" by throwing mud at African American bathers, and a black Mount Pleasant resident filed a complaint at the mayor's office after angry whites threatened and shoved her and a cousin for attempting to swim there. "Listen old nigger, you get out of here. No niggers are going to swim in this pool. I'll kill you," one antagonist allegedly told her. Whites behaved similarly in Glenville. In a 1930 incident, white youths at the Gordon Park beach on Lake Erie repeatedly ducked two young black girls whose mother insisted on their right to swim there, to the point where she felt compelled to wade out and thrash one of the bullies with her umbrella.[70]

Thus at least some black residents were willing to brave physical harm or take other actions to defend their legal rights. In fact, a few had already successfully gained pool access against the odds. During the week prior to the initial 1927 incident at Woodland Hills, slate roofer and enclave resident Emmett Meade, his wife, and their young son, with several of his friends, swam at the pool, albeit "after much difficulty." Meade had personally pushed to integrate the city's building trades unions, and after the mud-throwing incident the following year, he pressed the issue of pool access by forming a Mount Pleasant "Community Club" with the approval of *Gazette* editor Harry Smith, who urged black citizens, "particularly those in the vicinity," to "patronize it [the pool] far more liberally than they have been doing in the past, and thus support the stand in our favor, and that of law and order." Others turned to the political process or took legal action. The woman who filed an affidavit went to the mayor because police on duty at the pool had acted only to guard the dressing rooms while she and her cousin changed after deciding to leave, and to restrain the white bullies from following them off the premises. The mother who wielded her umbrella must also have lodged a formal complaint, because while police and lifeguards at the scene had declined to intervene, black Assistant Police Prosecutor Roger N. Dillard secured a warrant to arrest Barney

Gailwicz, the eighteen-year-old ringleader. Most dramatically, the aggrieved black youths in the 1927 melee, with the local NAACP branch's assistance, filed suit under the 1884 Ohio Mob Violence Act and won amounts ranging from $200 to $750 each, totaling more than $3,000.[71]

City officials were receptive, at least publicly, to black demands for redress in these incidents; although continuing enforcement would prove to be a perennial challenge, African Americans leveraged scarce political capital in attempting to produce a favorable outcome. In the wake of the 1927 incident, the city's park director issued a statement asserting that the facility was open to everyone—and Mike Baschko, the white assailant who had been stabbed, was convicted of assault and battery and sentenced to thirty days in the county workhouse. Meanwhile, black Glenville resident George Myers, who as owner of a barbershop in the posh Hotel Hollenden had ties to the city's white elites, sought to have African American officers assigned to the Woodland Hills Park police detail, being joined in this effort by Cedar-Central councilman Thomas W. Fleming. Their push resulted in the appointment of a "special duty" (white) officer—and as seen, did not prevent more trouble from materializing in 1928. On a brighter note, however, the mud-throwers were charged with disorderly conduct and each received five-day sentences in the workhouse.[72]

Frictions between African Americans and Southern and Eastern Europeans loom large in these pool conflicts. *Gazette* editor Smith blamed "the foreign element" in these disturbances, and the woman who went to the mayor's office similarly cited the ineffectiveness of the "evidently foreign" officers. Smith additionally derided Baschko as "a leader of the Buckeye Rd. gang," a reference to the Hungarian district on the northern border of Mount Pleasant centered along that thoroughfare.[73] In fact, Woodland Hills Park is best understood as lying at the juncture of several heavily immigrant or mixed ethnic neighborhoods where blacks were present only in tiny numbers. There was a sprinkling of African American families in Corlett, the thoroughly mixed Slavic and Italian neighborhood to the south, and in the industrial neighborhoods west of the park. However, virtually none lived in either the Italian enclave around Woodland Avenue and East 110th Street or in the vast Hungarian and Slovak colony along Buckeye Road.[74] Significantly, some of these ethnics either had lived in or were in the process of moving out of older, inner-city neighborhoods being subsumed into the Cedar-Central ghetto; both of the mud-throwers convicted in 1928 fit this profile, at least one of whom was of Italian ancestry. Complicating matters, cross-racial interactions in Cedar-Central were not generally hostile; while a former resident stated "no visiting" occurred between blacks and Italians, historians have uncovered instances of household barter as well as racially integrated youth gangs.[75] Nevertheless, for whites moving from older downtown neighborhoods to peripheral ones largely devoid of African Americans, the upward mobility noted by Kusmer had implications of racial separation as well as leaving a declining area. That Southern and Eastern Europeans increasingly understood segregation as the norm comes through in the surprise Gailwicz expressed upon his arrest in the 1930 Glenville incident, imagining he was merely enforcing accepted segregationist policy of one section of the beach for whites and another for blacks.

Despite securing some redress for incidents of racial harassment at swimming facilities in the early years, a lack of continuous enforcement left open the possibility of conflict, leaving many prospective African American bathers hesitant to test the waters. By 1934, Smith, of the *Gazette*, complained that only two swimming pools in Cedar-Central "of the eight or ten other public pools in the city . . . are open to our people and we have three members of the City Council." The conditions at one, Portland-Outhwaite, he described as "miserable." Smith's comments were motivated by a July incident in which Woodland Hills pool staff turned away black bathers from a pre-booked pool party, while police on duty deferred. This prompted recently elected Cedar-Central Councilman John E. Hubbard to approach Mayor Harry L. Davis, who subsequently issued an antidiscriminatory statement proclaiming city pools open to everyone. Smith, for his part, renewed his call for an on-duty black police officer at the facility. But incidents continued as black bathers were denied access to the Gordon Park beach in Glenville the following month. Once again, Councilman Hubbard pressed Mayor Davis, who reissued his previous statement and ordered the Safety Director to arrest anyone engaging in racial intimidation.[76]

African Americans' struggle in Cleveland's outlying city neighborhoods for access to public swimming facilities soon broadened beyond its community base, coalescing with the mid-to-late 1930s upsurge in left-wing, interracial political activism associated with the Communist Party's "Popular Front" phase.[77] In preparation for the summer 1935 swimming season, a "Neighborhood Committee," formed through the Communist-sponsored League of Struggle for Negro Rights, launched a campaign to ensure access to the pool. While the first meeting held at Mount Pleasant Methodist Episcopal Church was sparsely attended, organizers made more progress by the second meeting at Quinn Chapel AME in May. Led by Howard-educated Communist Party activist Maude White, the Neighborhood Committee chose the slogan "Make the Woodhill [sic] Swimming Pool Safe for Colored People." As a likely indication that it had tapped the degree of Communist Party support present to some extent within all the area's ethnic communities, the committee also "secured the endorsement of fourteen Hungarian and twelve colored organizations in its campaign." By July, the Legal Defense Committee of the local NAACP branch was also on board, demanding that the city's Parks and Public Property Department transfer a black police officer to the pool. Yet the campaign lacked traction, as complaints persisted. The following month, a delegation of Mount

Pleasant mothers, Councilman Hubbard, and black Assistant Police Prosecutor Perry B. Jackson lodged a complaint with the city's park director, for although African American youngsters went unmolested during the morning "free swim" sessions, a "determined element of whites in that neighborhood" repeatedly blocked black access in the afternoons and evenings. The mothers reported they were ordered out of the pool by white youths, threatened with ducking underwater, and told to go to the Outhwaite pool in Cedar-Central. After the meeting, Mayor Davis issued yet another statement and promised better protection.[78]

When the National Negro Congress (NNC) convention came to Cleveland in 1936, black community and left-wing activists grew even more determined to enforce the right of fair access. By broadening both momentum and mobilization, they extracted at least a symbolic victory. That year's campaign kicked off with an "Emergency Conference" held in May at the Cedar YMCA, led by the NAACP's Legal Defense Committee and followed by an assertive letter to Mayor Harold H. Burton. After a black youth was threatened near Woodland Hills Park in July, the Legal Defense Committee along with representatives from the NNC as well as the Communist Party–affiliated International Labor Defense (ILD) and American League Against War and Fascism met with Burton, who responded by assigning two African American policemen as well as several black lifeguards to the pool. When one of the policemen left after just one week and three of the lifeguards refused to transfer from Portland-Outhwaite for fear of being "mobbed," the activists made a bolder statement. On July 17, with the mayor's assurances, the local NAACP and *Call & Post* sponsored an official visit to the Woodland Hills pool. NAACP branch president and civil rights champion Chester K. Gillespie had sent a letter to the membership, urging participation lest the NAACP "be left holding the empty bag." With security guaranteed by twenty-six Cleveland police officers (three of them black), the *Call & Post* declared the visit a resounding success. Besides NAACP officers, the leading participants included black former city councilman and civil service commissioner Clayborne E. George, ILD attorney Sam Goldman, and Communist lawyer Yetta Land, who reported that the group was "not interfered with in any way." Black attendance subsequently increased in the short term. The following week, NAACP Youth Council members swam unmolested on two occasions and reported they were treated with the utmost courtesy by pool staff, while a group from the Future Outlook League, Cleveland's arm of the militant national "Don't Buy Where You Can't Work" boycott movement, also successfully visited the pool.[79]

But whenever enforcement slackened, conflicts at the city's swimming facilities resumed. Small-scale, left-wing direct action tactics continued the following summer at Woodland Hills, but, without substantial community backing and mayoral protection, these had little chance of success. One Jewish former resident remembered as "one of the most striking days of his life" an incident in the summer of 1937, when "two or three Jewish Communists and a couple blacks" entered the pool, prompting the other bathers to gather along the sides chanting, "Get out! Get out!" Outnumbered and without any police intervention, the activists in that instance had complied. The following summer, the *Call & Post* profiled the pool in a feature, asking, "Negro Bathers Shun Beautiful Woodland Hills Swimming Pool—Why?" The piece included a photograph of five on-duty police officers (all white), and reported, "There was not a single Negro bather to be seen. Nor, we learned upon questioning, had any appreciable number of Negro bathers used the pool since it opened this summer," despite its proximity to the historic African American enclave. No doubt many enclave residents hesitated risking bodily harm, considering the past record of police indifference. Meanwhile, black swimmers at Glenville's Gordon Park on Lake Erie reportedly still confined themselves to a rocky outcropping, because fights inevitably broke out when they tried to use the main beach. Sure enough, later that summer, white bathers chased from the beach a black mother with three small children. This incident prompted *Call & Post* editor William O. Walker to demand an inquiry of Mayor Harold Burton, following the revelation that the policeman on duty had refused to help and had told the woman that "she had no business in the water and should go where Negroes were permitted to swim."[80]

But it was another 1938 incident at Woodland Hills Park pool that revitalized neighborhood activism and the left-liberal alliance, again forcing the city administration to recognize black civil rights while underlining its reluctance to enforce the law. In early August, postal clerk and Mount Pleasant resident Raymond Hightower took his son and two of the son's friends to Woodland Hills for the occasion of the annual *Call & Post* newsboys' picnic. Hightower was also an officer of a local in the International Workers Order (IWO), a Communist Party–sponsored insurance provider and network of social clubs organized along ethnic and racial lines, of which there were forty in Cleveland at the time. Hightower and the boys were swimming with a dozen other youthful black poolgoers when they were suddenly surrounded and menaced by approximately fifty whites, who called them "niggers," told them the pool was for whites only, and threatened to drown them. The others left, but Hightower insisted on his right to swim and remained in the water, making two attempts in vain to seek (white) police assistance. When black patrolman John Jones arrived on the scene, the white antagonists splashed and taunted him when he attempted a reprimand. Finally, as Hightower reentered the pool a fourth time, he was tripped and struck in the back by one youth, at which point police reinforcements arrived and arrested six of the bullies.[81]

The left-liberal coalition swooped into action upon hearing that Mayor Burton was hoping "not to make an issue of the affair," and that the 29th Ward councilman where most of the arrestees lived was pressing for no charges to be filed. A delegation, including the NAACP's Chester Gillespie, Clayborne George, Yetta Land, and Rev. Grand Reynolds of Mount Zion Congregational Church, as well as representatives of the NNC and ILD, hurried to the chief prosecutor's office, demanding he pursue a case. After an hour of wrangling, the entire group of six arrestees was charged with "creating a disturbance," while the youth who had struck Hightower was additionally charged with assault and battery. Southern and Eastern Europeans were prominent among the group of bullies, as evidenced by the surnames Ambrescia, Monachino, Busky, Souco, and Solurky. Yet discouraging news came in the form of reports that pool staff had since started selectively applying "athlete's foot" checks in order to dissuade African American bathers, and that Harrison Harney, a black detective prominent in the arrest, had subsequently been reassigned. In the weeks before the trial, left-wing activists declared themselves ready to intervene at any sign of racial prejudice, while Harney's transfer led *Call & Post* editor William O. Walker to deride Public Safety Director Elliot Ness as "the great G-man [who] is turning out to be just another punk in so far as Negroes are concerned." Meanwhile, Hightower brought local black clergy in the Ministers' Alliance and Baptist Ministers' Conference on board.[82]

An interracial crowd of more than one hundred Hightower supporters came to the scheduled assault trial in early September, which was then postponed due to the small courtroom size and lack of an available jury. Held the following week and featuring black assistant police prosecutor Perry B. Jackson, the trial ended in acquittal for the defendant; six members of the all-white jury admitted during the selection process that they would personally avoid a racially integrated public pool, yet expressed confidence they could uphold the law with impartiality. While Smith in his *Gazette* bitterly blamed Mayor Burton for "his continued effort to cater to the foreign element in the community . . . while continuing to IGNORE our people," the *Call & Post* opined that "even though the case was lost, we believe it will have great effect upon the few lawless youths who heretofore have created the trouble." To publicize the October trial for the remaining five defendants, Hightower supporters organized a mass meeting at Saint John's AME Church with a special invitation to the mayor. Around 200 attended the event, where Mayor Burton went on record that "there is no basis for discrimination. . . . We are all interested in the principle . . . that a spirit of co-operation in mutual rights and obligations be developed." Representatives from the NAACP, Future Outlook League, NNC, American League for Peace and Democracy, and ILD also delivered speeches. When the second case came to trial, the defendants pled guilty to disorderly conduct on advice of counsel and received probation and $25 fines, which were waived on their lawyers' pleas for leniency, and paid court costs of about $5 each. Despite these minimal consequences, Smith lauded the outcome and credited the publicity generated by the previous week's mass meeting. Yet, despite their maximum exertion of political power, black Clevelanders clearly still lacked influence compared to Southern and Eastern Europeans, unable to extract anything more than a symbolic acknowledgment of their rights.[83]

While 1938 marked the height of racial conflict at Woodland Hills—the *Call & Post* newsboys again held their annual picnic at the park and successfully used the pool the following year—1939 saw one last flourish of left-wing civil rights activism, this time in response to an incident in Glenville. In July, two members of the local NAACP Youth Council, one black and one white, were assaulted when they attempted to use the public pool at Forest Hills Park. A white policeman on duty warned the young men that "there might be trouble" if they attempted to use the facility and then left the scene. Robert Fritzmeier, the white prospective bather, was viciously beaten by five Italian American youths when he defended their right to swim there—apparently by pointing out that Italians and other nonblacks used the Portland-Outhwaite pool in Cedar-Central without incident. "You must be a nigger yourself!" shouted one of the attackers as they beat Fritzmeier, sending him to the hospital and leaving him partially deaf. The two filed a complaint with Assistant Police Prosecutor Jackson and retained Yetta Land—a Communist Party member active in the Woodland Hills fight since 1936—as their lawyer. As the police investigation languished, activists organized a meeting demanding that Safety Director Ness take action, attracting members of the NAACP, Glenville Civic Club, 24th Ward Republican Club, Glenville Democratic Club, Glenville Garden Club, and the Young Communist League. These groups coalesced as the "Glenville Civil Liberties Council," which went on to sponsor an August 28 "Tolerance Day" at Forest Hills pool. Some five hundred participants competed in a friendly interracial swim meet and listened to speakers from the NAACP and the American Civil Liberties Union (ACLU). One of the attackers was finally arrested and convicted in October, but charges were dropped against another found to be already serving a burglary sentence in a nearby suburb.[84]

This regular, collective white violence against African Americans at swimming facilities in Mount Pleasant and Glenville from the late 1920s through the 1930s lies at the extreme end of a continuum which did not extend to other public spaces, or even to housing, with a few isolated exceptions. Evidence also suggests that trouble came not from whites who lived in closest proximity to blacks, but rather from those who lived in the wider vicinity or even visitors from older downtown neighborhoods being absorbed into Cedar-Central. Strict boundary policing offers another possible explanation for the observed discrepancy between swimming access and other aspects of neighborhood life, since whites had basically resigned themselves to the established nearby presence of African Americans, yet drew an extreme line at swimming pools. Local historian Russell H. Davis has written that "the pool incidents ceased when blacks used the pools in sufficient numbers so that white people hesitated to start trouble." While Woodland Hills ceased to be a point of conflict, clashes continued at Glenville pools and in even further outlying Garfield Park well into the 1950s. The Cleveland pattern once again contrasts strikingly with Chicago, which, according to Arnold Hirsch, saw few race-based pool conflicts until the 1950s and 1960s, after housing fights died down. Hirsch speculates that African Americans may have avoided these spaces until their numerical presence was sufficient to provide a modicum of safety, but his alternative explanation—that white residents simply did not consider black users threatening until they were present in large enough numbers to shake whites' sense of "community control"—seems especially inapplicable here.[85]

Persisting through Adversity

As in practically all major urban centers to which Southern migrants flocked during World War I, the Great Depression proved devastating to black Clevelanders as a group—raising the question of how African Americans in Glenville and Mount Pleasant weathered the crisis. While unemployment in Cleveland peaked at 45 percent on the whole, black unemployment ran as high as 85 percent in the poorest sections of Cedar-Central. According to one assessment, "The disproportionate rate of unemployment among Negroes . . . [was] the end product of the semiskilled occupational ceiling which had restricted Negroes to marginal jobs." To avoid eviction, working-class blacks improvised survival strategies that included taking odd jobs, bringing in family or boarders for extra money, even scavenging or throwing "rent parties." New Deal relief and job-creation programs provided a lifeline for thousands of poor households on the verge of starvation; by 1934, the local Urban League estimated that 80 percent of black Clevelanders were on either direct or indirect relief. But while African Americans did receive a proportionately greater share of jobs relative to their representation in the population, through agencies like the Works Progress Administration, their need was far greater. Furthermore, the available positions—for example, in street repair—were often short term, low paying, and tainted by the notion that blacks were suited only for manual labor.[86]

While poor and working-class African Americans were obviously hit hardest by the Depression, the striving and established middle class struggled mightily as well. The sorts of jobs that had provided a margin of economic security to Mount Pleasant residents proved especially vulnerable, as downward mobility increased competition for service jobs that white workers had previously scorned—for example, as waiters, attendants, and elevator operators. In the skilled trades, white workers redoubled their efforts to exclude blacks. Particularly devastated were the employment sectors into which African American workers had made inroads since World War I—transport, industrial work, and the construction industry—because as output contracted and the housing market collapsed, competition for the available jobs increased. White women also reentered domestic service in significant numbers, competing for work and adding to a general downward pressure on wages. As for the small number of nonlaboring positions available through New Deal programs, qualified African American jobseekers were rejected for white-collar or skilled trades work, or placed at a lower rank than their experience merited. With the tenuous economic condition of the African American population on the whole, black-owned businesses also suffered as their clients' expendable earnings declined. Small retailers went out of business in droves, barbers lost their shops, and beauticians were forced to dramatically lower their prices, while six of the city's most prominent undertakers—previously among the African American business elite—were bankrupted by the collapse of black-owned insurance companies whose policies once paid for funeral expenses. Even some established black churches struggled to pay their mortgages as congregants themselves cut back on regular donations.[87]

Key among collapsing black-owned businesses were mortgage-lending and real estate ventures that had served as important alternative sources of financing and had enabled some African American families to move to the urban periphery. In the comparatively prosperous 1920s, barber and political broker George Myers had counted two black-owned banks, two loan associations, and an insurance company; in 1930, writer Charles Chesnutt mentioned "three mortgage and loan companies, of which one expects shortly to meet all the requirements . . . to make it a regular bank." Postal-carrier-turned-businessman Herbert S. Chauncey was the powerhouse behind many of these ventures, the first of which was the Empire Savings & Loan Co., chartered in 1919; by 1926 it had opened a second branch office at East 90th Street and Cedar Avenue and reportedly held over $350,000 in assets at the time of Chauncey's premature death in 1930. With some depositors withdrawing funds and borrowers struggling to pay, Empire was reduced to insolvency and state receivership in 1934. An insurance company founded by Chauncey, as well as his Peoples Realty Co., also fell victim to the Depression. The latter, which he had envisioned as a means of promoting black access to farther-outlying neighborhoods, was forced to close after it defaulted on the mortgage for a tract of land it had acquired in Miles Heights, a former suburb recently annexed by Cleveland.[88]

In addition to poor economic conditions, federal and local housing policies contributed to a worsening housing situation for African Americans during the Depression. In a brilliant 1972 article anticipating "second ghetto" historiography, Christopher Wye demonstrated that so-called slum clearance and the construction of large public housing estates in Cedar-Central served to displace poor blacks into the farthest eastern reaches of the district, to the point where class stratification by occupation or educational level was no longer discernible by 1940. Meanwhile, fiscal and tenanting policies of the time ensured that not the poorest, but rather middle-class blacks experiencing downward mobility overwhelmingly made up the first generation of residents at Outhwaite Homes, the one public housing complex open to African Americans out of the initial three built. While location is not an exact proxy for class or status, a 1937 map by the Real Property Inventory of Metropolitan Cleveland reveals that out of 574 African American families moving into Outhwaite, 10 did indeed come from Glenville, while 54 relocated from Mount Pleasant; of the remainder, the overwhelming majority had lived in the formerly higher-status eastern reaches of Cedar-Central. Furthermore, lending policies formulated by New Deal agencies like the Home Owners Loan Corporation (HOLC) and Federal Housing Administration (FHA) served both to legitimize racial discrimination and further narrow African American homeowners' access to financing. In 1937, lawyer and NAACP member Chester K. Gillespie successfully got the state's director of commerce to intervene against the city's second-largest bank when it tried to deny a mortgage to a black purchaser for a house "north of Cedar Avenue," most likely in the still overwhelmingly white Hough neighborhood. The following year, however, black doctor Ira B. Scott filed a discrimination lawsuit against HOLC, and later in 1938 the *Call & Post* disapprovingly quoted Senator Robert J. Bulkley's letter to a Cedar-Central resident expressing "regret that you are among those whom the FHA does not benefit." In 1939, the paper decried the action of an agent with New York Life who had "refused point blank to sell a house in the Mt. Pleasant district and another in the Glenville area to colored."[89]

Wye subsequently described Cleveland's black housing dynamics during the Depression decade as a "contraction" of the ghetto—the number of census tracts inhabited by African Americans declined while their concentration increased—and dismissed black population increases in outlying Mount Pleasant, Glenville, Hough, and Miles Heights as insignificant. "Even if a movement of whites toward the suburbs had made additional housing available to Negroes in these sections during the Thirties, it is doubtful if many upper class Negroes could have afforded to move into them," Wye surmised. While the combined total African American population growth from 1930 to 1940 in all these outlying areas was only 1,400 individuals, or as Wye pointed out, an increase in their share of the city's black population from 6.6 to 7.3 percent, this expansion amid poor economic conditions and tightening lending discrimination was more significant than he allowed. It is true that African American gains in Hough, just shy of 300 individuals, were limited almost entirely to a single street, Blaine Avenue. Miles Heights was the youngest and still the smallest of these outlying clusters, seeing a population gain of less than 200. But with an increase approaching 600 and the number of blocks inhabited by African Americans nearly doubling over the decade, Mount Pleasant was described by the Welfare Federation as having "grown much faster" than the other black outlying areas. HOLC described African American "infiltration" there as having "progressed with moderate success" from 1928 until about 1936, at which point it became even "more pronounced" and steady. And in Glenville, where the black population grew by nearly 400, HOLC assessors noted that "foreclosures were very heavy in this area," with over one hundred properties "sold to colored, particularly where adjacent colored occupancy existed" from 1935 onward.[90] While statistically small, black population growth outside of Cedar-Central was anything but insignificant to these white observers.

A closer look at homeownership and patterns of geographic mobility for black residents of Mount Pleasant and Glenville indicates considerable resilience—more than previous assessments have assumed. African American influx into these neighborhoods was likely slowed by the Depression, and many families moved out as others moved in; renting also increased, with some departing whites apparently retaining ownership, as suggested by below-average levels of owner occupancy on some blocks by 1940.[91] But at the same time, black homeownership remained fairly stable; of the 238 African American homeowning families listed as living in these neighborhoods in 1930, 149 (63 percent) were still living at the same address in 1940. Eleven of the 1930 homeowners died in the intervening decade so cannot necessarily be counted as losing their homes. And as for those families who did change addresses, at least ten more moved into comparable or superior accommodations—a conclusion reached through location evaluation according to census tracts, ranked using the concept of "economic tenths" (deciles) developed by demographer Howard Whipple Green of the Real Property Inventory. By averaging rents and calculating equivalent values for owned homes by census tract, Green developed a ten-stage scale to estimate what he called "planes of living" in the metropolitan area. Combining the number of families who kept their homes with those who moved either within their tract or to a comparable or higher-ranked one, at least two-thirds (67 percent) were not geographically disadvantaged by the Great Depression. In fact, only sixteen of the total 1930 homeowning households (7 percent) demonstrably experienced downward mobility as evidenced by their move to a lower-ranked tract, although it is worth emphasizing that mobility proved indeterminable for 22 percent of the total.[92]

Some of the moves—both down and up—are revealing. The former homeowner who experienced the sharpest fall in mobility (six deciles) was Herbert H. Betts, who in 1930 worked as a furnace tender and lived on East 142nd Street in Kinsman Heights; ten years later he described himself as an "engineer" at the Independent Towel Supply Co. and had moved into the Outhwaite Homes, which made him typical of the first cohort of public housing tenants. In a comparable downward fall that actually seems worse than the four deciles indicated by the Real Property Inventory scheme, Oscar Fields went from working as a waiter in 1930 and owning a house on Garfield Avenue in Glenville, to toiling as a laborer and living on East 49th Street in Cedar-Central. Both mortician Elmer F. Boyd and dentist Jessie Bridgeman were forced to give up their Glenville homes for less prestigious accommodations in the main black district's eastern portion. Samuel D. Marlow of Kinsman Heights went from bricklayer to common laborer living on Quincy Avenue in Cedar-Central; his neighbor, carpenter William Gordon, was still plying his trade as of 1940, but had moved into rented quarters on Kinsman Road. The few cases of upward mobility are also worth mentioning. Self-employed painter and decorator James D. Hamilton moved from the main Mount Pleasant enclave to Englewood Avenue in Glenville, while Charlesetta Jones, a day worker already widowed in 1930, also succeeded in moving from there to East 146th Street in Kinsman Heights ten years later. The seemingly largest gain in geographic advantage (three deciles) was nothing of the sort, on closer examination. In 1930, chauffeur Henry B. Mason and his wife, Henrietta, owned a house on Pasadena Avenue in Glenville. He died five years later, and by 1940 Henrietta had been reduced to a live-in maid at the glitzy Moreland Courts apartments on Shaker Square.

A further indication that many black residents of Cleveland's outlying neighborhoods weathered the Depression and remained basically on an even keel—most strikingly in the original Mount Pleasant enclave—comes from a comparison of Real Property Inventory statistics collected in 1934 and 1940 (Table 1.4). While rates of homeownership among African American residents in the two census tracts containing the main Mount Pleasant black enclave saw a dip, to 30 percent, from the 1930 level of 33 percent, by 1940 this percentage was on the rise at 31 percent. Furthermore, the absolute number of homeowners increased during the Depression. In the other outlying black enclaves, the percentage of homeownership fluctuated downward, although the absolute number of homeowners there also grew substantially by 1940.

African American residents of neighborhoods like Mount Pleasant utilized various means to weather Depression-related economic adversity. One interviewee recalled that black families like his had sought supplementary menial work to maintain their position; his own grandfather shoveled coal into train cars, for example. Another former resident's father bolstered economic security through creative self-employment; having saved up enough money to buy his own truck after working as a driver for two different coal companies, he stockpiled cinders in his backyard to deliver as driveway filler for families in the suburbs. This man also used the truck to retrieve laundry that his wife washed for families in nearby Shaker Heights, and went on to haul scrap paper for extra money during World War II. In an even more dramatic story, an unemployed black bricklayer pawned his gold watch and bought a truck he used to peddle fruits and vegetables in Mount Pleasant. Gradually accumulating

Table 1.4. Black Households and Homeownership in Mount Pleasant and Glenville, 1930, 1934, 1940

Area	1930		1934		1940	
	Total	Homeowners	Total	Homeowners	Total	Homeowners
Mt. Pleasant (orig. encl.)	349	114 (32.7%)	371	112 (30.2%)	622	195 (31.4%)
Glenville (proper)	111	82 (73.9%)	134	72 (53.7%)	212	115 (54.2%)
Kinsman Hts.	70	30 (42.9%)	139	31 (22.3%)	193	57 (29.5%)
Glenville (orig. encl.)	45	13 (28.9%)	50	19 (38.0%)	48	8 (16.7%)

Sources: 1930 Manuscript Census; Howard Whipple Green, *Standards of Living in the Cleveland Metropolitan District . . . Special 1935 Report* (Cleveland, 1935); Howard Whipple Green, *Planes of Living in Cuyahoga County . . . Special 1940 Report*, pt. 2 (Cleveland, [1941]).
Notes: Compilers used "Other" (Nonwhite) instead of "Negro" for 1934. Black janitors living in all-white apartment buildings, a significant phenomenon in Glenville, could not be distinguished for 1934 and 1940.

savings, he bought land further out in Miles Heights and opened a store, which by 1948 he had upgraded into a brick grocery and ice cream parlor with living quarters on top.[93]

■

On the eve of World War II, African American families had securely established their presence in several of Cleveland's peripheral neighborhoods. While such areas still contained but a small percentage of the city's total black population—more than 80 percent continued to live in the Cedar-Central district in 1940—outlying black settlement had disproportionate significance for Cleveland's nascent black middle class, for a number of important reasons. The earliest African American residents benefited from arriving early, before the imposition of race-based deed restrictions or the establishment of clear customs of racial exclusion. In Mount Pleasant, middling and upper working-class black residents could bolster their economic security by using their properties for subsistence food production or as workspace to earn additional income, which proved especially crucial during the Depression. Meanwhile, more consistently middle-class Glenville emerged as a showcase for the city's black property owners. Early African American residents of outlying areas contested the solidifying notion among whites that black influx hurt property values and inexorably led to deteriorating living conditions. Such presumptions seemed to be borne out by developments in Cedar-Central and drove policies instituted by private lenders as well as New Deal agencies like the HOLC and the FHA by the 1930s.

Despite attempts to restrict their mobility, small but growing numbers of African Americans succeeded in gaining access to better housing, in part by moving to areas inhabited mainly by Southern and Eastern Europeans, and particularly Jews, who did not typically resist them. When faced with white antagonism, especially at local swimming facilities, African Americans organized themselves to demand their rights and found sympathetic white allies on the political left. In the process, they got a fair hearing and some consideration from city officials, although this particular battle proved to be a constant struggle. These residents' early presence in Mount Pleasant and Glenville also established the vectors of future black population expansion, and would eventually trigger a search for even newer, farther-outlying accommodations by upwardly mobile African American families—as World War II ushered in a renewed, and far more massive migration from the South.

2 : : :
Expanding Black Settlement in the 1940s

GLENVILLE AND MOUNT PLEASANT

The meeting of Glenville's Park Home Owners Association was barely under way one Sunday afternoon in April 1945 when Chester K. Gillespie threw the proceedings into tumult. According to an eyewitness report made to the Council Educational Alliance (CEA), a Jewish social service agency active in the neighborhood, association president Harold Beebe announced the purpose of the meeting: "to keep this area a white neighborhood," as "there had been a lot of trouble with hoodlums in the community which threatened the life and property of the people." A local police lieutenant was the first speaker to address the approximately 150 present, and he attempted to strike a conciliatory balance, pointing out that there were "plenty of white delinquents and wayward children" in Glenville and thus the problem was "[not] essentially one of a racial character." He did recommend, however, that "if any suspicious looking Negro gangs . . . were noticed the police should be notified immediately." One woman in the audience claimed that "twenty hoodlums" had "undermined the foundation of her home," while another complained about "potentially delinquent children" who "ran loose over the neighborhood while [their] mothers and fathers worked." The lack of racial specificity in these comments apparently caused some attendees to become "uneasy and impatient," leading Beebe to return to "the property angle and the problem of keeping Negroes out." It was only then that the otherwise all-white audience noticed Gillespie, an African American attorney who in 1944 had bought at 934 Herrick Road, right around the corner from Beebe. With Beebe demanding that Gillespie leave and the audience shouting remarks like "Get him out!" and "We don't want the Niggers," white councilman Harry T. Marshall stood and defended Gillespie as a model citizen, a former state senator, and city council member. Doubtless unbeknownst to the audience, he also had a history of litigating for civil rights.[1]

Gillespie rose amid continued shouts of opposition to his presence and promised he would leave if allowed several minutes to speak. He first thanked the police lieutenant for his relative impartiality, then expressed his own concerns about recent "disturbances" and pledged to maintain the desirability of the neighborhood. "If it is keeping up high standards that you are interested in," said Gillespie, "you'll not find a cleaner place than mine anywhere in this neighborhood—and as far as hoodlums are concerned, let's keep them out, white or black." With regard to the issue of black real estate agents pressuring white residents to sell their homes, Gillespie condemned the practice and additionally pointed out that "not only Negro real estate dealers but also whites who hire Negro field representatives" engaged in such tactics. One Park Home Owners Association member equivocated that "they didn't object to Negroes like him but it was the others," although someone else praised the South for knowing how to keep blacks "in their place," and Beebe apparently declared it was common knowledge that "Negroes are not social equals to the whites, they are ignorant, lacking of intelligence, and that it is a folly to build 'them' up because they were no good anyhow." At this point, the CEA observer countered Beebe by noting that modern science had disproven innate racial inferiority and caused a "general uproar" by answering "yes" when asked whether she would want black next-door neighbors. Another attendee said the gathering "had the character of a fascist demonstration" and someone else reminded the audience that American soldiers of both races were just concluding a war against Nazism. Gillespie finally became irritated and stalked out with the parting shot that "even though I am going the Negro race will still be represented by people you can't recognize as being Negroes," that is, individuals light enough to pass for white. He subsequently wrote Mayor Thomas A. Burke with the warning that "the Glenville area is a powder keg" where "a terrible race riot may be imminent."[2]

As discussed by a number of historians, white neighborhood "improvement" associations like the Park Home Owners Association became preoccupied with racial exclusion as early as the 1910s and multiplied in newer, outlying city neighborhoods in the decade after World War II.[3] In addition to using legal means such as zoning and racial restrictive covenants (prior to their outlawing in 1948), many came to rely on extralegal intimidation and violence as a way of discouraging would-be black neighbors. The Park Home Owners Association seemingly countenanced both approaches. The meeting concluded with Beebe's exhortation to strengthen the organization by "canvassing every street and getting property owners to pledge not to sell to colored people." But according to another observer, there had also been talk of an "Alert the Neighborhood" plan to be used in the event that "more than a normal number of Negroes . . . [were] seen congregated." The precise nature of the response was not made explicit, but in his opinion, "the definite impression was that sticks, brickbats are a part of it." However, the police lieutenant who addressed the meeting urged white residents to refrain from violence.[4]

A steady trickle of African Americans had been moving into Glenville since 1915. While approaching 300 families in 1940, blacks still made up just 2 percent of the neighborhood's population that census year. Increasing numbers of African Americans moved to Glenville during the war. But most continued to settle on the blocks just off East 105th Street and in the original black enclave near East 123rd Street and Superior. In the area represented by the Park Home Owners Association, from Kempton Avenue to the railroad tracks north of Saint Clair Avenue, between East 88th and East 102nd Streets, there were no more than twenty-five black families in 1940. Furthermore, only a few lived north of Saint Clair, where most of the Park Home Owners Association's defined territory lay. Also, while there was an underlying current of anti-Semitism at the meeting—some present openly blamed Jews for selling houses to blacks—the bulk of Glenville's Jewish population also lived elsewhere.[5] Thus while Beebe asserted that Jews "were just as much interested [in black exclusion] as the rest," the Association's membership likely drew mainly from the neighborhood's remaining old-stock Protestants and Catholics belonging to nearby Saint Aloysius and Saint Philip Neri parishes.[6]

What is striking about the Glenville case, and what distinguishes it from patterns observed in other cities prior to the 1960s, is that the Park Home Owners Association was not just countered, but actually marginalized by an interracial neighborhood organizing drive that effectively channeled white sentiment regarding the process of demographic change away from racist resistance. In Mount Pleasant, too, a similar strategy was deployed amid racial turnover. To the consternation of some, these neighborhoods were not successfully "stabilized," in that racial integration proved fleeting. As established destinations for African American home seekers, and with the operation of structural factors shaping population movements on a metropolitan level, Glenville and Mount Pleasant saw dramatic black population gains and steep white losses over the following decades. Some whites in these areas surely disapproved of such activism intended to mediate the process, and many more residents—both white and black—were either unreceptive or indifferent. However, these efforts ensured that demographic turnover occurred in both neighborhoods not without tension, but without collective violence. Described by activists themselves as undergoing an "orderly" transition, both areas thus fit the pattern of "undefended neighborhoods" that previous historians have largely disregarded.[7] Far from being insignificant, the unimpeded progress of racial residential transition in such areas forces us to rethink the assumption that white resistance was the most noteworthy aspect of neighborhood-level demographic change in the post–World War II city. Rather, the most pressing issues raised in interracial neighborhood organizing from the onset of integration—housing upkeep, city services, shopping options, neighborliness, and safety—would become increasingly synonymous with the core concerns, interpretation, and reform agenda that upwardly mobile middle-class blacks pursued in the face of postwar urban decline.

In fact, an effort to mobilize the Glenville community behind the slogan "Good Neighbors Are Good Americans" was under way even as the Park Home Owners Association met, with a "mass meeting" to form a community council already scheduled at Glenville High School for later that month. Beebe had even referenced it in his retort to Gillespie: "I'll see you at Glenville [High School]—they allow colored there—we don't want them." Impetus for the community council project came from several local groups: the Civilian Defense Block Plan, Council Educational Alliance, Jewish Community Council, and Urban League, as well as area PTAS and school administrators. Individual representatives from these bodies had been meeting since January to promote community cohesion, spurred by an awareness that "the changing neighborhood was bringing up problems which must be faced" and convinced that "an inter-racial program was necessary." In their discussions, the organizers had concluded that "every organization in the community should be represented, such as civic groups, churches, political organizations, social service organizations, clubs, fraternal organizations, libraries, schools, etc." They also recognized the need for special efforts to reach the area's growing black population, whose institutions were still located outside the neighborhood. In the weeks leading up to the community council's formation, its promoters made 10,000 phone calls through the local civilian defense organization and printed 20,000 handbills, which were distributed to every home and business in the neighborhood.[8]

Over a thousand neighborhood residents gathered on the evening of April 23 at Glenville High School to form the Glenville Area Community Council (GACC). Speakers identified a list of challenges facing the community: aggressive real estate sales tactics, conversion of housing to multifamily occupancy, and a dearth of recreational facilities. They included Mayor Thomas A. Burke himself; Leonard W. Mayo, dean of Western Reserve University's School of Applied Social Sciences who had been instrumental in the formation of the city's Community Relations Board the previous month; Sanford Solender of the Council Educational Alliance; Sidney R. Williams of the Urban League; and Russell H. Davis, the black principal of Central Junior High School who was active in Cedar-Central neighborhood organizing. Burke expressed pride that Glenville citizens were coming together for the occasion but also "deep humility that here in this great democracy such a meeting is necessary." Solender reminded the audience of the recent exclusionary efforts by the Park Home Owners Association and mentioned that African American residents were still being excluded from the neighborhood's parks and swimming pools. Williams expressed hope that "real neighborliness" might develop, imagining black and white housewives chatting over fences. Following the meeting, the *Cleveland Press* editorialized approvingly that Glenville had "recognized its problems and put democracy to work to solve them."[9]

While whites did not organize collective, violent resistance, smaller-scale racial conflicts did accompany the wartime influx of African Americans into Glenville. Adding urgency to the formation of the GACC was a narrowly averted conflagration in March 1945, a planned battle between dozens of white and black youths in Rockefeller Park at the neighborhood's western border. While initial reporting specifically mentioned young toughs from the nearby Sowinski Avenue Polish settlement as having gathered to meet Glenville blacks for a fight in the park, further investigation revealed that whites from inside the neighborhood itself, as well as Italians from Mayfield Road and African Americans from Cedar-Central had also showed up for the rumble, which was defused at the last moment by police. Following the incident, the local NAACP issued a press release stating, "The Branch is fully aware of the ramifications and final effects of such tension and strongly urges that all parents assume the full responsibility of explaining to their children the seriousness of these problems." Furthermore, they recommended that residents "exercise concentrated control over themselves and their children by keeping youngsters off the streets when necessary."[10]

Russell Davis additionally uncovered "street car incidents" between black and white youth, while two social work students doing research in the neighborhood around this time cited "conflict" over the use of a baseball diamond and "instances of racial discrimination" at the Forest Hills Park pool. They also reported "gangs from other areas" perpetrating "a slight wave of minor criminal acts, such as street-fighting, petty thieveries, the smashing of street lamps, etc.," while Harold Beebe of the Park Home Owners Association alleged that white youths had been beaten by blacks and that a white girl had recently been raped. Black neighborhood resident L. L. Yancey, an attorney and former deputy city treasurer, revealed in a private letter touching on the GACC that "several racial incidents with dire possibilities had occurred in elementary, junior high, and Glenville High schools, [as well as] in the neighborhood theaters" and local parks. Understandably, the GACC undertook among its earliest initiatives to investigate discriminatory treatment at Forest Hills, and to secure increased police patrols—which by the time of its second mass meeting in May 1945 were said to have led to a decline in "the type of disorder that previously seemed prevalent has been experienced lately." Yet homeowners' associations in Glenville's all-white, far eastern portion continued their efforts "to exclude Negroes seeking to rent or acquire property" there, the Community Relations Board reported.[11] Thus, despite auspicious beginnings, the long-term success of interracial strategies such as those employed by the GACC and its analogue, the Mount Pleasant Community Council (MPCC), remained tenuous.

Wartime Racial Tensions

Cleveland, like other Northern and Western defense industry centers, saw a massive influx of black Southern migrants during World War II. The city's African American population ballooned from 84,504 in 1940 to 147,847 in 1950, a 75 percent increase. During the war, accommodations became particularly scarce for African Americans whose housing options were constrained by white antagonism and racially discriminatory housing policies. The vast majority of black migrants ended up in Cedar-Central, further increasing segregation in the district and accelerating the deterioration of housing stock as apartments were "converted," or chopped up into smaller "kitchenette" units, to accommodate more renters. Another source of housing in Cedar-Central, the Cleveland Metropolitan Housing Authority (CMHA), had from its beginnings in the 1930s maintained a policy of racial segregation, with just token integration in the form of a handful of black or white tenant families strategically interspersed. CMHA continued its segregationist policies during World War II with the construction of so-called temporary war housing, reinforced by the city's War Housing Authority, which served as a clearinghouse for housing vacancies, and which basically exhausted all of its openings for black renters by mid-1943. Not until 1944 was a nondiscrimination policy put in place for the first of the CMHA-administered temporary war housing estates, Berea Homes—located on the West Side, where the African American population was already miniscule.[12]

Despite the housing hardships they endured, black Clevelanders' burgeoning numbers and collective economic power led to increased political influence. The city experienced a local version of the "Double V" campaign sweeping the nation, with African Americans vocally demanding equal rights during a war supposedly fought in the name of democracy. The local black press and NAACP spoke out against the extension of a whites-only policy to CMHA's Woodhill Homes estate, which opened in 1940 on the far eastern edge of Cedar-Central, with *Call & Post* owner-editor William O. Walker calling the housing authority "despotic" with "operations . . . more like Hitler's dictatorship than democratic America." CMHA's seizure of black-owned businesses along East 55th Street (including the eminent House of Wills funeral parlor), in order to build extensions to the Outhwaite Homes, similarly provoked outrage in 1941 and 1943. Meanwhile, the militant Future Outlook League, Cleveland's local manifestation of the "Don't Buy Where You Can't Work" boycott movement visible in Northern black neighborhoods since the 1930s, agitated against exorbitant rents and code violations in Cedar-Central. The Future Outlook League and Urban League simultaneously pushed for better job opportunities in the defense industry, as the wartime population influx also spurred a revival of black-owned businesses.[13]

In spite of the tight wartime black housing market, pent-up demand drove expansion out of Cedar-Central and into areas with an established African American presence. The War Housing Board noted a case in Glenville of a black man who purchased a house on Gooding Avenue in 1943, which caused the Jewish family renting there to scramble in search of accommodations; the new buyer moved his furniture in but generously agreed to stay with relatives until the Jewish renters succeeded in buying a house of their own. Commenting on wartime population shifts, *Call & Post* owner-editor William O. Walker noted in 1944 "the prodigious buying of residential properties by Negroes" in Glenville and Mount Pleasant, notwithstanding the refusal of institutional lenders to offer mortgages in these areas. "Again it is being proven that despite bans and restrictions you just can't coop people up in any given area if they want to buy and have the money to," approved Walker. He himself recognized the influx into Glenville as overflow from Cedar-Central and pointed out that "Negroes, no different from any other people, want to live in decent houses in desirable neighborhoods." Yet Walker discouraged hastiness, opining, "There is no need for all the white property owners in Glenville rushing to sell, [and] neither is there any reason for Negroes rushing in to purchase these properties at war inflated prices." One local historian explained the burgeoning black homeownership in Glenville and Mount Pleasant during and immediately after World War II as "a combination of eager home buyers and equally eager sellers," noting that African Americans and whites alike used wartime savings to upgrade their housing situations.[14]

As a result of this demographic shift, Glenville gained a reputation as the city's swankiest black neighborhood, dubbed the "Gold Coast." Poet Langston Hughes, who had lived in Cleveland as a teenager and retained an interest in the city, wrote in 1946 that a number of African American families had successfully purchased homes on East Boulevard with "spacious yards and trees and plenty of play space for children." The newest arrivals included Dr. Govan A. Myers, a prime mover in the establishment of the Forest City Hospital; Lawrence O. Payne, former city councilman and first black assistant prosecutor; and mortician William F. Boyd. In the only attempt at violent resistance during the World War II era, a dynamite bomb was placed in 1942 against the front door of a home purchased by black physician J. E. Brown, but it failed to detonate. The initial wave of African American newcomers to Glenville fit the previous pattern of having solid middle- to upper-class backgrounds. Playwright Adrienne Kennedy, whose father and mother were a YMCA secretary and schoolteacher, respectively, wrote about how in the summer of 1943 her family moved from Mount Pleasant to "the popular Glenville section," where the houses were larger and "even had a room with a fireplace, a room that ran the length of the house." Incoming African American homebuyers typically paid from $3,500 to as high as $7,500 for homes in Glenville. One purchaser, a federal employee at the time, related that he had been approached by a white business contact who was eager to unload his house and accepted a surprisingly low offer the federal employee made in an attempt to decline. This hesitation stemmed from an awareness that banks would not likely finance him—which indeed proved to be the case, although he was able to secure a loan through other means.[15]

African American business owners also gained footholds on East 105th Street, the neighborhood's main commercial strip—thus reinforcing the image of Glenville as the preserve of black Cleveland's entrepreneurial set, but also sparking some disagreements over what constituted "high class." A 1944 newspaper feature noted more than a dozen such establishments said to be "prospering": barbershops and beauty shops, a laundry and several dry-cleaning businesses, a confectionery and two restaurants. A dressmaker stated: "I opened my business here last January and I've been doing real well. . . . Several of the business people right close sent flowers when I opened, and they've treated me mighty fine." One of the city's black-owned newspapers, the *Cleveland Herald*, also relocated to East 105th Street from Cedar-Central. Apparently not all establishments were welcome, however. The *Call & Post* reported that one "Jitterbug Spot" had generated complaints and faced attempts to shut it down, even though it was "found to be guilty of no violations of any sort." More ominous was a trend of white-owned businesses lowering quality standards in response to the increasing presence of African Americans. Thus the *Call & Post* warned in 1944 that "the bad-food menace, usually flourishing in the areas most heavily populated by the Negro, has followed him in his escape to the 'Gold Coast,'" after a white East 105th Street grocer was fined for selling spoiled meat to a black housewife.[16]

Occurring between decennial censuses, the exact pace of wartime influx by African Americans into Glenville is difficult to determine, although a black real estate agent later recalled that the market "opened wide" to African American purchasers starting in 1941–42. Various estimates placed the neighborhood's black population at 10–18 percent and growing rapidly as of 1945. Black enrollments had risen in several neighborhood schools, to 30 percent in one instance. At the same time, Glenville's Jewish population—which began suburbanizing some ten years earlier, notably to Cleveland Heights—had decreased by nearly half, falling from more than 27,000 in the former year to approximately 15,000 at the war's end.[17] While partially attributable to racial anxieties, historians have explained this pattern by additionally pointing to Jews' above-average rates of upward mobility, as well as their generally smaller and thus comparatively "portable" institutions compared to more entrenched Roman Catholic ones.[18] Jews had particularly strong in-group commitments, whether defined in religious, social, or economic terms. As one black interviewee observed in retrospect: "When white families moved out of Glenville and other formerly all-white areas, they weren't always 'running away.' Many just wanted new homes in a suburb, or wanted to move where friends had moved." Meanwhile, as the Jewish share of the neighborhood's population declined from some 65 percent to below 40 percent between 1940 and 1945, non-Jewish whites (mostly Catholics) living in the area actually increased from one-third to nearly one-half the total.[19]

African Americans were also moving into Mount Pleasant and Jews were moving out during World War II, but demographic turnover there unfolded significantly more slowly. Even so, some white observers regarded this transition as ominous. In early 1945, as the Hiram House social settlement was establishing service in Mount Pleasant, one of its staff members wrote in a confidential letter, "The neighborhood Negro population is increasing very rapidly so that our work will be very much as it has been in the old neighborhood"—a reference to the dwindling of the original settlement's white ethnic constituency downtown. However, the bulk of this increase was in the census tract containing the historic black enclave, where African Americans' share of the population jumped from 27 to 56 percent between 1940 and 1950; this contrasts with Mount Pleasant as a whole, where their proportion rose from 8 to 22 percent.[20] Jewish residents were simultaneously flowing out of the neighborhood as blacks moved in, but as in Glenville, their departure began before racial residential transition was an issue. Demographer Howard Whipple Green found out that Mount Pleasant's Jewish population dropped by approximately one-third from 1926 to 1937, from 22,504 to 14,842—but instead of a sudden exodus to the Heights suburbs, this took the form of a "slow trend of mobility towards the east." Thus while Jewish enrollments declined at Lafayette Elementary School in the heart of the historic black enclave—and at Mount Pleasant Elementary in the older, less prestigious western portion of the neighborhood, where hardly any African Americans yet resided—they increased at Charles Dickens and Andrew Rickoff, newer schools in Mount Pleasant's eastern reaches, where the black population was actually growing. Even so, in 1944, staff at the Council Educational Alliance (CEA), which traditionally served the neighborhood's Jewish population, reported "antipathy . . . toward the Negro group which was moving into the neighborhood . . . with much tension resulting."[21]

White fears accompanying black population influx influenced behavior as much as any actual incident of racial conflict. Since the beginning of 1945, the local Civilian Defense Block Plan had been working on Glenville's Pasadena Avenue "to foster better relations by having everyone in the block get to know each other," because recently in the vicinity, "Jewish children were not being permitted out after dark to attend neighborhood activities or visiting because of fear of being attacked by Negro children." The previous year, this same body had organized a "racial unity forum" at Patrick Henry Junior High School attended by 600 neighborhood residents. Similarly in Mount Pleasant, one girls' club during the CEA's 1941–42 season organized a "Mother-Daughter tea . . . for the express purpose of 'showing' their mothers that 'it was all right to come there at night.'" While most observers agreed that white residents' fears were based more on rumor than in fact, these were powerful motivators nonetheless. Black politician Harry E. Davis, who lived in Glenville and participated in early community-organizing efforts, at one point suggested privately funded police patrols as a possible "method of combating the fear that people have of going out at night." In an attempt to "help relax race tensions," the Welfare Federation in July 1945 assigned a field worker to improve recreational access in Glenville, while the Cleveland Police Department's Race Relations Unit charged with "tracking down rumors" also operated in the area.[22]

Several other race-related issues stoked tensions in Glenville and Mount Pleasant during the war, setting the stage for the formation of the Glenville Area Community Council and the Mount Pleasant Community Council. In Glenville, for example, real estate brokers pressured white homeowners to sell their properties, although this was not nearly so widespread or organized as the "blockbusting" of subsequent postwar decades. Harold Beebe of the Park Home Owners Association claimed it had been formed in response to a "thoroughly organized effort . . . made to induce, by whatever means possible the white people of this community to sell their homes." At one point, seven owners on a block of fifty homes had simultaneously put their homes up for sale, although Beebe claimed the "panic" subsided after his group was formed in mid-1944. Russell Davis reported pressure on Yale Avenue white residents to sell, while black electrician Charles W. Brown of Englewood Avenue wrote the *Call & Post* to describe an incident in which a real estate broker canvassed his street—and expressed surprise that the Browns were sixteen-year residents. "These unscrupulous agents are promoting segregation in order to get a commission," Brown opined, before concluding, "There are many reasons why a stop should be put to this nuisance and let the owner make contacts if he wishes to sell." While some complaints singled out blacks, evidence turned up in field research by two Western Reserve University social work students suggests white brokers were as likely to be involved. Some of the aggressive tactics used included statements like "Your neighbors will be Negroes. They will damage your property and rob you. Your very lives and those of your families will be in danger." "This line of talk has, of course, not fostered better understanding between groups and among people," the students noted.[23]

Housing maintenance and especially conversion for multifamily occupancy stoked additional tensions having racial overtones. Widely blamed for fostering overcrowding and deterioration in Cedar-Central, housing conversion was actually promoted as a federal wartime imperative in order to accommodate additional in-migrant workers. In 1940, Glenville's housing stock was in relatively good condition; just 3 percent of dwellings needed repairs and 6 percent were overcrowded, approximately half the city average in each category. Five years later, a report on the neighborhood concluded that "Negro families for the most part are maintaining their homes in neatness and good repair," although "deterioration of property does occur when [white] families which intend to sell and move out feel there is no point in putting any more money into maintenance or when absentee owners feel that . . . opportunity must be seized to get as much income as possible out of residential property by creating multiple dwelling units." The Western Reserve University social work students similarly reported that some owners had "resorted to the familiar trick of converting one-family homes into multiple dwellings and turning loft areas over stores into a series of small suites," for which they charged exorbitant rents. However, white residents were more apt to blame African American newcomers for any existing deterioration. One fumed in a letter to Bishop Edward Hoban soon after the war: "We have lived on East 115th Street for over forty years, and have seen that particular section go steadily down from year to year and in the past two or three years now [with] the influx of colored people . . . many of the properties . . . have become so deteriorated that they should be abolished [demolished]."[24]

The number of wartime conversions is difficult to estimate. Social work students cited a 1946 survey that had counted an increase of 331 dwelling units in Glenville since 1940—two-thirds of them in the census tracts off East 105th Street into which many African Americans moved—and correctly observed, "This figure probably does not reflect the total increase as there was some doubling up and sub-dividing in homes that would not have been recorded." Mount Pleasant also experienced a degree of war-related overcrowding that alarmed some observers. In 1944, the local press reported on one shocking example in the neighborhood's historic black enclave: "The two houses at 3276 E. 126th street—though in a fairly good neighborhood—are so near to falling into their sewage-filled basements one hesitates to walk in them. Yet until Building inspector John Drees condemned them six weeks ago and ordered the occupants out, 20 people called these two shacks home." A black woman and her parents who moved into a duplex on East 132nd Street in 1945 recalled "lots of people" living in the house; they rented the third floor where there was no water or kitchen facilities, while some fifteen people from two extended families shared the rest of the space.[25]

Neighborhood Organizing and Community Councils

While the various tensions accompanying wartime demographic turnover in Glenville lent urgency to the formation of the Glenville Area Community Council (GACC), this effort at neighborhood organizing, as well as the analogous Mount Pleasant Community Council (formed in 1946), must be understood in the context of similar efforts around the country—none of which had yet prioritized racial residential transition, however.[26] Interracial coexistence was perceived as a wartime necessity, and many cities sought proactively to improve race relations during the war—especially after Detroit's horrific June 1943 race riot. Clevelanders were especially active along these lines, and their efforts predated Detroit's conflagration; furthermore, some participants were motivated by the humanistic goal of promoting mutual understanding between different racial and ethnic groups, not simply by short-term crisis prevention. As Charles W. White, a former Cleveland NAACP president and assistant city law director, explained at one meeting debating the adoption of an "Inter-racial Code" modeled on that of post-riot Detroit: "We have been trying to educate people for generations [about racial intolerance,] and most people have a lethargy about it. Both white and Negro have been apathetic because they accept the situation as hopeless. Owing to the influence of the War, more and more people are anxious to do something about it and more are becoming outspoken."[27]

As early as 1941, the Cleveland Federation of Churches, in a confidential memorandum, noted an increasingly militant mood among black organizations, concluding that lack of access to good industrial jobs, combined with increasing segregation and banks' discriminatory lending practices, was creating a "chasm . . . widening among the white and Negro community." Its authors recommended the formation of interracial teams to encourage "frank discussion of the facts" and to "increase goodwill." The organization subsequently appointed an interracial ministers' committee to promote dialogue at member congregations. By 1943, the Cleveland Federation of Settlements through its Committee on Race Relations was encouraging staff at its affiliates to treat all those using their services equally, in the interest of "broadening . . . social horizon[s]." Following the Detroit riot, this committee further convened a meeting of local social workers and public officials to discuss issues exacerbating racial tension, from unequal economic opportunity and poor housing conditions to insufficient police representation. For its part, the local NAACP branch interviewed black community leaders to gauge the potential for a mass outbreak of racial violence in the city. Most agreed that Cleveland's race relations were comparatively placid, though several warned that the younger generation, in particular, was becoming impatient and might retaliate if whites resorted to violence.[28]

Other observers were less optimistic. In July 1943, Mayor Frank Lausche convened one hundred community leaders, warning, "We must set in motion a courageous approach to the problem to guard against the possibility of someone touching off a spark that will set off an explosion." He subsequently appointed a Committee on Democratic Practices to investigate problems relating to housing, recreational facilities, and police protection. A confidential survey conducted by the YMCA also revealed a growing impatience among younger blacks, which concluded: "Negro leaders think that Cleveland passed a crisis on the July 4th week-end. Ugly rumors were circulated here at that time as had occurred in Detroit before the riot." While investigating anti-Semitism in the city the following year, a Racial Relations Panel, headed by Leonard Mayo, dean of the School of Applied Social Sciences at Western Reserve University, nevertheless concluded that "Negro race relations offered a more massive problem here." Meanwhile, Cleveland's social service umbrella, the Welfare Federation, instructed its Group Work Council to establish a Council on Race Relations, in order to facilitate interracial dialogue in its member agencies. In early 1945, the Cuyahoga County Council for Civilian Defense set up, through its Block Plan, "machinery to refer matters of inter-racial problems arising in the various areas" to the mayor's office.[29] Finally, Cleveland joined Chicago and many other cities in establishing its Community Relations Board later that spring, a valuable tool in mediating racial conflicts over the succeeding decades. Although the wartime atmosphere in the city remained tense, the largest-scale outbreaks of violence in the city proved to be three brawls following high school sports events in 1944 and 1945. While two of these were between black and white students, the third involved Jews and Italians and so was interethnic rather than interracial; furthermore, observers concluded that all these clashes were expressions of school or neighborhood rivalries as much as they were intergroup conflicts.[30]

Revisiting the formation of the GACC reveals the handiwork of several groups involved in citywide race relations efforts, as well as the intense commitments of neighborhood-based activists. A small cadre of eight to ten individuals from the Independent Voters Committee, who had helped mobilize support for Franklin D. Roosevelt's reelection in 1944, first took the initiative, including in their number both a teacher active as a volunteer with the Council Educational Alliance (CEA), as well as a "Jewish housewife" who chaired the local Civilian Defense Block Plan. By January 1945, some sixty individuals, consisting "largely of Jews and Negroes," formed the core group of activists; it was also noted that "almost none" of those involved came from "the predominantly white Catholic St. Clair section" and that "the Negroes on the Council represent largely the professional group" who were "long-time residents of the area, rather than the newly arrived element." The Jewish Community Council and Urban League soon came on board, while organizers approached local churches, synagogues, PTAs, and the Jewish Young Adult Bureau. Though it would prove futile, Sanford Solender of the CEA (who was a key GACC activist) even reached out to the exclusionary Park Home Owners Association, writing its president Harold Beebe to express "hope that all people of the Glenville section who are interested in the protection and betterment of the area will participate in the Glenville Community Council."[31]

Analogous efforts to form the Mount Pleasant Community Council (MPCC) were launched at a March 1946 meeting attended by several dozen residents. Here, too, the CEA was instrumental in promoting the project, along with the Hiram House social settlement, which had recently relocated to the neighborhood. By midyear, some 120 persons had been recruited onto the MPCC's organizing committee, one of whom stressed, "There is no crisis here, as there was in the Glenville area," but rather, "the main problem is the diverse population, consisting mostly of Italians, Negroes and Jews. . . . A community council could bind them together to solve some of the problems common to all." The organization was formally convened in a similar fashion to its GACC counterpart, with a "mass meeting" held on June 6, 1946, in the Alexander Hamilton Junior High School auditorium. Around 300 persons showed up for the event, where Solender, Frank Baldau of the Community Relations Board, and *Cleveland Press* editor Louis B. Seltzer spoke. Despite the generally upbeat tone, speakers did mention fears of housing deterioration and increasing absentee ownership, as well as concerns with liquor availability, juvenile delinquency, and "signs of intolerance and discrimination."[32]

The model adopted by the GACC and MPCC fit into the general approach of "intergroup relations" or "intercultural education," a project in which Jews were particularly active nationwide.[33] Tolerance efforts along these lines took an especially robust form in Cleveland, gaining ground since the 1930s. For example, the Welfare Federation organized the interracial and interethnic Intersettlement League of Mothers' Clubs in 1937, which brought together 2,000 mothers connected with neighborhood-based social settlements. As of 1942, this organization included members from twenty-five different ethnic groups, and in a radio program broadcast that same year to promote wartime unity, Ora McEwen, an African American past president, intoned: "We have worked together in harmony; barriers of prejudice and inherited hates have been broken down; we have had opportunity to appreciate the culture of other groups. . . . It's helping to make real Americans of us all." One participating Mount Pleasant mother said of the league in 1943: "Here white, black, Jew and Christian meet in fellowship and opportunity is given for practice of inter-racial relationships. . . . We have learned to break bread at our annual dinner with our Christian and colored friends and to like it."[34]

Other local practitioners of this approach included the Cleveland Church Federation, which first celebrated an "Interracial Week" in 1939, and whose Race Relations Committee in mid-1942 discussed forming a racially integrated church congregation. The federation, in early 1945, also sponsored a Race Relations Clinic at the city's Central YMCA. Brotherhood Week, an annual observance started by a Denver Catholic priest in 1934, was first marked in Cleveland with a 1941 City Club roundtable hosted by members from the National Conference of Christians and Jews. Starting in 1943, the local chapter of this organization held annual observances of Brotherhood Week, which became more elaborate after the war. That same year, the Cleveland NAACP branch celebrated the annual observance with a memorial service for the recently deceased Dr. George Washington Carver at the Masonic Temple Auditorium, an event attended by 1,000 people.[35] Seeming progress in race relations continued after the war. In April 1946, the Welfare Federation committed itself to an official policy of interracialism and nondiscrimination, and that summer, in a successful "inter-racial experiment," the city's Camp Cleveland in Warrensville Township was integrated for the first time.[36]

Such efforts also extended to the neighborhood level, prior to the formation of the GACC and MPCC. Brotherhood Week was observed by many of the city's Jewish congregations in 1943, including the Kinsman Jewish Center in Mount Pleasant, which had also earlier invited black youth from the Cedar YMCA to a meeting on "interracial problems." Residents also formed a 30th Ward Citizens Committee in 1944 "to unite all races, creeds, and nationalities and people of all political beliefs around the campaign to re-elect President Roosevelt" and subsequently requested that popular left-liberal councilman Joseph F. Krizek be considered for membership on the Community Relations Board. This group was likely synonymous with the Brotherhood Rally of the 30th Ward, which, along with labor unions and the Community Relations Board, lobbied Mayor Burke in 1946 to block right-wing firebrand Gerald L. K. Smith from speaking at the city's public auditorium. Demonstrating its commitment on the local level, the Community Relations Board scheduled talks with neighborhood groups in the interest of promoting good intergroup relations; its executive director, Frank Baldau, spoke to the Glenville Corner Club (a group of local business and civic leaders) in September 1945 and to the Glenville Youth Council in April 1946, with 250 attending the latter meeting.[37]

Citywide efforts by Jewish and African American organizations and leaders, to work together on matters of common concern amid the tense wartime atmosphere, extended beyond the CEA, which played such a crucial role in forming both the GACC and the MPCC. Perhaps most ambitiously, a Committee on Negro-Jewish Relations, formed by the Jewish Community Council, the NAACP, and the Urban League, set out to counteract black anti-Semitism, which they theorized had links to occasional "unfair treatment of domestic help by Jewish women, employment practices by Jews, and policies of some Jewish landlords in the Negro areas." One Jewish participant in the deliberations expressed his opinion at a 1941 meeting that "[as] victims of persecution and oppression themselves, Jews ought to be more understanding and careful to avoid any discriminatory acts toward other minorities." Yet friction between Jewish business owners and black customers persisted, despite suggestions to establish a "code of ethical practices," to educate through the Jewish press, or to enlist black attorneys as mediators. Finally, after a local black newspaper ran a 1944 exposé on "cheat merchants" that explicitly identified some as Jewish, the Committee on Negro-Jewish Relations decided to "call in the violators and to secure a cessation of their unfair practices." In the discussion that followed, "it was pointed out that while the Jewish community could not accept the responsibility for what individuals might do, it was in the interest of the Jewish community to encourage its members to maintain high standards of conduct in keeping with Jewish traditions."[38]

The GACC and MPCC also benefited from earlier neighborhood-based efforts to organize a community council in Glenville and, to a lesser extent, in Mount Pleasant. Early in 1938, activists from the East 105th Street branch of the CEA discussed the need for better recreational facilities in Glenville, alongside other pressing issues like unemployment. Over the course of the year, they coalesced into a Glenville-Doan Community Council (Doan being the former name of East 105th Street) with the assistance of local librarians, school and city officials, and rabbis and ministers. These youthful activists were regarded with some suspicion by adults in the stodgier Glenville Corner Club and by neighborhood Catholic clergy because of their Jewish leadership, the reputed presence of Communists in the group, and their insistence that African Americans be included in any community mobilizing effort. This latter demand caused an impasse until late 1939 when the Glenville Corner Club finally relented, reluctantly acceding to the participation of delegates from long-standing black organizations like the Glenville Garden Club. After an initial open meeting in early 1940 at the Glenville Branch Library, the organization was formally constituted as the Glenville Community Council the following month. Yet, despite offering some programming over the course of the year, the new organization folded by the following spring. The hint of a similar prior effort in Mount Pleasant comes from a 1937 plan of the Negro Welfare Association, precursor to the Urban League, to organize a "Mt. Pleasant Neighborhood Council," along with community groups in several other areas of black settlement, under Welfare Federation auspices. Such an initiative was in line with the Negro Welfare Association's successful formation, earlier in the decade, of similar groups in West Park and Miles Heights.[39]

Left-wing neighborhood activism is the final precursor explaining the GACC's and MPCC's origins, especially under the auspices of the Communist Party and the militant, boycott-oriented Future Outlook League, which continued into the early postwar period. As discussed, Communist Party activists were prominently involved in the mid-1930s fight to integrate the Woodland Hills Park pool in Mount Pleasant, and such activism was becoming more visible on the neighborhood level after the war—whether in the form of demonstrations by housewives from the Glenville Communist Political Association against the removal of price controls, or regular meetings of "the Glenville Communist Clubs" and the Communist Party–affiliated American Veterans' Committee (noted to consist "largely of Jews and Negroes") at the local CEA branch. The Communist presence in Mount Pleasant and Glenville persisted into the early postwar period, so that in 1948, when William Z. Foster, the Communist Party's general secretary, came for a Cleveland visit, the biggest fundraiser was the Mount Pleasant Club at $450. The Jewish Kinsman Club also donated $169, the Ward 29 Club representing Glenville donated $150, and the Lower Kinsman Club raised an unspecified amount. The Future Outlook League undertook similar neighborhood campaigns. It picketed one East 105th Street grocery in 1946 and succeeded in getting one of its members rehired, and as of 1947 it was negotiating with chain stores in both Glenville and Mount Pleasant in an attempt to win positions for black female clerks.[40]

Not only did the Communist Party and the Future Outlook League retain a visible presence in these neighborhoods into the early postwar period, but they also joined the GACC and MPCC on a number of prominent local causes until the brewing Red Scare neutralized the left-liberal coalition after 1948. For example, a November 1945 "Community Meeting" sponsored by the GACC to demand full employment and a permanent Fair Employment Practices Commission (FEPC) featured former Communist city council candidate Joseph Kres alongside Hazel Mountain Walker, the city's first black school principal, with the event moderated by the CEA's Sanford Solender. Similarly, in early 1946, the CEA, NAACP, Communist Party, and black churches organized a mass meeting for the "People of Glenville—Negro and White," held at a local Baptist church.[41] The 1946–48 push for a nondiscrimination ordinance, following a series of incidents at the city's Euclid Beach amusement park, brought both the GACC and MPCC together with the Communist Party, Future Outlook League, Congress of Racial Equality, Cleveland NAACP, National Negro Congress (Cleveland Chapter), and Social Action Department of the Cleveland Church Federation, among many other groups. In 1948, the MPCC and Jewish Peoples Fraternal Order joined with the Civil Rights Congress of Ohio to lend "full support and endorsement of the fight to see justice done" in the case of a black female graduate student at Western Reserve University who was denied service at a local tavern. The GACC was especially active in pushing for a state FEPC law, in 1950 bringing the increasingly radical W. E. B. Du Bois to keynote an FEPC rally at the neighborhood's black Cory Methodist Church. The GACC also opposed loyalty oaths and other "anti-subversive" measures used to purge local postal workers, exhibited a consistent interest in national causes like the Willie McGee case, and vocally condemned the poll tax and lynchings.[42]

Aside from these larger issues that mobilized other liberal and left-wing groups, the GACC and MPCC developed an intensely local, neighborhood-based reform agenda that would continue on for decades. In effect, these groups empowered upwardly mobile, middle-class blacks in these neighborhoods to fight for what they considered acceptable living conditions. Even before its official formation, the GACC's organizers had appointed a Recreation

Committee to tackle the issue of inadequate neighborhood facilities, which many observers believed exacerbated racial tensions and potentially encouraged juvenile delinquency. In one of its first actions, the Recreation Committee wrote the Board of Education, asking that school playgrounds be kept open on a supervised basis through the summer, because "the racial tensions in the area are an increasingly serious problem to the community, and we feel that a well-planned and directed recreational program can be a valuable offset to these disquieting conditions." Although the Board of Education granted this request, budgetary constraints prevented playgrounds from being kept open into the fall as the GACC had hoped, despite their efforts to recruit needed volunteer supervisors. The GACC Recreation Committee did convince one school to hire an additional recreation leader, persuaded another to open its gymnasium for basketball, had the city add a playground on Yale Avenue, and sponsored a "Play Festival" attended by 500 children during the GACC's first year.[43]

Another early priority that proved especially durable on the long-term black middle-class reform agenda was the restriction of liquor availability and the blocking of similarly "unsavory" neighborhood establishments. As early as October 1945, the GACC Executive Board sat down with police to discuss poolrooms as another nuisance, along with gambling and even prostitution in some area establishments. Russell Davis subsequently wrote the State Liquor Control Commission, "indicating our disapproval of the increase of liquor permits in our area," and the police shut down one business that was in violation of the law. By early 1946, the Legislative and Civic Affairs Committee of the GACC, which had taken up issues of zoning and housing code violations as well as liquor permits, was checking to see how many feet away two East 105th Street bars were from schools and religious institutions, in possible violation of city ordinances. "No rowdyism apparent at either place—Inter-Racial Clientele," their investigator incidentally noted. Sanford Solender of the CEA lent his support in a subsequent letter, writing, "The location of these bars in the immediate vicinity . . . attracts people of a type who should not be in contact with children and creates a general atmosphere destructive to the growth and development of young people." The GACC subsequently found out that the city's policy was not to enforce the ordinance outlawing bars within 300 feet of schools and churches, unless formal complaints had been lodged. Meanwhile, the GACC relented in the case of two veterans who sought their approval for a carry-out store selling beer but not liquor, asked three liquor-selling establishments to remove candy and "items conducive to children's trade," and planned a survey of the number and type of liquor permits already approved for Glenville.[44]

A third immediate interest of the GACC was the amelioration of racial tension, though this issue's urgency would diminish as Glenville became increasingly black during the 1950s. Interested in confronting prejudice and encouraging dialogue, the organization established an Intergroup Relations and Education Committee, tasked with addressing potential incidents, planning educational programming to improve tolerance and understanding, and handling tensions in local public schools. During the GACC's first year, this committee organized a Conference on Community Cooperation that brought together school personnel, PTAs, and social service agencies in the area. Working closely with the Community Relations Board, it also supplied "films, literature, and speakers on inter-group relations" as needed. By mid-1946, plans were being discussed to form "a choral group including different religious and racial backgrounds," which "might symbolize unity and be a more effective educational medium in the community than formal programs." The committee also planned adult activities, including "fun nights" and friendly tournaments, as "another means of helping neighbors become acquainted." In another accomplishment during its first year, the GACC established the Glenville Area Youth Council, which organized activities in the area's junior and senior high schools.[45]

In June 1946, the GACC held its first anniversary meeting with the theme "Speak Up For a Better Community" at the Glenville High School auditorium. The assembly opened with "Our Negro Neighbors," a play emphasizing racial tolerance, performed by Glenville High School students. A panel of "experts on civic problems," including city and school officials, fielded questions from the membership, and two resolutions were passed calling for tighter control over bars and for better recreational facilities in the neighborhood. Into its second year, the GACC expanded its focus, for example, creating a formal Neighborhood Conservation Committee to educate landlords, tenants, and homeowners, to organize block clubs, and to lobby for improved city services. By December, this new committee had organized "block conservation groups" on Grantwood and Morrison Avenues and was making further plans to "maintain the desirable residential qualities of the Glenville Area." Twelve such street organizations had been formed by the following spring, leading Conservation Committee chairman Norman L. McGhee to remark at a dinner conference held at the new home of the Cory Methodist Church (formerly a Jewish synagogue): "We are disproving the usual charge that a community deteriorates when a new group moves into it. . . . Our community will improve its appearance." Local radio personality Dorothy Fuldheim also spoke, commending the GACC's efforts toward "eliminating hostility between creeds and races" as the "[most] practical example of the brotherhood of man" she had ever seen.[46]

Of the 300 GACC participants in its second year (1946–47), 229 (76 percent) were actual residents, as opposed to other interested individuals living outside the neighborhood. Most of the latter were teachers and social service staff who worked in Glenville. Women were disproportionately active (at 62 percent), and teachers were a majority (61 percent) of the participating professionals.

The black participants included twelve clerical workers, nine teachers, nine service workers (mostly custodians), nine skilled/semiskilled workers, six social workers, five managers, and two each of ministers and lawyers, in addition to sixty-five housewives. Overall, roughly half (47 percent) the participants were African American, at a time when they made up approximately a quarter of the population in the area served by the GACC; about a quarter (26 percent) of the participants were Jewish. Regarding higher black participation rates, the social work students who collected this data as part of their master's thesis project ventured: "One of the factors affecting this is the fact that the Negro population generally is moving into the area with the intention of staying for some time and with the desire to maintain it as a good residential area, while many of the Jewish families are in the process of moving out." Noting that nearly two-thirds (65 percent) of the non-Jewish white participants lived outside of Glenville, the students worried that "lack of contact with the white group actually living in the area . . . means that communication for inter-group adjustment does not exist adequately."[47]

The GACC's second anniversary meeting in June 1947 incorporated a sense of growing urgency, with the proceedings staged as a "trial" presided over by an actual Court of Common Pleas judge, and with area councilmen and the associate editor of the *Cleveland Press* as "expert witnesses." "YOUR COMMUNITY WILL BE TRIED FOR FAILURE," warned the flyer announcing the event, "To keep streets clean[;] To protect itself against wayward children[;] To eliminate rats[;] To convert the gully North of Patrick Henry into a park[;] To keep facilities of Forest Hills Swimming Pool clean[;] [and] To limit the number of taverns." Residents were admonished, "Fail not [to attend] under penalty of your conscience," and were encouraged to contact the council's executive secretary if they wished to "testify." Held at Patrick Henry Junior High School, the proceedings generated a lively discussion, as residents and officials took turns siding with the "prosecution" and the "defense." Complaints were aired about children trampling lawns, an "excess of smoke shops, largely patronized by men from the suburbs," and the city burning rubbish in Forest Hills Park. In the end, "John Q. Citizen" (representing Glenville) was sentenced to five years' "probation" to improve the neighborhood.[48]

The GACC's 1947–48 membership drive conducted that winter—analyzed again in detail by the social work students—had the stated goal of reaching a broader segment of the community. While the organization did increase the white share of its membership, the drive ended up largely reinforcing existing patterns of participation and thus fell short of its potential to foster intergroup dialogue and tolerance. Over 500 members were signed up, 224 of them African American (42 percent), and they were disproportionately female (69 percent). Canvassers tended to approach members of their own racial, religious, or occupational group instead of working on a house-to-house basis; many

Jews who planned to move deferred signing up; and some volunteers concluded that recent Southern migrants would become receptive to neighborhood mobilization through the GACC "only after a more thorough orientation." More disturbingly, some canvassers expressed fears of going out after dark, exacerbated by incidents that fed perceptions of a rising crime rate, and which in turn led the GACC to form a Law Enforcement Committee in January 1948.[49]

The GACC thus approached the decade's end with a sense of pride in its accomplishments, while still struggling to recruit the neighborhood's remaining white residents and to categorically address some of the changing social realities in the area. By now, however, the organization had a dedicated core of activists and an established African American membership, ensuring that it would persist as a vehicle for black middle-class agency and blacks' visions of place, status, and good urban living. At its 1948 annual meeting, the GACC hosted city planning director John T. Howard, who answered in the affirmative his own question, "Can We Save Old Neighborhoods?" Over the next year, the organization successfully opposed a proposal to build a garbage incinerator in the neighborhood, convinced the city to resurface streets and install a traffic light, revoked one liquor license, and operated a rat-poisoning program on twelve blocks. At the fourth-anniversary meeting in 1949, Sanford Solender expressed his continuing faith that "the area community council is the most effective device yet discovered to make it possible for people to do something about their problems," while at the same time emphasizing, "Today the test is greater than ever whether we shall be able to live together with understanding and respect." In its annual report for that year, the GACC claimed to represent 8,000 individuals through its numerous community and civic body affiliates and stated that over 400 had actively participated in its initiatives.[50]

The Mount Pleasant Community Council (MPCC) followed a similar trajectory to the GACC in the mid-1940s. By 1946, when the organization was officially ratified, activists had already laid groundwork, having convinced the Board of Education to keep the Alexander Hamilton Junior High School playground open for the summer and having successfully prevented the granting of several liquor licenses. By March 1947, the MPCC had active Race Relations, Health, and Recreation Committees and claimed to be "progressing rather rapidly" with "proportionate representation of both Negro[e]s and whites," although it proved "difficult to activate the Italian population within the community." That same year, the organization also collaborated with the local NAACP in a Brotherhood Week celebration, was planning the first of an annual series of "Folk Festivals" for the coming summer, and in October sponsored its first Health Festival attended by 1,500 people. According to the local CEA branch, by early 1948 the MPCC had "developed into a stable and organized group which attempts to get the people in the Mt. Pleasant area to work together in . . . an effort to make it a better community."[51]

Glenville Area Community Council Meeting, 1952. Interracial community mobilizations in Cleveland's outlying neighborhoods helped mediate demographic transition from the 1940s onward, minimizing retaliatory violence. (Courtesy of the *Cleveland Press* Collection, Cleveland State University Library)

But similar to Glenville, although the MPCC developed a broadly conceived reform agenda and a solid organizational base, demographic change undermined the organization's interracial focus, as evidenced by creeping apathy among white residents and the departure of many, particularly Jews. Fear of crime also hampered white involvement. Councilman Joseph Horowitz, who was a key promoter of and activist in the MPCC, in 1950 called for better street lighting and increased police patrols and "better surveillance of liquor spots" to counteract illicit behavior. In 1950, the Welfare Federation conducted a study to determine how effective and representative of the neighborhood the MPCC was, in an effort to decide whether it would benefit from the assistance of a field worker; one finding to emerge was that a core of highly active individuals participated disproportionately. Furthermore, of the fifty-seven organizations and institutions identified in the multiethnic, broadly defined geographic scope of the neighborhood, thirty-nine were interested in or already affiliated with the MPCC, but the remainder expressed little or no desire to participate. Besides the annual folk and health festivals, the MPCC received high marks for having successfully lobbied the city to improve public transportation. Toward the end of 1950, the group reported to the Welfare Federation that it had organized six street clubs and had successfully prevented taverns from opening in the vicinity of churches and schools. Nevertheless, the following year the Welfare Federation withdrew the field worker it had provided, over the MPCC's objections that, considering the demographic changes already under way, "we are of the opinion that an ounce of prevention is worth a pound of cure . . . to avoid the development of another Central or Hough Area."[52]

Ongoing Transition in the Early Postwar Years

Demographic turnover in Glenville and Mount Pleasant accelerated after World War II. In Glenville, most dramatically, the African American population jumped from a total of 899 in 1940, to 22,060 in 1950, or 24 percent of the total population. However, black influx was strongly concentrated in "Central" Glenville, on the blocks abutting East 105th Street from East Boulevard to Parkwood Drive, between Superior and Saint Clair Avenues. In the corresponding four census tracts, they constituted the majority by 1950—overwhelmingly so in one, at 83 percent.[53] By then, Glenville's remaining white Protestants lived mainly in its easternmost reaches, which was also increasingly true for the Jewish population. In Mount Pleasant, the nonwhite population doubled over the same decade, increasing to just over 7,500, so that the neighborhood was 22 percent nonwhite in 1950. This increase occurred mainly in the census tracts containing the historic black enclave and the Kinsman Heights cluster, but also in an adjoining tract that was predominantly Italian. As for the neighborhood's Jews, the CEA noted in 1949 that "the population west of East 140th Street has been decreasing and is very small at the present time." Jewish enrollments in the local public schools correspondingly decreased, dramatically so at Alexander Hamilton Junior High School.[54]

An in-depth look at demographic turnover in one small section of Glenville confirms its rapid pace while tracking migration patterns of the black families settling there. Somerset and Ostend Avenues between East 99th and East 105th Streets experienced the largest numerical increase of African American households between 1940 and 1950 and had among the highest rates of change, with gains of over 80 percentage points. These streets were more or less typical for the neighborhood as a whole, with a mix of one- and two-family houses. Comparing the residents listed on that stretch of Somerset and Ostend Avenues in the 1940 and 1951 city directories (none was compiled for 1950), one is immediately struck by the extreme demographic transformation: only nine of the 278 households living there in 1940 remained eleven years later, a more than 97 percent turnover. In 1951, there were still at least eighteen white families living on this stretch of the two streets; fifteen of these were Jewish, of whom eight rented. Tracing back the last verifiable address for the new 1951 residents—excluding white households—is also revealing (see Map 2.1). While a handful of the new families moved from Mount Pleasant and isolated black settlements such as Thames Avenue and Saranac Road in Collinwood, the overwhelming majority came from Cedar-Central. Where in the main black district people had lived does not seem to have made much difference in terms of whether they bought or rented when they moved to Glenville; however, several dozen who did purchase homes had previously lived in the easternmost, formerly higher-status section of Cedar-Central. Five families moved directly from the Outhwaite Homes project, in keeping with anecdotal evidence that public housing's first generation of tenants consisted of middling types down on their luck, who subsequently experienced upward mobility after World War II. Finally, nineteen of the new families were already living in Glenville prior to moving onto Somerset or Ostend, with some residing on these same streets or in the nearby vicinity (Map 2.1, inset).[55]

A look at the occupational structure of residents on these blocks in 1951 also makes clear that the neighborhood's black, formerly elite class structure was beginning a downward shift (Table 2.1). By that year, less than one-fifth of the male heads were in white-collar and professional lines of work. They included a minister, a pharmacist, a photographer, managers of an A&P and a Kresge's store, two general contractors, two real estate agents, nine postal workers, and four proprietors—the owners of a garage, shoe repair shop, and two barbershops. A quarter of the male heads were operatives (including seventeen drivers classed in this category), and in the most dramatic divergence from the pre-1940 pattern, fully one-third were laborers. Of the female household heads, at least eighteen were widows, with eleven listing no occupation. While there was one female proprietor, the rest were nearly evenly split between clerical, operative, and service work; they included five clerks and five maids. Interestingly, few occupational distinctions distinguished homeowners and renters. While there were more managers (including proprietors), slightly more sales and craft workers, and slightly fewer laborers who owned, operatives and service workers owned and rented in roughly equal proportions. Surprisingly, there were actually more professionals and twice as many clerical workers who rented. Although houses on Somerset and Ostend were not among those that earned Glenville its "Gold Coast" nickname—and hence were not home to the neighborhood's wealthiest inhabitants—they were quite typical of the area on the whole. While still housing many middle-class families, the increase of working-class residents would contribute to Glenville's sagging reputation relative to other outlying areas of black settlement in the postwar decades, a trajectory previously seen in the eastern portion of Cedar-Central.

Even so, the percentage of owner-occupancy in Glenville rose by approximately 10 percent between 1940 and 1950, a reminder that neither homeownership nor occupation was an exact proxy for black middle-class status. Strikingly, even less-affluent black families succeeded in buying homes despite ongoing policies that furthered their borrowing disadvantage. In 1945 the *Call & Post* castigated the FHA along with the Cleveland Trust Co.—the city's largest bank, which in the pre–New Deal period had extended mortgages to a number of African American buyers in Glenville—for their discriminatory policies. By 1947, the paper was decrying the unfair administration of preferential veter-

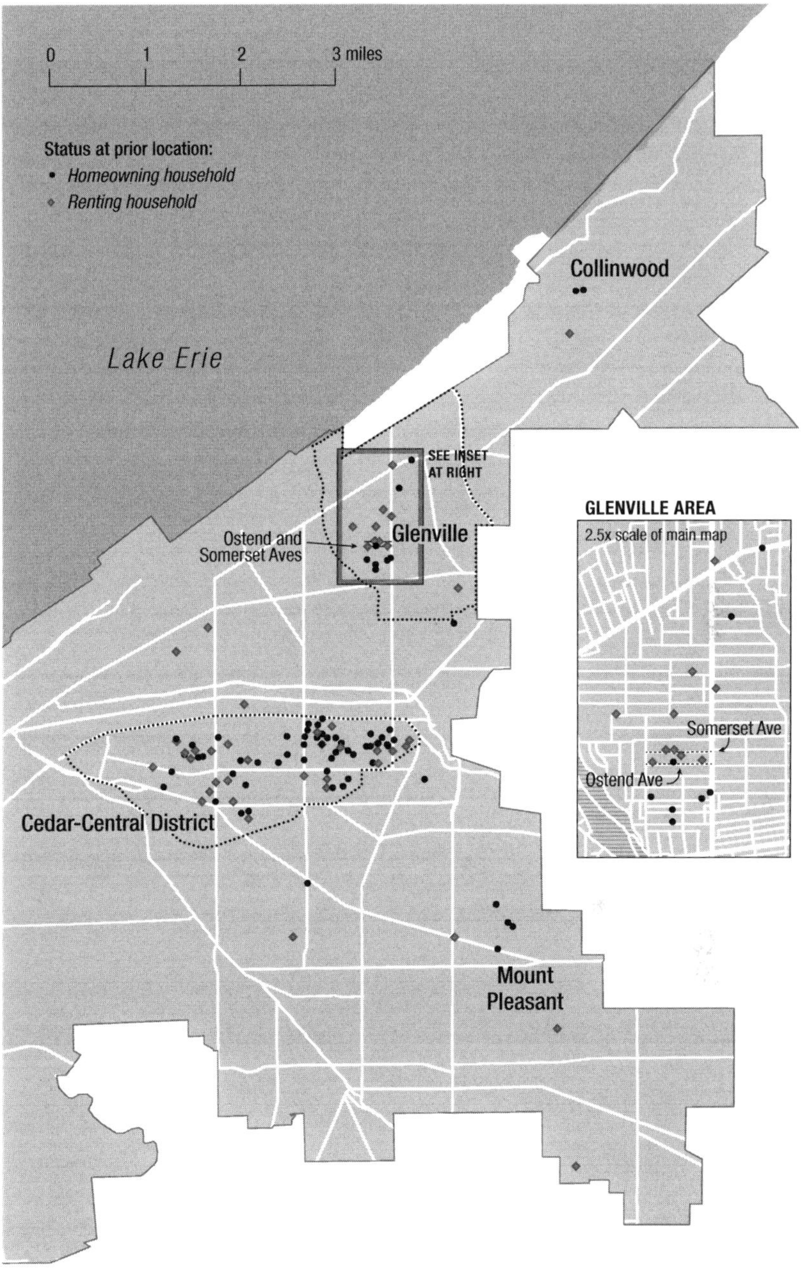

Map 2.1 Prior Location of Families Moving onto 9900–10499 Blocks of Somerset and Ostend Avenues, 1940–1951

Sources: Cleveland City Directories, 1940–49, 1951 (Cleveland City Directory Co.).

Table 2.1. Occupational Structure for Employed Somerset/Ostend Avenue Heads, 1951

	Male Heads (N=203)		Female Heads (N=21)		Owners (N=102)		Renters (N=122)	
Professional	2.0%	(4)	0		1.0%	(1)	2.5%	(3)
Manager	5.9%	(12)	4.8%	(1)	7.8%	(8)	4.1%	(5)
Clerical	7.4%	(15)	28.6%	(6)	6.9%	(7)	11.5%	(14)
Sales	2.0%	(4)	0		2.9%	(3)	0.8%	(1)
Craftwork	12.8%	(26)	0		14.7%	(15)	9.0%	(11)
Operator	25.6%	(52)	33.3%	(7)	25.5%	(26)	27.0%	(33)
Service	11.3%	(23)	33.3%	(7)	13.7%	(14)	13.1%	(16)
Nonhousehold:		23		2		11		14
Household:		0		5		3		2
Laborer	33.0%	(67)	0		27.5%	(28)	32.0%	(39)

Sources: Cleveland City Directory, 1951 (Cleveland: Cleveland City Directory Co.); Property Deeds, Cuyahoga County Recorders Office. Heads with obviously Jewish and Eastern European surnames were excluded from the calculations.

ans' homebuyer benefits, but it did note that "a handful of veterans are taking advantage of the G.I. Bill of Rights to acquire property for residential use in Glenville and Mount Pleasant." The *Call & Post* also renewed its assault on the Cleveland Trust Co. later that year, for fostering ghettoization through its lending practices. In the spring of 1947, the GACC's Neighborhood Conservation Committee claimed some success in convincing banks to loan on more favorable terms, but many black Glenville residents had to pursue their dreams of homeownership by using land contracts—potentially exploitative instruments that built no equity for buyers, who did not receive official title until the entire sum was paid off, and who could lose their entire investment if they missed even a single payment. In 1950, the *Call & Post* ran a cautionary tale about one such "foolish" home seeker. Other buyers tapped alternative sources of financing, as in the case of postman Walter Burks, who after the war purchased a Mount Pleasant lot on East 147th Street and then sidestepped discrimination by securing a mortgage through a black-owned insurance company to build his house. This proved so successful that Burks used the technique to help his friends build homes nearby.[56]

A proliferation of black-owned businesses and religious institutions also accompanied the expansion of African American settlement in outlying neighborhoods, which the local black press typically portrayed in terms of pride and accomplishment. Elmer E. Collins became the first African American physician on East 105th Street in mid-1945, although a year later the *Call & Post* was noting the "complete absence of any Negro-owned café spots in the Glenville section," which were regarded as "representative of . . . a 'secret pact' to circumvent their establishment." Indeed, the GACC had earlier that year formed a "Merchant's Committee" that would "attempt to take up such items as . . . allowing Negro merchants in the area without too much interference," although a subsequent inquiry into the matter found "most merchants were agreeable to such a group and were willing to work with it." The *Call & Post* further lauded instances where African Americans acquired investment properties in Glenville, such as when a doctor bought the sixty-two-unit Allen Apartments on East 105th Street in 1952 for $187,500. But considered most noteworthy were purchases by black congregations of white churches and synagogues. In October 1945, the Bethany Baptist Church became the first black congregation in Glenville, after a two-year fund-raising drive to purchase Zion Evangelical Church. Next came the Greater Abyssinia Baptist Church, which bought the Beth Hamidrash Hagodol Ohave Emuna synagogue for a reported $50,000 the following year. Most stunningly, in 1947 the Cory Methodist congregation moved into the former Glenville Jewish Center (Anshe Emeth) on East 105th Street, after purchasing the facility, which included a swimming pool and 2,000-seat auditorium, for $135,000—less than one-tenth its assessed value. Other Glenville arrivals during the 1940s included Central Christian Church, Saint Mark's Presbyterian, and Trinity C.M.E. By 1950, the *Call & Post* counted more than twenty such transfers as either pending or complete.[57]

But not all African American newcomers to Glenville and Mount Pleasant experienced outright success in either homeownership or business, and in the meantime anxieties about the future of these neighborhoods mounted. Black renters and buyers both suffered, as unfair lending policies and white unwillingness to relinquish sufficient living space perpetuated the city's artificial black housing shortage after World War II. In 1946, the *Call & Post* noted that overall scarcity was increasing rents not only in Cedar-Central, but in Glenville and Mount Pleasant as well. As a result, the issue of converting houses to multifamily occupancy also outlasted the war. Thus one Glenville "roomer" wrote to the paper in 1947, complaining that "the house has six families on the second floor and the women usually wash their clothes in the face bowl or leave dirty underwear in the bath room after taking a bath." Later that year came the report of a family renting a Glenville attic for $17 a week, an exorbitant price at the time. The wife had actually won an award from the *Pittsburgh Courier* as the "model mother of Cleveland for 1946," for her "cheerfulness despite the barriers of living." Yet another family in the neighborhood reportedly received an eviction notice after complaining to the Rent Board about overpaying. The tenants had themselves absorbed maintenance costs and had to use the fire escape in order to access kitchen facilities. Similar situations abounded in Mount Pleasant. After the war, it emerged that close to 90 percent of the nearly 800 new housing units created in the neighborhood from 1940 to 1950 were from conversions, with the Welfare Federation noting the "impending danger" of rooming houses. In 1951, the building inspector assigned to Mount Pleasant discovered a young family of five living in an "undersized garage" without heat, a toilet, or running water. They had actually been trying to buy the structure for delinquent taxes.[58]

Conversion to multifamily occupancy was not just a tactic of absentee landlords—many of whom were white former residents—but also of some African American homebuyers. For those who had overpaid on houses, or who held poorly compensated or insecure jobs, the temptation to bring in extra income this way often proved irresistible. Others bought property as an outright investment, unaware or unconcerned that conversion violated zoning or building codes. The issue divided black opinion in these neighborhoods, as reflected by ambivalence expressed in the *Call & Post*. In January 1948, the paper condemned this "degenerative housing trend," even as it recognized that a dearth of accessible housing drove it. It subsequently warned, "Many home-owners of recently acquired properties may lose their investments if they continue to rely on income from roomers and kitchenette utility suites." However, it blamed "ignorance of the law and loose mouth real estate operators" for creating the "delusion that they were free to take in as many roomers as they liked or break their homes up into investment properties." Some owners lost money when they began alterations but then were denied building permits, or when they attempted to complete the work surreptitiously and were bilked by unscrupulous contractors. Toward the end of 1948, the *Call & Post* equivocated on the practice, acknowledging the plight of those seeking scarce accommodations and stating that conversion "is not always a bad practice[,] providing owners are aware of the zoning ordinances and comply with the strict building code."[59]

Also troubling was the seeming tendency of the city to target black property owners for violations more readily than white absentee landlords. The city took its first such legal action in early 1948, following a complaint of the Miles Standish Conservation Association (affiliated with the GACC) against a black woman who lived in one half of her duplex on Parkgate Avenue and rented out the rest to three families. Though convicted, the owner did not have to pay court costs, which were suspended. In a case later that year, Mrs. Elizabeth Davenport, another black Glenville homeowner, won a restraining order against the city building commissioner's demand that she reconvert her six-suite property back into a duplex, on the ground that the changes were made before she purchased the house, and if completed would put four families out on the street. However, she lost her subsequent suit for $15,000 in damages against Detective George Ballard, the former owner, who was also black; she alleged he had sold her the property on Parkwood Drive using the lure of rental income.[60] Further illustrating the potential *intra*racial significance of such disputes, some Glenville renters vented their anger on their black landlords. One woman wrote the *Call & Post* in 1947 to ask, "What do the big shots on the 'Gold Coast' think a single woman is going to do. I pay $10 [per week] for one room and have no privileges whatsoever." She went on: "Some of the people pay as much as $100 and $125 a month for 5 rooms poorly furnished. Is it any surprise that many of these landlords ride around in big Cadillacs[?] They sure are robbing the poor people." Strong demand meant landlords could be choosy, with the paper noting the following year a "record-breaking number of Negro evictors [who] are Glenville landlords . . . using the reasons of non-payment of rent and quarters for immediate family as basis for eviction."[61]

With the increased pace of demographic turnover, race relations in both Glenville and Mount Pleasant remained tense after the war. While community organizing in these neighborhoods helped ensure that collective white resistance to black influx did not materialize, minor incidents continued into the immediate postwar years, and some social issues proved more vexing. Following a race-related clash between "several groups of school students" in Glenville, the Community Relations Board in June 1946 recommended that black and white police officers pair to patrol city parks. Racial transition in Glenville and Mount Pleasant also seemingly resolved former conflicts over swimming pools—although this was largely due to whites' decreasing usage of the pools in sections where blacks became numerically predominant. Both the Forest Hills and Woodland Hills pools were certified by the *Call & Post* in 1946 as accessible to black residents, and the GACC's main focus accordingly shifted toward renovation and adequate maintenance. The Community Relations Board touted the city's successful avoidance of racial clashes that year, after the Recreation Department's assurances that it would maintain open access to all facilities. "Though cities like Youngstown, St. Louis, Baltimore and Washington, D.C. had serious racial outbreaks in recreation facilities during the summer of 1949, Cleveland had none," the board congratulated itself. However, there was a hint this success came from carefully scheduled trips by interracial groups, not to mention incidents such as one, probably at Woodland Hills, where a black father brought along a stick to defend his daughter in the event that "trouble" should arise.[62]

Racial frictions in public schools also caused apprehension. In late 1945, the GACC sent a statement to the Board of Education observing that "the advent of Negro pupils into a school is not looked upon with favor by teachers, pupils and white families and is deplored both directly and by implication," and requesting the institution of an intercultural relations program and the hiring of more black teachers. At the start of the following school year and with Community Relations Board backing, the GACC pushed for additional transfers. More troubling was a "disturbance" that broke out between black and white students at Patrick Henry Junior High School in June 1946, although the *Call & Post* approvingly noted that Principal Oliver Deex (an active GACC member)

Beach at Gordon Park, 1947. Neighborhood swimming facilities experienced a short-lived period of racial integration as the presence of African Americans increased dramatically in Glenville during and after World War II. (Courtesy of the Cleveland Public Library/ Photograph Collection)

handled the incident "without favoritism to either faction." Later that same year, thirteen white and black youths were arrested at Empire Junior High School after a fight escalated into a fracas, though the investigator from the Police Department's Race Relations Unit "found little evidence of real racial tension or prejudice" in the matter. In a 1952 letter to the Welfare Federation, MPCC president Lowell A. Henry mentioned that there, too, "tensions around schools are sometimes apparent."[63]

Juvenile delinquency was a growing concern in both Glenville and Mount Pleasant after the war. At a 1945 GACC committee meeting, one observer opined that area youths' "conduct on the streets needs correction," even as Sanford Solender pointed out that "the young colored people felt that they were being discriminated against" by police. Later that year, the GACC executive board heard about "two bad focal spots for congregation of youth," one of which was Empire Junior High School. Similarly, an activist with the GACC's Recreation Committee stated that the Parkwood School playground had in the summer of 1946 been "a trouble spot with considerable gambling, profanity and bullying" and recommended that a complaint be submitted to the Board of Education's playground director. Despite the GACC's efforts, Glenville's share of official delinquency cases doubled from 1945 to 1947. As for Mount Pleasant, rates as of 1950 were average overall, but higher in the census tract containing the historic black enclave. The Welfare Federation study supplying these statistics also noted "gangs loitering more and more on street corners" and "patronage of [area] liquor spots by teen agers." Many observers understood the issue of juvenile delinquency in terms of a lack of adequate recreational facilities or adult supervision. With the exception of the Council Educational Alliance, which traditionally served the Jewish population, there was a dearth of recreational space in both neighborhoods, especially venues where black youth felt welcome. Those African Americans who patronized the YMCA may have continued using the Cedar-Central branch even after moving elsewhere; back in 1938 five Mount Pleasant groups had been affiliated there. Hi-Y clubs affiliated with the Cedar branch of the YMCA also existed at both Glenville High School and John Adams High School (serving Mount Pleasant) in the late 1930s. In 1945, the black Mount Pleasant Mothers Club asked the Phillis Wheatley Association to establish a branch in the neighborhood, to no avail. This shortage of facilities would continue for more than a decade in Mount Pleasant, and in Glenville until 1950, when the YMCA established the city's first interracial branch there.[64]

While juvenile delinquency was regarded mainly as a problem of wayward youth, crime also increased in Glenville and Mount Pleasant in the immediate postwar years, some of it violent. The murder of a Jewish tailor by a black youth in 1947 prompted the GACC's formation of a Law Enforcement Committee and purportedly "increased the fear of going out at night that existed among many Jewish people, some of whom were neither aware nor interested in the fact that their Negro neighbors shared that fear." Indeed, later that year, a black female Welfare Federation employee and active Urban League member was knocked down and her purse stolen, right in front of her house on Amor Avenue. Purse-snatchings, robberies, and, in the words of Councilman Joseph Horowitz, "attacks on women" were also allegedly on the rise in Mount Pleasant. In early 1948, the *Call & Post* ran a soul-searching article about high-profile crimes committed by African Americans. "Even the most liberal interpretation of the reports can hardly be made without an uncomfortable reflection on the entire community," stated the article, expressing fear that Glenville in particular was being lumped together with Cedar-Central. Later that year, the neighborhood received more bad publicity when it was rocked by two bombings—but not ones committed by white racists in this case. Among the neighborhood's new black homeowners were several racketeers in charge of "policy," or numbers gambling, and one of the year's five policy-related bombings occurred in Glenville, an apparent attack by one racketeer on a rival's Ostend Avenue home. A previous bombing, also in Glenville, had targeted the car of former councilman Thomas J. Davis but had also damaged his home and that of a neighbor.[65]

Two final sources provide detailed insights on the perceptions and attitudes of Glenville and Mount Pleasant residents from various backgrounds during the process of racial residential transition, revealing some of the challenges faced by activists seeking to mobilize these neighborhoods on an interracial basis. As part of their research project, the authors of the 1948 master's thesis on the GACC interviewed samples of non-Jewish white ("Gentile"), Jewish, and African American residents from the 1946–47 participants, seeking to determine their levels of "social distancing" as well as their impressions of their neighbors and neighborhood's trajectory. Keeping in mind that residents who opted to participate in GACC initiatives were almost certainly more open-minded on racial matters than those who did not, the findings are discouraging. Nearly all the white Gentiles and Jews interviewed stated they would accept African Americans as co-workers. However, on the other questions—asked whether they would readily accept blacks in the neighborhood, on their street, as dinner guests, or at a social gathering with their friends—affirmative responses from both groups hovered around one-third, with many qualifying their responses to indicate it would depend on the individual. One white respondent revealed her discomfort with sharing public spaces while expressing a near total disconnect between familiar black individuals and African Americans as a group: "I would have Mrs. X, a cultured Negro woman as my dinner guest and consider it an honor," she claimed, before continuing on: "When the coons get out of the movies on 105th Street they push you off the sidewalk and they jostle you in streetcars." Another expressed support for the ideal of toleration yet could not avoid generalizing, stating, "[I] teach my children that there are good and bad in every race . . . [but] I've seen so many bad Negroes that I've turned against all of them." That formal participation on an interracial basis did not necessarily equate with comfort in daily settings comes through in one Jewish woman's comment that "I meet and eat with Negro women all the time in organizations but I'm not yet ready for Negro neighbors. . . . It takes time to get used to them."[66]

While some whites have historically had trouble "seeing" class when observing African Americans—HOLC evaluators are one example—both the Jewish and the non-Jewish white interviewees proved highly cognizant of status distinctions, despite divergent assessments of the neighborhood's overall trajectory. "Glenville's Negroes are better than hill-billy white trash," professed one white respondent. "I wouldn't want white or colored trash as neighbors," said another. These may have been references to Appalachian whites who had also migrated to Cleveland during World War II, some of whom were concentrated in the Hough neighborhood immediately to the southwest, which also experienced multi-occupancy conversions during the war. "It's a question of class, not race," said one Jewish interviewee; two others, perceiving a shift in the types of black families arriving, stated, "Trashy as well as fine Negroes are moving to Glenville" and "Certain Negroes are all right but you can't be sure of who will follow them." Strikingly, the white interviewees disagreed overall on whether Glenville was "deteriorating," with equal proportions expressing beliefs that it had *not* and that it definitely had. Most identified some particular deteriorating influence, such as housing conversions, or specified that only particular sections of the neighborhood had deteriorated. Just one white Gentile respondent unequivocally linked deterioration to the presence of African Americans, while one Jewish respondent denied any significant change, stating, "I knew the same rowdy types in Glenville years ago when there were no Negroes there." The sense of uncertainty in such assessments helps explain the observable pattern: while they were temporarily willing to participate in the GACC with like-minded black residents, whites who had other options eventually made their way out.[67]

African American participants' responses contain hints of frustration with white distancing behaviors that ultimately made the GACC's interracialism unsustainable. Only about a quarter of the forty-five individuals interviewed in the sample had moved to Glenville within the four preceding years (the average was eight years), thus confirming the organization's hunch that long-standing black residents were more receptive to its program. Four out of five owned or were in the process of buying their homes. On the social distancing scale, the black respondents proved vastly more accepting, with only a handful balking at the thought of having whites over for dinner or to a social gathering; nine out of ten claimed to be ready to accept the presence of whites in all settings. However, some expressed skepticism that they would be extended the same courtesy, while others emphasized they were not opposed to socializing with whites but felt no strong desire to do so. "The white man needs to learn that the Negro believes in the right to choose one's own associates, but being good neighbors and citizens does not demand that you become a personal friend," said one. Others expressed bitterness at the rejection that white departures implied. "The Jews were here first, but they seem to be running from us now," said one respondent, while another recalled: "Don't see much of the Jews now, but I had excellent relations with them in the old block club." Most likely reflecting on the fact that many Glenville Jewish residents rented, yet another black respondent professed: "I would rather have Jews for neighbors. They don't keep their law[n]s and yards up so well but they know how to be neighborly. They build their home life around their children." Someone else disagreed: "Most ugly incidents have been with white Gentiles rather than with Jews. [But] Jews are not any better though." Such comments make clear that interracial neighborhood organizing efforts were incapable of fully mitigating the tense climate that accompanied demographic turnover, let alone convincing most whites to stay put.[68]

The African American sample also demonstrated a wide range of viewpoints on the problems and trajectory of the area. Many expressed disapproval at the trend toward housing conversion, with one stating that a "large number of Negroes bought and made improvements beyond their capacity to pay for these. They have taken in roomers indiscriminately in most cases, overcrowding the area and bringing people into the area who feel no responsibility towards it." However, again pointing to the dilemma of the often overextended black homeowner, someone else ventured, "It is okay to take in roomers if people are careful in selecting them." Yet another interviewee seemed exasperated, opining, "Some of our people just won't do right," but linked conversion to another growing black middle-class concern, excessive liquor availability: "Cutting up homes brings people into the area who soon tire of looking at just the walls of their rooms, so they go out to find entertainment and end up making the rounds of the bars." One called the East 105th Street business strip "awful," while another's comment underlines that black residents also harbored fears about crime: "I don't go out much after dark because I'm afraid, so I can't tell you much about 105th Street." Even so, respondents were unable to agree about causes or what constituted normality. "Most incidents are caused by people living outside of the area," insisted one, while yet another interviewee expressed the opinion that, "the area seems no worse in behavior than other areas. This however, may not continue to be true if the area becomes transient." Still another person thought Glenville was no different than the suburbs: "We have so much riffraff in the area, but you can find the same in all areas—East Cleveland and the Heights." Unquoted African American respondents apparently also mentioned the rural habits of recent migrants, poor discipline on the part of parents, and the church's lack of influence as factors shaping neighborhood outcomes, all explanations that would continue to characterize black middle-class understandings of urban decline into the following decades and the reform strategies they formulated.[69]

Observations by staff at the Council Educational Alliance (CEA), a social service agency traditionally serving Cleveland's Jewish population with branches in both Glenville and Mount Pleasant, demonstrate additional difficulties that arose as early as World War II in conjunction with interracial approaches. In keeping with increasingly typical social work practice, CEA staff strove to promote intercultural and interracial "toleration" but sometimes ran up against constituent bias. "It is very interesting and sometimes a bit discouraging to find how many deep-rooted prejudices are to be found among our own club members," one Mount Pleasant staffer wrote in a 1939–40 report, specifically of Jews toward African Americans and Italians. By 1944, increasing numbers of Italian youths were using the Mount Pleasant CEA branch and a group of African American Girl Scouts had even begun meeting at the facility. However, the presence of non-Jews not only created the potential for resentment but also raised questions about the agency's mission. Staff responded by forming a "House Inter-Cultural Committee" to alleviate tensions, in which the "amount of anti-Negro feeling" among both Jewish and Italian youth was discovered to be "surprisingly high—particularly among the girls." However, the CEA did successfully recruit delegates to participate in intercultural programming with multiethnic and multiracial youth from other social settlements around the city that year, and a mixed Jewish-Italian group even attended a pageant mounted by an African American group. By late 1945, the CEA had hashed out an interracial policy welcoming "any non-Jewish person wishing to join, after carefully interpreting to him our purpose as a Jewish agency and the Jewish nature of our program." However, while committing itself to this policy of non-exclusion, the CEA also stated that if Jewish participation became too small at a branch, it should be moved in order to more effectively serve the traditional constituency. Thus, like the GACC, the CEA, in seeking to promote interracial cooperation, constantly had to deal with white recalcitrance exacerbated by ongoing population turnover.[70]

Although CEA's efforts to promote intergroup contact and understanding continued—and even intensified—into the postwar period, progress proved a constant struggle. At the East 105th Street branch in Glenville soon after the war, "it was pointed out that some Negroes and non-Jews had been coming into the agency to participate in some of the activities and that there seemed to be a good deal of anti-Negro feelings on the part of the Jewish membership in the house, as well as negative feelings toward non-Jewish whites." In contrast to Mount Pleasant, the East 105th Street branch had no official black members and "there seemed to be more tensions present," with staff citing an incident in which black youths "attempted to bar" some Jewish girls from entering a CEA-sponsored party. At Mount Pleasant, too, "some objection" had been expressed to the policy of "permitting non-Jewish groups to meet in the building," although among twelve- to fourteen-year-olds, "both Negro and White children are thoroughly accepted in the activities." Into 1946 at the East 105th Street branch, "the staff could not help but notice the antagonisms stemming from the white Jews of the area," making them "painfully aware that some type of strong, positive inter-racial program must be attempted in the Alliance." To remedy the situation, the branch celebrated Brotherhood Week, conducted toleration-related programming including a display of the famous touring exhibit "Races of Mankind," and encouraged participation in the Glenville Youth Council. By the end of the year, staff claimed that tensions in the neighborhood had diminished, despite periodic "incidents." Successful interracial activities conducted in both Glenville and Mount Pleasant included dramatics, horseshoes, and playground usage.[71]

The specific prejudices and fears expressed were not always recorded in detail by CEA staff, but it is clear that whites had absorbed common stereotypes about African Americans even as they struggled to resolve them. Of the Jewish youth, one staff member observed that "among the girls the matter of intermarriage, dancing together, etc., is of great concern," and that "members tend to generalize a great deal (Negroes are drunkards, Negroes are dirty, have syphilis, etc.)." He also noted, "These youth know that they themselves are a minority but do not like to place themselves in the same category." Neighborhood-based status rivalries among Jewish CEA members had been an issue even before the advent of non-Jewish participation, and now with increasing outmigration to the suburbs, some neighborhood residents purposefully disassociated themselves. As the staff member explained: "The Mt. Pleasant neighborhood at the present time seems to be in a state of flux, as far as the Jewish Community living here is concerned. The influx of non-Jews and Negroes seems to have resulted in many of the groups not wanting to identify themselves as [a] 'Kinsman' fraternity or sorority." Another observer interpreted such attitudes and status-striving in general as an expression of Jewish postwar upward mobility. For their part, wrote the above-quoted CEA staff member at Mount Pleasant, "there seems to be some anti-Semitism by the Negro members" of junior-high school age, the precise nature of which he did not specify.[72]

Avoidance of contact with African Americans as well as perceptions of increasing danger similarly complicated the CEA's efforts. In a survey of parents at the East 105th Street branch, out of 164 responses explaining reasons for nonattendance, twenty-nine cited "Fear of Negroes in Neighborhood," eight mentioned "Plans to Move Soon," three said "Because Negroes attend C.E.A.," and two said "Gets Dark Too Early." The most frequent reason given, at forty-three responses, was "Too Far," which hints at the tendency of Jews to move into "Superior-Thru," the easternmost portion of the neighborhood. At the Mount Pleasant branch, in planning a day camp program for the summer of 1948 at Woodland Hills Park, staff worried that "many parents have very strong feelings against Negro[e]s and for this reason would not respond to a Day Camp held in this park." When it was pointed out that to propose an alternative site would be "submitting to this anti-Negro feeling," the staff decided to survey parents on the issue; as a result, they indeed found some such resistance, although it was "very subtly indicated." Despite their initial hopes of changing people's minds, ultimately not enough participants signed up to justify holding the camp.[73] Finally, a decision in late 1949 to discontinue the weekly "canteen" (dance) at the Mount Pleasant House was attributed to "tension in the area." Increased attendance by African Americans and fears of fights had precipitated a merger of the East 105th Street and Superior-Thru canteens several years earlier. While intended "to remove the chief point of possible interracial conflict," the merger was somewhat disingenuously "interpreted to members as a consolidation in order to serve both areas more effectively."[74]

Continued potential for interracial frictions and the CEA's limited ability to address them, combined with the relocation of these neighborhoods' Jewish populations, raised uncomfortable questions about how long services should continue at the two facilities. Having already moved the Glenville canteen, the CEA nevertheless retained its East 105th Street branch until 1947 when it purchased a new facility in Superior-Thru. However, the agency—renamed the Jewish Community Center (JCC) after a 1948 merger with three other organizations—continued to maintain an "extension" program in the East 105th Street neighborhood until 1950, in which the traditional youth-led clubs met at members' homes instead of at an actual JCC facility. In Mount Pleasant, the CEA/JCC branch stayed longer, despite Jewish outflow to nearby Lee-Harvard and suburban Shaker Heights, in part because a pocket of lower-income Jews remained in the vicinity of East 116th Street and Kinsman Road. Toward the end of 1949, the CEA/JCC followed the recommendation of its Mount Pleasant Advisory Committee and established a new branch on Lee Road, just inside the Shaker Heights border. Programming at the Mount Pleasant House was subsequently "curtailed," but the property was not sold until 1952, to a black Masonic lodge.[75]

While the CEA/JCC consistently couched its eastward shift of focus as a response to population trends, statistics indicate this strategy was anticipatory. CEA activity had declined during the war, and Jewish population movement out of both neighborhoods, as well as racial fears and aversions, as discussed earlier, certainly factored heavily. However, even at East 105th Street at the time of the 1947 branch relocation, the total numbers served were higher than at Superior-Thru. The shift of service to the new Lee Road facility also initially created difficulties, with one interracial group that had met at Mount Pleasant for years, the Senior Mothers, feeling "extremely threatened" by the looming sale of the building. Meanwhile, the matter of how to transport children still living in Mount Pleasant to Lee Road presented another challenge. The JCC clearly agonized over how to maintain a commitment to those Jewish families left behind, with a 1949 panel discussion on "Changing Neighborhoods" raising "much concern . . . that such services be not shifted away completely from the old neighborhoods." The panel concluded that "inadequate service is adding to the feeling of desertion and distress."[76]

■

By 1950, racial residential transition in parts of Mount Pleasant and the western portion of Glenville was well under way. As Jewish families and institutions moved out during and after World War II, these two neighborhoods emerged as black middle-class strongholds, with growing numbers of African

American home and business owners and the arrival of black churches. However, a sizable population of white Catholics remained in the vicinity, many of whom would stay through the 1950s. Their pattern of relations with African Americans had always been more tenuous—with a lack of participation by Catholics in the GACC and MPCC noted as a potential weakness faced by these organizations seeking to maintain neighborhood desirability and to promote "orderly" demographic transition. As will be seen, some Catholic residents expressed a more open hostility toward African Americans than did Jews, with a spate of racial clashes and incidents of vandalism accompanying ongoing demographic turnover during the following decade, although this opposition never approached the level of organized communal violence seen in Chicago and Detroit. For blacks, Glenville and especially the East Boulevard area retained its "Gold Coast" reputation into the 1950s, until newer, suburban-style housing became available in the southeasternmost portion of the city. But despite African Americans' improved access to better housing in Glenville and Mount Pleasant, the immediate postwar years brought worrisome trends—the conversion of housing to multifamily occupancy as well as a seeming uptick in juvenile delinquency and crime. These developments spurred residents to redouble neighborhood reform efforts and fed the continued relocation by upwardly mobile black families to even further outlying areas of the city that increasingly seemed more promising places to pursue their dreams of a better life.

3 : : :
Zoning, Development, and Residential Access

LEE-MILES IN THE 1950S AND 1960S

At a January 1953 meeting of homeowners' associations from Southeast Cleveland and the nearby suburb of Maple Heights, as part of an ongoing effort to halt construction of a public housing project, Henry Hawk, a former truck driver turned construction worker, rose to speak. "I made mine the hard way," he asserted, before claiming preposterously, "There are folks in these housing projects who own yachts." Hawk was a member of the Lee-Land Heights Civic Council, an organization that had recently supported industrial zoning to block African American settlement in the city's southeasternmost section where the proposed housing project was to be located. Containing a mixture of single-family homes, retail strips, and light industrial plants, this part of the city was still being developed in the 1950s, and it was overwhelmingly white. First and foremost, the fight against the public housing project—which, due to new federal mandates, was, at least in theory, supposed to have racially integrated occupancy—was a manifestation of the nearby white residents' racial anxieties. However, and surprisingly, considering the negative racial undertones that characterized much of the debate against the proposal, one other fact about Hawk needs to be taken into account: he was black.[1]

Predictably, Hawk's viewpoint and participation in the Lee-Land Heights Civic Council was met with skepticism in the larger African American community. Hawk was thrown on the defensive and felt compelled to tell the *Call & Post* that he attended meetings in the homes of white council members. Going further, Hawk additionally claimed that white residents in the area "welcome colored people who build their own homes, but [just] don't want a Project." The following week, he hosted a meeting of the organization at his own house, in an attempt to disprove charges that he was its token black member. While a handful of like-minded African American supporters did come, evidence indicates they had only a tiny presence on the council. Revealingly, at the September 1952 meeting where a petition drive against the housing project got its start, only six black sympathizers had been present—whom local NAACP head

Charles P. Lucas disapprovingly dismissed as a "few misguided souls" who "are being misled into becoming foes of their own interests, are being made dupes of vicious elements."[2]

While Henry Hawk's participation in the Lee-Land Heights Civic Council was undoubtedly unusual, his residence in the area was not. Since the early twentieth century, African Americans had lived in a compact, semirural enclave south of Seville Road, just west of Lee Road, a major thoroughfare. Like similar outlying black settlements, it consisted of families who in many cases built their own houses and maintained large gardens, like their forebears in the South. The community had served as an anchor for additional homebuilding by and for black families ever since. From 1944 to 1958, the Seville Homes temporary war housing project stood on a site immediately adjacent to this older settlement, dramatically augmenting the area's African American presence. Between 1940 and 1950, the black population jumped from 702 to 3,434, a nearly five-fold increase; not counting the Seville Homes' 2,000 occupants, the number of African American residents had doubled.[3] Hawk was among them; like several hundred neighbors, he had purchased a vacant lot on one of the side streets south of Seville Road. Two years earlier, he and his wife had built their brick bungalow at 4672 East 162nd Street with their own hands. Another black sympathizer who came to Hawk's meeting, Arthur Bussey, was a mason who had also built his own home on Myrtle Avenue and who would ultimately build dozens of homes in the area for other African American families. "People should buy or build their own homes instead of living in projects," was Bussey's adamant take on the proposal. Yet another black resident in attendance was Queenie Wade, also of Myrtle Avenue; a factory worker married to a truck driver, she and her husband had invested $30,000 in their property, even installing the sewer lines for their house themselves.[4]

Yet few black Clevelanders could go to such lengths to acquire housing that met their fullest expectations, as population dynamics ran up against the racialized constraints of the postwar housing market. Between 1940 and 1960, the city's African American population nearly tripled; Southern migrants continued coming in search of work, despite the initial onset of deindustrialization in the 1950s. In 1950, Cleveland's black population numbered 147,847, making up 16 percent of the total. By 1960, their number had risen to 250,818, or 29 percent. In a seemingly positive indication, a 1964 report by the Urban League found homeownership among African Americans had increased by 124 percent between 1950 and 1960 (from 8,872 to 19,621 homes). While the number of dwelling units occupied by African American Clevelanders increased by 91 percent during the same interval, their share of the population only increased 70 percent. But despite this decrease in overcrowding, the percentage of "deteriorating or dilapidated" housing occupied by African Americans remained high, at 28 percent, compared to just 7 percent for whites.[5] In sum, while some of the housing recently acquired by blacks was of high quality—such as the new homes built on the city's southeastern outskirts by owners like Henry Hawk and Arthur Bussey—a disproportionate amount was older, second-hand housing with a weightier maintenance burden. Furthermore, without strong legal protections against discriminatory practices, most African Americans had little choice at this time but to pay artificially inflated prices for property in racially segregated (or rapidly re-segregating) areas, in what experts increasingly termed a "dual" housing market.

White residents in the city's southeastern section enacted sweeping legislation over the course of a decade to impede African American access to the area, without having to resort to collective, extralegal violence. Thus, in the case of Southeast Cleveland, racial antagonism became sublimated in the political realm. In Chicago and Detroit, where historians have documented widespread organized and violent resistance by white residents, political means were additionally used with consistent success prior to the advent of civil rights legislation—with little evidence of countervailing power for black political agency.[6] In Southeast Cleveland, too, white residents generally extracted victories while African Americans suffered repeated defeats on legislative matters relating to residential housing development and open occupancy from the 1950s into the early 1960s. Still lacking political clout, black Clevelanders had few options to remedy their housing situation. Therefore, another way of increasing black residential access was to promote rapid housing turnover—"white flight"—using aggressive real estate practices. Although this strategy had serious drawbacks, it ultimately worked in the area's Lee-Harvard neighborhood. With so many roadblocks standing between African Americans and open access to good housing, it is obvious why Henry Hawk's participation in the white-dominated campaign to restrict public housing seemed traitorous to members of the organized black community, like NAACP head Charles Lucas. Indeed, Lucas's dismissal of such black sympathizers as "dupes of vicious elements" was consistently confirmed by white politicians, who seized upon the presence of African Americans to deny that race held any significance in the public housing issue.[7]

Yet such easy dismissal also risks further patronizing black residents like Henry Hawk. Besides misunderstanding or disregarding their motivations, it implies that political sentiment in the local black community was—or at least should have been—unanimous. While it is impossible to determine how representative the views of these upwardly mobile black homeowners living in what became known as Lee-Seville actually were, their early opposition to public housing offers a preview of opinions later expressed by a plurality of African American residents in the same area, when they rejected a 1968 public housing plan for Lee-Seville pushed by Cleveland's first black mayor, Carl B. Stokes. Already here we see the outlines of a worldview idealizing self-reliance and accomplishment through hard work, perhaps not so dissimilar from that which historians have identified among early white working-class suburbanites.[8] African Americans had to struggle even more mightily against discriminatory barriers in order to build successful lives for themselves in these outlying locations, and in the process, they laid the ground for subsequent newcomers to follow their lead. Though some black Lee-Seville residents allied themselves with nearby whites to oppose public housing for the area, they more often found themselves fighting against these former allies to preserve available vacant land for new black, single-family housing. Notwithstanding setbacks in the legislative arena, a number of black-owned construction companies—and, eventually, white outfits catering to an African American clientele—built hundreds of new homes for upwardly mobile black families in developments on either side of Lee Road, south of Miles Avenue. Thus, by 1953, a year also marked by the first successful African American purchase in the Lee-Harvard neighborhood immediately to the north, Southeast Cleveland had already begun its ascent toward becoming the city's most desirable black middle-class area, eclipsing Glenville (and, to a lesser degree, Mount Pleasant), which had previously held this distinction.

White Resistance, Black Response in the Legislative Arena

African Americans lived in Lee-Seville by the 1920s, when the area was contained within the short-lived municipality of Miles Heights. The original enclave began as the "Bella-Villa Allotment," a project of the Peoples Realty Co. founded by the city's leading African American businessman of that decade, Herbert S. Chauncey. With numerous lots remaining unsold when the Depression hit and in the wake of scandals following Chauncey's 1930 demise, the People's Realty Co. folded, unable to pay the mortgage on the Bella-Villa landholding.[9] Not unusual for developing suburbs of the time, Miles Heights attracted working-class buyers interested in cheap land and struggled to fund city services and public schooling. Like tiny Linndale on the West Side, which also bordered a black enclave, Miles Heights also became somewhat notorious for illicit activities like bootlegging. However, it was also the first Ohio municipality to elect an African American mayor—Arthur R. Johnston, a Jamaican immigrant, county road foreman, and former Mount Pleasant resident. Johnston sat on the school board and the village council before his appointment, completing the unexpired term of his predecessor; he was then elected to a term in 1929 with support from at least half of Miles Heights' white voters, as African Americans made up only about a third of the village's inhabitants at the time. Black residents suspected that Cleveland's drive to annex the territory in 1930–32 was due to Johnston's mayoralty, a belief he apparently shared, because he described his ultimately victorious, pro-annexation opponents as "klansmen." The enclave housed nearly 600 African Americans in 1930, and, like its Mount Pleasant counterpart, it actually grew during the Depression. Similarly, the established presence of African Americans preempted deed restrictions on developments in much of the surrounding area.[10]

Some Lee-Seville enclave residents pursued a semirural lifestyle into the 1960s, engaging in supplemental food production and putting their property to income-earning purposes. Known as the "Beehive" or "The Village" to residents, this community of self-sufficient African American homesteaders, including a considerable number of skilled workers, has been self-described as middle class.[11] However, outside observers typically characterized the Lee-Seville enclave as a rundown "Negro slum," emphasizing its missing sidewalks and storm sewers, unpaved streets, plus the lack of indoor plumbing and even electricity in some houses. In a 1939 report, HOLC cited "Shantytown" as another nickname for the area, asserting that "this community has had a very detrimental effect on surrounding area property values." The agency went so far as to claim that the enclave's presence had stalled development immediately across the border in suburban Garfield Heights, where, "at present, property can be sold only at sacrifice and mortgage money is not available[,] which indicate that potentially this neighborhood will eventually be taken over by Negroes with improvement in their financial condition." Statistics help to contextualize HOLC's assessment. Block-level data from the 1940 census confirms that 95 percent of the enclave's 175 dwelling units were occupied by nonwhites. Of this total, 76 percent of households had "no private bath," instead relying on outdoor toilet facilities. But contradicting HOLC's characterization, only 18 percent of the total units were described as "needing repair," and there was a high level of owner-occupancy (76 percent), with a relatively low number of mortgaged properties (33 percent).[12]

As for the Lee-Seville enclave's post-Depression effect on nearby residential construction, plans to build a housing project alongside it for African American foundry workers during World War II offer a preview of the fierce zoning and development battles that were fought in the postwar years. In late 1943, the Federal Public Housing Administration filed for the right to lease forty-nine acres of vacant land at Seville Road and East 153rd Street, a parcel on which the Cleveland Metropolitan Housing Authority (CMHA) reported: "It is remote from any high-priced residential developments, but adjoins an old, cheaply constructed and run-down neighborhood . . . in which values could not possibly be lowered by the proximity of temporary war housing." Nevertheless, the Cleveland Real Estate Board asked that plans be put on hold, and the City Council passed a resolution against the proposal, fearing, in the words of one white councilman, that "within a few years . . . [the project] would constitute a blighted area that would ruin the value of the entire neighborhood." William O. Walker, the *Call & Post* owner-editor and a city councilman at the time, wryly noted that "there is more concern about who is to occupy the houses than the type of the houses" and later wrote an editorial condemning the "dry-rot big-ots" opposing the project. When the contract was awarded in December, residents of Cleveland and nearby Garfield Heights and Maple Heights filed a tax-payers' lawsuit, winning an injunction that delayed construction until March, when a federal judge ruled it could proceed. One of the suburban mayors, John Pekarek, bluntly stated that the project was "bringing slums close to Maple Heights," while Congresswoman Frances P. Bolton called local housing officials "cold-blooded." When called to task by the *Call & Post*, she agreed to an interview in which she claimed: "This is not a Negro question. . . . It is a matter entirely concerned with the establishment of poorly constructed dwellings without proper facilities which will probably remain after the war and kill the property values of the surrounding areas."[13]

The Seville Homes temporary war housing project would indeed outlast the conflict and remain controversial. In the urgent wartime context, white opposition had a better chance of being overruled, a pattern seen not just in Cleveland but elsewhere around the country.[14] Ominously, however, the Community Relations Board had to intervene in May 1945, in one of its first mediating actions, to smooth frictions on the Miles Avenue bus line between the project's black tenants and white riders who accused them of "hogging" the available space. A letter from one angry white Southeast Cleveland resident to Mayor Thomas Burke indicates the depth of the animosity. "These Negroes are getting to[o] dam[n] fresh and bold here in Cleve," he opined; "this is getting to be noted all over the country as a nigger town, something has to be done about it, or your [*sic*] going to have some nice race riots on your hands." Although threatening violence, the letter-writer mentioned a more likely response to black influx: "This condition is forcing a lot of [white] people to get very disgusted and many of the people are putting there [*sic*] homes up for sale to get away from these niggers." Disapproving support for the project, he concluded: "It[']s a dirty shame the way these niggers are getting pampered and catered to by the City letting them move into good white neighborhoods and spoiling the whole section for miles around." Racial antagonism also factored into the Ward 30 council race that autumn, as left-liberal Democratic incumbent Joseph Krizek lost to Earnest Atkinson, who had fixated throughout his campaign on Krizek's support for the Seville Homes.[15]

While the deteriorating housing project was a source of consternation for nearby black as well as white residents until its demolition in 1958, the historic Lee-Seville enclave itself came under increased scrutiny as postwar plans materialized to develop the surrounding areas. In an effort to build sympathy for residents, the *Cleveland News* ran an exposé portraying the area in terms of municipal neglect but instead came across as embarrassing, labeling the enclave as Cleveland's "Tobacco Road" and calling conditions there "primitive" and "sordid." In response, the *Call & Post* ran an article giving Lee-Seville residents' side of the story, stating that, "while several of the homes in the area are unkempt and ramshackled, many of the homes are as modern as the homes of Negro families anywhere in Cleveland." The feature then responded directly to the cases mentioned in the *News* exposé. One elderly homeowner was chastised for not maintaining her property, while another household of scavengers and trash haulers received even stronger condemnation. However, a third family was defended against misrepresentation, with the conclusion that "individual cases of filth and disorder are exceptions rather than the general rule in Miles Heights." Black residents jumped to defend their settlement's reputation and lobbied the city for improved services. By 1947, the Miles Heights Progressive League was pushing for improvements, demanding sewers as well as better roads, sidewalks, and door-to-door mail service. The league called upon Mayor Burke and even convinced the indifferent (and possibly hostile) Councilman Atkinson to visit the area after a rainstorm, to view the deficiencies firsthand. As a result of the league's efforts, the city repaired streets, installed sidewalks, and instituted door-to-door mail service on most streets. Better streetlights and, finally, the first storm sewers were installed by the end of 1948. However, full water and sewer service was not extended until 1954, nor was the area incorporated into the Cleveland Transit System until 1955—allegedly because of a "gentlemen's agreement" with Shaker Heights which delayed a Lee Road bus line facilitating African American access to that suburb.[16]

Even as Lee-Seville residents sought to upgrade and expand their living space after the war, local whites organized to erect legal and political barriers to increased black settlement in Southeast Cleveland. As in many suburban communities, they used new powers of government over land use to restrict African American residential access in this still largely undeveloped section of the city.[17] In June 1951, Councilman Atkinson proposed that a parcel zoned for residential use at the corner of Lee and Seville Roads be rezoned as industrial to permit construction of a factory by the Electric Controller & Manufacturing Co. (see Map 3.1 for the location of this and other development controversies discussed in this chapter). White homeowner groups, including the Glen-Lee Civic Club and the Miles-Lee Civic Club, had successfully opposed industrial rezoning for the same site in 1948, when Coca-Cola had wanted to build a bottling plant there. In fact, these same homeowners initially opposed the Electric Controller plant, but in October they suddenly changed their position, on the racialized grounds that it "would be better than another housing project like the nearby Seville Homes." In addition to the Miles-Lee Civic Club, Lee-Land Heights Civic Council, and Lee-Land Business Men's Association, local Polish ethnic organizations went on record supporting the industrial rezoning. While the plant's proponents promoted it in terms of job creation and tax revenues, the City Planning Commission opposed the change because the area had long been designated for residential use and cited a 1948 survey that found that

Lawndale Avenue in the Lee-Seville Black Enclave, 1945. Cleveland's farthest-outlying pocket of black settlement played a significant role in providing African Americans living space on the suburban fringe—despite its derogatory designation as "slum" by many whites, due to its lack of infrastructure and sometimes improvised housing. (Courtesy of the Cleveland Public Library/Photograph Collection)

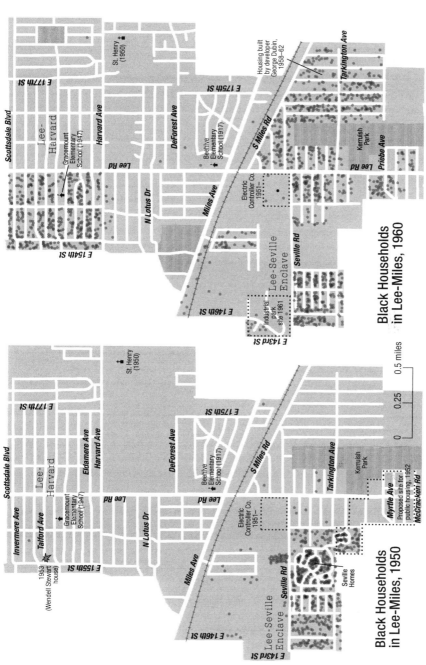

Map 3.1 Black Households in Lee-Miles, 1950 and 1960

Note: Dots scattered randomly within blocks, except in large vacant tracts, where placement was informed by the 1951 and 1959 aerial surveys viewable at http://cplorg.cdmhost.com/cdm/.

Sources: U.S. Bureau of the Census, *United States Census of Housing: 1950 Block Statistics, Cleveland, Ohio* (Washington, D.C., 1952); U.S. Bureau of the Census, *United States Census of Housing: 1960 City Blocks, Cleveland, Ohio* (Washington, D.C., 1961).

plenty of vacant land was available elsewhere in the city for industry. Mayor Burke also expressed disapproval. Meanwhile, the Electric Controller & Manufacturing Co. increased the pressure by threatening to leave the city altogether should rezoning plans be rejected.[18]

The rezoning plan catalyzed widespread black opposition, led by the Miles Heights Progressive League. Black councilman Harold T. Gassaway derided the zoning change as a "land steal" and "smoke screen" for the real objective of hampering black settlement in the area, one of the city's few areas with vacant land to which African Americans had access in a segregated housing market. Lee-Seville's African American population had increased substantially since 1940. Not only were black contractors like Arthur Bussey active in the vicinity, but some families moving out of the Seville Homes chose to remain in the area, rehabilitating old houses or building new ones with Veterans Administration (VA) financing. Of the approximately seventy houses occupied by African American families in the immediate vicinity of the area to be rezoned, one-third were "either built by them as individuals or by Negro contractors" and were in the $8,000–$14,000 range. Others continued to buy up vacant lots here and elsewhere, including at sheriff's sales, where tax-delinquent properties were sometimes auctioned off for as little as $100.[19] At the November 1951 hearing, where the rezoning passed, black councilman Charles V. Carr stated, "My people have invested a lot of money in this area for their modest homes," with others having "manifested an interest in building their homes in this area." Miles Heights Progressive League president C. M. Smart called the move "a death blow to efforts to provide incentive to the city's slum dwellers to build homes for themselves outside the city's crowded areas." Mayor Burke, despite claiming disapproval, was torn between balancing the interests of white and black residents and ultimately declined to veto the ordinance because "it affects only a part of an area."[20]

For black opponents of the rezoning, the controversy marked the beginning of a decade-long struggle over land and housing in Cleveland's southeastern corner. When a telegram campaign failed to persuade Burke, the NAACP, with the support of the interracial Cleveland Clearinghouse on Civil Liberties, launched a petition drive to repeal the ordinance. Key to the NAACP strategy was a citywide campaign; by the time a second public meeting was scheduled in February, petitions seeking to force City Council reconsideration were already circulating in neighborhoods with significant African American populations. Especially prominent here was Glenville, whose middle-class residents had a particular interest in making as much land available as possible for black occupancy elsewhere in the city, due to its own struggle with overcrowding.[21] Activists promoted the February meeting to black ministers, who took the matter to their congregations. The NAACP also sent notifications to the press, city council members, and Lee-Seville property owners, even renting a sound truck to promote the meeting in black neighborhoods. According to a "fact sheet" distributed at the meeting, African Americans made up about half of the total families in the affected area, but only four white families had moved out during 1951 prior to the rezoning proposal. However, more whites were now selling, and with the zoning change, black families were unable to access FHA financing. "These men and women knew that the banks won't lend money to Negroes in the section, and that the FHA was the last hope that Negro would-be home builders had," explained NAACP head Charles P. Lucas. "They knew, then, that if the area were made a factory section, Negro home-building would come to a standstill." At the February meeting, rezoning opponents submitted petitions with over 7,800 signatures, enough to force further hearings in City Council.[22]

The NAACP kept the pressure on into March, assisting a group of Lee-Seville residents in filing a taxpayers' lawsuit, which was refused by the city law director. Meanwhile, the building commissioner disregarded the dispute and issued the Electric Controller & Manufacturing Co. a permit. While continuing consultations with the Cleveland Clearinghouse on Civil Liberties on a possible legal strategy to derail the industrial project, the NAACP promoted attendance at the city council hearings scheduled for mid-March, sending more letters to ministers, petition circulators, and community leaders. By the first hearing, some 12,000 signatures had been collected on petitions opposing the rezoning. A handbill announcing the meeting stated forcefully: "The Lee-Seville Area MUST be rezoned back to RESIDENTIAL / PROTECT COLORED HOME BUILDERS AND HOME OWNERS / Keep in step with Urban Redevelopment. . . . Every true champion of Civil Rights and fair play must attend."[23] This mobilization must have had at least some effect on Mayor Burke, who made a bland conciliation: he announced to the Community Relations Board that while he could not revoke Electric Controller's building permit, he did favor repeal of the ordinance, which would allow the remainder of the rezoned tract to revert to residential use. Later that day at the packed hearing attended by some 300 people, numerous black community leaders, including NAACP staffers, councilmen, ministers, social service professionals, and representatives from the Miles Heights Progressive League and Lee-Seville Citizens Council, added their voices to those of neighborhood residents speaking out against the rezoning. They urged its revocation to prevent a racially divisive referendum on the matter, made possible by the collection of more than 10,000 signatures. Allegations also emerged of factory promoters attempting to bribe one of the white-dominated citizens associations, which proved unnecessary since these supported the industrial rezoning anyway.[24]

A second and final hearing in April sealed the deal for supporters of industrial zoning, at which they had their say prior to the City Council's vote. Already at the first hearing, the Electric Controller & Manufacturing Co. owners had circulated literature declaring this the only suitable location for a new factory; that the plant would be "noiseless, vibrationless, and smokeless" and thus entirely inoffensive to residents; and that it would supply much-needed jobs. Additionally, the owners disputed that mortgage lending in the vicinity was suffering. Ignoring the reality of racial discrimination, they pointed to numerous undeveloped lots in the area and in adjacent Garfield Heights, concluding, "There is no shortage of available land in this southeastern corner of Cleveland," while pronouncing as "doubtful" the prospects for ever developing residential housing on the disputed site. Again the NAACP worked hard to mobilize a large turnout, and some 250 on either side of the issue came. At the hearing, another firm, the Cleveland Cap Screw Co., disclosed it had also purchased land in the rezoned section for a plant. Some speakers in favor of the industrial rezoning, who included officers of the homeowners' associations, obliquely referenced race in voicing their opposition to further public housing built on vacant land, while others emphasized the job creation angle. For his part, Councilman Earnest Atkinson claimed that race was no consideration, because "we welcome all people to our ward." Following the testimony, the City Council's legislation committee killed the proposal to rezone the site back to residential use, and toward the end of the month, it voted not to reconsider the matter. Although the NAACP maintained its intention of placing the issue on the ballot, the Cleveland Clearinghouse on Civil Liberties backed away from what it considered a "divisive" approach, and the issue never made it to voters. Thus, despite a well-organized campaign, black homeowners and their allies proved unable to shift the discussion away from "colorblind" concerns with the city's jobs and tax base and thereby force acknowledgment of the particular handicaps they faced in the racially structured, dual housing market.[25]

Racial undercurrents influencing development policy in Southeast Cleveland were even more obvious in the mid-1952 brouhaha sparked by plans for a public housing development on vacant land off McCracken Road at the city's southeastern border—although here, too, white professions of "colorblind" innocence could be tendered because a handful of African American homeowners like Henry Hawk joined in opposing the project. Similar campaigns against public housing planned for outlying, vacant land were mounted all over the country, often at the instigation of the real estate industry.[26] The Cleveland Metropolitan Housing Authority (CMHA) had seized on the McCracken Road project as a potential solution to the relocation quandary catalyzed by urban redevelopment in the city's deteriorating core—as well as a way to rehouse residents of the dilapidating Seville Homes. CMHA hoped to house up to 900 displaced families in what its head, Ernest J. Bohn, promised would be "the finest housing project in the world," on three parcels of rugged terrain, which private builders had so far declined to develop. White opposition materialized immediately in the adjacent suburb of Maple Heights, with Mayor Walter K. Maser voicing his fears that the project would create a "slum district" and lower nearby property values. Some 200 homeowners came to Maple Heights city hall for an emergency council meeting, where residents discussed a lawsuit and passed a resolution urging Cleveland officials not to rezone the project site for multifamily occupancy. There, Maser argued that if the project were not stopped, "we must realize that our women will be unsafe and that we will have to triple our police force." Across the municipal line, officers of Southeast Cleveland's homeowners' associations also spoke out. Pointing to the Seville Homes as a supposed source of crime and blight, Johanna Wintrich of the Miles-Lee Civic Club said bluntly, "We don't want people from the slums moving out here." Vince J. Busa of the Lee-Land Heights Civic Council agreed with Ward 30 councilman Atkinson's statement that "slums should be cleared before vacant land is used"—and apparently with his preference that the historic black Lee-Seville enclave be demolished. Both Wintrich and Atkinson suggested ominously that the proposed project might give residents in Cleveland's southeastern section cause to consider seceding from the city altogether.[27]

Despite doubts that any legal action could be taken, since the land in question lay in Cleveland, opponents undertook a joint campaign heavily targeting the adjacent suburbs. A door-to-door fund-raising drive organized under the auspices of the Maple Heights Home Owners Association netted $1,250 in the week following the announcement. Over 1,000 persons attended a "mass meeting" held in the suburb's high school auditorium, after which the mayor of nearby Garfield Heights expressed that suburb's intention to join the opposition. By the end of June, the association had reportedly raised almost $4,000, which it used to retain attorney Wilson G. Stapleton, a Shaker Heights councilman and Cleveland Marshall Law School dean.[28] Meanwhile, in Cleveland, Lee-Land Heights Civic Council president Busa published a letter inviting CMHA head Ernest J. Bohn to debate at the organization's meeting scheduled for July 2. Glossing over the racial dimension to the conflict, Busa's letter began: "It may or may not interest you to know that we people of all faiths, color[s] and nationalit[ies] located in the Harvard-Lee area built or bought our homes out here to get away from the congestion of the big city." Accusing Bohn of attempting to bypass city government and failing to consult "the little people off the street," Busa concluded grandiloquently: "We heartily endorse any program that would clear our present slums and give all our people a decent place to live and raise their families[,] but not at the cost of destroying our little remaining fields and forests or modern residential areas." At the end of the month, a new white citizens' group, the South Side Civic Association, joined the opposing coalition at a meeting where talk of seceding from Cleveland remained rife. Meanwhile, the Miles Heights Progressive League, which for years had represented Lee-Seville black homeowners, voiced support for the proposed project.[29]

Mayor Burke's unwillingness to openly take their side drove public housing opponents to try at the ballot box. After he proved noncommittal at an early August meeting, reportedly stating, "I prefer to have homes built by private enterprise . . . but above all, we must have housing," opponents seized upon an extreme tactic: a petition drive for a referendum banning not just the proposed project, but any new public housing for Cleveland. Black homeowner Henry Hawk was one of the five sponsors of the resulting draft legislation. By September, volunteers set out to raise the 5,000 signatures needed to put the ordinance banning all future public housing on the November ballot (in the event that the City Council should fail to approve it), or else 10,000 signatures to force a special election.[30] However, their campaign proved far less organized than that of the NAACP in the earlier rezoning controversy. It took until the end of October for opponents of the McCracken Road project to get even 5,000 valid signatures—too late for the November 1952 election, which left the matter in City Council hands. Significantly, one of the issues on the ballot that autumn was a $7 million urban redevelopment bond issue; despite the public housing controversy, this issue passed with 60 percent approval, in fact surpassing the needed 55 percent threshold in all but eight of the city's thirty-three wards. Even in Ward 30, which contained the proposed McCracken project site and was the center of the anti–public housing campaign, the bond carried 46 percent of the vote, suggesting consensus on the city's approach to eradicating blight, including the construction of public housing. Therefore, even if the proposed total ban had made it onto the ballot, it would not likely have passed.[31]

Public housing opponents in Southeast Cleveland remained unbowed as powerful interests weighed in on both sides of the issue. With the first hearings on their proposed ban scheduled for mid-December, foes threatened to renew the referendum drive should the City Council reject their ordinance, and they picked up an important ally in the Home Builders Association, an organization of real estate developers. For his part, urban redevelopment coordinator Richard V. Hopkins seemed equivocal on the matter, declaring, "Whenever we see a sufficient supply of low income housing dwelling units, I will be the first to call for a reexamination of the public housing program." At the first hearing on the ordinance, CMHA head Bohn suggested that white homeowners were being used by their newfound ally. Others speaking against the ban were Mayor Burke, the heads of the Cleveland Federation of Labor and local CIO-PAC, and representatives from the League of Women Voters, Cleveland Area Church Federation, and Catholic Charities. Among those speaking in favor were Lee-Land Heights Civic Council head Busa, Home Builders Association president George Seltzer, and the new Ward 30 councilman, Anthony P. Lysowski. At a second hearing in early January 1953, the draft ordinance was sent back to the City Council's legislative committee with an amendment by Councilman Bronis J. Klementowicz that public housing be limited to "slum areas" only. Homeowners' groups seemed split on the proposal, with the Maple Heights Home Owners Association reportedly agreeing to it while Lee-Land Heights Civic Council head Busa expressed skepticism and threatened to move forward with the referendum drive.[32]

Then a sudden new amendment to the controversial ordinance—offered by Klementowicz right before hearings resumed in February—dramatically altered the equation. Taking advantage of a long-standing tradition in the Cleveland City Council giving its members discretion over any projects proposed for their individual wards, Klementowicz moved that all new public housing projects be preapproved by the City Council. His amendment narrowly passed at a meeting that found Mayor Burke highly conflicted over the compromise; Burke accepted it as "a lesser evil" because he feared the racial polarization that could result from putting the city's future public housing to a referendum. Lee-Land Heights president Busa declared his support for the amended ordinance so long as it "really means that public housing is kept out of our neighborhood." Black councilman Charles V. Carr, who led the fight against the compromise, demanded that the original ordinance be taken to the voters, buoyed by the passage of urban redevelopment funding the previous autumn. In the days prior to the final vote, tension mounted as the future of Cleveland's entire public housing program seemed on the line. One white councilman beseeched Bohn to drop the McCracken site, hinting that the ordinance might be withdrawn in return; as an alternative, he proposed revisiting an earlier plan to create a redevelopment site by exhuming the graves at the city's historic Woodland Cemetery, located in Cedar-Central. At the February 9 session, when the final vote was held, the amended ordinance passed by the narrowest of margins, 17–15. Following this outcome, the NAACP sought a veto from Burke, to no avail. The homeowners' associations agreed to abandon their referendum drive to ban all public housing but, with a reported $10,000 left in their treasury, vowed to renew their fight if the McCracken Road project should ever resurface.[33] Thus despite their comparative lack of political organization, these mostly white opponents of public housing in Southeast Cleveland achieved their objective by lobbying behind the scenes and threatening to push an issue the mayor found racially divisive.

The foiling of a plan to build low-rise apartments in the same vicinity, not long after the McCracken Road public housing project's demise, reveals that white Southeast Cleveland residents' opposition also extended to private development that could ostensibly lead to black occupancy—this despite indications that the builder, George Goudreau, harbored feelings toward the area's African American residents that were ambivalent at best. As early as 1944, amid the severe wartime housing crisis, Goudreau had floated the idea of building "a whole village near Seville Road" for black occupancy and even hired demographer Howard Whipple Green to calculate how many African American families could afford rents of $40 per month in the postwar period. However, the project never went forward. In 1948, Goudreau and his partner, Alex Treuhaft, unsuccessfully sought an industrial zoning change on the seventy-acre parcel they owned next to the Seville Homes, which was turned down by the City Planning Commission. Then, in 1952, the partners launched a plan to build up to 1,000 "garden-type" apartments on the site. As head of the Private Enterprise Redevelopment Corporation—recently formed to build accommodations for urban redevelopment displacees—Treuhaft proposed to the City Planning Commission that such families have first preference at the planned apartment complex, offering it as a preferable alternative to the McCracken public housing proposal, over which controversy loomed. Councilman Atkinson was in favor of the project but clearly did not have in mind the same potential tenants as Treuhaft, since he told the City Council, "We do not want our ward to be a dumping ground for slum-cleared families from downtown Cleveland." Furthermore, Atkinson went on to insist that both the Seville Homes and the adjacent Beehive be demolished as part of the development plans—in other words, a complete erasure of the African American presence in this farthest-outlying section of Southeast Cleveland. The *Call & Post* remained skeptical of Goudreau and Treuhaft, considering them in league with Atkinson. In response to the councilman's agenda, black organizations in the area, including the Lee-Seville Citizens Council and Miles Heights Progressive League, planned their defense of the Lee-Seville enclave, discussing "self-improvement" housing rehabilitation and continuing to lobby the city for improvements to the streets, sidewalks, and sewers there.[34]

Officials in charge of the city's redevelopment efforts actually considered these proposals to eradicate the historic Lee-Seville enclave. But while Atkinson seized upon the proposed development as a way to expel black residents, planners envisioned its potential to rehouse the comparatively affluent African Americans among those to be displaced from Cedar-Central. They concluded in an August 1952 report: "It may be possible to combine the 'Beehive' allotment and the temporary veterans housing section [Seville Homes] with the 60 acres of vacant land and erect a development of lasting worth for the middle income group." But by the time urban redevelopment chair Richard V. Hopkins met with Goudreau, Treuhaft, and Atkinson in October, he had concluded that the Beehive settlement "did not lend itself to Reconstruction"—in other words, demolition—due to more than 90 percent owner occupancy and a "large amount of new building of small homes." Soon thereafter, city officials met with homeowners in the area and went on record supporting voluntary rehabilitation efforts and stricter housing code enforcement, with a recommendation that the city "accelerate" infrastructure improvements upon evidence of progress. Into the following year, however, in order to "appreciate locality values," Goudreau continued to demand of Mayor Burke "that the city condemn and clear the Ohio Street 'Beehive' Area and make the land available to private builders as part of a complete redevelopment plan." Goudreau expected, "in the event all legal efforts in behalf of the above point fail," a wide-ranging plan, including housing rehabilitation, condemnation of properties with code violations, street and lot widening, infrastructure improvements, and a written commitment to demolish the Seville Homes. This last demand drew the ire of CMHA's Bohn, although he did eventually offer to gradually dismantle the temporary housing units on the condition that displacees receive first priority in the new development. The developers agreed, as long as Seville Homes displacees would be approved by a "credit department," finally accepting rehabilitation instead of demolition for the Beehive section.[35]

Putting the plans for an apartment project into effect proved another matter, foundering mainly on white racial anxieties. Lee-Land Heights Civic Council president Busa initially seemed amenable to a privately built project, but other activists demanded that only single-family homes be built in the area. In August, a meeting of that organization found residents too preoccupied with the McCracken Road public housing issue to scrutinize Treuhaft's proposals. In January 1953, the apartment project hit a snag when Atkinson's successor, Anthony P. Lysowski, suddenly withdrew his support for an ordinance to rezone the project site for multifamily use, on the grounds that Goudreau & Co. had not disclosed enough details about their development plans. Lysowski knew that urban redevelopment displacees would be among the tenants and may also have been dissuaded by the legal reality noted by the Cleveland Clearinghouse on Civil Liberties: that developers receiving public subsidies could no longer engage in openly segregationist rental practices. When Mayor Burke offered Goudreau & Co. the necessary utilities, sewers, and other improvements for the project in March, both Lysowski and Busa protested stridently. With the McCracken Road project having been sunk the previous month, the councilman stated, "Civic groups out here are opposed to an apartment project by either public housing or private builders." He claimed he had received over one hundred phone calls against the development. "This is practically a suburb. We don't want people moving out here and crowding into apartments," Lysowski concluded. Busa added, "We're worried about undesirable people infiltrating into the ward" as he renewed threats that Ward 30 might secede. The *Call & Post* remained skeptical that African Americans would actually be permitted as tenants in the proposed project, citing exclusionary policies at one of Goudreau's apartment complexes on the West Side.

Finally, in the wake of opposition and apathy, the developers abandoned their plans later that year after polling found Ward 30 residents divided over the proposed project.[36]

An expansion of housing options for middle-class blacks during the 1950s meant that the next major development controversy in Lee-Seville having racial undertones did not revolve primarily around preserving vacant land, but rather quality-of-life concerns. In early 1961, Ward 30 councilman Leo Dombrowski introduced a zoning change from residential to heavy industrial for a vacant sixty-nine-acre parcel, to make way for a proposed industrial park. Dombrowski had been elected in 1957 with black support, hitting the incumbent Lysowski for his opposition to not only public housing but also fair employment legislation. By this point, upwardly mobile black residents were gaining access to good-quality housing in eastern Glenville, Mount Pleasant, and, most recently, Lee-Harvard. As for Lee-Seville, African Americans were moving into brand-new homes to the east of the area's historic enclave; by 1960, the combined population of the neighborhood's two census tracts was 85 percent black. Expressing black middle-class fears, Lee-Seville Citizens Council chairman Arthur Bass referenced Cedar-Central in opposing Dombrowski's plan, saying that if the proposal went through, "in 20 years this area may look like another Woodland Avenue. . . . The rezoning will let in other undesirable uses." Clarence Thompson, the Lee-Seville Citizens Council's president and eventual successor to Dombrowski as ward councilman added: "We are trying to build up a nice neighborhood . . . [but] instead, we're being surrounded by factories." Within a week, the Lee-Seville Citizens Council garnered the support of five local black churches through the Lee-Seville Ministerial Alliance and had mobilized 150 officers of street clubs against the zoning change; a subsequent meeting on the issue at the Saint Paul Methodist Church drew 300 attendees. All this surprised the developer, who, like the owners of the Electric Controller & Manufacturing Co. ten years earlier, claimed the factory complex would be "beautiful, clean and truly something for the community to be proud of." Councilman Dombrowski emphasized job creation and tried to shift focus by accusing the Lee-Seville Ministerial Alliance of promoting public housing developments in the area against residents' will.[37]

The Lee-Seville Citizens Council and Lee-Seville Ministerial Alliance utilized the previous tactic of a citywide petition campaign, along with more confrontational tactics in keeping with the ascendant civil rights struggle, but ultimately failed to block Dombrowski's proposal. By the time the City Council held hearings on the zoning change in April, opponents had collected only 1,100 signatures, but 300 angry residents nevertheless appeared at the session to complain about inadequate sidewalks and sewers, excessive traffic, and an almost complete lack of access to the jobs promised by nearby firms like Electric Controller. Some voiced the traditional preference that the site be reserved for future black homebuyers, to which Dombrowski stubbornly (and disingenuously) replied: "Negro housing is an outdated term. Negroes can move anywhere they wish in Cleveland or the suburbs." While members of the City Plan Commission, among them CMHA head Bohn, opposed zoning for heavy industrial use, they did alternatively support a light industry project for the site with appropriate landscaping and traffic improvements—a compromise accepted by Dombrowski. Black councilmen Lowell Henry and Earl Hooper, representing Mount Pleasant and Hough, respectively, actually supported the move, both of them agreeing the land was unsuitable for residential development and could foster residential segregation. But opponents remained outraged, some threatening a lawsuit. "If we cannot have homes, let them plant trees," said Lee-Seville Citizens Council president Thompson, who subsequently led a protest march on a gas station in the area operated by Dombrowski's sons. Peaceful, and attended by 250 persons, the march was derided by Dombrowski as having been organized by "trouble makers" intent on causing "an Alabama incident"—an apparent reference to the Freedom Riders, whose daring protest had riveted the nation weeks earlier. As the legislation moved toward a City Council vote in June, black ministers from the Ministerial Alliance urged Mayor Anthony J. Celebrezze to veto the rezoning if it passed; when it did, without mayoral opposition, activists set out to gather the 20,000 signatures required to place the issue on the November ballot. But, despite a church-based strategy and the assistance of area councils in Glenville, Mount Pleasant, and Lee-Harvard, opponents of the measure came up a scant 1,500 signatures short by the July deadline.[38]

Though the residents lost this battle, as they had the one ten years earlier, rezoning measures remained hotly contested in the area around various proposals for an apartment complex, a retail development, and an office building. In 1966, residents successfully quashed a proposed change that would have allowed the construction of a gas station on the site of two brand-new yet vacant houses at the intersection of Lee Road and Seville Avenue, unsold because of high asking prices, residents alleged. The sum total of these zoning protests constitutes an important precedent, overlooked until now, that set the stage for the much-better-known controversy that erupted in 1968— when black Lee-Seville residents opposed Mayor Carl Stokes's attempt to build scatter-site public housing in the area.[39] These prior actions underline that African American residents had to work harder to influence land use policy than whites did—and that even when they were better organized and collected more signatures, their concerns and interests were not taken as seriously by city officials and developers.

To emphasize these defeats is not to discount the limited influence that black residents, led by organizations like the NAACP and the Urban League, exerted on housing politics and policy prior to the mid-1960s, such as the successful 1953 ouster of urban redevelopment director Richard V. Hopkins over a racially charged comment. Stumping for a second urban redevelopment bond issue on the ballot that November, Hopkins had reassured white Ward 30 residents that "in relocating people from the Central Area we will not move into your neighborhood any family that would upset the normal character of living of the neighborhood. Do you all understand what I mean?" Quoted in the mainstream press the following day, his words provoked an uproar. The NAACP immediately sent Mayor Burke a telegram asking for Hopkins's removal, foregrounding their expectations for improved residential access: "We are confident that if Mr. Hopkins remains as Director of Urban Redevelopment the seven million dollar bond issue which the Negro community has so faithfully supported will tragically be defeated. Desperately, eager as we are for Urban Redevelopment, we cannot entrust million[s] of the people's dollars to one who obviously means to use them to build an impassable wall of separation between white and colored Clevelanders." Other groups sent similar condemnatory messages to the mayor, including the black-led Cleveland Association of Real Estate Brokers, Cleveland Branch ACLU, and several labor union locals.[40]

Two days after the incident, Burke held a meeting with Hopkins, NAACP leaders, several black councilmen, and the head of the Community Relations Board. Hopkins apologized for his remarks, but his attempted clarification (that displaced Cedar-Central residents would be relocated to outlying areas "if at all possible") failed to impress the black representatives as sincere. With the fate of urban redevelopment in the balance, Burke asked Hopkins to resign, which he did the following day. Although this matter would appear to have been resolved quickly, the NAACP later reported it had been pressured to moderate its demand for Hopkins's ouster, and that "real estate interests" lobbied for weeks afterward for his retention. City Planning Commission head James Lister even temporarily reinstated Hopkins until another urban redevelopment director could be found.[41]

Black Builders and Building for the African American Market

Clearly African Americans prized Lee-Seville's vacant land, on which new homes for black families could be built. And despite formidable discriminatory barriers, upwardly mobile African Americans around the country moved into nearly 700,000 new housing units built during the 1950s. In Cleveland and elsewhere, one noteworthy source of new housing was African American building contractors and black-owned construction companies. Though of minor overall significance in augmenting the available housing stock, black builders took on symbolic prominence beyond their relatively small numbers—supplying hundreds of homes for interested buyers in Lee-Seville and elsewhere, although they struggled to meet increasing demand.[42] Some were former tradesmen who ambitiously expanded their operations to larger-scale housing development after World War II—incidentally, a common trajectory among smaller white-owned construction firms whose owners, frequently of Southern or Eastern European ancestry, made the jump into the boom-ing postwar home-building market.[43] Traditionally, black building trades-men's biggest jobs were African American churches and fraternal lodges. A 1949 article lauded five craftsmen who completed $125,000 worth of work on the Emmanuel Baptist Church, at the head of whom stood Arthur Bussey—a mason, the general contractor, and a church member. The struggle to secure bids in this niche amid competition from white construction firms was some-times heated and often couched in terms of community loyalty. Nearly a de-cade later, for example, Bussey, along with two other black contractors, George Fagan and Ralph H. Dickerson, blasted Antioch Baptist Church pastor Rev. Wade H. McKinney for awarding a lucrative job to a white-owned firm, in their words, thereby "excluding competent Negro contractors from participating in the greatest church building and expansion program in history."[44]

Many of Cleveland's black building tradesmen were born in the South, were formally educated in their craft, and, not surprisingly, had confronted racial discrimination in the local construction industry. A native of Augusta, Bus-sey had trained in masonry at Georgia State Industrial College before coming to Cleveland in 1917 and then earning a degree in architectural drafting from Chicago Technical College in 1932. Of the other tradesmen named in the 1949 Emmanuel Baptist Church job, carpenter H. Q. Rucker had similarly arrived in 1918 after graduating from Benedict College in Columbia, South Carolina, while plumber Sylvester Ward had learned his trade at Wilberforce University. Robert P. Morgan had studied to become an electrician at Tuskegee and came to Cleveland in 1924. He later became a key figure in the local struggle against the exclusion of black tradesmen from AFL craft unions and in 1949 first suc-ceeded in getting union cards for six of his employees from Local 38 of the Brotherhood of Electrical Workers. Bussey made the jump to general contrac-tor around 1947, and as of 1959, he was credited with erecting approximately forty houses, "all but eight or 10 [of them] for Negroes." That year, he was living in one of the several brick homes in the $35,000 range he had built on Myrtle Avenue, off Lee Road in the city's far southeastern corner. Remarkably, and illustrating the extreme measures that black builders sometimes took in order to succeed, Bussey personally financed the necessary extension of sewers for that street. The earlier mentioned George Fagan, a fellow bricklayer and native of Columbus, Georgia, who came to Cleveland in 1917, had supplied a dozen homes for black tenants evicted upon the demolition of the Berea Homes war housing project in 1956, around Guardian Boulevard and West 130th Street in the only historic black enclave on that side of town.[45]

New Homes on Myrtle Avenue, Built by Arthur Bussey, 1959. Black contractors supplied a limited but crucial portion of high-quality housing to upwardly mobile African American families, refuting white stereotypes that black neighborhoods were shoddily built and doomed to inevitable decline. (Courtesy of the *Cleveland Press* Collection, Cleveland State University Library)

Even those African American builders who successfully contracted for work faced challenges that limited the scale of their operations. Revealingly, the *Call & Post*, amid what it dubbed "the biggest boom in residential building for Negro occupancy seen ... in more than a quarter of a century," had in 1953 tallied only about forty-five new homes completed or in the process of being built, approximately thirty of them by three black-owned construction companies, which had plans for thirty-five more. Near the end of the 1954 building season, the three black-owned construction firms of Harris & Adams, Lee Road Builders, and Taborn Builders were each reported to have a couple dozen homes in the works, for a total approaching seventy. The city's Urban League chapter, which at the time was facilitating meetings between African American contractors and representatives of the Cleveland Home Builders Association, FHA, and local supply companies, emphasized black builders' difficulties in accessing land—as well as "gentlemen's agreements" between banks that either withheld financing or imposed higher rates of interest and smaller loan-value ratios, leaving them at a competitive disadvantage. According to the Urban League's housing specialist, K. C. Jones, in 1958, the numbers of black builders remained few, their enterprises still comparatively small scale, and their credit access to building materials limited.[46]

Clearly, black builders alone could not meet the new housing demands of African American families. A brief examination of the three previously named firms' record outlines the parameters within which black-owned construction firms operated, revealing their limitations, successes, and failures. The Harris & Adams Construction Co. was launched in 1953 as a collaboration between Morehouse-educated Thomas F. Adams of Selma, Alabama, and native Clevelander William A. Harris, a former football star at Miami University and real estate salesman. "We don't want to kid anybody—we are in business to make a profit," Adams explained to the local press. "But we also believe we are part of a civic program—getting people out of the slums." Tapping the expertise of mason Arthur Moore, active in the area for over thirty years and credited with getting black tradesmen admitted to local unions, the firm built to the specifications of individual customers, including in already-developed neighborhoods. But there were risks to this approach. In July 1954, four homes under construction by the firm were vandalized in a coordinated attack: one just south of Kinsman Avenue on East 112th Street, not far from the historic black Mount Pleasant settlement; another on West 118th Street, just outside the lone West Side enclave; and two more on East 154th Street near the Shaker Heights border. Dissatisfied with the level of police protection following these incidents, Harris & Adams hired private detectives to protect the still-unfinished houses. A week later, Cleveland police chief Frank Story assigned twenty-five additional beat policemen to the affected areas.[47]

Far more ambitious plans—that ultimately ended in ignominy—were hatched by Lee Road Builders, later known as Southeast Builders, Inc. The firm got its start in April 1952 when Tillman Carr and James Dillard, two young building tradesmen originally from Chattanooga, joined three World War II migrants with no formal training, but who had made a pact to help build each other's houses in Lee-Seville. Carr and Dillard, who were subcontracting for work in the vicinity, approached the three—most prominent among whom was Leslie Ephraim, formerly a schoolteacher in Camden, Alabama—with the idea of starting a construction company to improve their chances of securing credit from local banks. Getting off to an auspicious start, the firm built over twenty homes in its first year, constructed offices on Lee Road, recruited two African American real estate brokers to serve as its exclusive agents, and grew to include nine partners, including bricklayers, carpenters, and a plasterer. Near the end of the 1953 season, it announced a $50,000 stock issue to raise the capital needed to build "dozens of homes for 'modest income' families" in Mount Pleasant and the Lee-Seville vicinity. It reportedly had eighteen homes under construction at the time, for a grand total of fifty undertaken since the firm's inception. By the summer of 1954, Lee Road Builders employed white subcontractors as well as black, evidenced by an incident where white union plasterers walked off the job in response to the hiring of nonunion plumbers from the black-owned Hilliard Plumbing and Heating Co., who in turn used the issue to force Local 55 of the Journeymen Plumbers Association to vote on the issue of admitting blacks for membership.[48]

Yet problems with financing remained, even as the firm's ambitions grew apace. Despite securing credit with one of the area's largest lumber suppliers at unprecedentedly fair rates "in keeping with what the white competition has been using indefinitely," Ephraim complained in early 1954 that banks directed much of the available loan money toward "preferred builders"—larger firms that could more precisely estimate their budgets for the entire year. In August, Ephraim and four other members of the firm (which by then was doing business under the name Union Home Builders) entered into an agreement with white attorneys George Zimmerman and Sanford Likover to supply them with capital, in exchange for bonus payments from the profits. As part of the agreement, it reorganized as Southeast Builders, Inc. That winter, the firm announced plans for "Tarkington Heights," a project of one hundred colonial and ranch-style homes in the $15,000–$16,000 range, described by Southeast's sales manager as "the largest, most modern development of Negro Housing in the city." Having built eighty homes to date, the firm was said to be making a new departure in developing this entire neighborhood of new housing on vacant land adjacent to Kerruish Park, the goal being to preempt previous outcomes of "rapid depreciation of property value . . . caused by neighboring houses that, in most cases, were far from new." By January, Southeast had purchased 130 lots for the development off Lee Road and claimed it had an "unusually large" backlog of house orders; in April, it bought a second bulldozer and was reportedly acquiring milling equipment to produce doors and cabinets more economically.[49]

But already the first danger signals were apparent, as eight Southeast customers with a combined total of nearly $5,000 in down payments, dissatisfied with lengthy building delays, lodged a complaint with the Better Business Bureau. In the resulting hearing before the city's police prosecutor, Southeast got a "clean bill of health" and was assumed merely to have "bit off more than they could chew." It also emerged that the firm's primary customer base was veterans, and that financing was being guaranteed through the VA, but with resultant delays beyond the contract-specified ninety days after which a buyer could demand a refund. The prosecutor's positive assessment proved premature. Southeast Builders ceased all construction in May 1955, and by that fall was under investigation for a rash of new complaints. When it officially went under in March 1956, the firm owed some ninety-six customers a combined total of nearly $50,000—and to make matters worse, five home purchasers were facing foreclosure suits filed by subcontractors seeking to collect liens on the bankrupt company's unpaid debts.[50] A similar, but smaller-scale failure was seen in the case of the Frederick V. Tyler Co., which acquired title to some fifteen lots in the Mount Pleasant area and had three foundations under way in the summer of 1952 for homes in the $10,000–$14,500 range. The following year, Tyler offered lots for sale and had six homes under construction on East 147th Street; he also aspired to develop cooperative, "garden-type" apartments in the Lee Road area. After collecting down payments ranging from $300 to $1,500 from dozens of prospective buyers for this "Van Buren Estates," Tyler suddenly pled guilty to larceny in 1954, admitting he had used the funds to promote the project and staff an office. To make restitution, the builder obligingly offered up his two cars, building equipment, and the equity in four homes built by the firm.[51] As these examples illustrate, black building companies faced particular challenges in meeting their commitments. Thus having a home built, a routine matter for so many whites who moved to outlying neighborhoods or the suburbs, could be a process fraught with peril for African American buyers.

Without a doubt, the city's most successful black builder was Albert Taborn, a Michigan native who arrived around 1946. As the first African American admitted to the Cleveland Home Builders Association in 1953, Taborn had a real estate sales background as a founding member and former president of the predominantly black Cleveland Association of Real Estate Brokers. In the spring of 1954, he announced his intention to focus solely on building affordable new houses for black buyers in Mount Pleasant and the Lee Road vicinity—and at a July open house attended by 300 persons, he showcased the first ranch home of what would prove to be his exceedingly popular "Lorenzo" model. Teaming up with black mason George W. Fagan, Taborn successfully reduced construction costs using a special type of hollow brick, secured FHA and VA guarantees on loans extended through the black-owned Quincy Savings & Loan Co., and thereby enabled home seekers to buy with as little as $600 down. By the following year, the *Call & Post* was carrying regular features on happy black families and their "Lorenzos," of which several dozen were completed or under construction. "It is so thrilling," one young wife told the paper. "Everything is so completely NEW . . . just what WE wanted, not something someone [else] had picked and we got second-handed later."[52]

Continuing this successful trajectory, the Taborn Co. opened spacious new headquarters on East 105th Street in Glenville in March 1956, where it handled not just new home construction but numerous additional functions, including buying, selling, and trading real estate, home renovation, financing, property management, and more. At that point, Taborn had reportedly "produced more than 200 new homes for Negro occupancy in less than two years" and was in the process of acquiring a tract in Wickliffe (Lake County) for a new development. By 1958, Taborn's company had expanded to include branch offices in

Mount Pleasant and in the city of Akron, and that year he was one of fifty-three builders nationwide to win a "Blue Ribbon Award" from the *Saturday Evening Post* for his high-quality houses. The following year Taborn had a "Lee Heights" subdivision under way on East 176th Street at the city's far southeastern edge, with homes in the $15,000–$30,000 category. At least one other black builder, William Woodridge, got his start through the firm. A college-educated engineer from Saint Louis who was designing homes for Taborn in 1955, Woodridge struck out on his own by 1959, when his Engineering Enterprises Co. was reported to have built a dozen houses at prices ranging from $16,500 to $35,000.[53]

In addition to black contractors and individuals who built their own homes, some white-owned construction firms built specifically for African Americans near existing black settlements or, later, on an open-occupancy basis. Initial efforts along these lines, during the 1940s, had an uneven record of success. As noted earlier, George Goudreau had obtained priorities to build "Negro housing" in Lee-Seville during World War II, but he had never initiated construction.[54] The one white builder who did manage to do so during the war failed to satisfy his African American customers and came to feel that his efforts were not worth the "trouble." Maurice Fishman of the Precision Housing Corp. had thirty-two homes under way off Glendale Avenue in Mount Pleasant's secondary Kinsman Heights cluster as of November 1944, with FHA backing, no less. After inspecting some of the new houses as part of a black delegation, Rev. Wade H. McKinney, pastor of the prestigious Antioch Baptist Church, excoriated Fishman's houses as a swindle, where "for about $6,200 a Negro can buy a home without a garage or driveway and without interior paint." When the *Call & Post* investigated, Fishman angrily offered a free home to "anyone who can duplicate, for less" the homes he was building. Two years later, he blamed a speech McKinney gave at the City Club, which was broadcast over the radio, for causing potential buyers to back out, resulting in the completion of only sixty-one of his company's originally planned ninety-one homes. "I wouldn't build any houses for Negroes and there are no other local builders who would attempt construction of houses for Negroes," Fishman declared afterward. Stirred by these remarks, local black organizations, including the Urban League, stood by McKinney's original assessment and vowed to gather documentation on the various ways builders took advantage of African Americans.[55]

As of 1947, only one white-owned firm, the Grant Housing Co., marketed to African Americans. Grant had thirty-eight bungalows for sale in the West Park black enclave, at a starting price of $8,600, with a $1,000 down payment and VA guarantee. But apart from the availability of "suitable" land, the dilemmas of financing potential customers could dissuade even large white-owned building firms with plenty of capital. In the summer of 1954, the city's Community Relations Board (CRB) was approached by the regional FHA office for "advice and assistance . . . in easing financial problems encountered by one of the first large-scale home building companies which entered the Negro home building market." Black veterans' families typically had between 5 and 10 percent of the purchase price to put down and expected to get the minimum twenty- to twenty-five-year mortgages extended to white buyers; banks, however, typically demanded a 20 to 25 percent down payment on fifteen- to twenty-year mortgages, leading the CRB to conclude that "some solution in the conflict of interest needs to be arrived at if the building and purchase of homes for Negroes is to proceed at a pace commensurate with the needs." The following February, the CRB pledged to help facilitate the Housing and Home Finance Agency's new Voluntary Mortgage Credit Extension Committee, which in its words was intended "to aid a person or builder who has been denied twice in his attempts to secure a mortgage loan whenever minority groups are involved."[56]

A subsequent plan to build a subdivision for blacks, on seventy-one acres along Seville Road, harked back to zoning and development conflicts in the area. When Cranbrook Builders—a partnership of former urban redevelopment chief Richard V. Hopkins and developer Jerry Squires—announced the project of 275 two- and three-bedroom homes in the $15,000 range in April 1955, Councilman Anthony P. Lysowski declared his opposition and his intention to instead seek a light industrial project and street extension. But the CRB reported that, surprisingly, "the neighborhood groups who had objected heretofore to both public housing and private multifamily housing because of the interracial occupancy of such projects are in favor of this proposal." Perhaps the development was less controversial because it immediately bordered the historic Lee-Seville settlement. With the City Planning Commission strongly behind the planned development, Lysowski faced the prospect of appearing blatantly racist or else relenting, which he finally did after being confronted on the race issue at a July City Council meeting. A year later, however, Cranbrook Builders was having difficulties securing mortgage insurance from the Federal National Mortgage Association (Fannie Mac) and was being pressured by lenders to downgrade the development's quality and build on concrete slabs instead of foundations. Only nine houses had been started by then, and, despite strong promotion by the *Call & Post*, potential black purchasers were apparently dissuaded by what they considered a high price for the type of home offered, not to mention the twice-normal, $3,000 down payment required.[57]

By the late 1950s, however, growing demand and creditworthiness among Cleveland's black middle class attracted more stable and capable white firms to the market. Most successful was white developer George L. Dubin, who in May 1957 first announced his plan to build 500 homes for black occupancy on three streets south of Tarkington Avenue, east of Lee Road, in Southeast Cleveland. Although potential buyers might have had trepidations, had they recalled scandals involving Dubin in the late 1940s, this "Kerruish Park Development" unfolded as a public-private joint venture with the blessing of the nonprofit Cleveland Development Foundation, which ultimately lent the builder $100,000 to acquire the necessary land and install utilities. The *Call & Post* gave Dubin its stamp of approval, and the black-owned Quincy Savings & Loan Co. apparently made some loans to the buyers. Dubin recounted one appreciative client who told him, "You don't know what it means to have your husband come home from work, dirty and tired, and be able to take a shower in his own bathroom. We used to share a kitchen and bath with three other families in a rented house, and I worried every time my daughter and I went downstairs. There were always men in the hall. Now I don't have to worry." By the end of 1958, Dubin had completed 200 homes; adding 145 more in early 1959 made Dubin "the area's largest builder of homes for Negroes." Ranches and bungalows in the development cost from $14,000 to $16,000, or more, and had basements, although some were prefabricated. Notwithstanding the high financial qualifications of his black buyers, Dubin had been unable to arrange suitable loans through local banks in his first two years, and therefore had to approach Fannie Mae for assistance. By the time the originally planned 500 homes were completed in 1960, FHA financing was available on favorable terms, with just $950 down for a thirty-year mortgage at 5¾ percent interest. By 1962, the development had grown to more than 600 homes and was described by the Cleveland Development Foundation as an unqualified success.[58]

Dubin's example inspired other white builders to market new housing to African Americans. In 1959, K-D Builders, one of the largest construction firms in the state, announced plans for fifty ranches and bungalows in the $14,000 price range for West Park, to be marketed by the black-owned Ameer Realty; this followed the earlier success of a comparable number built on East 156th Street just south of Miles Avenue, in Lee-Seville. By 1960, Allstate Homes, Inc., was building $12,000 homes for African American families in Mount Pleasant, having sold some 200 by the end of that year by offering a free washer-dryer combination as an additional incentive. The following year, Allstate expanded its operations to Lee-Miles as well as the suburb of Maple Heights, where a small black enclave hemmed in by railroad tracks dated at least to the 1930s. By 1963, Federal Homes, Inc., a company founded by three Jewish Glenville High School graduates, had built 400 homes for black occupancy in Mount Pleasant, Lee-Harvard, and Maple Heights. At the time, it was building twenty-four homes in the $20,000–$25,000 range on DeForest Avenue off Lee Road and had twenty more planned for Priebe Avenue further south. Two brothers, Stanley and Charles Bernath, also had twenty homes under way that year in the same area, with plans for an additional fifty; the following year they opened a new "Stanley Homes Subdivision" in Lee-Seville. As another example of Jewish–African American collaboration in the black housing market, the

Bernaths teamed up with the M. Neidus Realty Co. to promote their properties through extensive advertising in the *Call & Post*. Both Federal Homes and the Bernaths' Stanley Building Co. offered black buyers VA-guaranteed financing with no money down.[59]

Gaining Access to Lee-Harvard

In addition to building on vacant land in Lee-Seville during the 1950s, African American homebuyers gained a foothold in the Lee-Harvard neighborhood immediately to the north that would subsequently prove crucial. This area was annexed to Cleveland only in the 1920s, and although most of its streets were laid out prior to the Great Depression, the neighborhood was mainly built up after World War II as "a suburb in the city." In its two easternmost census tracts, over two-thirds of the housing dated only to 1950–60. While historians like Arnold Hirsch have touched upon this distinction,[60] the recognition that some moves within the city were for all intents and purposes suburbanizing ones is of particular significance in evaluating the success African American home seekers had in improving their living conditions prior to the 1964 Civil Rights Act. Besides being one of the city's few sections with numerous vacant lots into the postwar period, Lee-Harvard shared another similarity with many suburbs: widespread deed restrictions barring sales to African Americans. Though invalidated by the 1948 *Shelley v. Kraemer* U.S. Supreme Court decision, these restrictions had a lingering effect into the early 1950s, letting African Americans know they were unwelcome.[61] In 1939, Home Owners Loan Corporation (HOLC) evaluators had designated Lee-Harvard's northerly portion one of the city's few top "A"-rated neighborhoods, due to its "rigid" deed and zoning restrictions; much of the rest of the area received a "B" rating, with existing racial restrictions set until 1950, which evaluators expected would help "maintain" property values. This portion of Southeast Cleveland included a mix of also-suspect Southern and Eastern Europeans (including Jews) who had migrated there from older, inner-city ethnic settlements beginning in the 1920s; tellingly, HOLC evaluators rated Lee-Harvard's southeastern portion as a "C," with its "better type Hungarian & Czech" population, uneven development, and large number of tax-delinquent lots, as well as a grade school (Beehive Elementary) "heavily attended by colored children" from the "D"-rated Lee-Seville enclave. Key to the neighborhood's postwar development was the opening of the Lee-Harvard shopping center in late 1949, which generated $6 million in gross sales during its first year of operation. Apart from some multifamily housing on its main thoroughfares, Lee-Harvard's residential streets featured relatively affordable ranch and colonial-style single-family homes built during the 1940s and 1950s.[62]

The first African American family moved to Lee-Harvard in the summer of 1953, igniting a furor that became the greatest test of the CRB's efficacy in its

Vacant Land along Lee Road, 1947. Large tracts of empty land remained in Cleveland's Lee-Miles section into the 1960s—making the area a contentious and racially polarized site for housing and industrial development, due to the established presence of African Americans there. (Courtesy of the Cleveland Public Library/Official City of Cleveland Photograph)

entire history.[63] When Wendell and Genevieve Stewart purchased a two-story colonial at 15508 Talford Avenue in early July 1953, they crossed an invisible line popularly dubbed the "38th parallel," with reference to the recent Korean War, which was the boundary where race-based deed restrictions formerly distinguished what was a "B"-rated HOLC neighborhood from the "C"-rated Mount Pleasant and Corlett to the immediate west. Wendell Stewart was the funeral director at the eminent House of Wills funeral home. A native of Urbana, Ohio, he had come to Cleveland in 1934. Stewart belonged to the NAACP, was a deacon at Antioch Baptist Church, and sat on the board of the Cedar YMCA. He was also light-skinned enough to be potentially mistaken for white. Stewart's wife, Genevieve, had come to Cleveland from Charleston, South Carolina, at the age of twelve and grew up in Glenville; during the 1940s, she was regularly mentioned in the *Call & Post* social columns. Mrs. Stewart worked as a supervisor at the Square Deal Department Store and hosted a weekly radio program sponsored by the House of Wills. The couple had no children and owned a house in Glenville, where they had been among the first African Americans on

Yale Avenue. In seeking to purchase the house on Talford, the Stewarts were refused loans by at least two banks, including Cleveland Trust, before they arranged financing through their life insurance company after borrowing a substantial amount of cash from Mr. Stewart's employer. This additional security was requested because—the 1948 *Shelley* decision notwithstanding—previous restrictions were still considered a "cloud on the title."[64]

As soon as white Talford Avenue residents discovered Stewart's purchase, they swamped a Friday evening meeting of the Lee-Land Heights Civic Council in the basement of a Czech gymnastic fraternity's hall in nearby Warrensville Heights, engaging in what the *Plain Dealer* called a "rip-saw discussion [which] whirled on for more than three hours." The following afternoon, residents gathered on the playground of Gracemount Elementary School, "where angry comments and bitter threats were made," before fifty or so proceeded with an unsuccessful attempt to confront and embarrass the seller, Richard J. Lepon, at his place of work. According to the Jewish Community Federation, Lepon was "a Jewish business man with a non-Jewish wife who, it was alleged, had sold the home to Negroes out of spite against his neighbors with whom he had had considerable difficulties." Over the weekend, reported the Jewish Community Federation, "tension mounted and calls were received . . . from Jewish residents in the area who felt extremely threatened by the growing restlessness, since such great resentment was expressed against 'Jews who pulled this dirty trick on us by selling to Negroes.'" Meanwhile, the CRB made arrangements for round-the-clock police protection of the Stewart house, at the request of the Cleveland NAACP. Consultations were also initiated with clergy at Saint Cecelia's, a Catholic parish in Mount Pleasant, which had a handful of African American parishioners and a record of interracial tolerance efforts.[65]

White residents continued their collective resistance, and the situation appeared increasingly ominous. A week's worth of nightly "mass meetings" began on Monday, July 13, in the Gracemount Elementary schoolyard, with 400 in attendance. "The crowd was fairly evenly divided between those who wanted to explore legitimate legal steps and those who demanded 'action' at once," the Jewish Community Federation reported. "Frequently, threats of violence were voiced by those who insisted that only by teaching the seller and the purchaser a lesson could further immigration of Negroes be prevented." A white NAACP observer at one such gathering was hounded as an "outsider" and later reported hearing statements like "They knew how to do it in Detroit" and "Let's throw a bomb." As crowds milled in front of the Stewarts' new property, neighborhood representatives began a series of closed-door sessions at City Hall with Stewart and his counsel, the CRB, and Mayor Burke. White residents first sent three lawyers from the neighborhood to ask Wendell Stewart to resell the house back to them; he politely indicated that he intended to stay, suggesting that the delegation instead "delay their offer to purchase his house for three months during which time they would have an opportunity to know him better." Stewart told the press, "I never expected anything like this. After all, there are colored people [living] just a few blocks away." The threat of violence was a constant undercurrent at the nightly gatherings, and even with police protection, there were a few "minor" cases of vandalism (egging of the house). More disturbing was the finding by a Mount Pleasant Community Council field worker that one of the police officers on duty considered the Stewarts "foolish" for trying to move into an all-white neighborhood, adding, "They'll never be comfortable here" and "We can't go on protecting them indefinitely." Meanwhile, the Stewarts, still living at their Glenville property, reported a barrage of harassing phone calls, along with numerous expressions of moral support.[66]

While African Americans were continually regarded as interlopers, notions of community were becoming more inclusive for ethnic whites. Just three years earlier, Talford Avenue residents had been featured in one of the city's major dailies as paragons of "neighborliness." In that article, they had been lauded for their thoughtful gifts to newcomers, mutual assistance in home improvement projects, and errands run on behalf of the street's senior citizens. The street included a number of avid gardeners who generously shared their produce with neighbors. At least two residents belonged to "a four-year-old neighborhood club that meets every two weeks, celebrates birthdays by going out to dinner, seeing a play or a movie." The article also emphasized the ethnic diversity of the street: "Representative of many nationality backgrounds, the women who preside over Talford's kitchens include European dishes in their menus" and "While Talford's feminine residents express their heritage through their cooking, their men folks reveal their backgrounds through music," a reference to two neighborhood polka musicians. The Lee-Land Heights Civic Council in fact served something of an assimilating function, as implied by president Vince J. Busa, who stated: "If anything I can think of, anything I can do, makes our association grow and leads our neighbors of all nationalities to know each other better, it makes me feel pretty happy." Busa, the son of Hungarian immigrants, was also—like many white Lee-Harvard residents—a World War II veteran. Thus while ethnic diversity existed on Talford, the resisting residents' opposition to the Stewarts' impending arrival was premised on their pan-ethnic mobilization as *whites*. This presumption of white racial solidarity in Lee-Harvard proved shaky, however, considering the dramatic turnover in population over the subsequent decade.[67]

The representatives mediating the Stewarts' situation were more reasonable, at least on the surface, than those who congregated nightly. Indeed, both Councilman Anthony P. Lysowski and leaders from the Lee-Land Heights Civic Council—who had directly undermined the ability of African Americans to settle in nearby Lee-Seville—consistently discouraged violence. But they hardly welcomed the Stewarts. Delbert Cohon, one of the attorneys in the initial delegation, commented to the press, "My legal opinion is that no court action is possible against Stewart. . . . However, I think the 2000 property owners of the Harvard-Lee section should each retain a lawyer and file damage suits against Lepon." But when addressing the crowd at Gracemount on July 13, Cohon had pleaded for calm, saying, "We are making a spectacle out of ourselves in front of the whole country." Similarly, Councilman Lysowski conceded that Stewart had "every right to occupy" the house he had bought, so "people should forget about it and learn to live with their neighbors in harmony." Busa had announced that the Lee-Land Heights Civic Council was "opposed to violence in any form" and urged the crowd to disperse, for which he was booed. Under CRB mediation at City Hall, however, the five-member Lee-Land Heights Civic Council team voiced their concerns that Stewart's presence would negatively impact property values and emphasized—while claiming they accepted him personally—that they could not vouch for the other residents. George Margolis, for example, volunteered that he was Jewish and had grown up with African Americans in Mount Pleasant, but now had all his life savings tied up in his house and thus asked Stewart to please resell, in order to spare the owners a supposed 25 percent drop in prices caused by his presence. Busa repeatedly insisted that Lee-Harvard was "not ready" for the Stewarts. And when pressed by the CRB as to whether having a "fine upstanding" black neighbor might not be an asset, Lysowski stated that all those present in the meeting could appreciate such, but that most of the neighborhood residents "accidentally or on purpose purchased their homes there because of the restrictive covenant clause in their deeds."[68]

In their own defense, Stewart and his legal counsel wove together two classic black rhetorical strategies sometimes presumed to be divergent, emphasizing both his middle-class respectability and his citizenly rights. In two meetings at City Hall, they noted that no one could force white homeowners to sell their properties, which meant that property values should not be a concern. They expressed disapproval of aggressive real estate tactics and emphasized that Stewart had bought the house to stay, not for speculative financial gain. Also, even if he were to leave, it was likely that other black families would eventually move in. "You gentlemen who live in this neighborhood moved there from where you were living because this neighborhood was better than the one you were living in," ventured Clayborne George, Stewart's attorney. "Of course, this is the most natural thing in the world. When someone gets enough money, no matter who he is, to buy outside the crime, disease-infested slums, he is going to move into a better location where the environment is better and where the property is equal to what he has to spend." Stewart's pastor, Rev. Wade H. McKinney, was more confrontational, stating: "We must always fight for principle in the face of an aggressive challenge by racial bigots. . . . Every so often there comes a challenge and a test and we must face it with courage and fortitude. Many people have called me and have talked with me and they have all stated plainly that they would rather see Mr. Stewart brought out in an ambulance or hearse than to make a cowardly retreat in a moving van." Stewart himself said simply, "My wife and I started about three years ago looking for a place and we took our time until we found what we wanted. . . . After a three-year struggle, I don't think I'm going to give it up overnight."[69]

By personally overseeing this mediation, Mayor Burke took a more pro-active approach than his counterparts in Chicago and Detroit, but his neutral stance satisfied neither Lee-Harvard's white homeowners nor the city's most vocal civil rights advocates. Burke had spaced the two meetings over five days in the hope of creating a "cooling-off period," and although he provided adequate police protection, he clearly dragged his feet on the matter of making a clear statement in support of the Stewarts' right to live in Lee-Harvard as urged by the CRB and local civil rights groups. He also expressed anger at the *Call & Post* for having "inflamed" the situation through its intensive coverage. In the time between the two meetings at City Hall, white residents gathered yet another time at Gracemount, where they heard a lawyer propose a voluntary restrictive agreement intended to circumvent *Shelley*. According to an eyewitness, the lawyer allegedly stated, "If anyone refuses to sign we want his name and address too because we will have to take care of him." Another account paraphrased him as saying that while the proposed agreement would not specifically mention race or religion, it would serve to "keep out those of bad moral or financial standing or those who could not qualify 'for one other reason,'" which met with "great laughter."[70]

Meanwhile, dozens of organizations, including the National Council of Negro Women, Baptist Ministers Conference, Ohio Bill of Rights Conference, Cleveland Civil Liberties Union, and several union locals went on record in support of the Stewarts. Ordinary residents also sent dozens of letters, both hate mail and expressions of support, to the Stewarts and Mayor Burke. Some threatened, but others attempted a more reasonable tone, as in the resident who wrote: "The area is so new and the mortgages so high that the people cannot afford to absorb any depreciation in their property out of line with other properties. Please, Mr. Stewart, for the sake of future good race relations and for the sake of the thousands of frightened people here, resell your home. You can buy another just as nice." One letter, signed "Many oldtime Clevelanders," implored Burke to consider the sometimes tenuous nature of white working-class upward mobility, even as it demonstrated how whites of all class backgrounds had fully internalized the real estate industry's logic regarding race: "I wonder if you know all the hardship and sorrow you have caused by allowing the colored people to take over and control so many of our best streets in Cleveland while we white Americans have to move out in the Styx and into rents we cannot afford[;] we have to give up our houses we have owned for years[;] we must sell them cheap and try to buy very expensive houses not well[-]built and far out. . . . Why must the black man spoil what we are giving up our sons for, our beloved houses and our freedom on the streets we have loved for years and years[?]" The Stewarts moved in during mediation, hiring a local heavyweight boxer to direct their moving crew. They had received offers of support and assistance from Charles Lucas of the local NAACP, Future Outlook League president John O. Holly, black councilmen John W. Kellogg and Theodore Williams, and real estate brokers James Lemon and Albert Taborn, among others. "The facts in the matter are plain," editorialized the *Call & Post*. "Unless Stewart can be bluffed or intimidated, the citizens have no other recourse than to reconcile themselves to the inevitable, and to rejoice that the 'invaders' are thoroughly high-class citizens who will grace, rather than depreciate the neighborhood."[71]

Subsequent events further underline just how different of an approach Cleveland's political leadership took on the matter of racial residential transition compared to other cities at the time. At the conclusion of CRB mediation, Mayor Burke summoned the Lee-Land Heights Civic Council delegation and Stewart's team to read a compromise statement, which was subsequently released to the local press. It acknowledged white residents' fears of a negative impact on property values but also affirmed "that Wendell Stewart has purchased this property and has moved into this property with his family and . . . there is no power in the United States that can cause him to withdraw from that property." Furthermore, it continued, Stewart was to be "afforded the full protection of the law," and, in keeping with the city's broad-minded traditions, the residents were encouraged to "co-operate with us in maintaining good community relations, and in doing so we are confident that this problem will be solved." Councilman Lysowski then thanked both the CRB and Stewart for their efforts, and Stewart's lawyer expressed his "appreciation to these gentlemen who have brought this problem to the Board [CRB], for . . . this is the place where these matters ought to be talked out." Then Burke, acknowledging that the white delegation had gotten a "rough deal," offered to present the statement in person to the residents at a July 21 session in the Gracemount School auditorium.[72]

Burke was greeted with resounding boos and catcalls from over 500 people upon his arrival at the school that evening. Once inside, the crowd remained raucous and belligerent. Burke said he was "not unsympathetic" to the white residents' situation but asserted that he would enforce the law. While many prevailed on the mayor to protect their collective "rights" over those of Stewart, at least one went further, stating: "The papers call us bigoted. But *we* are the ones discriminated against. This is all part of a well[-]laid Communist plot, carefully worked out, to invade our neighborhood and take away our rights." Another audience member added, "We came out of the slums and have built a fine neighborhood. We don't want another slum here for our sons." Yet another said: "I am an Italian. When I was not wanted in Shaker Heights, I was decent enough to get out. Why can't this man? Are 2,000 families to be sacrificed for one?" When Burke reminded the audience of the bigotry faced by their immigrant forebears and asked how their attitudes were any different, he received the retort: "*We're* all white." The mayor said he believed what he was hearing was "economics, not bigotry," and recommended that residents not become "panicky" and put their homes up for sale, but seemed to countenance their attempt at restriction with a statement that earned him trenchant criticism in the *Call & Post*: "You can best protect your property values by getting together as a neighborhood group and supervising the selling of houses in your area." Councilman Lysowski was likewise booed, while the crowd also heckled the featured speaker, locally renowned housing reformer and human relations activist Monsignor Robert B. Navin. Busa of the Lee-Land Heights Civic Council also addressed the gathering, as well as the head of the Glen-Lee Civic Association, the latter announcing that a batch of "This House Is Not for Sale" signs had been ordered for area residents—an ambiguous message which could be interpreted both as an attempt to stem panic selling and as exclusionary. Over the next week or so, 600 of these signs were distributed to Lee-Harvard residents, along with a letter urging vigilance against blockbusting tactics.[73]

The city administration's balancing act seemed to achieve the desired effect, although the police patrols provided for the Stewarts into the autumn was probably the most significant factor in controlling the tense situation. No overt antagonism toward the new black residents surfaced over the next several months, until mid-November, when five weeks after police protection had been discontinued at Wendell Stewart's request, vandals defaced the house's new paint job and broke the front window with a brick. Genevieve Stewart told the *Call & Post* that they had been "getting along unusually well with our neighbors," mentioning that their house had been an especially popular stop for trick-or-treaters on Halloween. Stewart said he suspected several teenagers had perpetrated the incident, although other observers believed the subsequent resumption of hate mail and harassing phone calls implied an organized campaign. One chilling anonymous letter threatened: "Listen, N____r, you will miss your legs, or your arms one of these days. We will get you some day when your guard is down. No white man likes to live close to no N____r . . . the N____s are going for to try to live and marry white girls. Some day we expect to put the N____s in their place like the Indians." It added, for good measure: "Your councilman Lysowski can't and will not protect you for he too will get his some day. We will get him, too." The Cleveland Clearinghouse on Civil Liberties reported rumors of an anti-Stewart group holding secret meetings and expressed concern that police might be "in collusion" with this effort. More openly, an organization called the Shaker-Lee Home Owners Association was reportedly circulating a restrictive agreement that required prospective sellers to gather the signatures of ten neighbors before putting their property on the market. Despite the *Shelley* ruling, this effort's organizers expected the measure would have a deterrent value regardless of legality.[74]

Apparently these new developments were troubling enough to cause the Stewarts to consider selling their house. Anticipating this possibility, the local NAACP and Cleveland Clearinghouse on Civil Liberties discussed forming a "Cleveland Conscience Fund" to enable another black family to purchase the house in the event the Stewarts decided to move. On a more militant note, the NAACP reported that some people had sought its approval for a retaliatory action against white-owned homes in the area. Newly elected Mayor Anthony J. Celebrezze quickly restored police protection for the Stewart house, stating, "I am ordering that these vandals be found and punished. . . . Nobody in Cleveland is going to be permitted to interfere with the right of a family to live where they please." Mayor Burke, in one of his outgoing actions, strengthened tolerance training for police officers to ensure that law enforcement properly conducted its duties in this regard. Celebrezze maintained police patrols into March 1954, and by May, Stewart reported to the CRB that "neighborly feelings have begun to develop, especially with the Italian family who lives immediately east of him, one of the most hostile families in that area when protests were being made." While this turn of events marked the end of harassment for the Stewart family, the CRB went on to state ominously that "there is still continued tension in the general area because of the possibility of other Negro families moving into the area."[75]

The successful containment of violent retaliation in the Stewart case was touted as a notable success by the CRB and proved to be the most serious example of organized, collective resistance mounted by white residents during the 1950s. Thus Cleveland did not descend to Chicago's or Detroit's level of an "era of hidden violence," to use Arnold Hirsch's phrase, during that decade—although the city did see a number of incidents of vandalism or worse against African American–owned properties into the 1960s and beyond. Of the thirty-four such crimes perpetrated from 1951 through 1964, twenty-two occurred from 1953 to 1956, which means the reaction to the Stewarts' move took place amid a climate of rising tension and fear in both Cleveland and the nation as a whole. Less than two months before Wendell and Genevieve Stewart purchased their new home, a black-owned house in the Wade Park section to the south of Glenville was dynamited. A night club serving an interracial clientele, located in the Euclid Avenue/East 105th Street entertainment district, was also bombed on two occasions that spring, with another unsuccessful third attempt. In addition, vandals painted a racist message on a house bought by an African American family, and a bottle with a threatening note was thrown through the window of a black woman's house; both incidents occurred in the Hough neighborhood, which also was integrating at the time. These occurrences led the CRB to note that "it is approximately twenty-five years since this kind of vandalism could be attributed to interracial hostility in connection with home ownership" and worry that the city's "distinctive" record "in the lack of vandalism occurring as a reaction toward large scale and rapid interracial population shifts" might be coming to an end.[76]

Such attacks help explain why some observers in the African American community and the *Call & Post* in particular became impatient with Mayor Burke's cautious approach in the Stewart case. Indeed, some black commentators disputed the city's supposedly good record of race relations. Local NAACP head Charles P. Lucas, in his *Call & Post* "Civil Rights Watch Dog" column, wrote in 1951, shortly after white residents in Cicero, Illinois, violently attacked an apartment complex into which a black couple had moved, that the incident "could have happened right here in Cleveland," noting further that "we find many sections of our great city still closed to Negro families who can afford to live in better residential districts." In a column the following year, Lucas excoriated existing human relations efforts as ineffectual, writing: "Let's stop kidding ourselves. This business of brotherhood is a year-round job. It is not for the one-week fakers who attempt to salve their consciences with a temporary pause from hating." He then lumped Cleveland together with cities that had experienced race-related clashes, including Cicero. Following the Stewart incident and other violent expressions of white antagonism from that year, Lucas observed: "Time was, when smug Clevelanders made ugly references to Chicago and its unhealthy housing pattern. . . . That was in the past. Today Cleveland has on her hands one of the most explosive situations of any place in the country." The *Call & Post's* retrospective feature on the events of 1953 heavily emphasized the past year's seemingly worsening race relations.[77]

Troubling incidents of racial intimidation continued into 1954. In April, a mansion under negotiation for use as a new church site by the black Mount Zion congregation was bombed in the Wade Park section. Vandals broke windows and smeared with paint four houses owned by African American families in Glenville, one of them on four separate occasions. Several houses under construction by the black-owned Harris & Adams firm were vandalized in July, while an additional house in Mount Pleasant twice had windows and the door smashed. The Mount Zion case prompted the City Council to discuss writing a specially tailored ordinance against bombings, while *Call & Post* owner-editor W. O. Walker penned an angry editorial stating, "It is up to the mayor and his police department to make Cleveland too hot for those who are so prejudiced in their souls that they cannot live with their neighbors in peace and as brothers. . . . Cleveland's record as a liberal city must be maintained. Not only must it be maintained, but by our leadership and example, we must set the pace for other cities to follow." Concerned groups wrote Mayor Celebrezze, like the financial secretary of an Elks lodge from Cedar-Central who wrote, "For 'The best location in the nation,' it is hardly conceivable that such traits of character blot out the motto of our City. . . . We deem it necessary that the Office of the Mayor of the City of Cleveland, call upon his cabinet and see that necessary action is taken, less [sic] Cleveland finds itself in the same predicament of Chicago, Ill., with regard to living conditions." Still, the CRB sought to put these "unfortunate" incidents in perspective, insisting that Cleveland could avoid "the extremes which are experienced in other cities," such as the destruction of a house in Philadelphia that year and sixty-three incidents of "housing tension" during the first half of 1954 in Chicago, "the majority of which involved either arson or bombing."[78]

Cleveland's proportionally smaller wave of white resistance wound down in 1955 with three documented instances of vandalism and then a final bombing case in January 1956 followed by a three-year hiatus. In the latter incident, African American attorney John W. Pegg's garage was dynamited, which was attached to his house under construction on Corby Road in the prestigious Ludlow area off Shaker Square. Speculation centered around whether the bombing was specifically race-related or motivated by a labor dispute; quite possibly it was both, since the African American contractor H. D. Dobbins employed black nonunion tradesmen for the work. Some observers claimed the neighbors had taken issue with the garage's frontage, which was at odds with others on the street. In any case, white residents in this area had attempted to institute a restrictive agreement the previous year, similar to Lee-Harvard. While the building or purchase of homes by African Americans in the neighborhood panicked some white residents, it also sparked the formation of the Ludlow Community Association in 1957, which succeeded in keeping the area racially integrated into the 1990s, and helped transform Shaker Heights' reputation from one of resistance into a nationally renowned model of stable and neighborly race relations.[79]

■

Cleveland's limited number of race-related conflicts over housing in the 1950s "era of hidden violence" did not result from its white residents being more open-minded about race, regardless of what boosters might have said about the city's supposed reputation for tolerance. Instead, racial antagonisms became sublimated in the legislative arena, taking the form of rival campaigns over public housing placement and land use as regulated by zoning. African American residents living in the city's southeasternmost corner, concentrated in the Lee-Seville neighborhood, found themselves frequently overpowered in these political battles, failing to sway outcomes even when their petitioning efforts were better organized than successful white initiatives. In a city council where black representatives were outnumbered and where voting often broke down along racial lines, whites commanded enough clout to hamper black access to this still-developing and attractive part of the city. However, despite such setbacks in the political arena, African Americans in Lee-Seville made an important difference by their very presence. The handful of black Lee-Land Heights Civic Council supporters in the fight against public housing in the area, despite the appearance of tokenism, did moderate the racialized rhetoric used by opponents, or at least force white residents to couch their fears and prejudices in euphemistic terms, or what in our present parlance is called "colorblind racism." More importantly, the new homes successfully built for hundreds of black residents on the area's precious vacant land offered a visible challenge to the stereotypes many whites associated with African Americans living in deteriorating inner-city neighborhoods.

African American home seekers in the 1950s also first gained access to Lee-Harvard and Ludlow, among the city's newest, most prestigious, and previously restricted areas—an accomplishment that proved more controversial and which did raise the specter of violent white resistance. While attempts by the city administration to mediate the resulting disputes were not nearly as supportive of new black homeowners as African American civil rights advocates would have liked, they were sufficient to reduce race-related violence to a much lower level than in many other major U.S. cities experiencing black population influx and racial residential integration and did allow Cleveland to maintain its reputation for comparatively placid race relations. By the 1960s, the process of racial residential transition was a flood of outward migration involving tens of thousands of people. How and why this dynamic played out differently in the various neighborhoods to which upwardly mobile African American families moved is explored in the next chapter.

4 : : :
Racial Residential Transition at the Periphery

NEIGHBORHOOD CONTRASTS

Interviewed some thirty-five years after the fact, Murtis H. Taylor reflected on her early experiences directing the Alexander Hamilton Community Center and its successor, the Mount Pleasant Community Centers, a position she held from 1949 until 1971. Asked the original focus of the agency, Taylor stated, "The purpose in coming to [the] Mt. Pleasant community . . . was to see whether or not we could integrate activities, [and] prevent the exodus of [whites from] housing." Taylor was African American, born in Macon, Georgia, but raised in Cleveland from an early age. A graduate of Western Reserve University, she had previously worked at Karamu House, the renowned Cedar-Central social settlement that since the 1920s had mounted interracial theatrical productions. At the Community Center, Taylor headed a racially integrated staff fitting for what she termed a "melting-pot" neighborhood, which included a Polish-American Catholic, a Japanese-American Baptist, a white Quaker, and herself. In a bold first step, Taylor eliminated the all-black weekend dances once sponsored at Alexander Hamilton Junior High School and instead organized interracial "interest groups" revolving around art, sports, drama, and square dancing.[1]

To make participation more racially "balanced," Taylor reconfigured the program from 1949–50, recalling, "If we felt that too many Negroes were coming we would run and recruit whites. If we found out that too many whites were coming we would run out and recruit more Negroes." However, her efforts to sustain integration ultimately failed because of "pressure from . . . the colored teenagers," who wanted a place to dance, considering that "the white teenagers had Canteens all over the neighborhood," particularly at Catholic schools, where African Americans were unwelcome. "And so we [re]opened the canteen because of the pressure," Taylor explained. "A few whites would come and they would try to dance, and our colored kids would laugh at them. . . . [So] pretty soon they stopped coming to the dances." With only a youth square dancing group remaining integrated, Taylor redirected attention toward adults and elementary school children, who seemed more receptive. The weekly all-black teenage dances soon returned to the earlier pattern, as confirmed by an African American former resident who attended Alexander Hamilton between 1953 and 1956. He confirmed these were all-black, even though African American students were still in the minority at the school. While the dances were officially for junior high school students only, he recalled that black East Side high school students regularly attended, often provoking fights based on neighborhood rivalries. While teenage turf battles were not unusual at the time, the existence of such pointed conflicts underlines the prevalence of class and status issues for African Americans and whites alike.[2]

Racial residential transition continued during the 1950s in Mount Pleasant, notwithstanding community efforts like those attempted by the Mount Pleasant Community Centers to promote interracial sociability and tolerance. Strikingly, the African American teenagers in Taylor's account were more interested in recreational space than in the ideal of racial integration; they were keenly aware of the outlets white youth enjoyed, and instead of access to those venues, they demanded parity. Furthermore, the anecdote indicates how separate black and white social lives remained, despite the increasing potential for cross-racial contact within the neighborhood. Although this particular example specifically concerns youth, the pattern of white withdrawal and image of a growing and increasingly autonomous black community, largely indifferent to racial integration and shaped by internal status rivalries, was a recurrent pattern in Glenville and the neighborhoods of Southeast Cleveland as they transitioned.

Because these outlying areas experienced a relatively quick and nearly total population turnover with little organized white resistance, they fall into the category of "undefended neighborhoods," a topic which has received barely a nod from scholars; however, the observable differences accompanying the demographic transformation of these Cleveland neighborhoods, some even adjacent to one another, demand scrutiny.[3] As discussed, the Stewart family's 1953 move to Lee-Harvard catalyzed significant opposition among white residents, amid city officials' growing concern that violent resistance to residential integration might erupt on the greater scale seen elsewhere. Thankfully, however, that case represented the high point of such organized opposition, a level that was never again reached. To be sure, even in the neighborhoods discussed below, some incidents of vandalism and racial clashes did accompany demographic transition—with white Catholics more openly antagonistic than Jews, in keeping with previous findings.[4] At the same time, neighborhood activists and social workers continued their efforts to minimize racial tensions, and in some ways population turnover proved to be surprisingly smooth. The following analysis investigates continuing demographic transition in the various neighborhoods that served as black middle-class expansion areas, focusing on both race-related frictions and additional contextual factors, including ethnicity and class. In Glenville, transition in the western portion flanking East 105th Street was basically complete by the early 1950s but continued in the area's eastern portion through the end of the decade. In Mount Pleasant, turnover had already begun during World War II, but overall it unfolded at a slower pace. In Lee-Harvard, there was a rapid and almost complete changeover during the 1960s; and in Corlett, a more homogeneous ethnic area to the south of Mount Pleasant, the process was a combination of patterns seen elsewhere.

Attempts to identify a consistent and predictable "tipping point" in racial residential transition have proven illusory.[5] Any comprehensive analysis of the process in a given neighborhood must take into account a constellation of factors, including the composition of the incoming and outgoing population in terms of race, ethnicity, religion, age, income, occupation, and family type; the condition and mix of housing stock there; and the relative desirability or prestige attached to the neighborhood in terms of newness, location, and access to education, shopping, and transportation facilities. While it can be difficult to determine exactly how all of these variables interact to shape outcomes, it is important to examine how and why the process unfolded differently, sometimes even in abutting sections. Racial residential transition was not inevitable, of course, but rather resulted from the particular decisions and actions of thousands of individuals on all sides of the issue. Despite occasional bursts of optimism from some quarters that racial integration could be maintained in these outlying Cleveland neighborhoods, by the mid-1960s they had either become, or were well on their way to becoming, virtually all-black—at the same time evincing an increasingly vocal determination to remain middle-class.

Eastern Glenville

Black population influx during and immediately after World War II occurred almost entirely in western Glenville, on blocks off East 105th Street and south of Saint Clair Avenue. This portion had traditionally been heavily Jewish, and by 1960 it was over 90 percent black. Meanwhile, African Americans began moving in substantial numbers across several geographic boundaries, namely north of Saint Clair Avenue into a traditionally more heavily Protestant and Catholic area, as well as south of Superior Avenue and across Lakeview Road to the east, all the way to the city limits at the East Cleveland border (see Map 4.1). This population expansion was facilitated by ongoing white departures, as well as a continuing influx of Southern migrants, placing pressures of overcrowding on older, inner-city areas. As of 1954, the Family Service Association estimated that Glenville's population was 50 percent black, 40 percent non-Jewish white, and 10 percent Jewish. While newcomers were overwhelmingly African American, around 10 percent of the total influx consisted of white Southerners, Catholic ethnics from coal-mining regions of Pennsylvania, as well as "displaced persons" from Europe.[6] Increasing numbers of Afri-

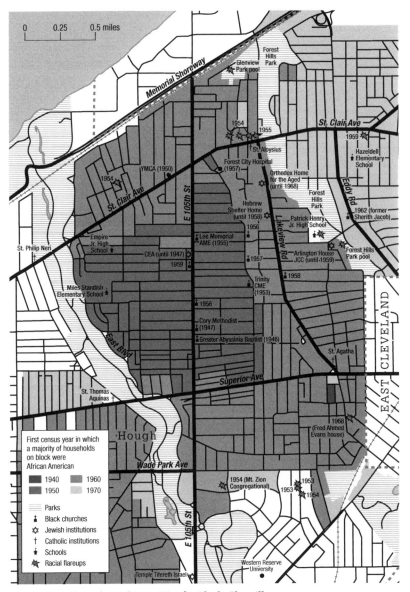

Map 4.1 Racial Residential Transition by Block, Glenville, 1940–1970

Note: Black churches depicted are former Jewish synagogues, with year of transfer.

Sources: U.S. Bureau of the Census, *United States Census of Housing: 1950 Block Statistics, Cleveland, Ohio* (Washington, D.C., 1952); U.S. Bureau of the Census, *United States Census of Housing: 1960 City Blocks, Cleveland, Ohio* (Washington, D.C., 1961); U.S. Bureau of the Census, *1970 Census of Housing: Block Statistics, Cleveland, Ohio, Urbanized Area* (Washington, D.C., 1971); Jeffrey S. Morris, "Haymarket to the Heights: The Movement of Cleveland's Orthodox Synagogues from Their Initial Meeting Place to the Heights" (February 2014).

can American families purchased in the Wade Park section south of Superior, where the Garvin family—infamously harassed in 1926—had for decades been the sole black occupants. By early 1955, African Americans had crossed Lakeview to occupy the streets abutting Forest Hills Park, which, according to a report by the Regional Church Planning Office, whites considered "as a tacitly agreed upon barrier" demarcating the eastern limit of black settlement. African Americans crossed the parkway into eastern Glenville by 1958, and after 1961 that entire section rapidly transitioned to become majority black. In 1956, an African American real estate broker told *Cleveland Press* reporter Julian Krawcheck that any given block in Glenville turned over within three years, in contrast to Mount Pleasant, where the process took "much longer."[7]

While Jews had rapidly moved out of western Glenville during and after World War II, substantial numbers still lived east of Lakeview Road. But even as eastern Glenville's remaining Jewish population was estimated at over 9,000 in 1952, a downward trend was apparent. While staff at the Jewish Community Center (formerly the Council Educational Alliance) observed in 1954 that "population decline . . . did not appear to be too drastic as yet," participation at its Arlington House branch had dipped and the Jewish portion of Glenville High School's student body was estimated at just 6 percent, down from 60 percent in 1944. Enrollments at Patrick Henry Junior High School had also fallen precipitously, although the number of Jewish students at several Glenville elementary schools held steady.[8] More indicative of the demographic trend was the community's changing age structure, as the Family Service Association noted: "The older Jewish people have tended to stay in their homes and apartments between Lakeview and Eddy Road." By 1955, "accelerated" movement out of both Glenville and Mount Pleasant was anticipated, into the traditional Heights suburbs and beyond. By 1956, very few Jewish families lived in the area east of Forest Hill Park, and by 1958 even the Holocaust survivors who had gravitated to the area's comparatively affordable rents were moving on.[9]

The trajectory at Arlington House paralleled the earlier pattern at East 105th Street, in terms of Jewish members' reaction to African American influx and staff dilemmas about how to serve the traditional clientele while maintaining policies of nonexclusion and interracial tolerance. Imagining the prospect of demographic transition as early as 1950, staff wrote: "Ways must be found whereby our Jewish population can live creatively and happily with real fulfillment of their Jewish aspirations and at the same time [promote] recognition of the need for neighborliness and cooperation with other neighborhood groups." The branch initially thrived, with a fluctuating dynamic of new Jewish families moving into the area even as others moved away. But its location on East 123rd Street at Arlington Avenue—immediately west of Forest Hills Park, which many whites imagined as a racial buffer zone—served to foster parental trepidations about children's safety, as seen earlier at both East 105th Street and Mount Pleasant. In a 1952–53 inside look at one Jewish preteen girls' group, a staff member noted that the group felt "invaded (in their terms) by another minority group which has lower status. . . . These nine and ten year old girls show expressions of these feelings, in refusing to sit near a Negro in the bus, and showing surprise and concern when a Negro is seen in the agency." Following newspaper reports of several assaults in the neighborhood, the girls told the group leader that their parents had forbidden them to play in Forest Hills Park. Black-white rumbles and other incidents of racial friction at nearby Patrick Henry Junior High School were also cited as contributing factors to declining participation and Jewish relocation. Arlington staff thus resolved to minimize rumor and further decline by "interpret[ing] to those in the area the true facts of the situation."[10]

At the same time, Arlington House also saw an increase in non-Jewish participation, especially among African Americans. Although there were no black members as of 1955, five or six black children (out of 140) had participated in the branch's day camp program since 1951, and "there were indications . . . that Negro residents were interested in using the agency," though they were "unsure of their reception." Later that year, four black families joined at Arlington, for a total of twelve non-Jewish member families—stirring Jewish parents' fears "that Negro teen-agers would next be . . . mingling with their own children." These parents felt that "since the children have to be mixed in the schools, the agency should provide an opportunity where they [Jews] can have clubs among their own people." Considering this recalcitrance, Arlington staff toward the end of 1955 pondered solutions, asking: "How can more friendly relations be established and people helped to be more comfortable together? . . . How do we maintain racial balance in agency groups and membership?" The situation was further complicated by the fact that some Jewish families remained active at Arlington even after moving out of the area. Yet the staff hesitated to relocate prematurely, recognizing the area's dearth of recreational programming as well as the fact that some Jewish families could not afford to leave "even though they have the desire to do so."[11]

But JCC's Arlington branch soon joined the exodus of Jewish institutions from eastern Glenville, closing its doors in 1959. By January 1958, the active membership had fallen to sixty-four families: forty-seven Jewish, four non-Jewish white, and thirteen African American, compared to a peak of 229 family memberships in 1950. Staff additionally noted that parents' fears of extralocal contact increased with age, so that "as children became eligible for Junior High School the families tended to move out." Glenville's remaining Jewish institutions faced similar dilemmas. As of 1955, Sherith Jacob was the only large synagogue left, with most of its membership already residing in the Heights suburbs. Other synagogues sold their facilities to incoming black church congregations, like Trinity CME, which purchased Oheb Zedek for $60,000 in 1953, or Memorial AME, which moved into a former synagogue in 1955. Jewish-owned businesses, on the other hand, thrived in the neighborhood into the 1960s.[12]

Other social service agencies active in Glenville during the 1950s also promoted interracial socialization and tolerance. The first truly integrated YMCA branch in the city—and among the earliest in the country—opened at 10211 Saint Clair Avenue in mid-1950, nearly three years after the Glenville Area Community Council nixed a plan for the historically black Cedar YMCA to develop a segregated "outpost" in the vicinity. The new branch offered recreational facilities and programming and also continued the tradition of celebrating Brotherhood Week, holding a "Brotherhood Bake Sale" in 1952, for example. That summer, staff also worked to positively redirect two local youth gangs (black and Italian) that had recently fought on the Patrick Henry school grounds. But the YMCA similarly struggled to maintain interracial participation amid increasing African American residency. The agency's initial membership was 80 percent white and 20 percent black, but within three years these proportions had nearly reversed to 30 and 70 percent, respectively. White participation was also low at the neighborhood's YWCA branch, established in 1951; meanwhile the Glenville Community Center initiated a teenage program at Patrick Henry in 1950 but had less than 10 percent white participation five years later. In 1954, a Glenville YMCA staff member reported to the Group Work Council's Committee on Intercultural and Interracial Relations: "Y.M.C.A. has tried to keep [the] program interracial but finds the result of large Negro membership threatening to white members. Should club group activities, such as dancing, be limited to provide a comfortable climate for all groups and if so, how?" While those present agreed that they had "some responsibility to provide a good interracial experience for minority white groups," no recommendations were made and the chair simply noted that "these are pointed problems for which we need answers."[13]

Founded to address wartime tensions, the Glenville Area Community Council (GACC) actually expanded its wide-ranging reform agenda as the neighborhood became increasingly black but also had to adapt amid changing demographics. In its most prominent showcase of the neighborhood's remaining diversity which harked back to the World War II unity ideal, the GACC sponsored three "Stars and Stunts Festivals" from 1951 to 1953. Dozens of street clubs, PTAs, Girl Scouts, the YMCA and YWCA, Arlington House, the National Council of Negro Women, Kiwanis, local churches, and the public library collaborated on this annual event, with approximately 1,000 attendees in 1951. The GACC's Community Relations Committee also remained active, chaired by longtime black Glenville resident Rev. Isaiah Pogue of the Northern Ohio Presbytery. As of 1957–58, the committee sought to "offset the idea that the committee functioned only in time of tension or after some racial disorder," that season sponsoring a panel entitled "Being a Good Neighbor in a Changing Community." While Arlington House collaborated with the GACC, it had greater difficulty generating enthusiasm than its predecessor on East 105th Street. Arlington House lent its facilities for meetings and assisted in the GACC's ongoing project of organizing block clubs; in 1957 one such club on Hopkins Avenue reported that middle-class black residents were "active" and young Jewish residents were "very active," but described the older (and more religious) Jews and Appalachian whites as "non-participating." However, the GACC also felt the need to remind Arlington staffers that it was originally "predominantly a Jewish constituency," declaring its intention to reach "the population on the other side of the Forest Hills Park, which has not been interested in participating."[14]

While many white residents simply withdrew in the face of residential integration, some responded with overt hostility. A handful of violent housing-related incidents accompanied demographic transition, the worst occurring in 1953 and 1954 in the University Circle district, just across Glenville's southern border, marked by Wade Park Avenue. On May 24, 1953, someone detonated a bomb in the basement window of a house on East 115th Street recently purchased by Rev. S. E. Ware of Antioch Baptist Church, causing some $4,000 in damage. Six more sticks of dynamite were piled on the porch of another black-owned house next door, but failed to detonate. However, while mentioning the infamous Garvin case nearly three decades earlier, the *Call & Post* also noted that seven African American families already lived on the block. Apparently they were all recent arrivals, with threats having been made against the first white seller, along with an unsuccessful attempt by the neighbors to buy back the first black purchaser's house. Despite this indication of hostility, black residents reported to the paper that "their relations with the whites had been very congenial until the Sunday morning bombing." Mayor Thomas Burke immediately followed the city's traditional response, sending police and making a strong statement of the city's commitment to protect the rights of homeowners regardless of race and vowing to "vigorously" pursue the perpetrators. After further investigation, and consulting with local social service and religious professionals as well as the GACC, the Community Relations Board (CRB) concluded that racial antagonism was not the "sole motive" in the incident, since "Negro ownership has been in effect [in the area] for about a year and a half, and while the bombing was committed against the most recently purchased property, no previous evidence of hostility is known to have occurred."[15]

But the following spring, another bombing rocked the same area, following the black Mount Zion Congregational Church's purchase of a mansion on Magnolia Drive for its future church home. Though not technically a residential situation, white homeowners had disputed the sale because plans for a

church would require zoning board approval, and for fear it would hurt property values. Clearly, they specifically opposed the presence of a black congregation, as other religious edifices already existed in the vicinity and many of
the stately houses in the area already had multiple uses as clubs, fraternity
houses, and rest homes. On March 25, 1954, after the zoning board approved
the church plans, someone dropped a bomb through a basement window,
causing $6,000 worth of damage and endangering the caretaker in residence.
A third blast, this time at the home of a numbers policy operator also on East
115th Street, led the *Call & Post* to conclude the attacks were "apparently the
work of the same dynamite expert" and were "aimed at stopping Negro pene-
tration into the Wade Park area." Mayor Anthony J. Celebrezze subsequently
provided two months' worth of round-the-clock police protection and issued
a strong statement of condemnation, as did a group of neighborhood residents. The Mount Zion congregation, for its part, refused to be intimidated
and completed the sale; after all, two years previously their bid to buy an existing church in Glenville had been torpedoed by prejudiced white neighbors.[16]

Vandalism also accompanied black influx into Glenville proper, with a rash
of incidents in the heavily Catholic section north of Saint Clair Avenue likely
committed by a single group of perpetrators. George Harrison, a factory worker
employed at Thompson Products who became the first African American purchaser on a section of East 107th Street in the area, had paint splashed on his
house and rocks thrown through his windows in two separate incidents in May
1954. Although Harrison was first on the block, a number of African American
families already lived on Elk Avenue just a few hundred feet away, and he told
the *Call & Post* that while he had not seen much of his white neighbors, "those
I have seen have been very friendly." The CRB initially suspected the "backyard
neighbor" on East 108th Street, who the previous fall had threatened a white
family rumored to be selling to a black buyer. A week later, despite augmented
police protection, two more houses in blocks just north were similarly vandalized, one on East 109th Street and another on Glenview Avenue; police ques-
tioned a suspect, but made no arrests. Twenty-five white and black residents
met to discuss prevention of future attacks, at which both GACC and NAACP
representatives spoke. In addition, volunteers from the group Christian Social
Action in Action, consisting of Unitarians, Quakers, and several Baptist ministers, later spent the Fourth of July weekend repairing damage to one of the
houses. Meanwhile, vandals smeared yet another house on East 107th Street
with paint, just before its new black owners moved in. Police ultimately concluded that teenagers were behind these incidents, with a nearby city dump
site as the likely source of paint used in the attacks.[17]

In evaluating these incidents, the CRB concluded that "there seemed to be
nothing paralleling the Stewart case," in that the presence of African Americans had prompted neither neighborhood meetings nor threats, and there

were already some thirty-five to forty black families living in the section. "Unfortunately, vandalism committed against houses acquired for occupancy by Negroes in areas where they have not previously resided occurs regularly in many American cities," the CRB observed. "Chicago is, of course, the most notorious, but incidents comparable to Cleveland are also to be found in Detroit, Philadelphia, Cincinnati, etc." Referring to the volunteerism of Christian Social Action in Action, the CRB practically bragged: "Cleveland has again demonstrated its capacity to develop a practical example of action which can help to overcome the blighting effect of overt bigotry." But that December a black family who had recently moved north of Saint Clair onto Cobb Court, some fifteen blocks to the west, got a particularly vicious reception when vandals broke their windows on four separate occasions in two weeks, police protection notwithstanding. As in the previous cases, the *Call & Post* described the attacks as "more mysterious by the fact that already there are several colored families in the immediate neighborhood, and relations between them and their neighbors have always been good." Finally, the following June, police arrested three white youths aged fifteen and sixteen for breaking windows and smashing lightbulbs filled with paint against the house of a black family on East 110th Street. They all had previous police records and were widely presumed to be the perpetrators of the previous summer's incidents. As a result, they were sentenced to terms at the Boys' Industrial School outside Columbus, and the black couple whose house was targeted filed for $21,000 in damages against their parents.[18]

Thankfully, there were no more incidents of race-related vandalism as residential transition wound down in Glenville west of Forest Hills Park. Beyond isolated telephone threats, the most worrisome matter handled by the CRB was a case on East 128th Street in the summer of 1957, in which the first black family's purchase to the east of the park sparked a meeting of 400 white residents at a local Protestant church. An anonymous white observer reported to the *Call & Post* that "one anti-Negro slander followed the other" at the meeting, with one speaker asking the crowd, "Do you want colored men knocking off your wives? Do you want them cornering you and robbing you?" White residents subsequently tried to convince the Women's Federal Savings & Loan to renege on the loan it had extended for the purchase, leading the CRB to intervene on the borrowers' behalf. But no further collective resistance materialized. The CRB reported the following month that "the [black] family has been almost entirely unmolested by any threats or intimidation in the neighborhood and has already rented the upstairs suite to a Negro family."[19]

August 1959, however, saw an ugly conflagration resembling contemporaneous "communal" protests against residential integration in Chicago and Detroit. But like the earlier Wendell and Genevieve Stewart case, it was contained through strategic intervention. World War II veteran Henry McCarthy must have known his attempt to purchase a house on East 125th Street in far northeastern Glenville could prove controversial. After all, he was seeking to buy it from another black buyer, the first on the block, who had never moved in; that man, in turn, had purchased the home in a "spite sale" from the previous Jewish owner, who had a running feud with his neighbors. Furthermore, when the real estate broker arranged to show the McCarthys the property, he made sure that the head of the local NAACP was present. Perhaps none of them, however, had anticipated the level of hostility their visit would elicit from the "lower-middle or upper-lower [class]" residents, many elderly and foreign born, along with recent Appalachian white arrivals. "Old men and women with babies in their arms joined scores of cycle-riding children . . . to hurl violent abuses and downright filthy words at the McCarthys as they inspected their new home," the *Call & Post* reported. As many as forty white bystanders yelled for them to "Go back to Woodland or Scovill," references to major thoroughfares in Cedar-Central. One man told a reporter that if the McCarthys moved in, "we'll throw bricks through their windows," while another "menaced" the patrol car summoned to the scene, prompting officers to call for backup. For her part, Mrs. McCarthy retorted to the crowd: "The for sale sign will be on your property before it will mine because we intend to stay right here."[20]

Following this initial encounter, the CRB stepped in to advise the McCarthys, along with the Urban League, Cleveland Church Federation, and Jewish Community Federation, once the couple expressed their determination to follow through with the purchase. But even with police patrols, vandals ransacked the still-vacant house several nights later, methodically breaking every window and tearing down blinds and curtains; meanwhile, the Jewish former owners received anonymous phone threats. An interracial group of ministers assisted in the cleanup and arranged to replace the McCarthys' broken windows and doors. Following complaints by the Urban League and NAACP to Mayor Celebrezze and the city's police chief, round-the-clock patrols were instituted; eight white neighborhood youths were apprehended and ultimately arraigned in Juvenile Court, ordered to pay damages, and fined $25 each. However, even after the McCarthys moved in several weeks later, neighbors remained hostile: local children leveled insults and refused—at their parents' behest—to play with the family's young daughter. Tensions continued to run high. "The CRB should be planning a program with the street clubs, the church groups, etc. to bring about a better feeling among the people in the area so that the same thing won't happen again," warned the ward councilman. Sure enough, the CRB had to step in again the following spring after callers leveled phone threats at a white woman who sold to a black family on nearby East 120th Street.[21]

In contrast to other cities, white homeowners' associations were an insignificant presence in Glenville, with one possible exception, the Northeast

Property Owners Civic Association (NPOCA). Operating in this same area beyond Eddy Road, this organization had come under scrutiny shortly after its founding, with the GACC noting in 1945: "Any anti-Negro expressions have been kept in closed meetings. . . . Outwardly it is a civic betterment group." By 1954, the CRB was expressing "concern" that the primary goal of the NPOCA was "to hold back the acquisition of homes by Negroes" in the area. Indeed, when a black family purchased on East 128th Street in mid-1957, both the NPOCA and another group, the Perry Home Owners Improvement Association, protested. But just as it had against the Park Home Owners Association fifteen years earlier, the GACC successfully thwarted the NPOCA's exclusionary efforts. In 1959, the GACC's Rehabilitation-Conservation Committee made the decision to approach sympathetic individuals within NPOCA, concluding that "there are, in this group, many people of intelligence who would wish to participate in our work."[22]

At a tumultuous meeting the following May, the GACC's behind-the-scenes overtures succeeded in breaking the NPOCA into factions, with one agreeing to a program of interracial cooperation. Held at Saint John's Lutheran Church, the meeting was attended by some 150 "disorderly" white residents—early in the proceedings, one elderly man attempted to hit NPOCA president Gordon Kennedy with a chair, as a local Catholic priest pleaded for calm. Many present demanded the immediate impeachment of the organization's officers, who favored including African American homeowners and had in fact "distributed handbills announcing the meeting to residents west of 120th Street, composed largely of Negro property owners." Several African Americans were present, including recently elected Ward 24 councilman and GACC activist Leo Jackson, who received applause for his statement that "there is nothing in local or state laws that forces white persons to socialize with new Negro neighbors." After two hours of "acrimonious, personal, and sometimes riotous debate," the meeting was forcibly adjourned without any resolution. While the majority of the membership rejected integration and demanded new leadership, a smaller faction just as "vociferously" defended it; intensifying the squabble was the existence of a $3,500 treasury. Two years later, the NPOCA had split into two separate organizations: one integrated with about a hundred active members focused on preventing panic selling, and the other all-white and on the verge of acquiring the original group's funds to promote white-only purchases in the area. As late as 1963, by which point race relations in Glenville had stabilized, this "splinter group" still disdained the GACC, though its exclusionary power had been neutralized.[23]

Blockbusting did become an issue in Glenville, highlighting the considerable racial tension that accompanied residential transition even with minimal collective white resistance compared to what other cities experienced.[24] According to the city's black assistant law director, interviewed by *Cleveland*

Press reporter Julian Krawcheck in 1956, the first African American families secured a toehold in the Eddy Road section after a black congregation began negotiations to purchase a Lutheran church; the church then backed out after black real estate brokers "circulated in [the] neighborhood," convincing six white families to sell their homes. On a block of East 115th Street just south of Saint Clair, immediately east of Forest Hills Park, the CRB reported in 1960 that thirty-seven (presumably white) homeowners out of fifty-seven had recently been approached by real estate agents, with thirty-three reporting they were "being continually harassed." That same year, a white man planning to move off Eddy Road told Krawcheck that a white real estate operator had bought the house next door and threatened to sell to "undesirables" when he declined to partner with the buyer on purchasing an adjoining vacant lot. The broker indeed sold to two black brothers-in-law several months later. Councilman Leo Jackson, for his part, reported rampant blockbusting in northeastern Glenville, even claiming that "unscrupulous" black and white real estate firms were in collusion to turn over "suckers" to each other. "I'm convinced we can't have the strongest possible community (ward) if it is all-Negro," he opined. "No special group should be allowed to drive another special group out."[25]

Krawcheck's investigations also reveal some of the nonstandard and often racially divisive tactics employed by real estate brokers in so-called transitional areas at the time. K. C. Jones of the Urban League claimed that some brokers relinquished half their commission to ensure that black buyers got financing, confident the initial sale would produce subsequent profitable transactions. Leo Jackson stated he knew of instances where brokers would "sell on a land contract to a couple with a dozen kids, knowing the family can't keep up the payments" in order to get whites to "start running" and list their houses for sale. Jackson claimed to have successfully discouraged black operators from using such tactics, so that "most of the offenders now are white real estate firms." One white agent active in the Eddy Road vicinity revealed that investors and brokers were buying up homes worth $12,000–$13,000 for around $8,000. "When an area becomes a fringe area, (transitional), a lot of white buyers will buy solely for investment, then sell on land contract to Negroes," he explained, because a "bona fide white buyer doesn't want to buy if Negroes have moved in." Yet another white broker said her firm had begun taking "Negro listings" because financing had "loosened up"—although typically not until a given block was 25 percent African American, to avoid accusations of blockbusting. However, she did admit passing unsold homes to a cash-paying investor known to deal in land contracts.[26]

Additional signs of racial tension accompanied Glenville's ongoing demographic transition. In a 1956 incident, a presumably black perpetrator tossed a brick through the window of an East 105th Street property that posted a whites-only rental sign. Underlining that retaliation was sometimes directed at white sellers rather than African American buyers, a former resident recalled that the only "unpleasant incident" accompanying the arrival of blacks on East 110th Street was the "stench-bomb[ing]" of a house by angry white neighbors after the owner said that "Negroes couldn't be kept out of [the] area no matter what." Upon becoming the first African American to move into one apartment building on East Boulevard, an assistant city law director was informed by a neighbor that her bridge club had decided they would no longer attend get-togethers there. Other white residents wrote letters to public officials, complaining about the purported effects of black occupancy. One wrote Mayor Thomas Burke in 1953 to inquire whether deed restrictions were still enforceable, blaming "colored real estate agents" for illegally converting homes to multifamily occupancy on Thornwood Avenue.[27]

However, other white residents remained unperturbed or perhaps resigned to racial residential transition. One real estate agent told *Cleveland Press* reporter Krawcheck that many departing whites were older couples who cited a desire for downsizing, not black residency, as a primary motivating factor. He claimed to have run into "very little bitterness," and said strong demand ensured white families got good prices for their homes. While recalling several cases of black newcomers violating zoning laws to allow their relatives to live with them, the agent believed this was unusual; on the contrary, most of his buyers had renovated or otherwise improved their properties. In fact, a major observation of Krawcheck's first investigations, published as a series of articles in September 1956, was that black homebuyers typically maintained their properties in exemplary fashion. One former white resident of Herrick Road told Krawcheck: "I think the colored families who have moved in have kept their homes up better than the people they replaced. . . . The old white owners . . . were putting a minimum of money into improvements. And the Negroes, moving in, were perhaps owning property for the first time and eager to fix it up." A white doctor who moved in 1952, but kept his office in Glenville, confirmed that his former property and old neighborhood looked "just as good, if not better" than at any time he could recall, and quoted his sister-in-law's grudging compliment, "I'd give anything if I could dress as smartly as they do or get my grass to grow as well." One black couple who had remodeled extensively, even knocking out a wall to create a breakfast nook, recalled white next-door neighbors' initial fears that they planned to "operate a rooming house or at least take in another family," but after being invited in to inspect the work, soon expressed interest to "duplicate the kitchen remodeling."[28]

Whites who stuck around found some of the black newcomers quite gracious. One set of parents instructed their teenage son to cut the elderly white neighbors' lawn, and in another instance a black man provided emergency assistance when his white neighbor fell off a ladder. The president of the Castlewood Street Club, where eleven white families out of forty remained in

1956, claimed that the early "tendency of the whites to run" had abated once they found their new black neighbors were "easy to live with." She stated that the block club had "helped a lot in getting the whites and colored families together," with the members sponsoring an annual picnic and even pooling their money to buy a snowplow and fertilizer spreader. A white drugstore proprietor told Krawcheck, "The Negro families are easy to wait on and accord me greater respect as a pharmacist than the whites did," additionally noting that there was "no more rowdyism or noise" in the area than before. Naturally, African Americans sometimes found such reactions patronizing. In response to Krawcheck's 1961 series on blockbusting, one man wrote: "The rapidly increasing middle-class segment of Negroes with high education, good incomes and high social standards has made the general racial stereotypes more illusion than fact. . . . More articles of this type would go a long way toward dispelling many of the illogical fears that form the basis for racial difficulties." A black resident of East 115th Street wrote the *Press* to say, "I don't know when people are going to wake up & realize that times are changing and the Negro is tired of being the under dog." "I feel I'm just as good or better than some of them," she said of her white neighbors. "In most cases white people get the wrong ideas about Negroes. They are not have [*sic*] as bad as the white man wants them to be."[29]

Eastern Glenville also experienced racial friction over swimming pool access as well as in the public schools. In 1952, a police captain stated the "problem" dated back to the Alta House social settlement closing its pool three years earlier, which prompted young toughs from the Little Italy neighborhood to start using the facilities at Forest Hills, on Arlington Avenue across from Patrick Henry Junior High. Two years later, Forest Hills seems to have been designated by white neighborhood residents as the "black" pool, with trouble shifting to Glenview Pool in the East 110th Street–Saint Clair section—the locus of race-related housing vandalism, as discussed. In June 1954, whites chased an African American man away from the Glenview pool and on another occasion assaulted a thirteen-year-old boy for riding his bicycle near it. Subsequent investigations revealed that few African Americans attempted to use the facilities at Glenview, and that those who did were typically pointed toward Forest Hills pool instead. The CRB subsequently got two black staff members assigned to Glenview, and the Police Department placed an African American foot patrolman on duty. After the Recreation Department reiterated that *all* citizens were "legally entitled to use the swimming facilities" and that "the city was ready to protect their rights," two different delegations set out in July to test access at Glenview, one consisting of NAACP members and the other an interracial group of about twenty Progressive Party members. The demonstrations went smoothly—albeit with the NAACP stridently disassociating itself from the other activists, successors to the left-labor coalition now under scrutiny amid

McCarthyism. No other flare-ups occurred that summer, although both the CRB and the *Call & Post* noted that African Americans still generally avoided Glenview pool. The following summer, the NAACP received Mayor Celebrezze's assurance of adequate protection for black swimmers, and while the CRB reported no pool or park incidents for 1955, it remains unclear how many African Americans actually sought access at Glenview.[30]

As already mentioned, Patrick Henry Junior High School had experienced racial tensions as early as 1946, which became more pronounced in the following decade. In late 1950, an argument between white and black girls in gym class came to blows, but Principal Oliver J. Deex handled the incident effectively by refusing requests from white parents to have their children transferred out of the school, enlisting the help of the PTA and GACC. But in October 1951, the beating of two black youths on the school's football field by four white youths triggered retaliations, which escalated into an after-school standoff, in which "scores" of white and black toughs "armed with sticks, stones, bottles, pocket-knives and a few army-surplus bayonets" menaced each other from opposite sides of the street until police dispersed them; some of the white antagonists apparently later caught and beat several Jewish students. The GACC and clergy from the area subsequently sponsored meetings to try to defuse the tension, after anxious parents made 200 calls to the police, characterizing the disorder as a "riot." Following the near-rumble, many kept their children home from school for several days.[31]

Despite this shocking event, an NAACP investigation concluded that racial tensions at Patrick Henry were "greatly exaggerated," a complaint echoed by both the CRB and school officials over the next several years. Whether misreporting by the *Plain Dealer* in October 1953—when an incident of a sole black man assaulting four white youths outside the school was characterized as involving a "Gang of 50"—or later coverage describing a school boycott by twenty white students as a "strike," rumors abounded, as Patrick Henry approached a near-even split between black and white students and as worries about juvenile delinquency mounted in the neighborhood. A caucus involving Principal Deex and staff from the CRB, GACC, NAACP, and Arlington House determined that "largely false accounts or misinterpretations of minor incidents" exacerbated tensions, further magnified by anxious parents and nearby residents resentful of black students. Problems in the school were attributed to new black residents, especially recent Southern migrants, as well as white students from all-white elementary schools like Hazeldell in the far northeastern portion of the neighborhood, who had no prior encounters with African Americans. The caucus agreed that newspapers should provide "sober and factual news treatment," a request resulting in a five-article, March 1955 *Cleveland Press* series on positive intergroup relations at several Cleveland public schools, which debunked the exaggerated reporting of incidents at Patrick Henry and elsewhere.[32]

By the early 1960s, racial residential transition in eastern Glenville was essentially complete. Interviews conducted by the CRB in 1963 with twenty-three school officials, police officers, politicians, businessmen, and street club members concluded that "racial tensions . . . are at a minimum," with demographic turnover "no longer as noticeable as it once was because the people involved are all Negroes." The most common attitude among the remaining white residents was "aloofness," as the CRB observed in its annual report: "Some of the remaining white people in the area have chosen to isolate themselves and stay cool and unfriendly toward their new neighbors." A 1961 interview with the pastor at one of Glenville's five remaining white Protestant churches typified this stance, as he confirmed that "some of the Negroes in the neighborhood have come [to services] from time to time and we treat them as we should, but we certainly don't encourage that sort of thing." Quite a different outcome emerged at the Episcopal Church of the Incarnation, as virtually the entire white membership pulled out in the space of one month in 1957, soon to be replaced by African American congregants. Meanwhile, the Werner Methodist Church and Fellowship Lutheran Church succeeded in retaining a portion of their white congregants after integration, even though many commuted from the suburbs. Roman Catholic parishes also shrank but made a more thoroughgoing accommodation to new African American residents. In 1960, the pastor at Saint Aloysius decided to make "special efforts to serve the newcomers in the parish," launching an "Operation Doorbell Catholic Revival Program," which included black canvassers seeking new converts. By 1961, 40 percent of the parish's 1,200 remaining families were African American, as were 300 of the 700 students at the parochial school. In fact, racial "incidents" at Patrick Henry Junior High supposedly ceased once Saint Aloysius was integrated. Saint Agatha's also had black students by 1963.[33]

Mount Pleasant

Regardless of whether one traces its outline using specific census tracts or the city's "neighborhood planning area," the pattern of demographic turnover seen in Mount Pleasant from 1950 to 1965 differed from that in Glenville. Put simply, it initially proceeded more gradually and consisted of an outward expansion of the two substantial, existing black enclaves (see Map 4.2). As of 1950, the Federation for Community Planning put Mount Pleasant's nonwhite population at 22 percent, based on census data. In 1956, black real estate broker J. W. Carmack claimed that "Negro families have lived on many streets off Kinsman for 20 years or more without the whole street going Negro." However, the pace of demographic change picked up by the mid-1950s. By

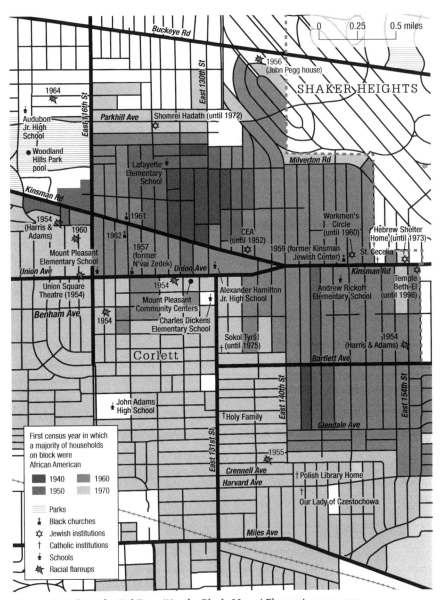

Map 4.2 Racial Residential Transition by Block, Mount Pleasant, 1940–1970

Note: Black churches depicted are former Jewish synagogues, with year of transfer.

Sources: U.S. Bureau of the Census, *United States Census of Housing: 1950 Block Statistics;* U.S. Bureau of the Census, *United States Census of Housing: 1960 City Blocks;* U.S. Bureau of the Census, *1970 Census of Housing: Block Statistics;* Morris, "Haymarket to the Heights."

1959, African Americans made up 55 percent of Mount Pleasant's population in terms of census tracts; using the boundaries of the city's "social planning area," which lay slightly further south and west, Mount Pleasant's population as of 1960 was 71 percent black and would rise to 89 percent by 1965. A racial imbalance was also increasingly evident in the neighborhood public schools, with three out of seven in 1961 said to be "almost entirely Negro" and another two schools over two-thirds white, with the remaining two roughly balanced.[34]

Similar to Glenville, Jews were among the first to move out of Mount Pleasant. As one man who left East 147th Street around 1952 for the suburb of South Euclid recalled: "We'd forsaken Kinsman, as most Jewish families had by that time. . . . I didn't want to join that rush, but Ma needed Jewish neighbors and she'd always looked forward to 'moving to the Heights.'" Even so, considerable numbers of Jewish families remained in Mount Pleasant into the 1950s, creating a dilemma for the Jewish Community Center (JCC), the successor to the Council Educational Alliance. As previously discussed, in 1949 the JCC decided to wind down programming at its Mount Pleasant House and counter population shifts by opening a new facility to serve Shaker Heights and the Lee-Harvard neighborhood. A committee planning for the new location had stressed that "the population west of East 140th Street has been decreasing and is very small." Even so, school enrollment statistics for the previous academic year indicated that there were still twenty-one Jewish students at Lafayette Elementary School, in the heart of the historic black enclave, as well as seventy-seven at Mount Pleasant Elementary in far western Mount Pleasant. Furthermore, a survey conducted in 1951 to determine the location of Mount Pleasant JCC members revealed a "concentration" of Jews still living between East 117th and East 119th Streets. Even though Jewish departures subsequently accelerated, as of 1954 an estimated 5,000 Jews still lived in Mount Pleasant, and as late as 1958 nearly 10 percent of students attending the neighborhood's public schools were Jewish.[35]

All of Mount Pleasant's traditional Jewish institutions struggled in the face of demographic transition. The Workmen's Circle School One (3467 East 147th Street) found it necessary to offer transportation to the increasing number of its students who lived beyond walking distance, and in 1953 it temporarily suspended operation because so many of its pupils had moved to Cleveland Heights. The Kinsman Jewish Center (B'nai Jacob Kol Israel) still had 500 families on its roster as of 1950, but in late 1952 it voted to merge with the smaller N'vai Zedek congregation in order "to achieve a strong organization in the Kinsman Shaker area." By 1955, so many orthodox Jews had moved beyond walking distance—a religious stricture pertaining to Sabbath observance— that the rabbi initiated High Holiday services at the JCC's Shaker-Lee House. Finally, in 1959, the merged congregation moved to the suburbs, picking up a third Mount Pleasant synagogue to become the Warrensville Center Synagogue. An explanatory letter promised, however, to maintain the original N'vai Zedek facility on East 119th Street "as long as members wish to worship there." Perhaps the last Jewish institution to leave Mount Pleasant was the Hebrew Shelter Home, which offered inexpensive lodgings and a kosher kitchen. Still located on Kinsman Road at the Shaker Heights border as of 1967, by that point it was apparently used mainly by Israeli tourists.[36] Jewish-owned businesses in Mount Pleasant, on the other hand, were common into the 1960s, with some remaining into the 1980s, as in the case of Greenstein's Hardware. And in contrast to the pattern in other neighborhoods—like Hough, where black-Jewish business dealings soured—relations between Mount Pleasant's white merchants and African American newcomers remained cordial, according to a Jewish egg wholesaler who employed many black neighborhood residents.[37]

As in Glenville, a number of organizations, agencies, and institutions attempted to mediate the neighborhood's ongoing demographic transition and promote tolerance. Paralleling its Glenville counterpart, the Mount Pleasant Community Council (MPCC) had been at the forefront here—although by 1951 its Race Relations Committee was defunct, with a newspaper article from that year acknowledging that "instead of making a frontal attack, which might only aggravate [racial] tensions, they [area councils] hope to bring about gradual solution of such problems by simply ignoring them." By 1953, however, the MPCC returned to a more direct approach by sponsoring a human relations workshop—the centerpiece of which was a series of skits depicting various instances of discrimination and prejudice, including "what can happen when a family of another 'group' moves next door or across the street." Attended by approximately 150 residents split evenly between black and white, the workshop sought a frank discussion of racial problems.[38] In 1957, the MPCC revived its annual Folk Festival to celebrate the observance of Brotherhood Week. Co-chaired by a committee consisting of African American judge Perry B. Jackson, Rabbi Jacob Muskin, and Saint Cecelia pastor Rev. John J. Tivenan, the event mobilized nearly twenty nationality, fraternal, and religious organizations, along with black churches, and was attended by over 2,000 people. Especially notable was the involvement of the Shaker-Lee JCC, which retained a stake in Mount Pleasant intergroup relations even after most Jews had moved out. Shaker-Lee House actually hosted the observance in 1959 and for several years afterward, reformulating it as a dinner honoring the late Joseph Sokol, an activist in the MPCC's various toleration efforts.[39]

The Mount Pleasant Community Centers, established in 1948 as the Alexander Hamilton Community Center, also sought to promote positive interactions among the neighborhood's various ethnic, racial, and religious groups, from human relations workshops to racially integrated recreational activities for adults and children. Clubs served as a means to mingle neighborhood youths on an interethnic and interracial basis, or at least expose them to individuals

BROTHERHOOD IN OUR NEIGHBORHOOD

BELIEVE IT!

LIVE IT!

SUPPORT IT!

Spectacular

Mt. Pleasant and Shaker-Lee

FOLK FESTIVAL

Wednesday, February 12, 1958

8:00 P. M.

at

JOHN ADAMS HIGH SCHOOL

AUDITORIUM

Doors open at 6:30 p. m. for viewing of exhibits. A film will be shown at 7:00 p.m.

☆ ☆ ☆

BRATRSTVÍ V NAŠEM SOUSEDSTVÍ

FRATERNITA NEL NOSTRO VICINANZA

BRATERSTWO W NASZYM SĄSIEDSTWIE

TESTVÉRISÉG A MI KÖRNYEKÜNKÖN

БРАТСТВО В НАШЕМ СОСЕДСТВЕ

Featuring

ISRAELI FOLK DANCES

GYMNASTIC FEATS

ITALIAN SONG GROUP

MODERN DANCE GROUP

MANDOLIN ORCHESTRA

POLISH SINGING GROUP

CHORAL ENSEMBLES

AUSPICES

Mt. Pleasant and Shaker-Lee Brotherhood Week Committee

Mount Pleasant Community Council Program, 1958. As whites increasingly left outlying neighborhoods on Cleveland's East Side for the suburbs, community organizations attempted to mobilize remaining residents along interracial and interethnic lines. (Courtesy of the Western Reserve Historical Society, Cleveland, Ohio) from different backgrounds. In 1954, one such club consisting of twelve Italian boys shared attitudes "prevalent among insecure whites," although they eventually accepted an African American group leader and were persuaded to play sports and take a field trip with black kids. Another group, reluctant to admit black members, eventually accepted a group leader who inspired them to adopt "more positive attitudes." Adults had similar reservations. Murtis Taylor recalled one white Catholic woman who expressed reluctance to join a square dancing group where she might have to hold hands with black men, without realizing Taylor herself was African American. As the two women walked home together, holding hands at one point, Taylor successfully recruited her into the program. Then, at their second meeting, Taylor graciously welcomed the embarrassed resident, who by then had realized her gaffe. Taylor and her staff kept programming integrated for "as long as possible," noting that the interracial summer camp for younger children was particularly successful. But with whites moving out of the neighborhood, their efforts ultimately proved unsustainable.[40]

The Mount Pleasant Community Centers sought ways to continue working with those whites who remained and to bring together Mount Pleasant residents and open-minded individuals from other neighborhoods. Beginning in 1959, the Centers joined with various interested partners on a number of initiatives intended to foster better intergroup relations. The local chapter of the National Conference of Christians and Jews (NCCJ) signed onto a training program for teachers and principals designed to address the "problems they are meeting in a changing neighborhood," which subsequently grew into a full-blown "Five-Year Plan for Intergroup Relations in the Mt. Pleasant Area." Kicked off by a "town meeting" attended by over 200 people at Saint Cecelia's Catholic Church, the plan was described by the NCCJ regional director as "an attempt to get all of the neighborhood's forces into action on the common problems they face." Some particular points of concern were raised at a follow-up meeting, namely vandalism, frictions after sports events, prejudices children absorbed from their parents, and "discipline problems and more aggressive behavior" in the public schools. By 1962, concerns about a growing "lack of interracial contact" in the neighborhood itself led to a reciprocal exchange with the JCC, in the form of an annual Passover dinner observance followed by a group picnic, which continued at least through 1967. And in 1966, the Mount Pleasant Community Centers sponsored an interracial camping program with Alta House, the settlement serving Little Italy that had a history of fractious race relations.[41]

Additional interested players helped promote intercultural tolerance in the neighborhood. The Cleveland Public Library's Mount Pleasant branch first sponsored a joint Christmas-Hanukkah program in 1948, which continued at least until 1962. The annual observance included singing and other performances by choir groups from neighborhood churches, schools, and Jewish institutions like the Workmen's Circle. Notably, by 1957 the Jewish representation appeared to be from the Shaker-Lee JCC. Neighborhood public schools, PTAS, and several churches observed Brotherhood Week during the 1950s; on one occasion a black and a white congregation exchanged pastors. In another intergroup relations initiative, the Group Work Council sponsored a project in 1955 at A. J. Rickoff Elementary School involving fifty children, thirty of them African American and twenty white. Split evenly by sex, the children were organized into interracial groups with the goal of addressing "maladjustments." Such initiatives, at both school and home, along with "close contact with parents," provided opportunities to discuss "interracial attitudes" and encouraged teachers to enroll their students in the program. By the end of the 1950s, Mount Pleasant residents were winning a quarter of all citywide scholarships awarded by the Council on Human Relations, a group which had splintered off from the NCCJ in 1955 in order to pursue a more proactive form of interracial activism.[42]

Despite such efforts, however, Mount Pleasant also saw a rash of vandalism and harassment directed at incoming black families during the mid-1950s, similar to Glenville; yet here, too, such incidents had a random aspect in that they did not accompany the initial arrival of African Americans. In July 1954, vandals attacked with "paint bombs" an African American couple's nearly completed house, which was under construction by the black-owned Harris & Adams Construction Co. Located on East 112th Street just south of Kinsman Road, it was less than ten blocks from the historic African American enclave dating to the turn of the century. As previously mentioned, this was one of four Harris & Adams houses vandalized in a coordinated attack; the house's owners, the Pontones, who were moving from Glenville and had come to Cleveland just five years prior from Jacksonville, Florida, expressed their determination to move in, despite threatening phone calls. "This is our first house and we don't plan to let it set [sic] idle," Mr. Pontone told the Call & Post. "I can't understand it. Negroes already live less than a block away," he continued, suggesting that maybe "it was some kids who thought they were doing something smart." In fact, as the CRB determined, two other black families had been living on the same street for over twenty years. Vandals nevertheless hit the Pontones' house again the following week, immediately after it had been repainted, breaking more windows and smearing it with tar. But the couple refused to be intimidated and went through with their move, subsequently reporting: "We are happy in our new home. Not only have we had no trouble with vandals any more, but more than a dozen of our neighbors have telephoned to welcome us to the area and assure us of their friendship."[43]

Later that year, in September, vandals struck another black-owned home, on East 117th Street south of Union Avenue. The owners, the Halls, were the second African American family to purchase on the street and had lived there since the previous June without incident, although someone had attached a threatening note to their door when they first moved in. Robert Hall worked for a nearby business and, ironically, had resignedly bought in Mount Pleasant only after fighting a two-year battle against the village of Solon, a far-outlying suburb where he owned a lot but was blocked by racist officials from initiating construction of a new house. In this latest incident, vandals simultaneously threw rocks through the Halls' bedroom and living room windows while they and their daughter and son-in-law were at home, nearly injuring them. Despite subsequent police protection and the involvement of both the CRB and NAACP, vandals attacked their house a second time ten days later, throwing a brick through an upper-story window. In response, Councilman Joseph Horowitz demanded better protection, stating: "Nobody has the right to halt any peaceable family from living where they like in this ward. Any act to annoy them is un-American and will not be tolerated." The following month, Horowitz again prevailed on the city's safety director for a police investigation, following the bombing of a building on Union Avenue. Although an "old feud" with the owner was the presumptive explanation, Horowitz suspected "racial and religious feeling" was the actual motive. Thankfully, race-related vandalism proved unusual, as only two additional instances were perpetrated, in 1960 and 1964, when African Americans moved into formerly all-white portions of the neighborhood.[44]

In addition to vandalism, blockbusting, though not as prevalent as in Glenville, was an incipient issue in Mount Pleasant as early as 1953. At one session of a "human relations institute" held in the neighborhood that year, the guest speaker, local Urban League executive secretary Arnold Walker suggested an informational campaign "as [a] means of meeting exploitation of a neighborhood by 'unscrupulous' real estate dealers who attempt to stir up hysteria." Many former residents interviewed for this study did not recall aggressive real estate pressures during the 1950s, while others thought such tactics were limited to areas immediately adjacent to existing African American settlements (as in the Kinsman Heights enclave centered around East 142nd Street), or thought families who rented were less susceptible to panic than owners. Two black sisters whose family moved from Glenville to East 142nd Street and Bartlett Avenue in 1953 had no recollection whatsoever of blockbusting speeding the departure of white families, which they dated to 1956.[45]

Such tactics were on the rise, however, by the time *Cleveland Press* reporter Julian Krawcheck began research for his 1961 blockbusting series, concurrent with patterns in eastern Glenville and Lee-Harvard. He interviewed one (apparently Italian) resident on East 147th Street south of Kinsman Road who was approached by both a "dignified colored man" and a "bald Jewish realtor" who asked her to sell, followed by "telephone calls day and night from various realtors." She and her husband refused, with Krawcheck noting, "The street is now

90% colored. The first Negro family bought eight or nine years ago." Another white resident observed that "some white families, mostly older people . . . don't want to sell and have resisted overtures of realtors to date," but claimed there was "no undue pressure" involved. However, a white reader responding to the series wrote that on her street, East 133rd south of Union Avenue, signs advertising houses for sale "mushroomed one after another" less than a year after the first black family's appearance. The Urban League's Shelton Granger described practices similar to those in Glenville: "Broker deliberately sold to a low-income Negro in order to panic whites. He knew the low-income Negro family could not maintain payments but deliberately sold it anyway to . . . promote sales." In seeming confirmation, an African American correspondent claimed to know of a black real estate agent operating in Mount Pleasant who exploited the sexual anxieties of white residents by "finding a family on the street with teenage girls . . . [and] telling them a house is being sold down the street to a colored family [from Cedar-Central] with teenage boys."[46]

As in Glenville, white residents who stayed put were often pleasantly surprised by the initial black newcomers' high standards, and some even developed friendly relations. "I was impressed by the cleanliness of the homes of the newer residents," Councilman Horowitz remarked in 1950. "They maintain their homes in a tidy condition neat and clean; the outside of their homes are also well[-]kept, lawns are planted where possible, and the shrubbery is cared for." He added that while "it is the common belief . . . that Negroes deteriorate a neighborhood and 'run it down,' I can truthfully say . . . that on the contrary their homes are superior, many times, to [those of] longer residents of the area." An African American former resident who moved to Mount Pleasant as a newlywed in 1953 thought many whites were on the verge of moving out anyway and said they typically remained for up to five years after the first blacks arrived. She recalled that neighbors even exchanged food, for example, sweet potato pie for Italian Christmas bread. Another whose family moved to the neighborhood in 1956 recalled that "Soika [Avenue] was a beautiful street; neighbors—black and white—would greet one another daily, sharing stories. The neighbors next door to us were Hungarian; they taught my family a little Hungarian and a lot about growing roses." A black man who built a house on East 154th Street at the Shaker Heights border recalled he "never had any problems" with his Italian neighbors; in fact, as a Catholic he knew them from Saint Cecelia's Church.[47]

The northeasterly section of the neighborhood bordering Shaker Heights saw the most dramatic, but seemingly peaceful racial turnover between 1950 and 1960. This portion featured spacious two-family houses and numerous apartment buildings along Kinsman Road, and it was also the most heavily Jewish. Considerable numbers of brand-new single-family ranches and colonials had also recently been built here, proving highly attractive to upwardly mobile middle-class blacks. When Krawcheck visited the area in 1956 as part of his research for a series on racial residential transition, he found "pretty new frame houses" on East 147th Street between Milverton Road and Spear Avenue, built right after World War II. Although the first black purchase had occurred just two years earlier, only six white families remained, with Krawcheck nevertheless noting active interracial participation in the block club. One white neighbor stated there was no "unpleasantness" on the street, because the African American owners were "high class and intent on keeping up and improving their properties." In fact, she believed the neighborhood's appearance had "improved 100%" because the black newcomers painted their houses regularly, remodeled interiors, made exterior alterations, and sometimes built additions. The lawns, she added, looked "like velvet." As the owner of a grocery store, she also described warm relations with her new black customers, although she expected "the remaining whites will undoubtedly move out soon." An African American couple (the husband a lawyer) interviewed by Krawcheck on the same street verified that incoming black families had installed recreation rooms and storm windows, adding an estimated average of $2,500 to the value of houses they had purchased for around $15,000.[48]

The large proportion of two-family houses in Mount Pleasant, at half or more in two of its four census tracts, also helped to moderate the pace of demographic turnover. On the one hand, renting enabled whites to move away more easily; but, according to some white former residents interviewed for this study, it also reduced anxiety about population transfers, because it muted fears about property values. For example, one Jewish man who grew up on East 146th Street said his family had remained there until 1952 or 1953. When the landlord sold the house to an African American family, his family rented just down the street for a year, before moving onto Hildana Road, less than ten blocks to the east in Shaker Heights. An Italian man who had rented from his father-in-law on East 147th Street said he was "perfectly happy" in 1955, when the neighborhood was split evenly between black and white; he fondly recalled how the elderly African American couple who lived downstairs had "adopted" his kids. Four years later, however, the neighborhood had become practically all-black. "It's not that they were hurting us or mean to us," this man explained in justifying his move. "It's just when you're 10 percent [of the neighborhood population], you know it's time to move on." In a further complication, all-white apartment buildings were common in Mount Pleasant as late as 1957, largely due to discriminatory tenanting; interviews with black former residents confirm that well into the 1950s, the apartments along Kinsman Road typically had all-white occupancy, with the exception of custodians.[49]

Even so, white trepidation amid black influx was a more common response, with sporadic conflicts contributing to an atmosphere of tension. As early as 1950, Murtis Taylor had warned of "malicious rumors" accompanying demographic turnover. Social workers described the area around Lafayette Elementary as "the heart of a changing community," noting that children there "do not share the playground with each other," although with the qualification that "this problem is being very effectively handled by skilled playground workers." An Italian man who grew up on East 147th Street south of Kinsman recalled that "people didn't like it" when African Americans began moving in, that "nobody wanted to live there," and that some whites "just panicked and left." In one instance, neighbors on the street raised $600 to convince a white renter to buy on the street instead of moving. Tellingly, one responsibility of a new aide to the Mount Pleasant Community Council in 1954 was "to help settle racial problems, [and] iron out squabbles between residents and merchants." And later that year, a fracas at the Union Square Theatre (11417 Union Avenue) spurred a direct intervention by the CRB. After an assault on an African American youth precipitated a brawl, police apprehended only the black youths involved. In response, angry black parents notified the CRB, which persuaded the district police captain to identify and arrest the white youths. Such incidents led the Board to describe the southern portion of Mount Pleasant as "in a general state of tension." In 1963, the CRB was again summoned as a mediator, following complaints from white residents in the vicinity of Benham Avenue and East 116th Street that black schoolchildren were "walking on lawns, jaywalking, and obstructing the flow of traffic."[50]

Racial clashes at Woodland Hills pool had declined by World War II, so that at least for a time, it saw integrated use. A 1952 study commended the Division of Recreation for its "forthright policies" in enforcing equal access.[51] A black former resident who frequented Woodland Hills during the early 1950s recalls that African Americans no longer had any problems swimming among the still-numerous white bathers there but claimed blacks were barred from playing tennis. A 1955 newspaper photograph depicted an interracial group of preteens signing a petition to restore checkroom facilities at the pool, which when cut by the city had led to an increased incidence of theft.[52]

But as African Americans increasingly used Woodland Hills, whites switched to the pool at Garfield Park, just outside the city limits in Garfield Heights, on land owned by the City of Cleveland; incidentally, this facility was also the closest for black residents of the Lee-Seville enclave. To an even greater degree than Woodland Hills, Garfield Park had a checkered history, with sporadic racial clashes dating at least to World War II.[53] In a summer 1950 incident, members of an interracial club, most likely from Mount Pleasant, decided to go swimming at Garfield Park, despite their adult leader's reservations "because he had heard that there was a great deal of tension in the area around the use of the pool by Negroes." The Recreation Board was duly notified, and the group of four boys, aged nine to thirteen, three white and one black, set off for the park with their adult leader. Upon entering the pool, a handful of youths in their late teens singled out the leader and angrily asked him why he had brought the African American boy along, with one adding: "They [blacks] got Woodhill [sic] to swim in." Up to twenty white bathers soon surrounded the group, and as the leader tried to gather his charges and escort them out, he was dealt a blow that knocked him unconscious. Police then arrived to guard the dressing room until the group left the park.[54]

This case provides a rare glimpse at the mentality underlying racialized white territoriality. Several days later, a social worker from a settlement house closer to Garfield Park unexpectedly got to speak with one of the antagonists, a nineteen-year-old of Polish ancestry. It had all been the group leader's fault for "bringing those nigger kids out there," asserted the youth, and when the social worker countered that the facility, being public, was supported by black tax-payers as well as white, the youth elaborated further: "I know, and I guess it's not so bad just bringing one or two of them in, but as soon as we let a couple of them in they all start coming in and before you know it the place is crowded with nothing but niggers. Look at Woodland Hills Pool. They started to let nig-gers in up there and now they have taken it over completely. We don't want that to happen here at Garfield." The antagonist readily made class distinctions be-tween African Americans, yet still exhibited assumptions of inevitability akin to those many whites formed in facing racial residential transition. The social worker reported: "In the conversation that followed, John [the youth] admitted that he knew that some colored people are 'better' and 'cleaner' than some white people and that he wouldn't mind them swimming in the pool but that along with them would come a lot of 'dirty niggers' and then there wouldn't be any way of keeping them out of the pool."[55]

Racial residential transition continued in Mount Pleasant and was effec-tively complete by the mid-1960s. In 1955, committee members planning a new recreation center for the neighborhood expressed fear that locating the facility near Alexander Hamilton Junior High "would mean that the Center would be used predominantly by Negroes" and worried that "within two years the area would be occupied by Negroes all the way to Shaker Heights." Indeed, a grant proposal by the Mount Pleasant Community Centers from 1956 observed not only that the white population was "rapidly moving out," but also that "whites remaining in the area [tend] to withdraw from all community activities and not to identify with [the] area." When the recreation center did finally open in 1958, social work professionals concluded that white youths indeed avoided it because of its "racial composition."[56] By the early 1960s, those European ethnic institutions remaining in the vicinity, such as the Czech gymnastic organiza-tion Sokol Tyrš, proved increasingly disinclined to participate in the MPCC as their membership moved away. Saint Cecelia's Catholic Church, which had counted African American congregants since the 1920s, and whose pastors had long promoted tolerance through the Saint Augustine Guild, struggled to re-

cruit converts among the new black residents in the face of a steep parish-
ioner decline. Racial residential transition seemed to have run its course by
1964, when a newspaper article reported that apart from the "stable Hungarian
settlement around Parkhill Ave. in the northern part of the area," whites in
Mount Pleasant, "mainly of Italian and Slavic descent, are scattered."[57]

Lee-Harvard

In contrast to older Glenville and Mount Pleasant, racial residential
transition proceeded far more rapidly in Lee-Harvard, which saw a nearly
complete demographic turnover between 1961 and 1965 (see Table 4.1). One
key factor explaining the different pattern here is the much more intensive and
systematic approach undertaken by real estate operators. Following the Stewarts' 1953 purchase on Talford Avenue, additional black families began moving into the neighborhood's northwestern section. Looking back nearly fifty
years, *Plain Dealer* columnist Dick Feagler recounted his family's experiences
on Invermere Avenue, three blocks north of Talford. "A ripple of fear vibrated
through the neighborhood," he wrote. "After supper, the doorbell would ring,
and somebody would be standing there usually with his wife, asking us to sign
a piece of paper pledging that we would not sell our home simply because we
were afraid of black people." This confirms reports by the CRB that "certain
groups were seeking to mobilize home owners in the area south of Lee and
West of Harvard [*sic*] and using the 'restriction' agreement developed immediately after the Stewart case."[58] Not long afterward, Feagler's family began receiving flyers with slogans like "Harvard and Lee by '53, Negroes Make Good
Neighbors." His father sold when approached while cutting the lawn, in this
instance by two black real estate agents who convinced him he would lose
money if the family stayed. The *Call & Post*, investigating a suspected 1955 case
of vandalism on East 154th Street, just inside the neighborhood, determined
it to be merely a prank—but nevertheless the paper uncovered considerable
tensions stirred up by aggressive white and black real estate salespersons. "We
have had fine relations with our new colored neighbors," one woman stated.
"But our lives are made miserable by real estate agents pressuring us. . . .
It's really making a terrible situation here." The CRB investigated but could
do little, noting: "One particularly trouble-making salesman was reported to
the State Real Estate Board only to find the only charge that could be lodged
against him was that of overzealous salesmanship."[59]

African American purchases in these first few years nevertheless remained
infrequent and were limited to the blocks west of Lee Road and north of Harvard Avenue. By 1957, more African American families were moving into this
northwestern quadrant, with the CRB counting five on Talford Avenue by
year's end. African American prospective buyers still faced difficulties obtaining credit, as revealed by a former president of the local NAACP who was re-

Table 4.1. Percent Black-Occupied Dwelling Units in
Lee-Harvard Census Tracts, 1950–1970

	1950	1960	1970
U-7	0.1	30.2	94
U-8	0	0.1	92
U-9	0	1.6	87
V-1	0	0.4	91

Sources: U.S. Bureau of the Census, *United States Census of
Housing: 1950 Block Statistics, Cleveland, Ohio* (Washington, D.C.,
1952); U.S. Bureau of the Census, *United States Census of Housing:
1960 City Blocks, Cleveland, Ohio* (Washington, D.C., 1961); U.S.
Bureau of the Census, *1970 Census of Housing: Block Statistics,
Cleveland, Ohio Urbanized Area* (Washington, D.C., 1971).

peatedly refused bank loans to buy on Talford. Reluctance among lenders undoubtedly explains the fact that as late as 1962, African Americans still did not
constitute a majority of homeowners on any street in the section. But the trend
was clear, with "a growing restlessness" evident among white homeowners by
1958, as noted by staff at the JCC's Shaker-Lee House, located just outside the
neighborhood. Parents felt pressure to move as their children grew older, the
staff explained, "to avoid using the nearby Junior High School where the Negro
population has been growing." The following year, the Cleveland Baptist Association initiated confidential discussions on how to convince white homeowners to stay, anticipating an African American influx.[60]

Already in 1958, a white homeowner was ostracized for trying to sell his
home east of Lee Road, which, the CRB reported, "certain elements consider
to be the boundary where there should be no movement of Negroes." He was
temporarily unable to sell the house, which was left vacant when he moved
anyway. The first successful black purchase east of Lee Road did not take place
until December 1960, but blockbusting tactics quickly commenced throughout the entirety of Lee-Harvard. Some residents posted "Not for Sale" signs,
though one observer noted "almost as many 'For Sale' signs in [the] streets
south of Scottsdale as there are trees" by summer, prompting officials in the
adjacent suburb of Shaker Heights to begin drafting antiblockbusting legislation. By the time Julian Krawcheck began interviews for a follow-up series on
blockbusting in mid-1962, he was presented with statistics showing that on the
eight streets north of Harvard Avenue, east of Lee Road to East 177th Street,
about one-third of the roughly 800 houses had already been purchased by
African American families—an amazing, tenfold increase over the previous
summer. The originator of these figures, Harvard-Scott-Lee Home Owners Association president Joseph Novak, professed: "I hate to say it, but I'm afraid the

area is past preserving as an integrated area. Too many [white] families have moved away and too many Negroes have bought, in too short a time." Novak expressed hope that integration could be maintained in the adjacent section from East 177th Street to the Warrensville Heights border, where only several dozen black families had bought. Novak qualified, however, that he was "not hopeful for the area generally" because too many whites had "given up."[61]

Krawcheck's interviews for the two *Cleveland Press* series provide a rich record of the mind-set of white homeowners in this era of rapid neighborhood turnover. Similar to earlier patterns, and despite reports of "tension," there was little overt resistance toward black newcomers, and only two reported instances of vandalism: in 1961, the first black couple on Eldamere Avenue east of Lee Road had the words "Nigger Go Home" chalked onto the outside of their house on two occasions, and in a more serious incident that same year, vandals paint-bombed the soon-to-be home of a black family on Wyatt Avenue, south of Harvard and east of Lee. Other incidents underlined tensions among white residents as well as those between blacks and whites, including shunning, intimidation, and retaliation. For example, when the DelGarbino family on De-Forest Avenue, south of Harvard and east of Lee, put their house on the market in 1961, they received phone threats of arson, including one from the woman next door, who threatened to toss a brick through their soon-to-be-born baby's window. Someone also put sand in the gas tank of their brand-new car. Mrs. DelGarbino blamed her subsequent miscarriage on the stress surrounding this harassment. On the same block, the Klima family received similar threats when they considered moving out, one caller warning, "I'd advise you to watch your children." Recognizing the voice as a neighbor's, he pressed charges, but the case was dismissed as hearsay. Both families delayed selling as a result of the intimidation, thus accomplishing the intended effect.[62]

Ethnicity also played into these conflicts. Because Jews were often first to move out, they were sometimes blamed by other white residents for "selling out" to blacks—a problem serious enough to warrant the attention of the Jewish Community Federation's Community Relations Committee by 1958. Ambivalent about its responsibility in such matters, the committee sought to avert "violence and hasty selling and to help produce a calm atmosphere" but made clear that "the final decision must be the homeowner's or the landlord's" on the question of selling or renting to African Americans. "Our role is to supply the pertinent facts, including the commitment of the organized Jewish community to free housing opportunities," declared the committee. "At the same time," it continued, "those breaking long-established neighborhood patterns should be fully informed as to possible community reactions." While considerable animosity was directed toward Jews, ethnic prejudices also extended to others. Krawcheck interviewed one white Catholic couple who planned to move away, in part because "until three years ago, Invermere was a 'lovely

neighborhood.' . . . Then some of the nicer people moved out and were succeeded by another element, impliedly the Slavic element who were clannish."
The couple went on to claim that these "Slavic" residents "became suspicious
of everyone else, and got real nasty" when prospective black buyers began
combing the area. In a sense summarizing the religio-ethnic dynamics of Lee-
Harvard, a white Protestant minister and resident mentioned that "there never
was a great deal of community cohesiveness in H[arvard]-S[cott]-L[ee], even
before the first colored families came. There were significant percentages of
Jewish, Catholic, and Protestant people—all moving in separate directions and
tending to mingle primarily with their own groups."[63]

Here, as in the case of more ethnically homogeneous Corlett, organized attempts to combat blockbusting took a nonracist approach, at least officially.
An early flyer produced by "The Invermere Committee," led by Joseph Novak,
advocated action on the logic that "if we respond to, instead of ignoring these
tactics and act hastily, then we put ourselves at the mercy of these realtors
whose interests are not those of the seller nor of the buyer, but only in the
amount of commissions they can collect." This flyer helped spur the founding
of the Harvard-Scott-Lee Home Owners Association in early 1961, following a
meeting at Saint Henry Catholic School. According to Novak, who was elected
president, the organizers had to convince the parish priest that their intentions
were nondiscriminatory—or, as Novak put it, that they "were not trying to find
ways to keep Negroes out . . . but rather how to keep the whites in." By summer,
approximately 300 families had joined, each paying $1 in dues, although Novak
expressed pessimism that "people are not working hard enough" in convincing white families to stay. Another resident claimed that the membership was
divided on the question of selling to African Americans, but that all sought
"an orderly transition." When Krawcheck asked the group's leaders whether
they were trying to prevent more blacks from moving in, they replied, "No, we
welcome qualified, respectable people of all kind[s]. We merely want to prevent panic and large-scale dumping of houses on the market." The CRB shared
these modest goals, later deeming the neighborhood's transition "peaceful."
In 1962, as African Americans moved even into Lee-Harvard's farthest reaches,
community meetings remained focused on convincing white residents to
stay put.[64]

Krawcheck found a range of sentiments around the issue of racial residential transition among the white residents of Lee-Harvard. Several saw a "con-
spiracy" behind the moves, as in the man who had heard rumors that "the
NAACP pays $20,000 to the first Negro family to crack a neighborhood" and
that the city's most prominent black funeral home, the House of Wills, had
financially rewarded the first African American family to move into the nearby
Ludlow area—apparently a jumbled rendition of Wendell Stewart's financing
arrangement. Another woman wrote: "I think this whole thing was part of a

long range plan on the part of the colored. . . . They picked the first [north-ernmost] street in our Shaker area, Invermere, . . . [which] gave them access to both Shaker Heights and Warrensville Heights." Mrs. Novak, of all people, expressed nostalgia for their previous block in Corlett, saying, "It is still white. Sometimes we wish we were back there." Quite a few white interviewees—likely more open, if willing to talk—claimed not to oppose black residency, at least in moderate proportions. Typical was one woman who found little to dis-like about the highly educated, middle-class black families moving in: "We like our children to be exposed to other children of all colors and creeds, including Negroes . . . but we don't want to be a minority anywhere. Wouldn't want to live in an all-Catholic or all-Jewish neighborhood." Another resident who had posted a "Not for Sale" sign likewise claimed: "We're not opposed to having a few Negro families on the street, but a deluge doesn't help anyone."[65]

Numerous white residents also expressed concern at the increasing propor-tion of African American students at Gracemount Elementary School. "Some of the Negro families that have moved in are nicer than some white families, and we wouldn't mind at all if the area were, say, 50% white and 50% colored," one resident told Krawcheck. "But Gracemount school, where our youngest child is in kindergarten, is about 85% colored, and the ratio seems to be increasing. Naturally, we wouldn't want to live in a ghetto of any kind," she continued. Afri-can American enrollment at Gracemount increased because the school drew largely from the neighborhood's increasingly black northwestern section, and because many of the area's white children attended Catholic schools. Some white residents claimed transition could be slowed if additional school facili-ties were provided for the section immediately east of Lee Road, with one cor-respondent revealing that residents had unsuccessfully sought to extend the school district for E. M. Williams Elementary, which served the area's eastern section, westward to Lee. Other white residents claimed that Gracemount was "overcrowded," and, while everyone agreed that the quality of education re-mained excellent, some expressed fears that the school could "decline" with a continued influx of black students. Gracemount's principal contended that de-spite the dramatic increase in the school's proportion of African American stu-dents—she confirmed a jump from 67 percent to an estimated 80 percent from 1961 to 1962—levels of academic achievement had remained consistently high, with the addition of a fourth "Major Work" (advanced placement) class for the coming year. Meanwhile, Gracemount PTA president Mrs. Ciarlillo added that "Negro mothers [are] very active in PTA, very cooperative. White mothers who have dropped out . . . were never active anyway. I see no change at all in the scholarship level at the school; if anything, it might be better."[66]

Interestingly, some white residents who spoke with Krawcheck revealed they had purchased in the area despite warnings by lenders and real estate agents that African Americans would move in. One woman stated: "When we bought the house, we knew Negroes would be moving into the area sooner or later, but we didn't care. We intended to stay only about five years anyway." A minister living in the area confirmed that "the houses in the area were 'good as a first house but not the sort of thing you want permanently.' The young professional people got out fast." In seeming verification, a former resident told Krawcheck that Lee-Harvard had been "all young couples" when she and her husband first moved there, who left as they "got better off financially." Some remaining whites suggested they might move out when their children reached school age, or when they needed a larger house. On the other hand, Harvard-Scott-Lee Home Owners Association president Joseph Novak mentioned several families he expected would remain because they had invested substantially in home renovation, had children in college, or were elderly. "But the majority of [white] people evidently plan to move eventually," Novak conceded, before admitting that he, too, would consider selling "if somebody came along and made us a good offer."[67]

Several white residents actually claimed they had chosen Lee-Harvard precisely because it was integrating, while still others expected they would remain after the fact. Said one woman whose children attended Catholic schools: "I asked my daughter Kathy, 17, if she was embarrassed having her dates know there were colored people in the neighborhood, and she said no. . . . I have a feeling we will stay right here—unless, of course, the area gets totally Negro and unpleasant." Other white residents reported that their children had black playmates, and that neighborly relations were cordial enough, an assessment verified by the handful of new black residents Krawcheck interviewed. One claimed, "The friendship and kindness of those we know is very genuine and sincere," with neighborliness "just as high as it was in the old, all-Negro neighborhood." One white resident expressed concern, however, that "over-the-fence sociability" was impeded by the larger proportion of black wives who worked, while another woman who wrote the *Cleveland Press* dismissed interracial pleasantries as superficial: "You show a picture of Eldamere 'where whites and Negroes live side by side harmoniously.' Maybe they say 'hello' and exchange a few words. But do they exchange coffee breaks in the morning? Do they walk to the shopping center together? Do they watch each other's children when one is away for a time? No. I feel as if I am in alien territory." Still another woman gave proof that too much interracial sociability might provide motivation for moving out, when she explained her decision to leave for the suburbs to Krawcheck: "We wanted to be friendly and democratic with the Negro but when it's a case of children not having [any] white friends, you think twice about remaining in such an area."[68]

The Krawcheck interviews also broaden our understanding of how white residents understood the peculiar interplay of economic impulses that accompanied the process of racial residential transition. One family wanting to sell their home was rejected by realty firms, with one agent telling them: "We don't want your house because we could only sell to a white buyer at a great loss, and we won't sell to a Negro." This corroborates other evidence that immediately prior to the first appearance of African American residents in a given neighborhood, white property owners could find themselves stuck with "white elephant" properties, unable to interest white buyers and unable (or unwilling) to sell to blacks. As Krawcheck discovered, some whites decided to move without selling and temporarily took on the burden of two mortgages. Numerous interviewees mentioned being offered several thousand dollars less than market value for their homes, by potentially interested white investors seeking to capitalize on fears of impending racial change. Such buyers might turn a significant profit as prices rebounded when the first African Americans actually arrived, as in one case on Eldamere where the white owner bought in 1958 for $16,500 and sold just three years later to a black family for $19,500. As one angry letter-writer described the situation east of Lee Road: "Homes were worth from $18,000 to $23,000. Then suddenly it began to drop in value. . . . Beautiful homes complete in every detail on which owners had lavished care, were being sold in those times of inflation for $14,000 to $16,000. . . . Now suddenly, some of the sharper sellers have found that the colored will pay what the homes are really worth." Nevertheless, the correspondent deflected blame, concluding, "It was the fault of the colored that the decline in value came about in the first place."[69]

Some white owners approached this situation cynically with two asking prices, one for whites and a higher one for blacks. As one man put it, "I know my house is not worth more than $25,000 but if I have to sell it to a Negro I'm going to get $30,000 for it." This demand may have been extreme, but the first white sellers did generally get "top dollar" for their homes, from black buyers who were willing and able to pay more. As the first African American buyer on Invermere east of stated: "We accepted the price, $25,000, feeling that perhaps it was a little more than a white family would have to pay but we weren't too perturbed about that. I guess when you want something bad enough, you will pay the price if it isn't exorbitant." But once blacks started moving in, aggressive real estate agents sought to manipulate prices. As one anonymous writer put it: "Yes if you are one of the very first to sell to colored, you may get a price even above the value, but stay a year or so & try to sell, the colored man comes to your door & tells you that you can[']t expect to get your price as this is [a] 'colored neighborhood' now!"[70]

This correspondent continued on to identify the crux of the dilemma faced by many white residents contemplating moves, which undoubtedly helped to sustain the belief that racial residential transition led to declining property values: while no one lost money on the original sale, it could be extremely difficult to find comparable housing at an affordable price. Thus the anonymous letter-writer had invested $6,000 in his former house from the time he bought in 1920, and he sold in 1958 for $9,250, yet he still felt shortchanged when he wrote: "Allright I made [$]3000—but now I bought a smaller house [with] 2 bedrooms[,] 1 single garage, all worn out, for $13,800, to live in a white neighborhood." Similarly, a white resident on Talford claimed that the "people [who] moved from west of Lee now haven't got a nickel for chewing gum. They sunk all their money into a house they can't afford elsewhere."[71] Thus some white residents did experience economic hardships associated with racial residential transition; but instead of blaming the segregated, "dual" housing market for erratic prices, they reserved their ire for the incoming black residents. To understand how the mentality of white residents facing racial residential transition in neighborhoods like Lee-Harvard helped to drive that process, we may turn to an insightful 1957 article by sociologist Eleanor P. Wolf, who compared racially motivated panic selling to such phenomena as a bank run or a stampede caused by someone yelling "fire" in a crowded theater: white residents were implicated in the process of racial residential transition even as they were affected by it. While "self-fulfilling," their actions were not totally irrational, she argued, but rather derived from expectations based on previous outcomes and a drive to protect their perceived self-interests. Furthermore, Wolf found that in the middle-class Detroit neighborhood she studied, "most [white] residents are well aware of individual differences among Negroes, recognize the personal worth of many of their [black] neighbors, etc.," yet still harbored intensely pessimistic expectations regarding racial transition, making them prone to move.[72]

Corlett

Located immediately south of Mount Pleasant and spanning Harvard Avenue approximately from East 116th Street to 154th Street, Corlett is best understood as a second-tier neighborhood to which many individuals moved from more cohesive ethnic communities. Not annexed to the city until 1909, land development here resembled patterns in both adjacent Mount Pleasant and Lee-Harvard. The bulk of Corlett, west of East 140th Street, was developed during the 1920s with a mixture of double- and single-family homes. In contrast, the neighborhood's eastern portion—particularly beyond East 147th Street—still contained considerable vacant land in 1940 and was built up with numerous single-family, ranch and colonial-style homes, much as adjacent Lee-Harvard had been. Between 1950 and 1960, in fact, there was still housing under construction, with 444 units built in the neighborhood's easternmost census tract alone, some 30 percent of the 1960 total.[73] The predominant ethnic groups in Corlett were Czech and Polish, many of them having moved out of their nearby, older Broadway Avenue settlements into the neighborhood by 1950; smaller numbers of Italians also lived in the area.[74]

Small numbers of African Americans also lived in Corlett from early on. In 1940, twenty-four black families were sprinkled through the blocks north of Harvard Avenue and west of East 140th Street, and they apparently coexisted peacefully with their white neighbors. One such African American family that Julian Krawcheck interviewed in 1956 had been living at 13507 Crennell Avenue since 1917, tipped off to the destination by a black plasterer friend who had done work in the area. This family had been directed by the Guardian Savings & Trust Co., one of Cleveland's most prominent turn-of-the century banks, to a "sub-rosa," subsidiary mortgage company for financing. By 1956, the street had about a dozen additional African American households, but the immediate area was described by the original black family as "90% white" and having the "very finest [race] relations." Home values had steadily risen, and new black residents maintained their properties admirably. Incidentally, other researchers have documented this pattern of "isolated" African American families being accepted by their white neighbors in other Northern cities.[75]

Due to its mixed housing stock and population, Corlett was described by the early 1960s as "actually two communities," with disproportionately elderly white ethnic residents predominating in the mix of older, one- and two-family houses in the neighborhood's western portion, and upwardly mobile black families in the newer, single family houses in the eastern section bordering Lee-Harvard. The *Cleveland Press* reported, "Negroes first moved into the E. 147th St. area before 1950 and spread south to the [newer] Judson Dr. area," and, indeed, the relevant census tract went from 0.4 percent black in 1950 to 24 percent in 1960, indicating a rapid racial transition with spillover from the Kinsman Heights enclave in Mount Pleasant. One Italian former resident, whose family moved onto East 147th Street in 1942, estimated the street had been 5 percent black at that time. His family remained until 1957 and claimed that interracial relations were neighborly but not intimate; they eventually saw an African American family move in next door—whose son grew up to be a doctor—and further down the street, former Olympic champion Jesse Owens. The interviewee stated that there was no blockbusting on his street, but rather that white families gradually moved away in a pattern similar to Mount Pleasant, like his did when they decided to stop renting and build a house in Warrensville Heights.[76]

In several other aspects, however, Corlett's demographic transition resembled Lee-Harvard's. By 1962, social service professionals were reporting "a sharp racial change during the last 10 years, with resulting racial incidents. Some realtors have worsened the situation by their 'block-busting' tactics." Several interviewees for this study did recall blockbusting in the neighborhood; one Italian man who remained in Corlett until 1960 said real estate agents had come "once a week" and that many white residents, like him, felt "lucky to get out"—in his case, to the West Side suburb of Parma. Another Italian man whose family moved the same year thought the high proportion of renters in the neighborhood's western section, where two-family houses predominated, made it easier for them to move away. As early as 1953, one African American family anonymously wrote the *Call & Post* to say they had lived on Glendale Avenue since 1931 and been "accepted and trusted by our [white] friends"—but now due to increasing fears of black crime, they were facing "loss of our standing in the community and [of] credit at our stores." They lamented: "We plan on moving after all these years, but where to? This means pioneering all over again." In a 1955 case of *intra*racial retaliation, vandals smeared tar on a Benwood Avenue house owned by a Polish widow, after she showed it to a prospective black buyer.[77]

Several other controversies predating full-blown racial transition in the neighborhood offer further evidence of now-familiar patterns: white rejection followed by withdrawal, amid upwardly mobile black newcomers' anxieties over acceptable living conditions. In 1958, some 125 property owners in Corlett's northeastern reaches (likely in the vicinity of Kinsman Heights), a supposed "90%" of whom were African American, lobbied Councilman Leo Dombrowski to "rezone their area from two-family to one-family houses," a preemptive move against conversion to multifamily occupancy paralleling code enforcement efforts in Glenville and Mount Pleasant. Meanwhile, African Americans had not yet even gained access to other parts of Corlett. In mid-1960, a prospective black buyer attempting to buy in a brand-new development in the southeastern portion of the neighborhood filed a lawsuit against the builders when he was turned away because of his race. Everette Gregory was a World War II veteran and a thirteen-year employee at Republic Steel, and his wife worked at the Fisher Body plant. Despite securing financing under VA terms, Gregory was rebuffed by the developer whom he allegedly overheard say: "Why should I risk a $150,000 investment by selling to Negroes? It might cause a disturbance among the other residents and I am no crusader." Illustrating an exclusionary tactic used by whites who lingered once integration got under way, an African American Catholic mother wrote the bishop in 1961 to complain that her children had been denied admission to Holy Family parochial school, on the questionable ground that it was an exclusively Bohemian (Czech) parish.[78]

Initial efforts to counteract blockbusting in Corlett first emerged in late 1960 and bore direct links to ethnic institutions. Meetings of a newly organized Corlett Homeowners Improvement Association (CHIA) were held at the Polish Library Home on East 141st Street, while the primary organizing locus centered on Our Lady of Czestochowa parish. A member of the association's organizing committee told the press, "We are not organizing a group to promote racial or religious discrimination," and, "Our purpose is to stop this harassment, then work on such projects as maintenance of homes and zoning laws." At the initial meeting, attended by approximately 400 white residents, this emphasis on racial tolerance was upheld with the blessing of the CRB, although the meeting "occasionally became heated over the racial issue," leading the chairman to declare: "We are going to stick to this one purpose—helping the neighborhood. . . . And our association will be open to any homeowners living here." More ominously, a scheduled speaker from the Perry Home Owners Improvement Association declined when informed his remarks might be quoted by newspapers. But tolerance paid off by the organization's second meeting, when it received assistance from the majority-black Cleveland Association of Real Estate Brokers to rein in any members alleged to be blockbusting in the area. That evening, one African American resident was reportedly among the 200 in attendance, as the organization won a pledge of support from the CRB, established a complaint bureau to be open two evenings per week, and organized block representatives for the entire area. At one point, the proceedings were translated into Polish for the benefit of some of the older residents present. Over the next month, the CHIA planned smaller-scale "parlor meetings" with the assistance of the CRB and the Welfare Federation. Elected officers recruited at least twenty-five volunteers and 150 dues-paying members and incorporated as a nonprofit. At a subsequent meeting, the group voted down an attempt by some of those present to bar African Americans from membership.[79]

Of course, undercurrents of racial tension persisted in Corlett. When Krawcheck conducted interviews for the *Cleveland Press* series on blockbusting the following year, he learned that many white residents attending the initial meeting of the CHIA "assumed the organization was being formed to keep blacks out." Councilman Dombrowski appeared defensive when he told Krawcheck, "I've taken a lot of abuse from some white people because I have said that a Negro has a right to move into any area where he can afford to buy." At the same time, he continued, "I've also said that no one has a right to harass people or force them to sell their houses." Attempts to curb blockbusting achieved mixed results. Although property turnover continued, an officer of the CHIA told Krawcheck that blockbusting complaints had declined and that real estate agents were routinely asked to desist when problems arose. The organization by then held weekly sessions to address blockbusting complaints and other issues such as zoning violations, and it claimed a membership of 250 families. Social service agencies continued to report "tension" in the area during 1961, however. Some African Americans apparently harbored suspicions about antiblockbusting efforts, with the NAACP's Housing Committee, for one, expressing concern in 1962 that the neighborhood's program of "'conservation' . . . includes maintaining discriminatory housing practices." A contemporaneous flyer printed by the CHIA did not contain any outwardly racist rhetoric but did express concern with problems that whites and upwardly mobile African Americans alike associated with poor black neighborhoods: property negligence, overcrowding, and noncompliant or illegal use of premises, all of which were to be reported to the zoning board.[80]

Racial tension was ultimately contained in Corlett. In early 1963, alleged blockbusting tactics just outside the neighborhood, in the vicinity of Union Avenue and East 116th Street, provided the catalyst for Councilman Anthony Pecyk to demand an investigation by the CRB, which paved the way for his subsequent attempts to bring antiblockbusting legislation before the City Council that spring. After surveying over a hundred residents, the CRB concluded: "There was constant harassment on the part of real estate agents in an attempt to create panic selling by injecting racism in sales arguments, profuse use of the myth of property values depreciating as a result of Negroes buying into an area, regular telephone contacts, and door-to-door soliciting of property by real estate agents." One elderly white woman had received an incredible ninety calls pressuring her to sell; meanwhile, African American purchasers had paid inflated prices, in one case nearly twice market value. With his ordinance stuck in committee the following year, Pecyk claimed that blockbusting in his ward was escalating further. In the wake of such developments, many white residents pondered moving away, as reported in a letter to Mayor Ralph Locher recounting a bus stop conversation with a woman who was "living in the Corlett district for many years, and is Polish and a Catholic like I am and so when these colored people moved into the neighborhood, her husband and her said they are also created by God so they will continue to live there, after all they were both in their 80[s,] but now after a few years they see it is just unbearable and the way she explains it to me, I couldn't help but crying because she told me we are old, and should be buying a grave for ourselves, instead of a new home."[81] Demographic turnover in Corlett subsequently continued, but at a relatively slow rate, especially in its western portion. The attenuating factors here included intact ethnic institutions; the presence of preexisting, albeit isolated African American residents; a lower-income, working-class white population, including a considerable number of elderly residents; and, quite significantly, a preponderance of older housing stock both less desirable to upwardly mobile blacks and potentially more susceptible to the structural forces underlying urban decline.

■

The neighborhoods discussed in this chapter, "undefended" in the sense that racial residential transition proceeded with minimal violent resistance compared to other locales, nevertheless saw quite different trajectories and timing, relating to a multiplicity of factors. In Glenville and Mount Pleasant, which had long-standing established black settlements, a steady influx of African American newcomers from World War II to the mid-1960s transformed these neighborhoods into nearly all-black but still mostly middle-class preserves. Exhibiting a complex dynamic that engaged the status aspirations of both white and black residents, this demographic transformation unfolded at a comparatively slower pace in Mount Pleasant, despite similarities in the white ethnic population mix of the two areas and housing stock of a roughly comparable age. In Corlett, which also had a small black presence before 1940, considerable ethnic cohesion and a relative lack of mobility options for elderly and lower-income white residents similarly served to slow transition. But here, too, the age and type of housing stock made a difference, as the vanguard of upwardly mobile black buyers initially bypassed the neighborhood's older western portion, instead favoring the new, suburban-style single family homes on its eastern fringe.

Lee-Harvard, developed during and after World War II and practically indistinguishable from the suburbs that bordered it, experienced a vastly accelerated demographic turnover, in which the physical attributes of its housing factored considerably. The neighborhood offered new yet relatively affordable housing, as well as newer and higher-quality schools proving attractive to members of the city's diverse Southern and Eastern European ethnic groups. Their rapid movement out of Lee-Harvard in the face of black influx was shaped by their previous experience in past locations—whether a lack of prior engagement with African Americans in a residential setting, or else as something they sought to leave behind in their ongoing quest for respectability. As evidenced by their assumptions about property values, white residents associated black influx with eventual neighborhood "decline." Perhaps ironically, many of Cleveland's middle-class blacks, even as they grasped the opportunity to move into better, increasingly available housing in Glenville, Mount Pleasant, Corlett, and Lee-Harvard, drew not so dissimilar conclusions as they were squeezed by the complex structural and human forces underlying the urban crisis. It is with this background in mind that we can proceed to examine class dynamics in these communities, after they became virtually all black.

5 : : :
Mobility and Insecurity
DILEMMAS OF THE BLACK MIDDLE CLASS

In April 1966, Morris Thorington Jr. testified at a hearing of the U.S. Commission on Civil Rights at Cleveland City Hall. As a black business owner and lifelong resident of the city, he starkly expressed many of the realities, dilemmas, and frustrations faced by upwardly mobile African American families striving to get ahead in a deteriorating local economy and segregated housing market. The Thoringtons owned a home on Eldamere Avenue in the city's Lee-Harvard section, and he was the proprietor of a beverage store and delicatessen in Hough—the neighborhood that would explode several months later in the city's first urban uprising. Yet Thorington felt the need to bolster his economic security by working as a driver and salesman for a potato chip company; using income-pooling, like many middle-class African American families, Thorington's wife ran the store during the day, while he took over in the evenings. Asked by the commission to name the biggest problem facing his business, Thorington responded, "Financing," the need for "a quick small loan," which arose from buying "a warmed-over business in a warmed-over neighborhood," by which he meant one that had "deteriorated to the point that the previous [white] merchants have decided it is no longer to their advantage to stay there so they sell out to some Negro who is trying to move a step up the ladder." He cited difficulties in obtaining insurance and reemphasized how crucial credit was for businesses whose customers relied heavily on welfare and social security. Asked if his business was located in an urban renewal area, Thorington corrected the questioner that it was an "urban destruction area," drawing applause from the audience. "All they've done down there," Thorington said of the city's redevelopment projects, "is chase the people over into Glenville and other areas and made slums out of them; tear down a few houses, make the streets more deserted, fewer people and more vulnerable to hoodlums."[1]

Continuing on, Thorington opined, "You are just moving your ghetto from Hough to Glenville, to Mount Pleasant, and finally to Lee-Harvard and Shaker Heights[,] and God knows where to from there. But the whole thing is eventually going to erode the whole city." Asked whether he would like to see public housing built in Hough, Thorington replied, "I don't like projects. . . . Everybody in a poor economic bracket does not want to live in a project. They want a home so they can have gardens, with a yard for the kids to play in or have a dog or something of that nature." Asked what he desired for his children, whom he and his wife sent to the suburban East Cleveland schools because they considered the Cleveland public school system "inferior," Thorington responded: "A little better life than I had. A chance to go into business . . . [to] live in an integrated community, to attend an integrated church, an integrated school if they desire, [but] not forcibly." Looking back on his 1920s childhood in Cedar-Central, Thorington recalled: "I grew up in a neighborhood where there were Italian[s], there were Polish, there were Swedes—just about every nationality you could think of. We went to school together, we visited together, fought together, played together, and got along together. . . . But my children don't have this privilege. There are only two white families in the immediate area." "Now," he continued, "this is how far integration has progressed. I think we have lost ground."[2]

Thorington's testimony underlines the challenges as well as the lengths that upwardly mobile black families felt they had to go to maintain their economic security and ensure the prosperity of future generations. Two years before the hearing, the local Urban League chapter had prepared a report emphasizing the widening gulf between black and white Clevelanders, over an interval that saw robust and unprecedented economic growth in the country as a whole. The report enumerated the pervasive inequalities African Americans endured in employment, education, health care, and housing. It pointed out that residential segregation had actually increased between 1950 and 1963, with blacks overwhelmingly shut out of ongoing suburbanization and paying more for lesser-quality housing stock. True, black homeownership had increased by 124 percent over the course of the decade from 1950 to 1960, and overcrowding had subsided. Yet, despite such gains, segregation disadvantaged African Americans regardless of class, so if a person lived in one of the city's six overwhelmingly black neighborhoods in 1963, "the odds are 90 against 10 that this individual will be a Negro; will have attended a school 90 percent or more Negro; will make $1,400 less than his white counterpart; and will work in some semiskilled or unskilled jobs. If he is a professional, that is, a doctor, lawyer, nurse, school teacher, or social worker, chances are that he will be working for a government agency or for an all-Negro organization."[3]

Struggles for Access to Better Housing

Notwithstanding racial inequality and the debacle of urban renewal in Cedar-Central, which exacerbated housing scarcity, African Americans moved into new, previously all-white or overwhelmingly white areas of Cleveland's East Side in the three decades after World War II. As discussed, racial residential transition continued in Glenville and Mount Pleasant and proceeded far more rapidly in Lee-Harvard. Even so, expanding housing options came nowhere close to meeting the needs of the thousands of black residents trapped in overcrowded inner-city neighborhoods. Although the process of racial residential transition has been popularly termed "white flight," it generally unfolded on a block-by-block basis—despite white fears of "invasion" and "saturation." In an era of discriminatory lending, it could hardly have been any other way; financing typically became available only when African Americans established a majority presence in a given area. As the Urban League stated wryly in 1957: "We'll sell the Negro middle class clothes and middle class cars, but he must settle for lower class housing. He can have the white man's home only after all the newness and comfort have been wrung from it. . . . A Cleveland Negro's moving into a new house which was built for him or purchased directly from the contractor is an event of a frequency less than the birth of twins." Even when they did get mortgage financing, African Americans paid interest rates up to two percentage points higher than whites, according to Frank C. Lyons, attorney for the black-owned Harris & Adams Construction Co.[4] Notwithstanding such disadvantages, large numbers of black Clevelanders successfully arranged to move from more densely populated inner-city neighborhoods to outlying areas of the city during the 1950s and early 1960s, even before the advent of state fair housing laws and federal civil rights protections.

Despite nominal governmental involvement, racial discrimination impeded conventional financing for African Americans. As early as 1945, the Reverend Wade H. McKinney, pastor of the prestigious black Antioch Baptist Church and a Mount Pleasant resident, had complained bitterly to an audience of Kiwanis members, "Bankers refuse loans for home improvements in the central areas, although finance companies loan to Negroes on cars." That same year, the black owner of a prosperous florist shop tried to buy an apartment building in an exclusive white neighborhood and was refused a loan by the Cleveland Trust Co.—the largest bank in town, which, in the pre–New Deal era, had extended mortgages to some African American borrowers. On a 1951 visit, the nation's leading African American builder, Atlanta native W. H. Aiken, castigated local banks for withholding monies, threatening that "unless this situation improves very soon, I will personally head a group of Negro financiers who will put a half-million dollars or more into the Cleveland area and set up our own lending institution." Specific details as to how local banks made loan determinations emerged at 1953 hearings held to investigate discriminatory lending practices in the city, presided over by Housing and Home Finance Agency head Albert M. Cole. There, it came out that the Cleveland Trust Co. would not lend to African Americans on any street until it became 50 percent black-occupied. Not surprisingly, the bank made such determinations using what was later called "redlining," verified when a mortgage officer admitted such, but dismissed the significance of a charge made by the Cleveland Labor Committee for Human Rights that it "has a map of Cleveland showing occupancy of neighborhoods by race." Even in cases where banks did consider loans to blacks, only those with "one-third of an already too high purchase price" could qualify, another witness testified.[5]

The particulars of discriminatory lending were further documented by *Cleveland Press* reporter Julian Krawcheck in the process of conducting research for his 1956 "Negro Neighbors" series. Off the record, a senior vice president with Cleveland Trust told Krawcheck that the bank's policy did not permit financing the first black purchaser in a white neighborhood—"for public relations reasons"—but that the 50 percent threshold by that point was no longer insisted upon, or "any arbitrary statistical line." "We have [made] thousands of loans to Negroes and welcome their business, and we play square with them always," the bank officer claimed. However, Krawcheck was informed by Armond L. Robinson of the black-owned Quincy Savings & Loan Co. that "not a day passes that two or more Negroes don't come in and say they can't get a home-financing loan at one of the so-called white banks." Estimating that African Americans had some $65 million invested in white-owned banks and savings and loan associations, Robinson pointed out: "Ironically, when they wish to buy in a white area, these Negroes often find they can't borrow their own money." On the flip side, "any good credit risk could go into any good bank in Cleveland and get a mortgage provided that the house he wants to buy is in what is in the mind of the bank an accepted area for Negroes," as Urban League housing specialist K. C. Jones put it in 1958. Perhaps this explains the overly simplistic statement by Frank Baldau, head of the Community Relations Board (CRB), that "finance is not the major problem of the housing shortage of the Negro in any large scale, but rather that of land—building sites."[6]

The existence of the Quincy Savings & Loan Co. highlights the significance of limited but nevertheless crucial sources of alternative financing tapped by some black Clevelanders. In addition, Quincy's decisions on where to lend helped shape black loan access more generally. The company, originally founded by Czech immigrants in 1919, was purchased in 1952 by a group of eleven African American investors. Some five years later, its assets had mushroomed to $3.3 million, a nearly tenfold increase, and it had made loans on 1,200 private homes, most of them in Lee-Seville, West Park, Mount Pleasant, and Glenville, but some in Shaker Heights and even farther outlying suburbs such as Woodmere. It had invested money in Longwood Estates, a private urban renewal project built for lower middle-class blacks; and as revealed by Robinson, it had "worked with Negro groups who formed clubs to buy tracts of land for new homes," including a black builder, possibly Arthur Bussey, who "organized the purchase of an entire street for the construction of Negro housing." In 1953, the FHA approved Quincy for its mortgage insurance on loans, and in 1958 it was additionally authorized to extend home improvement loans backed by that agency. The company at the end of 1959 had Councilman Charles V. Carr as its vice president and general counsel, controlled over $5 million in assets, and besides home loans offered services including safety deposit boxes, money orders, and utility bill payment.[7]

Interviewed in 1958 for a study on local leadership, Carr felt certain that Quincy had "stimulated some of the other lending institutions to go forward," mentioning the posh houses and apartments on Ashbury Avenue and East Boulevard in Glenville as new areas "broken in" by its extension of loans. Surprisingly, considering his sponsorship of a fair housing ordinance, Councilman Carr refused to question Quincy or any other bank's prerogatives in making or refusing loans and denied that the company was "trying to do any race relations job" or "break down the barriers." Expecting that outsiders "couldn't understand why we did certain things," he insisted the institution's only responsibility was to its investors, and that applicants considered the "best risk" received priority without regard to "where a man is going to buy and whether his neighbors want him." Another Quincy board member, A. B. Heard, confirmed this approach, saying, "We don't care whether it's an area that has been penetrated [already] or not. We've made loans in the Central area and loans in the Heights area. . . . It's the individual, the merits of the individual and the appraisal of the property, that's what we're primarily concerned about." He even mentioned that a small number of white customers had deposits there and had been extended loans, and that Quincy—like all savings and loans companies— had to deposit with a commercial bank and therefore did business with Cleveland Trust, despite that institution's discriminatory record. Heard dismissed the suggestion that Quincy could threaten to place its deposits elsewhere, in order to leverage fairer lending policies. "We're not fighting a race war here, this is a business, a legitimate business, with permanent stockholders just like any other company. And they want to make money, that's what they invest for," he told the interviewer.[8]

Some black Clevelanders successfully obtained loans from out-of-town banks (reportedly a common strategy in Lee-Seville), or negotiated less conventional financing through black-owned insurance companies where they held policies. In fact, the city's black-owned Dunbar Life Insurance Co., founded in 1934 and named in honor of acclaimed African American poet Paul Laurence Dunbar, got involved in mortgage lending as early as 1941 when it formed the Bardun Mortgage & Investment Co. By 1947, Dunbar Life reportedly held some $275,000 in homes purchased by approximately one hundred black families. "Today, neighborhoods which have been predominantly white contain residences of Negroes," the *Call & Post* lauded the company's actions, most likely in reference to Glenville. As of 1949, it reportedly had "a considerable portion of its assets in FHA approved first mortgages." Further, "In many instances, where FHA guarantees are not available, Dunbar Life . . . extends mortgage loans to policyholders able to meet the requirements necessary for sound loans." Only one other black-owned insurance company in Cleveland lent on mortgages as of 1955. By 1957, Dunbar had offices around the state and held more than $1.6 million in mortgages, which represented half of its total assets. It claimed to have initiated just two foreclosures and took credit for placing deserving black families in such places as Milverton Road on the city's border with the upscale suburb of Shaker Heights.[9]

For many African American borrowers, however, the installment land contract remained the most widely available form of alternative financing. In the worst cases of abuse, this instrument embodied the ultimate early example of predatory lending. Land contracts often targeted desperate borrowers, and especially those of modest means, by offering a small down payment but high monthly rates; the lender, frequently a speculator, retained the deed until the contract was paid in full and could repossess the property on default of a single payment.[10] Until state law changed in 1961, these contracts did not even have to be publicly recorded—thus making legal recourse difficult for borrowers and allowing lenders to assess additional arbitrary fees and charges on the already-inflated monthly payments. All of these aspects made land contracts an extremely dangerous purchasing method for African Americans, who were vulnerable to job insecurity due to both employment discrimination and larger structural shifts in the economy.

Black Clevelanders were cognizant of the dangers of land contracts, and some sought assistance to address the abuse. As early as 1950, the *Call & Post* warned prospective buyers to resist the pressures of land contracts, cautioning them to have a lawyer inspect any financing arrangement before signing. The local NAACP sponsored a 1953 "emergency meeting" to raise awareness of the risks here, in the wake of cases like one in which "a woman had been offered a few hundred dollars for her land-contract equity in a home," which was then "sold for many thousands of dollars in a quick-turnover deal." In 1954, a rash of complaints led the Ohio Division of Securities to investigate such abuses, and the Cleveland City Council subsequently held hearings—at which one (white) councilman argued that land contracts were "causing the spread of slums to all parts of the city" since they inherently encouraged purchasers to subdivide houses into multiple living units to meet payments. Less than two months later, the city's Grand Jury Commission issued indictments in several cases where slick operators sold individual "apartments" in such subdivided properties to land contract buyers, on a supposed cooperative basis, at three to four times their actual value. Further details emerge from the two cases that subsequently went to trial. Bess and Sam Hirsch, Romanian immigrants and residents of suburban Cleveland Heights, had sold a house divided into eight suites on Glenville's Linn Drive, for an average of $6,000 per suite, but retained their stake in the property through the issuance of bogus "stock" as a condition of purchase. In addition, they padded the $51 monthly payments with "extras" that raised these as high as $83 or more. Another violator, Hirsch M. Silverberg, proffered contracts similarly offering buyers stock instead of the actual properties, on houses in Hough and on Glenville's Barrett Avenue. Assistant Prosecutor Fred Frey reported he had received "scores" of additional complaints as a result of the publicity generated by these cases, expressing surprise at the fact that these came not from Cedar-Central but overwhelmingly from Hough, Glenville, and Mount Pleasant.[11]

Complex and overlapping financial interests could result from the use of land contracts. For example, the Hirsch case had initially come to light because one of the black couples who bought bogus "stock" in the Linn Drive property were getting divorced, and the wife's lawyer looked into the ownership of this asset, which they presumed they were paying off. In a particularly convoluted 1958 case, a family of ten faced the loss of a Glenville home on which they had been paying the land contract for five years, but not through any failure to make consistent payments. Neal and Aline Hudson had signed the contract for the property on East 90th Street for $13,500, paying $2,000 down to the owners, who were also black, Lucious and Gloria Sturdivant. The Sturdivants had paid the previous owners $11,500, taking out an $8,800 first mortgage, but by 1954 had overextended themselves on other investments and owed creditors a total approaching $20,000. They therefore took out a second mortgage on the Glenville property for $4,000, with one Joseph Kline. In late 1956, Kline foreclosed on the Sturdivants and moved to evict the Hudsons. However, the Hudsons had already filed to have the original land contract rescinded and arranged to have their payments held in escrow by a court referee. This set up the matter of whether their land contract, toward which they had paid $6,000, or Kline's outstanding mortgage had first legal priority. The case was so complex and uncertain that the Hudsons retained a succession of nine different lawyers to represent them. Some African Americans actually bought investment properties on land contract, which could similarly generate legal complications. In 1945, Clara Mosley and Rhena Hudson went in together on a Glenville property, intending to use it as a "rooming house." Two years later they had a falling out, and Hudson sought to evict Mosley, whose name was on the land contract used to purchase the property. In response, Mosley filed suit to halt the eviction and asked that "an accounting be made to determine her share of the investment." Yet another Glenville resident, Dr. C. Alexander Simpson, was named in the original document as "agreeing to pay $3,400 in the event the women failed to meet the payment."[12]

In 1956, a federal housing official visiting Cleveland declared that "nowhere have I seen the land contract business practiced to the extent it is here," pointing out that, on paper at least, FHA loans could be had for a lower monthly payment than the typical land contract terms. And despite the dangers, many black families did successfully acquire homes this way. In fact, a 1959 newspaper feature on the expansion of black middle-class settlement in Cleveland reported that up to half of all black home purchases were likely made on land contracts. Although the state began mandating the recording of land contracts in 1961, Cleveland's urban renewal commissioner reported two years later that their continued use forced buyers to pay up to 35 percent in excess of fair market values, a side effect being that the city could not afford to acquire properties for its planned redevelopment projects. Despite an increased flow of credit into city neighborhoods as encouraged by the federal government after 1966, state and local legislators had still not solved the problem of land contracts at the end of the decade.[13]

No matter how black families financed homes in new areas, these purchases were likely to be controversial when they took place in formerly all-white neighborhoods. Notably, the previous examples of new housing built specifically for African Americans on vacant land at the urban periphery conveniently avoided this matter. Notions widely held by many whites associating black residency with neighborhood "decline" proved difficult to surmount, even in places like the farthest reaches of Southeast Cleveland, where upwardly mobile blacks, some of them living in brand-new housing, offered a visible refutation of this stereotype. Such notions proved widespread and resilient despite efforts to debunk them, such as contemporary research demonstrating no immediately observable impact of demographic transition on property values. At a 1953 meeting of the local American Jewish Committee chapter, where tensions surrounding the Stewart family's move into Lee-Harvard came up for discussion, guest speaker Charles Abrams, a nationally known housing reformer whose pathbreaking study *Forbidden Neighbors* was published two years later, found it necessary to reassure those in attendance that "the mere presence of Negroes in certain areas should not affect property values. . . . What does affect property values is the creation of the fear that values will be affected by the advent of Negroes in so-called white neighborhoods." Abrams correctly identified the real estate industry's designation of race (and earlier, ethnicity) as a negative factor, well-established by the 1920s, as the source of white fears about property decline.[14]

In 1956, the *Cleveland Press* ran an unprecedented five-part series by Julian Krawcheck that attempted to refute widely held notions linking racial residential transition and neighborhood decline. The series was apparently inspired by a letter to the newspaper's editor by Judge Perry B. Jackson, a black Mount Pleasant resident, in which he expressed concern over a one-sided fixation on "slum" neighborhoods inhabited by African Americans. Krawcheck conducted extensive interviews with local officials and both black and white residents in

Corlett, the far reaches of Mount Pleasant, eastern Glenville and Forest Hills, and the Ludlow neighborhood on Cleveland's border with Shaker Heights. Exuding an optimistic tone, the series emphasized that selling prices held steady and even increased in transitional neighborhoods; that upwardly mobile black residents not only maintained their properties, but sometimes did so even more meticulously than the whites they had replaced; and that polite, neighborly relations not infrequently developed between the remaining white residents and their new black neighbors once the initial discomfort waned. In reaction to this series, letters flooded in to the *Cleveland Press*, some from white residents disputing Krawcheck's conclusions and including hate mail.[15]

No one group can be credited with opening more housing for African American occupancy than black real estate brokers and firms, along with those white operators willing to sell to an African American clientele—an increasingly common possibility by the 1960s. In seeking to expand black housing options into previously all-white areas, such brokers often leveraged, whether implicitly or deliberately, prevailing stereotypes that associated racial residential transition and declining property values. And despite institutionalized discrimination in the mainstream real estate industry, changing demographics and black desire for better housing often proved sufficient to force turnover.[16] The *Call & Post* frequently reported on notable real estate deals, considering unprecedented access gained to new areas or particularly valuable acquisitions as a point of community pride.[17] Through the 1950s, the city's most successful African American real estate salesman was John W. Carmack, who had first gone into the business in 1925, not long after his arrival from Tuscaloosa, Alabama. Among his more notable transactions, Carmack arranged for the purchase of the Glenville Jewish Center by Cory United Methodist Church (of which he was a member) in 1946. He later became a director of Quincy Savings & Loan. Carmack's place was subsequently usurped by the younger Isaac Haggins, a native of New Bern, North Carolina, who came to Cleveland in 1954 and started a business in 1960 after a brief stint selling for another firm. With branch offices in Glenville and Mount Pleasant, Haggins's company by 1963 was the leader among the estimated fifty real estate firms with an exclusively black clientele, annually selling more than $6 million worth of property. In September 1964 alone, the Isaac Haggins Realty Co. sold homes worth a total of $826,800. Notably, in his 1961 series for the *Cleveland Press* on blockbusting, reporter Julian Krawcheck discovered that both Carmack and Haggins had reputations for using racially divisive and strong-arm sales tactics.[18]

Tensions remained between fair access to housing and, considering inadequate legal protections, what means were defensible to facilitate that access. African Americans were banned from the Cleveland Real Estate Board until late 1963 and, like black real estate brokers around the country, were barred from applying the legally trademarked title "realtor" to themselves—forcing them to coin the term "realtist."[19] Black real estate agents thus organized their own Cleveland Association of Real Estate Brokers (CAREB) in 1948, yet from the outset they expressed their interest in promoting "high standards of conduct in real estate transactions" and went on record as "pledged to the preservation of the residential character of a given area." At the same time, they sought to improve African American access to financing—and held discussions to that end with the local FHA race relations adviser, DeHart Hubbard, at their second annual seminar following the Supreme Court's landmark *Shelley v. Kraemer* decision from 1948. At a conference jointly sponsored by CAREB and the local Urban League in 1955, two years after the Wendell and Genevieve Stewart brouhaha in Lee-Harvard, those in attendance still divided over whether it was "ethical" to sell to a black buyer in the case of a white owner motivated by spite, with the Cleveland NAACP executive secretary expressing the view that "we will never achieve the 'good neighbor' background necessary to make 'open occupancy' a fact instead of a slogan by trying to slip in the back way."[20] In 1957, CAREB launched a listing service for its members, which they hoped would "improve relations in areas which are integrating and in some sections where ill-will has resulted from misinformation and over zealous sales pressures." Even so, CAREB astutely understood blockbusting as a symptom of a larger problem, stating in 1958: "Anti-discrimination laws in a community will tend to eliminate even the occasional temporary depression of values resulting from panic selling. They will disperse the demand of minority groups among all neighborhoods, and will, at the same time, eliminate areas of majority exclusiveness to which the panic-stricken may run." In late 1960, amid charges of unscrupulous sales tactics in the Corlett neighborhood, CAREB further agreed to reprimand any of its members engaging in such.[21]

The local Urban League also consistently advised on improving housing access for African Americans, notably in its 1956 launch of the "Three Year Project in Housing." In this early fair housing effort, the Urban League, with the backing of the local NAACP and black neighborhood organizations, including the Mount Pleasant Area Community Council, convinced a skeptical social service and philanthropic establishment to provide $10,500 in grant funding that enabled the hiring of K. C. Jones Jr.—who was white, incidentally—as director of housing activities. Its ambitious program sought to build constructive relationships with lending institutions, real estate interests, the building industry, and other interested agencies; to formulate "educational programs" to empower black homeowners, facilitate housing rehabilitation, and promote "good housekeeping standards"; and, finally, to create a "registry" of available properties for black families seeking housing. An elaborate pamphlet was distributed to skittish white neighbors. Ultimately the Three Year Project's impact was minimal, as it succeeded in placing only about two dozen African American families outside of the developing black expansion areas—this proved controversial enough prior to the passage of federal civil rights protections—with no apparent backlash. Directly anticipating the later "Operation Equality" project (1966–76) that the Urban League's national office sponsored in eight cities, including Cleveland, this local initiative, along with black councilman Charles V. Carr's push for a fair housing ordinance beginning in 1958, should revise assumptions—concerning Cleveland, at least—that the genesis of fair housing efforts was in the interracial liberal coalitions of the mid-1960s.[22]

But perhaps the most striking emphasis in the Urban League's "Three Year Program" was its imploring of black real estate brokers to conform to a code of sales conduct. In outlining its specific program in March 1957, the League urged: "1. Careful selectivity of Negro buyers in open occupancy areas; 2. Abandonment of 'scare' techniques and 'panic selling' in newly Negro-occupied areas; 3. A liaison between the realtists and the Urban League to facilitate our entering an area coincident with the move of Negroes into that area so that by personal contacts incidents may be kept to a minimum or eliminated; 4. A general urging of highest professional standards in sales techniques: a. Refrain from selling more than the buyer can afford; b. Refrain from suggesting code violations as a means of easing the financial burden; c. Call potential buyers' attention to any existing code violations as well as to zoning codes." Thus, even as the Urban League sought to protect the rights of African Americans to purchase homes without restriction, concerns about controversial sales techniques loomed large. By the end of that same month, Director of Housing Activities K. C. Jones had drafted a letter elaborating these points, addressing "all Brokers dealing in Real Estate sales to members of minority groups." The letter appealed to professional decorum and ended on a note of race pride, stating: "I am sure that you will agree that we need to do everything possible to show the community that a man's quality as a neighbor has no direct relationship to his color." As noted earlier, CAREB itself had sought to distance itself from blockbusting practices, so it is not surprising to see the Urban League reporting "progress in establishing a working relationship" with the organization as of 1960, including co-sponsoring a well-attended luncheon.[23]

The following year, CAREB officially renounced blockbusting tactics, but at the same time it asserted the right of black real estate agents to show houses anywhere and continued to identify discrimination and segregation as the underlying problems. Yet blockbusting still proved difficult to stop. Only 40 percent of Cleveland's black real estate brokers belonged to CAREB in 1961, which, according to then-president Albert Taborn, had just seventy-five members, a few of whom were white. Some in the industry were even more marginal, as Taborn explained: "There are probably 500 Negro 'brokers' who work at the Post Office and have a realty license but only 150 of us actually work full time at it." Furthermore, some white real estate companies, in seeking a share of this lucrative market, fostered blockbusting practices, not uncommonly employing black agents to promote panic selling.[24]

In their August 1961 series, titled "Is It Blockbusting?" *Cleveland Press* reporters Julian Krawcheck and Bill Tanner investigated the aggressive real estate sales techniques that often accompanied racial residential transition, which was well under way in Lee-Harvard at the time. These tactics invariably involved active solicitation in person, by telephone, by leafleting, or through the mail. The approach was systematic, targeting entire blocks, and utilized the "criss-cross" indexes in city directories, which listed a given street's occupants by name. At least one real estate agent admitted to searching out "For Sale by Owner" signs and pressuring such homeowners for their listings, or even approaching them with a prospective buyer. These schemes, all legal, grew increasingly controversial when they played upon white homeowners' racial fears in order to generate a rapid turnover, or when they leveraged the segregated, "dual" housing market to take unfair financial advantage of both white sellers and black buyers. Many whites reported being pressured with lines like "Sell now . . . the area will be black by spring . . . your property won't be worth anything . . . you know what Negroes do to a neighborhood . . . you don't want your children playing with colored kids, do you?" Many also suspected that African Americans, some specially picked to confirm white stereotypes, were being paid to drive through white neighborhoods, a phenomenon the residents termed "Black Sundays." While the authors and the *Cleveland Press* editors condemned these aggressive tactics as unscrupulous, they acknowledged the underlying prejudice and segregation that drove them. "The Negro long has been LEGALLY entitled to much more than he has been able to achieve, including the right to decent housing," wrote the editors, noting that only a fair housing market could resolve the dilemma. "Meanwhile," they suggested, "white homeowners can serve their own and the community's best interests by . . . brushing off, as forcefully as they know how, those who try to make them panic."[25]

But the series may have raised as many questions as it answered. While conducting their interviews, Krawcheck and Tanner found discrepancies among white homeowners' understandings of solicitation as "harassment," even on the same block. Many of the alleged blockbusters, in turn, denied acting unethically, pointing out that some such outcomes either had rational explanations or were out of their control. Several suggested that prospective black buyers exploring newly integrated neighborhoods could be coincidental. CAREB president Taborn opined, "You know a few cars driven by Negroes in a white area can look like a whole lot more than that to people who are jumpy." Some white residents' imaginations did indeed run rampant, as in one instance where the appearance of a black domestic in the neighborhood catalyzed a wave of rumors, and another where a group intending to pass out religious literature was mistaken for a group of new black residents. The executive director of the local Urban League, Shelton Granger, perceptively commented: "Whenever Negroes have bought attractive real estate, the charge is made that blockbusting tactics were used. . . . A lot of people talk [about] and deplore but don't define blockbusting. . . . To them, blockbusting is what happens whenever Negroes move into 'racially pure' neighborhoods like Shaker Heights."[26]

Readers' reactions to the series, and to a follow-up in August 1962, ranged widely. Some white readers found the coverage either enlightening or timely; similarly, one black reader wrote to say, "Your recent columns exposing the vicious Cleveland real estate racket is wonderful. . . . I am a colored woman but I have too much pride to condone the actions of a group of money hungry men . . . who sell the race down the river and pad their pockets." She even claimed to know people who had been paid to participate in "Black Sundays." In contrast, a black real estate agent dismissed the series as "a smear campaign against the real estate brokerage profession," while another reported that white residents had organized a phone harassment campaign against *her* for taking a listing in the easternmost, still-white reaches of Lee-Harvard. Others blamed Krawcheck and Tanner for exacerbating the situation, like one white homeowner who telephoned the *Cleveland Press* to complain: "1½ years ago he could have sold his house for $5000 profit. After our article last year, he could have sold it at neither a profit [n]or a loss to white buyers. Last week, he could have sold it at $1000 loss to a Negro family. Tonight, they called him and told him to drop his price another $1000." Similarly, another white seller claimed, "We had our house virtually sold" but then "the Negro buyer called today and said he would hold off until the rest of the series appears." Other responses were more blunt and angry: "Hope your [sic] satisfied ruining a neighbor hood [sic] where so many had bought homes to retire, I hope they surround you & I hope you drop dead. . . . Rats are more respectable." The *Call & Post* cautiously praised the 1961 series but ultimately concluded of blockbusting that "any real onus for its existence must be placed squarely in the laps of the forces that created it. . . . 'Blockbusting' hurts nobody as much as it does the poor devil who is forced to pay through the nose for the dubious advantage of occupying a white family's second-hand house."[27]

City officials were in a quandary over the issue. The CRB tentatively supported legal efforts to curb blockbusting in the neighboring suburbs of Shaker Heights and Warrensville Heights yet doubted the constitutionality of such measures. The *Call & Post*, too, soon concluded that such efforts were a "foolish waste of energy," suspecting exclusionary intent behind such legislation. In early 1963, Corlett councilman Anthony Pecyk introduced an ordinance to make intimidating sales tactics punishable by fines, after complaining that blockbusters enabled "negative people" to move into his ward—language that offended Mount Pleasant councilman Lowell Henry and quickly turned the session into a shouting match. Pecyk's proposed ordinance was shelved until the following October, despite his repeated attempts to free it. While the CRB supported such legislation, the Urban League by then was neutral, also having come to understand blockbusting as a symptom of discrimination. Meanwhile, local black real estate agents voiced their opposition and proposed that complaints instead be handled through the Ohio Real Estate Commission. The City Council's legislation committee deferred action on the bill in January 1965, bottling it up until May, when it narrowly passed in a 5–4 split along racial lines. African American representatives on that committee ultimately decided to oppose it when they were unable to attach an amendment banning retaliation against blacks moving into white neighborhoods or white homeowners selling to blacks. The City Council then voted to return the bill to the legislative committee, where it was preempted by the Ohio fair housing law passed later that year.[28]

Middle-Class Insecurity

Middle-class status among African Americans has historically been complex, extending beyond such straightforward indicators as income and occupation. That said, the arrival of working-class blacks in neighborhoods like Glenville, Mount Pleasant, and Lee-Harvard was an eventuality not always welcomed by their middle-class counterparts. Demographic transition worked as a complex dynamic, made possible by the housing opportunities that arose as more affluent whites sought new housing in farther outlying areas and other whites fled with the arrival of new black neighbors. For their part, African Americans—long constrained by the "dual" housing market in which generally only the oldest, most run-down houses had been available to them—rushed into these newly opened areas, despite often having to rely on unconventional and potentially exploitative financing. This cyclical process happened block by block, in neighborhood after neighborhood, despite different timing and dynamics in each case. The artificial yet severe housing shortage created by lending discrimination and white opposition to African American occupancy virtually guaranteed that any crack in the walls of segregation would soon give way to a flood—in turn ensuring that class relations in post-transitional black neighborhoods would constitute a crucial part of the story.

Middle-class black views of (and even prejudices toward) their less-fortunate brethren might seem initially reminiscent of the stereotypes white neighbors typically harbored. Some writers have drawn such parallels between resisting white residents and sometimes-resistant middle-class blacks—noting, for example, the supposed irony of African American opposition in the Lee-Seville neighborhood to a public housing plan, promoted by black mayor Carl B. Stokes in the late 1960s,[29] just fifteen years after white residents torpedoed a similar public housing project for the area. But attempted exclusion was but one approach taken by middle-class blacks—as was "black flight" to the suburbs, which became increasingly common by the 1970s, and which also seems to parallel the approach pursued by whites.

In neighborhoods like Glenville, Mount Pleasant, and Lee-Harvard, many black residents made an altogether different choice during the 1960s and 1970s—they stayed put despite conditions they felt were threatening the overall quality of life there. Without resorting to what some observers have derided as a "golden ghetto" formulation—the idea famously promoted by sociologist William Julius Wilson that segregation, by limiting black middle-class housing options, ensured that African American neighborhoods of an earlier era featured greater institutional depth and more individual examples of positive role models[30]—a considerable body of sociological research has emphasized that upwardly mobile African Americans, unlike their white counterparts, had fewer means to exclude working-class blacks or to flee, even if they wanted to.[31] Furthermore, most middle-class blacks had themselves felt the debilitating effects of discrimination, and many maintained links to older, inner-city neighborhoods, including relatives, business interests, or institutional affiliations (most commonly church membership). Thus we must explore the subjective impressions that upwardly mobile African Americans in areas of expanding black settlement formed during racial residential transition and its aftermath, as well as the structural factors operating on a citywide basis that helped speed the arrival of less-affluent black newcomers to the urban periphery.

While it is difficult to generalize African American perspectives on the process of demographic turnover, fragmentary and anecdotal evidence does suggest a sometimes contradictory tone of both disappointment and a kind of tongue-in-cheek sympathy for the choices of their white neighbors. One black woman shrugged off white departures from Lee-Harvard in 1962, observing, "With limited areas to move into, Negroes are bound to concentrate in those areas open to them. Besides, white families have a right to live where they want to. If they don't choose to live in a neighborhood with colored families, that is their right." She and her husband had been the first African American family to move east of Lee Road on Invermere Avenue. Another black resident of the area said he was well aware of white residents' motivations, including social pressure from friends to move and the specter of falling property values; he even echoed Jewish former residents' assertions that they had moved primarily to live near friends, although he believed incoming blacks found this explanation disingenuous. One woman related a humorous situation to the *Call & Post*, of seeing former white residents driving through Lee-Harvard after they claimed they were moving out of state. "They've been told so many different things about us," she ventured, "I think they're just confused." A former Mount Pleasant resident claimed African American homeowners like herself had considered the presence of white families on the street in the 1950s as a "stabilizing" factor; furthermore, she recalled that racial residential transition was a relatively smooth process in Mount Pleasant and even Lee-Harvard, mentioning that it was not uncommon for elderly white residents to live out their years in these neighborhoods. Another resident who grew up in the farther reaches of Mount Pleasant from the early 1950s on felt black residents had fully expected that whites would move out as soon as they could afford it.[32]

Indeed, a special 1965 mail-in census found that white families remaining in post-transitional Mount Pleasant, Glenville, and Hough had a lower average income and higher unemployment rate than their black neighbors. Meanwhile, a 1966 newspaper article on Lee-Harvard—where racial residential transition was winding down—quoted a white boy, the only one remaining in his public school class, who complained that black students "call us white trash."[33] In 1958–59, a YMCA project seeking to mitigate the anxieties accompanying population changes had discovered a group of white teenage boys living on the streets south of Miles Avenue and east of Lee Road, around Kerruish Park. As an area built up mostly by and for African Americans after World War II, these boys were said to be "from families that had to stay because of financial difficulties when the social change began to take place in the area." All were said to carry "strong negative attitudes toward the racial group which now occupies the area," to have "grouped together for social and protective reasons" against harassment by a group of black youths on the way home from school, and to have been "involved in many law violations." Their delinquency included overturning their African American neighbors' garbage cans, an act of racial animosity with possible symbolic significance (black-occupied premises as dirty and unkempt). The Mount Pleasant Community Centers in 1958 initiated an "Unreached Youth" project with the aim to accommodate "cliques" of similarly bad-behaved white boys whose "conversation depicted hatred of Negroes, parents, teachers, and the police." In 1965, three young white men burned stakes with kerosene-soaked towels attached—an apparent imitation of Ku Klux Klan cross-burning—in two black homeowners' backyards on East 187th Street, in the far eastern reaches of Lee-Harvard. Amazingly, the *Call & Post* uncovered that the area was "about 70% Negro," with an African American neighbor who had shooed the men off surmising they came from the "several white families who have not been able to sell their homes . . . and are bitter about it."[34]

At some point, the number of whites remaining in post-transitional neighborhoods diminished to the point that they became something of a curiosity. One woman growing up in Mount Pleasant during the 1950s fondly recalled her sole white playmate, "little white Janie," who lived two blocks north of her on Lambert Avenue. She also remembered some older white residents and mixed-race families living in the neighborhood, and in particular a widow who continued living there after the death of her black husband. Another man who spent his early years in the northern reaches of Mount Pleasant described whites as "peppered in" along Imperial Avenue and recalled two white playmates next door. He additionally remembered an older, "ethnic" couple with a grapevine who let his family pick the grapes every year to make jelly. Yet another woman growing up in Lee-Harvard in the early 1970s related that as a child, she had thought of whites mainly as "authority figures," particularly teachers and policemen, having personally encountered few others besides the occasional elderly resident. Whites revisiting these neighborhoods also took particular note of those remaining; one man was surprised to see a very old Italian resident, who lived in the top floor of a two-family house on East 143rd Street in Mount Pleasant, getting his weekly wine delivery in 1962.[35]

Ample evidence highlights the various "push" and "pull" factors that motivated upwardly mobile African Americans to move into newly opened neighborhoods. As an early promoter of fair housing efforts, the Cleveland Urban League sponsored a 1958 panel entitled "Where Will the Negro Live Tomorrow?" at which one commentator likely confounded prevailing expectations by stating that blacks moving into new areas were "looking for good housing with what money they have to pay. They aren't consciously, necessarily seeking integration as an experience but they learn that they can't find, in the distorted market conditions, the kind of dollar value . . . they're entitled to." In supporting a proposed fair housing ordinance two years later, the Urban League emphasized further: "Negro home buyers seek housing for the same reason as other home buyers. . . . We have not found a single example of Negroes seeking neighborhood integration for the sole purpose of interracial association. They seek to upgrade their housing circumstances and are lured by the same advertisements as others, because the middle income Negro is identical in his social and economic aspirations with his white counterpart." Significantly, and in what might have come as a surprise to panicky white homeowners, the Urban League additionally noted "a marked reluctance" on the part of prospective black buyers "to look at houses outside of established areas of Negro occupancy or on the fringes of such areas." These assessments were apparently based on their Department of Housing Activities' recent findings, that the twenty-one families they counseled from 1959 to 1960 were motivated by a desire for better schools, housing, shopping facilities, and public transportation—but that these families typically waited to move until the perceived disadvantages of their previous location outweighed the risk of white hostility in a new neighborhood. In 1963, an African American real estate broker who was the first to move into affluent Shaker Heights' Moreland section noted that some families in Lee-Harvard had "over-improved" their homes instead of buying in more expensive suburban areas where they could have afforded to live, but where they felt they would be unwelcome.[36]

The Urban League and other organizations involved in 1960s fair housing efforts repeatedly encountered this cautious tendency, in the face of which they sometimes expressed frustration that verged on blaming the victim. For example, Dr. Winston H. Richie, a black dentist and the chair of Fair Housing, Inc., remarked in 1965 following the passage of a state fair housing law: "While I realize that there are good reasons why a Negro family would move into a colored neighborhood, I do feel that those that do are less than 100% dedicated to solving the housing and school segregation problems that face us." In his view, "Any Negro who is interested in solving the problem of segregation should refuse to participate in it by buying a home in a colored area." True to his philosophy, Richie himself lived deep within Shaker Heights, in an otherwise exclusively white neighborhood. Around the same time, the Urban League approvingly noted the movement of African Americans into certain suburban areas, but added that diminishing "fears of the suburbs" had "not yet overcome the general reticence" of black families who did not want to be pioneers. Such reluctance thus acted "to increase Negro demand for housing in presently (already) integrated neighborhoods." The Urban League insisted that "until Negro leaders pioneer instead of meekly following, open housing cannot be a reality." In 1966, the Fair Housing Council likewise noted, "Negroes have not shown great initiative to seek compliance" with the new fair housing laws, at least "unaided and on an individual basis." "The result," they went on to say, "has been solid, expanding areas of middle-class Negro neighborhoods on Cleveland's east and southeast side, rapid turnover of homes from white to Negro families in transitional neighborhoods, few bridges of understanding or communication between the Negro and white communities and mounting dissatisfaction among younger Negroes."[37]

In striking contrast to such momentous assessments of what was at stake, black homebuyers offered mostly mundane reasons for buying in newly integrated areas. Consider how the previously quoted woman who bought on Invermere described her family's relocation from East 135th Street in Mount Pleasant to the Lee-Harvard area: "We had been looking for a suitable house for some time. . . . We looked at some houses in Shaker Heights but didn't like the talk going on about neighborhood resentment and we didn't like the prospect of paying big taxes. We just wanted an older-type brick house with an extra-size lot. . . . We weren't thinking of stirring up trouble by being the first Negroes in the area—we didn't even know that we were [the first]." Another "accidental" pioneer family moving in 1961 to Lee-Harvard from Mount Pleasant said they had decided two years earlier that "an apartment was no place to raise children" and that "we weren't greatly concerned with the racial angle at all. We simply liked the house . . . and saw that it met our needs and that the price seemed to be fair." The wife in another black family on the same block, having moved to Lee-Harvard the same year, explained that upwardly mobile

African Americans were typically seeking better housing and schools, and that "usually he [a black buyer] has a better chance to obtain these things in an integrated area, but he does not prefer an integrated neighborhood for any status-symbol reason." A. B. Heard, of Quincy Savings & Loan, claimed, "I don't give a darn if we all have segregated housing so to speak. . . . I think that we can have just as nice an area with all Negro people and if a white person wants to move in fine—if he doesn't want to move in, it's all right with me." He even expressed his wish that a "decent" black family would replace his noisy Italian neighbors. Further illustrating the sheer indifference some black residents could show on the question, yet another early mover into Lee-Harvard simply said: "I have no objection to an integrated area. It wasn't my intention to run white people out, and it isn't my intention now."[38]

Many African American families who moved into previously all-white areas risked serious economic setbacks, due to their being denied access to affordable credit or having to pay inflated prices.[39] In 1954, a representative from one black-owned construction firm reported that buyers of the firm's new houses in Mount Pleasant were being asked by banks to put down as much as 50 percent, if they were not outright rejected. "When people can't get decent financing," he pointed out, "they frequently are forced into land contracts and second mortgages which make their payments so high [that] they take in roomers and overcrowd the house." The effects of exploitative lending outlasted the process of racial residential transition itself, beyond the point when a neighborhood became solidly black, as noted in a 1961 report, which stated: "The Mount Pleasant Area is very burdened with the discrimination situation, and the consequences of Negroes moving into a formerly largely 'white' area." The racially discriminatory dual housing market also led to disproportionately high tax valuations on overpriced houses bought by African Americans. Glenville residents campaigned from 1953 to 1956 to reduce these taxes, but to no avail. Homeowners there paid up to $50 per foot of lot frontage, compared to as low as $5 in some of the newest outlying (and often racially exclusive) suburbs like Broadview Heights.[40] The economic insecurity of upwardly mobile black homeowners comes through in an anecdote from a woman whose family was among the first wave of African Americans to move onto Westview Avenue in the Lee-Harvard neighborhood in 1961. Knowing full well the financial sacrifices such families had made to live there, one of their former neighbors back in Mount Pleasant teasingly asked, "Still eating them steaks out in Lee-Harvard?" In the 1940s, the sumptuous homes along East Boulevard in Glenville were nicknamed "Oatmeal Row"—a barb that could apparently also be applied to outlying sections like the Kinsman Heights cluster in Mount Pleasant—suggesting that their well-off new black inhabitants could afford little else to eat after making their house payments.[41]

Although the Urban League claimed that black access to credit improved significantly after 1960, discrimination in lending remained a formidable obstacle. In 1964, the NAACP sent letters to all Cleveland's major banks demanding they commit to equalizing loan access and threatening protests should they refuse to comply. But discriminatory lending continued and, paired with income inequality, effectively shut African American buyers out of many Cleveland suburbs—as Operation Equality noted, with frustration, in 1967. Credit starvation lingered even in post-transitional, black middle-class city neighborhoods. Out of ten Lee-Harvard real estate agents interviewed in 1971, all but two said 90 percent or more of their clients were unable to get conventional bank loans and thus depended on FHA and VA backing. Such government-sponsored lifelines became critical for black borrowers as soon as the original, race-based restrictions were lifted in the early 1950s. Just how critical was revealed by the 1967 uproar catalyzed when the FHA reclassified Glenville and about 10 percent of Mount Pleasant as "high risk" for lending purposes, replacing favorable "203" type mortgages with the shorter-term, smaller-limit "221" type. In response, beleaguered homeowners working through the Urban League prevailed upon Glenville councilman Leo Jackson, chair of the City Council's Community Development (formerly Urban Renewal) committee. Thankfully, a subsequent City Council resolution passed against the change, and entreaties to the FHA prompted a restoration of the discontinued loan programs. The following year, however, Jackson found himself facing a related issue: the loss of insurance coverage by home and business owners in such areas.[42]

Despite these economic hardships, neighborhoods like Glenville, Mount Pleasant, and Lee-Harvard became, during the first two postwar decades, in the words of one observer, "communities of black homeowners." Accompanying this outcome, average levels of educational attainment rose in Mount Pleasant from 1950 to 1960, particularly college education, which jumped by nearly 60 percent. This was both a percentage and numerical increase, as compared to the city as a whole—which experienced "a negligible percentage gain, but actual loss in numbers," during this period. The occupational structure also changed, with increases in professional and service jobs, categories typical for upwardly mobile African Americans at the time. Alongside these were decreases in the numbers of clerical and sales workers, skilled tradesmen, foremen, and factory operatives, all categories where whites predominated because job discrimination—or its residual effect in the guise of low seniority—seriously disadvantaged blacks. Data collected on post-transitional Lee-Harvard some ten years after the fact yielded similar results: "As middle class blacks moved in[,] there was an increase in educational level, with larger numbers having completed at least one year of college. Similarly the influx of blacks was accompanied by a large increase in the number of residents employed as professional and technical workers. The general pattern was middle-class blacks replacing working class whites." In 1959, those same African Americans—who at that point were still limited to the section west of Lee and north of Harvard—were of inordinately high status, with a high representation of "professional and clerical workers, as well as school teachers and skilled workers." Newspaper reports consistently found that initial black buyers in the area had not just maintained their properties, but in fact raised the standards of upkeep; and in 1964, the Cleveland Area Church Federation asserted in a research study that the comparatively high status of Lee-Harvard black residents correlated with feelings of "jealousy" among the area's remaining whites. In 1967, the area claimed to be "unique in the high percentage of professional folk who make their homes in Lee-Harvard, doctors, lawyers, pharmacists, dentists, teachers, engineers, social workers, ministers, school principals and many others."[43]

Racial residential transition also brought initial increases in average income,[44] although the considerations here are more complex. While the negative effects of job discrimination and lack of seniority have already been noted, additional factors disadvantaged even the highest economic strata in African American communities, underlining the fact that income inequality characterized blacks as a group, if not always as individuals. Black professionals and business owners were historically relegated to serving their own communities; as seen in the case of Morris Thorington Jr., whose testimony opened this chapter, since these were inordinately low-income, their clientele had less money to spend. Also, squeezed by lending discrimination and forced to buy at artificially inflated prices in a dual housing market, African Americans typically had to devote a larger proportion of income toward housing costs. Finally, inflation makes computing price comparisons over time more difficult. In Mount Pleasant, for example, median income rose from $3,506 in 1950 to $5,850 in 1960—an increase of more than $1,000 beyond what would be expected considering the inflation rates for that decade, but not nearly as much as it might look at first glance. A 1969 "feasibility study and market analysis" for the area noted that the median income for Mount Pleasant rose again between 1960 and 1965, to $6,504—but calculated that this was a gain of only $250 with the 1960 dollar value held constant. Placing this figure in the larger context, Mount Pleasant's 1965 median income was far above the average for Cleveland blacks, which stood at $5,489; however, it lagged behind the $7,459 figure for whites living in the city, and even the city median of $6,895. And considering the city and suburbs together, Mount Pleasant's median income as a percentage of Cuyahoga County's declined from 98 percent in 1950, to 89 percent in 1960, to 75 percent in 1970.[45]

In a distinctly different trajectory, Lee-Harvard's median income saw a decline from 133 percent of the city median in 1950 to 116 percent in 1960, as the highest-earning white families moved on to the suburbs. The figure subsequently rose again, however, to 127 percent in 1970, bearing out the previously quoted assessment of "middle-class blacks replacing working class whites." The Urban League recorded similarly dramatic upward income shifts for Lee-Harvard families between 1960 and 1970, pushing the area into the eighth-ranked decile (tenth) for the county as a whole; the Urban League further noted: "Of the county's richest families, Cleveland has only one tract in each of the two top tenths. Over half of the Cleveland families in the richest three tenths of the county's census tracts live in the Lee-Harvard-Miles area." A similarly high ranking was attached to the eastern portion of Lee-Seville around Kerruish Park, noted earlier as having been built up in the 1950s by developers like George Dubin, with new homes available to blacks from the very beginning. Largely as a result of this portion, Lee-Seville's median income as a percentage of Cuyahoga County's rose from 90 percent in 1950, to 97 percent in 1960, to 104 percent in 1970. Taken together, Mount Pleasant, Lee-Harvard, Lee-Seville, and Corlett formed a compact cluster that Operation Equality targeted for special recruiting attention in its suburbanizing fair housing efforts of the mid-to-late 1960s: "This, the South-East Office area . . . is reported to be the *highest income residential area in Ohio where Negroes live* and one would assume the higher educational standing or rating. Median income is thought to be $7–8,000.00 per year."[46]

But again we must not lose sight of the fact that even upwardly mobile black families in these Southeast Cleveland neighborhoods confronted economic insecurity, of which observers made recurring note. A 1961 Mount Pleasant study bemoaned the rise of "latch-key children," resulting from "the inflated costs of houses or rents, [that] require both parents to work to stay solvent," while the city planning department, in surveying the community soon thereafter, noted, "Some incomes are often supplemented by minor members of the family." In a 1962 interview, a new black resident of Lee-Harvard defended dual-income couples and resisted the suggestion that her children "suffered" as a result of her career: "It is true that the average colored man doesn't make enough to buy a house on one salary. It usually takes two salaries to lead a half-way decent life. For instance, I work as a nurse six hours a day because I want to help build a better life for us and a better future for our children. But I see that the children are looked after when I'm not at home." A 1965 report on Lee-Harvard further emphasized the prevalence of working husbands and wives, with the assessment that such families had "over-reached themselves economically to obtain better housing." And a 1969 grant request for a summertime youth employment program in Lee-Seville emphasized the economic urgency faced by families in such positions, stating: "Probably a majority of the married women in the area work outside of the home. Many men work at two or more jobs. A large portion of the youn[g] people to be served by this program depend on summer earnings to help pay for school expenses and clothing and some need to help supplement their family income." This sentiment proved durable, as expressed by Harvard Community Services Center director and longtime resident Rubie J. McCullough in 1985: "My concept of middle-class is that my husband works and I have time to go volunteer at a hospital or something. . . . [But] in this neighborhood, middle-class means everybody works."[47]

While middle-class black families living in these neighborhoods may have adapted to precarious economic circumstances, they still had to deal with the effects of larger, structural forces operating on a metropolitan scale. Despite the passage of federal civil rights legislation in the mid-1960s, the ongoing prevalence of lending discrimination, as well as white reluctance to live alongside African Americans, ensured that the artificial housing shortage for blacks would continue and that race-related economic disparities—rooted in a legacy of employment discrimination and the contracting industrial base of the local economy—would combine to make work scarcer and push affordable housing beyond the reach of many black Clevelanders. These realities assured that not long after the first wave of upwardly mobile black families moved into a new area, less prosperous families would make their appearance. While areas like Mount Pleasant and Lee-Harvard continued as middle-class strongholds in the 1960s, troubling trends materialized in the form of rising unemployment and a concomitant increase in the percentage of neighborhood residents on welfare. In 1961, for instance, Mount Pleasant's Aid to Dependent Children rate was only 19.2 families per thousand. Yet just four years later, in 1965, that figure had tripled, to a rate of 59.6. By then, 15 percent of Mount Pleasant families lived below the poverty level, compared to 20 percent in Glenville and 25 percent for the city's black population as a whole; this figure rose to 18 percent in 1970 for Mount Pleasant, smaller than Glenville's increase to 31 percent, but still worrisome.[48]

Some of the new African American arrivals in outlying neighborhoods were recent migrants from the American South, either directly or by way of older, inner-city areas. Hopeful Southern migrants, both black and white, continued coming to Cleveland and other Northern cities during the 1950s and 1960s before the full extent of the region's industrial decline became apparent.[49] The city's NAACP branch actually formed an "In-Migration Committee" in 1956 and sponsored an "emergency conference" in March 1957, out of which the Cleveland Citizens' Committee on Newcomers arose with the mission of determining how to "best meet the challenge of new arrivals and the subsequent problems of adjustment associated with them." The Mount Pleasant Community Council (MPCC) was at the forefront of the many social service agencies and community organizations participating in these efforts, working hard to be "sensitive to the problem and particularly as it affects housing." At the MPCC's 1957 annual meeting, local Urban League director Arnold Walker urged members to reach out to the recent migrants in their midst who "bring their disadvantages with them . . . not only of poverty but also lack of education and training." In 1958, the *Call & Post* correlated recent Southern arrivals with the proliferation of storefront churches in Hough, Glenville, and Mount Pleasant. Despite these perceptions, expansion neighborhoods like Mount Pleasant and Glenville seem to have been a secondary destination for Southern migrants. The 1960 census revealed that only 8 percent of those Mount Pleasant residents who had moved into the neighborhood since 1955 originated from outside the Cleveland metropolitan area; as for Glenville, the figure was even smaller, at 6 percent. Research conducted in 1967–68 did find larger numbers of Southerners living in Hough and to a lesser extent in Glenville, although they actually proved better economically adjusted than their Northern-born counterparts.[50]

Regardless of the actual scope of the phenomenon, reform-minded black observers continued to express concerns about the effects of in-migration over the next decade. Some, like Municipal Court judge Perry B. Jackson—a Mount Pleasant resident—advocated a more tolerant approach involving welcome committees and benign resocialization to eliminate supposedly dysfunctional, rural-origin behaviors, but others advocated more forceful measures and advanced strongly moralistic interpretations. For example, Antioch Baptist Church pastor Rev. Wade Hampton McKinney—who also lived in Mount Pleasant—saw in-migration as closely linked to rising crime rates and advocated stricter policing. Along similar lines, Glenville councilman Leo Jackson rebutted Judge Jackson by suggesting that more stringent law enforcement would accomplish better results than resocialization. Councilman Jackson did share the view, however, that certain supposedly rural Southern behaviors relating to garbage disposal, loitering, noise, child rearing, and sex were detrimental in an urban setting. After detailing these in a 1961 speech, the councilman concluded: "It is time we developed more assertive and aggressive programs in the [social] service agencies and institutions of the city. Not to force compliance on the in-migrant, but at least to win confidence and participation." Harvard Community Services Center director Rubie J. McCullough's 1966 articulation of the need to teach families "how to live in a new urban environment," in conjunction with reform efforts in Lee-Harvard, as well as similar pronouncements by the Urban League's Housing Committee the following year, illustrate how "urban adjustment" continued as an undercurrent of reformist agendas through the late 1960s.[51]

The city's extensive urban renewal program also drove these population flows. Although redevelopment almost exclusively targeted Cedar-Central, population displacement associated with the various projects reverberated throughout areas of African American settlement on the city's East Side. As early as 1952, 150 Glenville residents had come to interrogate the city's redevelopment chief, Richard V. Hopkins, at a meeting sponsored by the Glenville Area Community Council. Someone there noted it was unlikely that displacees would be able to afford rents in the redeveloped area, giving them no choice but to "try to move into the attics and basements of the houses already over-crowded in Glenville and Mount Pleasant." Later that year, Rev. McKinney condemned the city's plans before the interracial Ministerial Association as sounding "more like slum transference than slum clearance." In 1957, a black field representative with the city's Urban Redevelopment Division expressed alarm that residents relocated from the Longwood project site were crowding into Hough, Glenville, and Mount Pleasant, neighborhoods already "bulging at the seams and bringing new substandard housing." Although only 23 of the 409 families displaced by the Longwood project were known to have definitely relocated in Mount Pleasant (122 were unaccounted for), social service providers in the area did mention, as of 1960, "a shift in recent years, with lower income Negro families coming in from [the] Central Areas." They noted further that "some of these families and their children may bring problems with them that they have developed in other sections of the city." In 1961, another report claimed that many families displaced from rental housing in Cedar-Central "have been forced to buy, and buy at highly inflated rates in the Mt. Pleasant Area." The following year, Councilman Lowell Henry blamed overcrowding and the subsequent deterioration of housing stock in one section of the neighborhood on the arrival of typically larger families displaced by urban renewal. He did emphasize, however, that absentee landlords did not adequately maintain the apartments into which these families moved.[52]

A 1963 newspaper report cited urban renewal as a significant factor driving racial residential transition in Lee-Harvard, and by 1965, the Urban League's Stabilization Committee named "pressure of urban renewal relocations on Mt. Pleasant and Glenville" as chief among the reasons behind an incipient demand among black Clevelanders for homes in the suburbs. In 1964, Leo Jackson proposed that relief workers be required to inspect the properties into which urban renewal displacees planned to move, before reimbursing moving expenses. And in 1967, as the head of the City Council's urban renewal committee, Jackson threatened to withhold funding and thereby sink the entire University-Euclid project—planned for the troubled Hough neighborhood immediately adjacent to Cedar-Central—on the grounds that "the urban renewal program is undermined in the minds of people throughout the city because of the adverse impact it has on other areas," particularly Glenville and Mount Pleasant. Yet it is important to note that the displacements associated with urban renewal seem to have had more of an indirect effect, at least on Southeast Cleveland. Of the first batch of residents leaving the Dike project site in 1966, only 10 percent moved to Mount Pleasant and only 2 percent moved to Lee-Harvard; the majority, 54 percent, actually remained within Cedar-Central. In fact, of 1,027 families displaced from five different urban renewal projects, only 55 (5 percent) went to Mount Pleasant, only 33 (3 percent) went to Lee-Harvard, only 14 (1 percent) went to Corlett, and only 5 went to Lee-

Seville. Even in Glenville, this influx was insubstantial, at just 132 families (13 percent).[53]

In effect, urban renewal further decreased the overall supply of housing available to African American Clevelanders, triggering a chain reaction of migration into middle-class black neighborhoods, not necessarily by those directly displaced, but by others experiencing the resultant overcrowding and deteriorated living conditions. Newcomers to Mount Pleasant in 1964, for example, originated not just from Cedar-Central but also from Hough and Glenville, where, it was claimed, property values had sunk. The acting director of the Urban League similarly commented on the 1962 transition in Lee-Harvard this way: "One factor . . . is the fact that many Negro buyers in H[arvard]-S[cott]-L[ee] are families buying their second homes, having become dissatisfied with the original homes they bought in older sections of the city." A former black resident has written about his parents' decision to move to Lee-Harvard: they were "alarmed at the deterioration of the Mount Pleasant neighborhood . . . as it filled with black newcomers from the inner city." In perhaps the most nuanced analysis of urban renewal's effects, however, a 1967 grant application discussed the contradictory trends at work. First, the insufficient relocation efforts of the urban renewal department meant that "families which cannot afford the rent being charged for Mt. Pleasant properties must [nevertheless] move into the community for lack of decent housing in other parts of Cleveland." But at the same time, "Other persons and families move from urban renewal areas to Mt. Pleasant because of declining property values. Property values in this community have remained stable."[54]

Black leaders and some residents in expansion areas were highly cognizant of developments in older neighborhoods, which sometimes took on cautionary significance in their telling. *Call & Post* editor William O. Walker lamented in 1964: "The Glenville area in Cleveland at one time was the hope of Negroes who wanted a decent place in which to live. . . . Today, Glenville is in the throes of becoming a slum ghetto. E. 105th Street, its main artery, resembles very much [Cedar-Central's] Scovill Ave. in years gone by." In 1966, Lee-Harvard Community Association (LHCA) president Rubie J. McCullough warned, "We have all the problems of Hough and Glenville . . . on a smaller degree but growing fast." Assistant School Superintendent James R. Tanner, who was black, similarly told a meeting of the LHCA: "Other areas—I'll not mention names— were once model communities. They are not today. The main reason for their deterioration was their failure to maintain community standards." McCullough additionally wrote in a 1967 letter that "many people moved to Lee-Harvard from inner-city areas to escape these [various] problems only to find them rapidly catching up with them again." That same year, Cleveland Urban League director Ernest Cooper reported at its annual meeting: "We are doing the same thing in Glenville and Mt. Pleasant as we did in Hough—nothing. We

Houses on Glenville's East 107th Street, 1964. Many of Glenville's remaining middle-class black homeowners continued to maintain their houses admirably, even as others moved away when confronted by larger structural forces. (Courtesy of the *Cleveland Press* Collection, Cleveland State University Library)

are creating new Houghs." One Mount Pleasant resident wrote to Mayor Carl B. Stokes, also in 1967, declaring: "The people in the Mt. Pleasant area want to do their part to help save the inner city from decay, and are prepared to take proper action to help prevent the erosion of their home and property. They are willing to make an effort to forestall this area from become [*sic*] another Hough or Glenville slum." At a 1968 City Council meeting, Leo Jackson's remark that "we are now at the point where Glenville and Mt. Pleasant are going through the very things that the Central and Hough neighborhoods went through" drew a pledge from Mayor Stokes to "use every tool available to help the areas of Glenville, Mount Pleasant, and the Lee-Harvard [area] remain stable." And in a similar evaluation, a 1969 grant application warned: "Mt. Pleasant's condition is very similar to that which existed in the now deteriorated communities fifteen to twenty years ago."[55]

Such assessments of Cleveland's various black middle-class neighborhoods return us to the question of perception and, by extension, whether the noteworthy flow of Glenville and Mount Pleasant black families into Lee-Harvard during the 1960s was "preemptive" in nature. A grant proposal from the end of the decade touched on this issue while conveying uncertainty about the neigh-

Abandoned Apartment Building on Glenville's East 106th Street, 1964. Multifamily housing often deteriorated rapidly as landlords evicted white tenants so they could rent units at exorbitant prices to African Americans and stopped investing in routine maintenance. This property sat less than two blocks from the houses on East 107th Street. (Courtesy of the *Cleveland Press* Collection, Cleveland State University Library)

borhood's future: "Mt. Pleasant is at the critical stage: the concrete conditions of decline are still on a scale limited enough that the significant strengths of the area should, or at least could, stop the steady drift toward deterioration. . . . What residents think is going to happen is as important as what concrete conditions indicate. On both scores Mt. Pleasant is at the stage where more is working in its favor than against it. But the balance is much closer to shifting than most suspect." Interestingly, however, while one-half of a group of thirty-nine Mount Pleasant residents surveyed in late 1967 admitted that they had considered moving, and one-third seriously so, "only a few mentioned wanting to get out of [a] declining area." Rather, they cited changing family needs and the attractiveness of newer housing and schools in Lee-Harvard or the suburbs as motivators, leading the interviewers to conclude: "It used to be that Mt. Pleasant was one of the few areas where middle income Negroes could find good housing. Now the range of choice is much wider as other areas open up. There would be a natural tendency for people to move out even if no deterioration was taking place."[56] Mapping the previous addresses of residents living on Talford Avenue—the first street in Lee-Harvard to integrate—in 1970

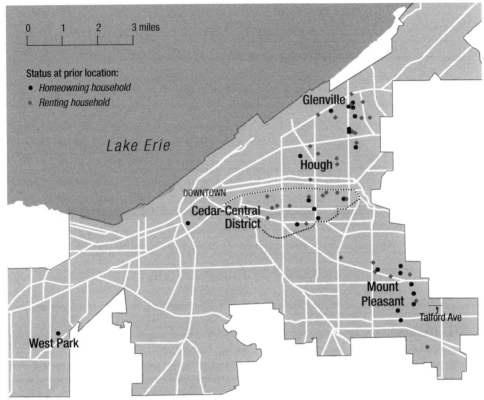

Map 5.1 Prior Location of Families Moving onto 15500–16499 Blocks
of Talford Avenue, 1957–1970
Sources: *Cleveland City Directories, 1957–70* (Cleveland City Directory Co.).

reveals that more than half came from Glenville or Mount Pleasant, and that
nearly a third had previously owned homes in those neighborhoods (Map 5.1).

Former residents were split on the question of relative status distinctions associated with these areas. A woman whose family moved to Lee-Harvard from
Mount Pleasant in 1961 claimed that Lee-Harvard's newer housing was considered "better" than Mount Pleasant's, that the neighborhood was safer, and that
shopping facilities were more ample and modern. A man whose family made
a similar move the very same year stated: "Lee-Harvard was clearly a step up
from Mount Pleasant. You had a sense that you were on the next level up."
Others, however, thought of Lee-Harvard's "matchbox" colonials and ranches
as small and cramped, and best suited for retirees. They pointed out that both
neighborhoods eventually experienced population influxes from "down the
way," and observed that one did not have to live in Lee-Harvard to take advantage of its shopping facilities. One former resident who grew up on East 154th
Street, at the eastern edge of Mount Pleasant, considered her neighborhood

and Lee-Harvard as a contiguous whole. Because of how the school districts were drawn, she attended Gracemount Elementary and Charles Eliot Junior High School with children who lived in Lee-Harvard proper.[57]

Considerable intraracial class and cultural conflicts also accompanied the ongoing process of African American influx in outlying, expansion neighborhoods. Block clubs on two virtually all-black streets in Glenville during the 1950s prioritized the nuisances of loose dogs and "chickens in yards," a working-class subsistence practice. As early as 1948, the *Call & Post* reported disapprovingly on one Glenville family's tendency to hang laundry on the front porch and "the advent of non-descript fences" in the neighborhood, motivating a defensive telephone call from one homeowner. Neighborhood groups met regularly to address "problems" such as destructive and rowdy behavior, "loud talking," and a "lack of intelligible speech in the home." Numbers gambling, loud parties, "smoke shops," bootleg liquor sales, and teenage fights were becoming commonplace in Glenville, according to both residents and observers. A 1951 editorial by W. O. Walker asserted that Glenville and Mount Pleasant were "the residential show places for our people in Cleveland," and "for selfish reasons, then, everything should be done by them [homeowners] to preserve and protect their investment." While he saw overcrowding as the root of the problem, some of Walker's critiques were more specific: "Simple things like observing the parking laws, dressing decently when going to [the] store; keeping lawns and trees in good appearance; painting and keeping property up, are not as easily learned by some people as you would think. Many people have the very bad habit of putting discarded overstuffed furniture on the front porch, or littering up the back yard with useless junk; or putting garbage and rubbish together, thus creating a health menace." In a 1959 column, F. V. Tyler counseled residents to confront those who did not respect their neighborhood's appearance: "For the owner whose lack of respect for others is so gross—who refuses to repair his gutters, remove and replace rotten clapboard, repair termite infested window sills or replace broken windows—should not be permitted to go unchallenged and you, if necessary, should take the initiative yourself." On a lighter note of disapproval, someone's decision to plant a vegetable garden in their Lee-Harvard front yard was ridiculed in a 1962 installment of the newspaper's "Cleveland Confidential" column.[58]

For some of the reasons mentioned earlier, class status among African Americans did not historically link directly to more measurable indicators like income and occupation, although these certainly carried weight. Due to discrimination that severely restricted African American access to many fields of employment, certain jobs that would be considered "low status" in the society as a whole historically took on relatively higher status in black communities. Middle-class women taking on work, even of a menial sort as domestics or laundresses, could generate the extra income needed for upward mobility; and in dual-income families, a wife who worked as a teacher and a husband who worked as a manual laborer would generally qualify as middle class.[59] Yet divisions persisted, as noted by participants in a 1958 race relations workshop on class and "caste" among African Americans: "People may live near each other and seem to feel comfortable together, but in many cases, they have different value systems in what they think is right and wrong and what they are taught in institutions, churches, and homes." Furthermore, "We often find people who have escaped from one class to another but who find they haven't measured up or don't belong. They have left behind all that they are accustomed to and will often return to the old neighborhood to visit friends. These people often behave in a way different from the class group in which they live." One black former Mount Pleasant resident thought the distinction lay not in where a person or family lived, but whether or not they were "decent" in their lifestyle and habits. Another thought middle-class blacks were simply those who "kept going forward, who knocked on the door until they got in." And yet another said more cryptically that Mount Pleasant blacks had considered theirs to be a middle-class community, because "we have different reasons [other than income] to define ourselves in a certain way."[60]

Late in 1956, a grant proposal by the Mount Pleasant Community Centers was already noting, besides the fact that whites were moving out, that "the area is also changing from one socio-economic group to another; middle class, lower middle class, and upper lower class Negroes are moving into the area. There are evidences of subtle conflicts between these class groups, each with a different set of values." Observers noted feelings of "insecurity and non-acceptance among many of the newcomers" to the neighborhood, some examples of which African American board members of the Mount Pleasant Community Centers discussed explicitly in late 1960. "The newcomers bring a different set of values," stated director Murtis H. Taylor, "[and] it shows in maintenance of property, yards, garbage disposal, aggressive behavior, attitude toward learning, [and] attitude toward authority." Another board member offered his personal experience, mentioning how "we live in a nice building but there is noise and low standards on behalf of other tenants" and expressing frustration that "we can't escape [the] pressure brought about by ghetto living." Articulating the predicament of middle-class blacks whose housing alternatives were limited, he tellingly added: "If we were white we would [just] move." Making the same point more forcefully, a black Glenville homeowner had responded to Cleveland Press reporter Julian Krawcheck's 1956 "Negro Neighbors" series by noting: "The normal solution for a dissatisfied resident, when conditions are not satisfactory, is to move elsewhere. Is that our answer? Could we move to Beachwood, Shaker Heights, Parma, or any of the neighboring suburbs without fear of bombs and other threats on our lives and property?" She concluded that "we in the neighborhood have accepted the fact that we are living in a Negro Ghetto. . . . Yet, in view of all this, we have sacrificed to enhance the beauty of the area."[61]

Although some residents did move out, neighborhood organizations and social service agencies placed considerable emphasis on resocializing incoming residents as a sort of alternative to upwardly mobile departure. In 1960, the Mount Pleasant Community Centers cited a street club that had contacted them for help in dealing with a group of unruly elementary schoolchildren "who were out late at night—noisy, destroying property, arrogant in their attitude toward authority, fighting and loitering." Noting that these children's families "had come from an area where standards and values were different from the middle class area in[to] which they had moved," the Community Centers concluded: "These children are not emotionally disturbed but need help in becoming integrated into their new community." By way of a solution, the agency hoped "to help the children adopt new neighborhood habit patterns through working with them in groups," and to recruit the children's parents for membership in the street club. Similar culture clashes characterized other middle-class black neighborhoods, as suggested by a 1967 Lee-Harvard Community Association pamphlet, which spelled out that "A GOOD NEIGHBOR: 1. Keeps his sidewalks clean in the winter. 2. Sprinkles his lawn and not his neighbor's or sidewalk pedestrians. 3. Does not entertain the neighborhood with his radio, television or record player. 4. Does not park his car in front of his neighbor's house overnight. 5. Does not start his lawn mower before 9:00 on Sunday morning."[62]

Socialization to new behavioral norms could be coercive. The language introducing a 1962 camping excursion planned by the Mount Pleasant Community Centers—for boys having behavioral issues in the local schools—stated outright: "During the camp, strict middle-class standards will be observed in regard to manners. The group members will practice and will be taught the meaning of proper behavior, of cleanliness, of politeness, table manners, etc." Considering this approach, it is perhaps not surprising that when unemployed high-school-age youths were asked what sort of people they "disliked," in conjunction with another such program the following year, "The majority indicated people who thought they were on a higher level, or people who tried to be what they were not." With no apparent irony, the Mount Pleasant Community Centers went on to state: "It is interesting to see how many of them feel persecuted by some system or group of people."[63]

Not all observers were so relentless in their insistence on class or culturalist explanations. Harold B. Williams, the Cleveland NAACP's executive secretary, claimed in a 1961 speech to the MPCC that "citizens of Mt. Pleasant are concerned, as neighbors should be, about unemployment of its residents. The answer to this problem may well affect your neighbor's lawn, a coat of paint for his house, etc." Williams went on to beseech the audience: "Mt. Pleasant is not an Island. It does not stand alone. It is a vital part of the community, with problems and issues beyond its boundaries. . . . I ask you at this annual meeting to toil here in fellowship and spread your interest abroad." Similarly, an extended report on the neighborhood from that same year tried to consider both sides. "If one has invested hard earned resources to improve one's life conditions, one has a reason to be concerned when new neighbors are actually much less socialized, have lower standards of behavior, or lower the physical conditions of the neighborhood," the report ventured, before continuing on to say, "There are families who feel trapped in the community because they cannot find decent housing open to them [elsewhere]." But on the other hand, many recent arrivals expressed not feeling accepted, but rather only "tolerated" by their neighbors. As the report recognized, "Adaptation to a new neighborhood with different standards is not easy—and many newcomers to Mount Pleasant find it so. Upward mobility calls for knowledge about 'proper behavior'—'how to live in this kind of community.' This can produce tension among all members of the upwardly mobile family. . . . Group norms are developed partially through group pressures." These class conflicts arose at a 1967 meeting of the Urban League's Housing Committee, which discussed "rejection by middle-income neighborhoods of low-income families." While some members complained about newcomers who needed to be resocialized, and others emphasized that overcrowding strained city services, the meeting's chair instead "deplored society's containment of low-income families in certain neighborhoods and stated that probably 99% of all middle-class Negroes were at one time of low-income status."[64]

Although the voices of less-affluent incoming residents themselves are even scarcer, a 1968 grant proposal stressed that practically all Mount Pleasant residents shared an interest in "high standards," regardless of income. But, unfortunately, "Many middle-income residents have not discovered what the survey indicated: that most of their recently arrived neighbors, even those receiving welfare, place as much stress as they do on matters such as good schools and recreation for their children, safety in the neighborhood, and above all property maintenance and ownership. Instead they focus on what is more visible—that their new neighbors are having difficulty maintaining their property at the highest level." As for low-income residents, the proposal explained: "Many have moved recently from the inner city and feel that the area is much better than the one they left. Owning a home matters almost more coming from the inner city than it does to those who have been in Mt. Pleasant for some time." Furthermore, "The comments of the renters interviewed in the survey including mothers receiving ADC [Aid to Dependent Children] made clear that those who have to rent want especially to live in Mt. Pleasant because homeowners predominate in the area." Another proposal from the previous year had noted similarly high aspirations regarding education: "Families with school age children desire to live in Mt. Pleasant in part from a belief that school conditions [there] are not as critical." A woman whose parents had grown up in the neighborhood, but who had to move to the King-Kennedy public housing project in the late 1960s when her family fell on hard times, thought of Mount Pleasant as "where the people who worked at the steel mills lived. . . . They carried home paychecks full of overtime and spent them on long, green Ford Gran Torinos, Buicks, Chryslers, and sometimes Cadillacs." She dreamed of the day when her family might be able to move back and "buy our own two-story, two-toned house with a bright painted porch and, in the evenings, sit right out on it." The pride of many economically challenged residents who did make it into the neighborhood is reflected in a remark Mount Pleasant Community Centers director Murtis H. Taylor made to reporters, that residents "don't like to have their problems publicized, even to their own neighbors. Although many families here in Mt. Pleasant are on ADC, few advertise the fact."[65] All of the foregoing evidence would seem to dispute William Julius Wilson's assessment: middle-class mores continued to be promoted even as upwardly mobile families moved away, and considerable numbers of less well-off (or even poor) newcomers internalized conventional notions about how to achieve success.

Some of the complexities accompanying the in-migration of lower-income residents into outlying black expansion neighborhoods come through in a handful of anecdotes from former residents, which suggest, significantly, that children may have experienced the process differently. For example, one African American woman who grew up in Mount Pleasant during the 1950s recalled being excited that large numbers of potential playmates were moving into the neighborhood. She said that contact with the newcomers transformed her very mode of expression, that their parlance became "our way of speaking"—sometimes to her mother's chagrin, as she once discovered upon saying "ain't." Although there might be neighborhood speculation as to whether a new family was on relief, she was never forbidden from playing with anyone. A man who grew up in Lee-Seville's Kerruish Park section in the late 1950s, however, was instructed by his parents to "avoid" certain families. Yet another Mount Pleasant resident, who grew up there in the late 1940s when it was still majority-white, associated frequent visits to his grandparents in Cedar-Central with "freedom," since he was allowed to go barefoot there—which he termed a "Southern thing"—and to stay out in the evening long after his usual bedtime back in Mount Pleasant. He also distinctly recalled a sudden influx of "Woodland Avenue" blacks into his fourth-grade class, many of whom he found "amazing" in their defiance of authority and inclination to fight—even the girls, one of whom challenged him, putting him in a bind. Looking back, he thought these kids acted out because of fear and resentment at the loss of their former associations and support networks. A black former resident of Lee-Harvard whose family moved there in 1962 painted a similar picture of "groups of boys, 13 to 15 years old, wearing jeans and ragged T-shirts, [who] swaggered with a stride called the 'pimp walk.'" "Their long steps and swinging arms," he continued, "announced their angry possession of Lee-Harvard. . . . Even the streets seemed to submit to their transistor radio blaring R&B."[66]

■

From the 1950s into the 1960s, upwardly mobile African American Clevelanders seeking to improve their housing situation experienced mixed outcomes. Even as the city's black population continued to grow, overcrowding decreased and homeownership rose modestly. Some black families successfully bought or built new housing, but as a group, African Americans remained disproportionately saddled with the city's oldest and hardest-to-maintain housing stock. In a dual, racially structured housing market, the supply of decent available housing remained woefully inadequate; the Cleveland Real Property Inventory's 1956 estimated vacancy rate for nonwhites was just 0.5 percent, as compared to 5–10 percent for whites. Strikingly, panelists at a 1958 conference entitled "Where Will the Negro Live Tomorrow?" could not agree on either the pace of racial residential transition in Cleveland or how close the city might be to achieving open occupancy. Still other observers exhibited a cautiously hopeful tone when assessing the state of the housing market, as in the 1959 Workshop on Intergroup Relations sponsored by the local chapter of the National Conference of Christians and Jews. Pointing to the recent expansion of black settlement in Glenville, Mount Pleasant, Lee-Harvard, Ludlow, and Hough, this group concluded, "Today a Negro in Cleveland can live in a neighborhood suited to his income and interests, with neighbors whose backgrounds are similar to his. . . . Yet there is much to be done to clear existing slums and encourage integrated housing."[67]

Despite hard-won advances, upwardly mobile blacks found their possibilities for further outward expansion constrained by continued discrimination in lending and the force of white opposition, notably in the suburbs. Meanwhile, large-scale forces operating in the city as a whole, most importantly urban renewal–related demolitions and an ongoing population influx from the South, helped push less-affluent African Americans toward the new black middle-class expansion areas, even as they, too, were simultaneously pulled by the lure of better housing conditions and schools. Established residents sometimes regarded these less-well-off newcomers with dismay or condescension, leading to increased class and status conflicts in post-transitional neighborhoods. Facing the human consequences of a nascent urban crisis even at the city's periphery, organized middle-class black residents in Glenville and the various neighborhoods of Southeast Cleveland seized upon an ambitious reform agenda to address these areas' "problems" as they perceived them.

6 : : :
Urban Change and Reform Agendas in Cleveland's Black Middle-Class Neighborhoods, 1950–1980

In November 1972, the Lee-Harvard Shopping Center in Southeast Cleveland became, according to the local press, the "largest black-owned commercial complex in the nation." The culmination of three years of planning, the property's new owners, a group of African American professionals and shareholders from the surrounding neighborhood organized as Southeast Renaissance, Inc., had purchased it with a $700,000 loan from the Cleveland Trust Co. and an additional $250,000 from an anonymous benefactor. Immediately upon acquiring the shopping center, the new owners resurfaced the parking lot, upgraded landscaping, and hired more security personnel. All but one of the twenty-one stores, including five formerly vacant, had tenants within a month, and the last remaining vacancy was slated to be filled. The twelve-acre complex included three supermarkets, a drugstore, and a bank, all of which were "triple-A" tenants having assets in the millions of dollars. The new owners' optimism seemed boundless, with their grandiose master plan calling for future additions of a high-rise apartment building, medical center, and more retail stores. The group even talked of acquiring an additional, adjoining property, the now-vacant, former Federal Department Store. "One of the big department stores could set up a branch store here; or several could, through a consortium, help . . . to start the project," suggested Dr. Tillman Bauknight, a local dentist and chairman of the Southeast Renaissance board. With this accomplished, Bauknight expected shoppers would come from miles around to patronize the complex.[1]

The Lee-Harvard Shopping Center project stands out as one example of the various "black capitalist" ventures undertaken in American cities from the late 1960s into the 1970s.[2] An overarching theme of pride in Black culture, concurrent with nationwide trends in African American communities, became even more apparent when another group formed in June 1973 to purchase and renovate the Federal Department Store property. Equally ambitious, its plans called for seventeen shops, including an African boutique, a soul food restaurant, a party and recreation center, and a performing arts theater, as well as a finance company. Fund-raising for the project was slow to start, however, with the result that these particular designs never came to fruition. New hope came in March 1975, though, when heavyweight boxing champion Muhammad Ali suddenly bought the Federal property for $2 million, with intentions to convert it into a mosque and shopping complex. Expressing the delight of many in the community, Councilman Robert C. McCall, who had been involved in previous efforts to purchase the property, said of Ali's sect, the Nation of Islam: "We wish much success to these proud, devout people whose trademark is thrift and industry." That summer, Muhammad's Temple No. 18 from the Buckeye Road neighborhood held a "Grand Bazaar" on the site, at the same time expressing to McCall their "appreciation for the great and honorable welcome the merchants and businessmen have bestowed upon us." As of that December, Ali was reportedly considering expansive development plans that included a bowling alley, as well as a possible roller and ice rink for the site. The prospects these various projects had for success were deemed especially good by their promoters, because they were situated in the heart of Cleveland's most prosperous middle-class black community. The 1970 census had revealed the surrounding neighborhood's median income to be $14,000, more than double the city average of $6,400. In addition, a 1969 study had counted some 19,000 potential customers in the immediate area, and discovered that 53,000 vehicles traversed the intersection daily.[3]

However, the background against which Southeast Renaissance, Inc., had originally stepped in to buy the Lee-Harvard Shopping Center was one of economic uncertainty and decline—as assessed by the black buyers themselves. "We don't like the decay and blight of the commercial area and we don't like to lose stores," Dr. Bauknight had stated when announcing the project in 1971. "Many businesses left when blacks moved into the community," he continued, before adding, "We don't want this to be a black thing. We want to draw quality stores and businesses from everywhere." The shopping center's 1974 financial statement emphasized it was a "community owned and operated facility" and invited investors "to join us in our efforts to make this commercial area one of the finest in the country." With "hard work and pride," the statement continued, "we shall overcome the blight and deterioration that plagues the Lee-Harvard commercial area." In a slightly different vein, Councilman McCall had stated in connection with the original efforts to purchase the Federal property: "This is primarily a race problem. White businesses are moving out because they refuse to change their merchandising habits to sell what blacks want to buy." Optimistically, he went on to predict, "Blacks will support a shopping center because it is black, as long as they are given good service."[4]

Sadly, neither of the two projects was successful. Muhammad Ali's plans for the Federal property evaporated just as suddenly as they had materialized; after less than a year of use for public events, the building was boarded up and inexplicably left dormant by its owner. Six months into the Lee-Harvard Shopping Center project, Bauknight was expressing disappointment that more African American politicians, organizations, businesses, and churches had not come on board. Only half of the original 2,000 stock shares in the venture had been bought up by that point, and plans to open a liquor store at the complex had been quashed "by some pretty influential black people for no reason he can understand." Nearing the end of its first year of operations, the shopping center was reportedly $1,500 a month shy of breaking even and struggling to pay its two mortgages, which amounted to $860,000. A year later, Lee-Harvard's Urban League branch cited rumors that two major stores might be moving out at the end of 1974. With continuing reports of "deterioration" at the complex in 1977, Southeast Renaissance, Inc., finally put the property up for sale in early 1978, apparently under the threat of foreclosure.[5]

In his final assessment of the project, Bauknight commended its community-oriented focus, particularly his organization's decision to sell stock to nearby residents at $10 a share, and the many jobs it had provided for black contractors. As to what went wrong, he returned to the paradox of Lee-Harvard's high per capita income, levels of education, and homeownership rate, and concluded that redlining (lender discrimination) was the primary reason for the project's downfall. Particularly bitter that no financing could be secured to bring a department store back to the site, Bauknight gibed: "What baffles me is that the lending institutions will fund a barbecue joint in the ghetto and will not fund a project that can become viable." Revealingly, a 1971 "abandonment study" conducted by the Urban League of Cleveland—just as Southeast Renaissance, Inc., was planning to buy the property—had already made extensive mention of redlining practices by banks and insurance companies among area business owners. In fact, many observers were well aware of various underlying structural factors that hampered entrepreneurship and economic stability in the area. In 1971, the Lee-Harvard Community Association (LHCA) complained that "most of the businesses are owned by absentee landlords who have no desire to improve the area." As early as 1968, Councilman McCall had worried about "second hand stores" replacing general retail establishments, a diagnosis the Lee-Harvard Urban League branch would repeat in 1974 when it noted the lack of a dime store and that "more stable shops were needed rather than wig and incense shops." The branch also called for extended business hours and emphasized that residents spending their money outside the area furthered instability; they acknowledged this latter dilemma was related to poor-quality merchandise being offered but suggested that residents demand better instead of shopping elsewhere. Finally, the Harvard Community Services Center correctly predicted that the 1976 opening of the gigantic Randall Park Mall, just two miles from the Lee-Harvard intersection in a nearby suburb, would further hurt business—underlining that the accelerating suburbanization of the community's highest-income black families was yet another core problem facing Lee-Harvard retailers.[6]

Large-scale structural factors have figured prominently in the most compelling analyses of the postwar "urban crisis" in American cities—investment flows, occupational structure, and labor markets, to name a few. How these factors interacted with race—particularly in terms of lender and job discrimination, but also with regard to the deindustrialization that we now know began much earlier than previously thought—goes a long way toward explaining why so many American cities became increasingly "poor and black" in the postwar decades.[7] Such studies emphasizing structure have been implicitly written against popular and some scholarly explanations interpreting "white flight" to the suburbs and the "white backlash" against New Deal liberalism as a reaction to the civil rights movement's increasingly radical turn—which some whites ostensibly conflated with street crime in inner-city neighborhoods and the spectacular urban uprisings of the mid-to-late 1960s.[8] Historians Arnold Hirsch and Thomas Sugrue first countered this line of reasoning by emphasizing that white resistance to the expansion of black settlement in the urban North began as early as World War II and intensified in the 1950s; as seen, while there were definite parallels in Cleveland, the relatively greater availability of housing for African Americans in Glenville, Mount Pleasant, and Lee-Seville made the process far less violent than in Detroit and Chicago.

More striking, however, is the apparent willingness of many African American residents in upwardly mobile neighborhoods like Lee-Harvard to offer noneconomic, and even cultural explanations for social phenomena, including crime and juvenile delinquency. In seeking to discuss such topics, one treads on extremely precarious ground. There is a considerable risk of reinforcing stereotypes about black "criminality" and notions still widespread, to this very day, that neighborhoods inevitably "decline" following racial residential transition. One must carefully assess the connections between larger structural factors and personal agency, realizing that some individuals when faced with constricted life and livelihood options choose to participate in illicit, "underground" economies instead of formal ones. In discussing particular incidents, the statistics required to place these in proper, comparative context are not always available. The very definitions of what sorts of behavior constitute "juvenile delinquency" are potentially laden with class or cultural judgments; likewise, it is sometimes difficult to ascribe motives for why exactly individuals act in certain ways. Yet even while acknowledging these pitfalls, the sheer frequency with which crime, juvenile delinquency, and other perceived threats to quality of life came up in discussions held by African Americans themselves requires that these issues be considered. Perceptions of reality powerfully influence personal decisions, whether or not individuals take into account all the relevant factors that should ideally inform their actions.

Juvenile delinquency and the Lee Road commercial strip's viability were issues raised as early as 1962 in a "community workshop" jointly sponsored by the LHCA and the Cleveland NAACP, at which point their concern was preemptive and based on the experiences of older black neighborhoods. By 1966, the LHCA was expressing alarm at some area businesses' decision to install steel gratings on their windows. "They have a connotation and are atrocious," LHCA president Rubie J. McCullough stated, adding, "You drive through Lee-Harvard and see these window guards and know you're in a colored district now." Yet even as she asked whether local merchants might be motivated by fear rather than actual incidents, McCullough revealed that her organization had recently met with police to voice concerns about delinquent behavior by area youth, and she additionally expressed her beliefs that poor discipline on the part of parents and problems surrounding "how to live in a new urban environment" underlay such neighborhood problems. While a subsequent pamphlet produced by LHCA claimed that relations with area businessmen had improved, "increased effort by parents to improve the conduct of their children to and from school" was listed as an ongoing priority. In 1968, McCullough reported that rowdy after-school behavior by teens at the Lee-Harvard Shopping Center—especially fights, but sometimes even the formation of traffic-impeding "human chains" across streets—was being taken up by the LHCA. Shortly before the Federal Department Store closed in 1970, McCullough's successor as LHCA president, Albert Moore, revealed that Federal banned unsupervised schoolchildren from the premises and incidentally had become a "haven" for abandoned cars. A grant application that same year echoed past suspicions (at least to 1965) that the very basis of Lee-Harvard residents' economic security and relative affluence might be factors here: "The frequent employment of both parents creates key-carrying youngsters who steal from merchants and home owners, and the very high drop-out rate in the schools creates idle, unemployed young people . . . who are responsible for break-ins, vandalism, gambling, and disorders in the area of John F. Kennedy High School."[9]

Thus when Southeast Renaissance, Inc., bought the Lee-Harvard Shopping Center, it confronted a complex legacy, some aspects of which extended beyond and were only indirectly linked to admittedly crucial larger, structural factors. Although Dr. Bauknight took credit for there being "no major crime or violence" at the complex during the years his group had owned it, continuing concerns with juvenile delinquency and increased crime rates in the surrounding area were contributing factors to an insecure business climate, visible in pullouts and closings.[10] Such issues as the decline of commercial strips, juvenile delinquency, and crime fell within a broad spectrum of concerns identified by reform-minded activists in Cleveland's upwardly mobile black neighborhoods. In addition, maintaining high-quality housing stock and education in these areas ranked high as areas for constant vigilance and corrective action. Starting in the 1940s, activists addressed these issues through neighborhood-based civic groups like the Glenville Area Community Council, Mount Pleasant Community Council, Lee-Harvard Community Association, and their constituent networks of block and street clubs.

Such locally led organizations had close links to social service agencies and municipal government but seemed to work most effectively when they were not dominated by these bodies, instead taking the initiative to set their own reform agenda. These neighborhood-based civic groups were often connected to African American churches, business associations, and nationally prominent civic organizations like the Urban League. Their growth and florescence generally coincided with the racial residential transition that opened large portions of the East Side to African American occupancy starting in the 1940s; in fact, these organizations really only hit their full potential once the neighborhoods in which they were centered became overwhelmingly black. Strongly shaped by the moral outlooks and class interests of their members, their prescriptions did often parallel those of the local social service establishment. Strikingly, even the activists within these organizations did not always consider the larger structural factors impeding successful reform efforts.

Still, the attempts these residents made to take charge of their communities deserve closer attention, especially in light of recurrent criticism that scholarship emphasizing structural inequality too often discounts the significance of black agency, with the implication that African American residents were essentially powerless against the force of urban change.[11] Furthermore, such studies have left off at the point where city neighborhoods transitioned to become virtually all-black and have read the ongoing, post-1980 trajectory of decline back into the earlier stages, at which point the subsequent state of affairs by no means appeared as foreordained. While residents of neighborhoods like Glenville, Mount Pleasant, and Lee-Harvard expressed pessimism about existing problems even in the earliest stages of the process, their activism nevertheless helped to maintain these communities as livable and economically stable into the 1970s and beyond.

Wellsprings of Reform in Black Middle-Class Communities

It is important to locate such activism within the African American community, even though such efforts often began as interracial mobilizations in the context of neighborhood-level, demographic change. Without enough time or momentum to develop in the city itself, the interracial approach ultimately bore fruit in certain Cleveland suburbs, most famously Shaker Heights. Even when whites intended to eventually move away, some in newly integrating areas could not help but acknowledge black residents' civic activism. A man interviewed by the *Cleveland Press* in 1956 observed: "We never had a street association to police zoning violations and look after the general welfare of the street until the Negroes moved in and started such a club. . . . We may not mix socially but we are good neighbors." Similarly, the city's Community Relations Board noted the following year: "Parenthetically, the most active area councils, where street clubs have multiplied most quickly, are in areas such as Glenville, Mt. Pleasant, Central and Hough. These areas are substantially Negro areas (or rapidly becoming so due to the 'ghetto' developing on Cleveland's east side). It is indeed ironic to have Negro leaders charged as failing 'their' responsibilities when the extent to which Negroes are actively battling the tide of social breakdown equals, if indeed it does not exceed, the proportion of such effort expended throughout the greater Cleveland community." Many observers felt Mount Pleasant exemplified such activism. A 1963 grant application emphasized: "The Mt. Pleasant neighborhood is a sound community with wholesome values, strengths, and aspirations." Again and again, the neighborhood's "informed citizenry," its "active churches and civic organizations," and its "fine tradition of civic interest and involvement" was referenced. Similarly, a 1969 proposal for Glenville noted the neighborhood's "numerous indigenous community organizations (block clubs, Glenville Area Development Corporation, churches, etc.), in addition to a score of organizations and agencies which have a broader community base."[12]

As comparatively older areas, positioned that much closer to the city's inner core, Mount Pleasant and Glenville experienced the social, demographic, physical, and economic pressures shaping the postwar metropolis both earlier and more intensively than further-outlying Lee-Harvard. To be sure, newer middle-class black neighborhoods also chalked up fine records of citizen activism around a variety of issues and, in fact, mobilized around the same issues first confronted in Glenville and Mount Pleasant. But tellingly, relatively higher economic security in the newer expansion neighborhoods was sometimes blamed for a lack of urgency in community reform efforts. Somewhat unfairly, one observer in 1971 characterized "Lee-Miles" (Lee-Harvard and Lee-Seville) as a "fragmented and disorganized community" beset with "apathy and social isolationism." "One of the most significant difficulties in this area," this assessment concluded, "is the lingering suburban mentality which breeds a lack of commitment and involvement in organizations and [the] community." In a similar vein, one community-minded resident wrote Rubie J. McCullough in 1973 to say: "It has been often repeated at the 'brainstorming' meetings of neighborhood leadership that although the members of our neighborhood proved skillful in overcoming adversity, we are having difficulty adjusting to our relative degree of affluence. The individual initiative which helped each of us to make the migration from the inner-cities to Harvard-Lee-Seville is resistant to being transformed into collective action to maintain and improve our neighborhood."[13] Especially on the issue of juvenile delinquency, as will be seen, some observers suspected that some of the "problems," in Lee-Harvard at least, related directly to this relative affluence—making the community seem even more similar to those suburbs also feeling the effects of youth behavioral rebellion in the 1960s and 1970s.

Largely responsible for coordinating and focusing reform efforts were umbrella organizations like the Glenville Area Community Council (GACC), Mount Pleasant Community Council (MPCC), and Lee-Harvard Community Association (LHCA). As discussed previously, the GACC and MPCC were organized in 1945 and 1946, respectively, with the stated purpose "to strengthen and build the general unity of the community." But as racial residential transition neared completion in these neighborhoods, the two organizations actually broadened their scope and ambitions and experienced a growth in membership. The GACC kicked into high gear in 1958, more than doubling its number of affiliated street clubs to ninety-six and printing 10,000 copies of a newsletter for distribution to interested neighborhood residents. The organization's budget stood at about $3,000, which was raised in an annual door-to-door membership drive. As for the MPCC, its membership drives were increasingly well-organized by 1955, with 1,000 new members added in that year alone. The organization had 2,000 members by 1958, and in the succeeding years it set more and more ambitious membership targets. By 1965, the MPCC was seeking 4,000 new members and was said to be the city's largest community organization. Throughout their history, both bodies had various committees for such specific concerns as zoning, schools, health and welfare, housing, and recreation. They also periodically sponsored popular events that brought their respective communities together, such as the GACC's Home and Yard Show, begun in 1954, and the MPCC's Garden Show, initiated the following year. The MPCC held an annual picnic, which by the mid-1960s included a parade that drew thousands of spectators. Another example of a communitywide initiative was the GACC's sponsoring a forum for City Council candidates in 1957, which the MPCC likewise institutionalized into a tradition beginning in 1964. The MPCC even founded a credit union and established a "hotline" for neighborhood complaints in 1966.[14]

Other black middle-class expansion areas took up this community council tradition. The LHCA existed by 1962, also starting originally as an interracial organization. Like the GACC and MPCC, it held an annual banquet and coordinated the neighborhood's street clubs. By 1965 it was conducting membership drives, and despite continually falling short of its recruitment targets, counted 2,300 members by 1969. As will be seen, the LHCA focused activity around a variety of issues and similarly held a "candidate night," in addition to an annual Summer Arts Festival, beginning in 1968. Furthermore, the organization co-sponsored a "drop-in" center for local youths prior to the opening of the Harvard Community Services Center in 1968, and in fact it was deeply involved in the establishment of that facility.[15] The Lee-Seville neighborhood had an equivalent organization, the Lee-Seville Citizens Council, although its record of activity is spottier. It already existed by 1958 and, as of 1967 was seeking 1,000 members. Less well known was the Corlett Area Council, also formed as an interracial organization in 1968. Funded through the United Area Citizens Agency beginning the following year, the Corlett Area Council was forced to sever its ties with that body by 1976 because it could no longer fulfill the requirement that its membership be interracial.[16]

These community-based organizations rested on networks of dozens of block and street clubs that helped mobilize residents behind neighborhood goals or else acted on a more localized level. In the mid-1950s, the GACC and MPCC regularly summarized street club activities in their monthly newsletters, giving some sense of their scope and activity. For example, in 1954 the East 137th Street Club reported: "Plans have been made for the annual children's party in June after the closing of school. The club donated $25.00 to the Girl Scout Camp Development Fund. Also for the benefit of the club's treasury, a raffle was held and will have their garden party in August." A black attorney and member of the East 147th Street Club in the farther, still-integrated reaches of Mount Pleasant told the *Cleveland Press* in 1956: "The [East 147th] street association polices safety and building restrictions to see that there is no doubling up in individual homes. We had a speeding problem, and the club worked to lick that by contacting police. Our club donated $150 for a Christmas party for all the children, white and colored, on the street, and staged an Easter egg hunt." In early 1957, the GACC reported that Castlewood Street Club members were sharing the snowplow they had collectively purchased; meanwhile the Garfield Avenue Association had collected five bushels of food for distribution to "some of their less fortunate neighbors." Some street clubs extended their consciousness far beyond the neighborhood, as in the example of one that sent a small contribution in support of the Montgomery Bus Boycott. Street clubs formed the basis of recruitment efforts for both the GACC's and MPCC's annual membership drives and sometimes assisted with special projects, as in supplying the addresses of "shut-ins" to junior high school students, who organized a Christmas caroling group in 1958.[17]

It is difficult to pinpoint how many street clubs functioned in Cleveland's black middle-class neighborhoods from the 1950s through the 1970s, but the indications are that there were many dozens. The number affiliated with the GACC ranged around thirty in the early 1950s, hitting one hundred by 1959. The MPCC testified to the existence of fifty-three street clubs as of 1960; two years later, that number had expanded to at least seventy-two, judging by the number of delegates who signed up for an MPCC-sponsored street club organizing workshop. While Mount Pleasant's street clubs persisted into the 1970s, a grant application toward the end of that decade would lament that that over 200 street clubs had once existed in the neighborhood, implying their decline.

As for Lee-Harvard, only nineteen street clubs were affiliated with the LHCA as of 1965; more apparently existed, however, since the LHCA sought to tap into these for its membership drive the following year and ended up having twenty-eight affiliated clubs. By 1967, the LHCA counted thirty-six, meaning more than half of the area's streets were organized; and as of 1970, the neighborhood's fledgling newspaper, the *Lee-Harvard Community Star*, listed forty affiliated street club presidents by name. Despite less information on other neighborhoods, surviving evidence suggests a similarly important role; in 1966 the Miles Heights Improvement Club (Lee-Seville) was formed from a federation of eight street clubs, while that same year the councilman for Ward 13—including part of Corlett—reported that his constituents were highly enthusiastic about street clubs. Street clubs also acted independently of the overarching area councils, with one Corlett resident recalling how in the early 1970s, his block club on Crennell Avenue sponsored annual events and even saved the red-brick street from being paved over on several occasions.[18]

Considering the central place traditionally occupied by churches in African American communities, it is not surprising to see local congregations collaborating with these secular neighborhood organizations. Such cooperation was extensive and took place on a number of levels. It could be small scale and targeted, as when the Saint Peter's AME Zion Church co-sponsored a Cub Scout pack with the East 144th Street Improvement Club in 1953. More commonly, churches provided space, facilities, and potential recruits for organizing efforts. At least several neighborhood organizations were formed out of meetings held at local churches: The Lee-Seville Civic Council out of Saint Paul Methodist Church (1961); Mount Pleasant Citizens of Concern out of Saint Peter's AME Zion (1968); and the Southeast Community Forum, also out of Saint Paul Methodist (1970). Secular community organizations also held regular meetings at local churches, as in the case of the LHCA, which was effectively run out of the Lee Road Baptist Church, or the GACC, which had a close relationship with Antioch Baptist Church. Churches might host events sponsored by organizations like the MPCC—as in a 1969 workshop on community leadership held at Olivet Baptist Church—or else organize their own, as in a 1965 panel on juvenile delinquency at the Lee-Seville Baptist Church planned in conjunction with four other congregations. For that matter, black churches and their affiliated organizations sometimes became directly involved in political battles, as when five neighborhood churches signed on to protest industrial rezoning for Lee-Seville in 1961, or when the Lee-Seville Ministerial Alliance came out in favor of public housing proposed for the area in 1968.[19]

In two notable cases, individual activists participating in these community-based organizations used them as springboards into local politics: Ward 24's Leo A. Jackson, who had chaired the GACC's Public Safety Committee and sat on its executive committee, and Ward 10's Lowell Henry, who was a leading

MPCC activist. Significantly, both men were elected in 1957, displacing long-time Jewish incumbents. Jackson, a lawyer and Florida native who had come to Cleveland in 1946, ran against Harry T. Marshall at the insistence of his neighbors, who organized a petition drive and gathered spare change to jumpstart his campaign. With the slogan "Let's Have Action—Vote for Jackson," the upstart seized the initiative; a campaign cartoon portrayed the popular incumbent reading a paper titled "Political Opportunities" with his back turned on the neighborhood, which had chimneys belching smoke labeled "Slum Development! Dirty Streets! Traffic & Parking Problems! Limited Youth Opportunities!" Jackson went on to win, with 54 percent of the vote. His early career would be marked by confrontational crusading, which he carried over from his previous GACC experience with the state liquor inspectors, city's zoning board, and Police Department. In 1961, Jackson called from the floor of the City Council for the dissolution of the Zoning Board of Appeals, on the grounds that it was capricious and inconsistently enforced the housing code in African American neighborhoods—a prelude to his later brash holdup of funding for the city's urban renewal program on similar grounds. Jackson was a polarizing figure, with some other black local politicians considering his tactics either embarrassing or counterproductive. In a 1962 *Call & Post* column, he was accused of victimizing the "little man," charges echoed the following year in an electoral challenge from fellow GACC activist Frances K. Williams, who defended a black insurance agent whom Jackson had labeled an "exploiter" and invited skeptics to "find the first instance in which the Councilman of Ward 24 has gotten a press notice for doing something other than attacking a fellow Negro in council, in business or in community life." Later in his career, Jackson increasingly appeared as a supporter of the status quo, especially to younger civil rights activists. In 1967, his home was firebombed, allegedly by black militants whose tactics he stridently opposed.[20]

In a similar pattern, a nonpartisan "citizens' committee" urged Ohio Bell commercial aide Lowell Henry to run against incumbent Joseph Horowitz in 1957. Henry had lived in Mount Pleasant for over a decade and had long been active in the MPCC, even serving as its president. He also held a seat on the City Planning Commission and had briefly served as the local NAACP branch's "at large" Housing Committee member. Henry's platform called for improved lighting, bus service, and sewers, as well as better enforcement of traffic and parking laws; in addition, he benefited from the expertise of future black Cleveland mayor Carl B. Stokes, who served as his campaign manager and came up with the idea to emphasize Horowitz's ownership of "slum" properties. Henry emerged victorious, with 59 percent of the vote, thereby pulling off an even greater upset than Leo Jackson. However, the MPCC's refusal to publicly release the names of its affiliated street clubs' presidents the following year brought allegations in the *Call & Post* that Henry was using the organization as a personal political "machine," as well as inappropriately utilizing the services of a staff member whose salary was paid by the Welfare Federation. As further evidence of political disagreements among black Clevelanders, such insinuations led the MPCC in early 1959 to formally abjure "the use of the community council program for political ambitions" and to call instead for "more 'togetherness' and objectivity in the group."[21]

The Complexities of Housing Stock and Rehabilitation Efforts

While reform-minded black neighborhood residents identified a wide range of issues that could have a negative impact on a community's quality of life, the condition of housing stands out as perhaps the most basic—and one that was extremely difficult to solve. Housing and choice of neighborhood are prime expressions of upward mobility and status; at the same time, the quality and upkeep of housing stock in a given neighborhood is linked to a complex array of factors, which may include income and employment status of the residents; access to credit for maintenance or home improvement loans; the age and mix of housing types; tenancy and owner occupancy; and previous owners' record of upkeep. Not surprisingly, the relatively new single-family houses in the Lee-Harvard area had few problems in this regard during the period under study. Besides, its colonials and ranches were not readily convertible to multifamily occupancy, a process that rapidly wore out the housing stock in older areas. The 1960 census revealed 98.6 percent of Lee-Harvard's housing stock to be sound, with three out of its four census tracts at or above 99 percent—including the northeasternmost one, into which African Americans had been moving since 1953. Only *one house* out of the area's nearly 15,000 was categorized as "dilapidated." Even so, the majority-black homeowners in the Lee-Harvard Community Association expressed interest in "neighborhood conservation" and worried in a 1965 newsletter: "We must be alert to certain growing adverse conditions that will eventually damage property value. . . . HELP PROTECT YOUR INVESTMENT!" In its 1969 program "Lee-Harvard Yesterday, Today, and Tomorrow," the association declared its primary aim to be "rehabilitation," presumably of the housing stock. Yet as late as 1977, the only problems mentioned specifically relating to property upkeep were "unpainted homes" and "broken garage doors," which were said to be on the rise.[22]

Similar to Lee-Harvard, Lee-Seville's eastern portion abutting Kerruish Park contained nearly new, ranch-style housing, although this was less characteristic of the section west of Lee Road, which included the area's historic African American enclave. A 1966 assessment by the Urban League, in conjunction with planning for a controversial scatter-site public housing project there during Carl Stokes's mayoralty, captured some of the complexities here: "The present development of houses immediately west of the City's land is neat and well-maintained; however, that development south of the tract shows signs of blight—some houses in a far-advanced stage of deterioration." A 1969 newspaper report, while noting littered vacant lots in the older section, remained generally positive about the neighborhood's housing stock, drawing attention to the fact that "dotted among the one and two-story cottage-type homes, many about 50 years old . . . are several newly built unobtrusive ranch-types blending into the calm." Further complicating the matter, city planners that same year, in seeking federal rehabilitation funds from the Department of Housing and Urban Development, declared a whopping 67 percent of the area's historic Miles Heights enclave to be "blighted"; only so-called blighted areas were eligible for the funding, which surely influenced this designation.[23]

Corlett was another neighborhood with an assortment of housing types, varying in age but in better overall shape. The 1960 census revealed that only 6 percent of Corlett's homes were "deteriorating," and these were mostly in one small pocket. Furthermore, some 70 percent of the total were owner-occupied. That the neighborhood's older, two-family homes in its western (historically Czech and Polish) portion were potentially vulnerable to conversion was, however, a prime factor behind Councilman George W. White's formation of a "Negro Community Federation" there in 1966. "It is a constant struggle," White explained, with reference to the destructive results of subdividing houses in older sections of the city like Cedar-Central, Hough, and perhaps Glenville. "But the enthusiasm of street groups makes the homeowners more conscious of policing their responsibilities," he continued, before concluding, "We think we have a fine area."[24]

Among Cleveland's black middle-class neighborhoods, Glenville and Mount Pleasant faced the greatest challenges with regard to housing, and their residents went the farthest in attempting to maintain the housing stock. As early as 1948, research for a master's thesis project discovered that, despite the Glenville Area Community Council's (GACC) initial focus on other issues, "conservation of properties and neighborhood is foremost in the minds of the Negro participants." In both 1950 and 1953, the East Boulevard Improvement Association won cases before the Board of Zoning Appeals that prevented apartment house owners from doubling the number of units in their buildings by chopping the existing suites in half, a bid to preserve the area's "Gold Coast" reputation. In the latter instance, one resident recounted how he once lived on East 86th Street in Cedar-Central but "had to move when the area deteriorated." He had next relocated to Earle Avenue in Glenville but subsequently felt the need to move to a "better" section. Now that even East Boulevard was "threatened," he expressed frustration that "I am getting too old to start all over again in this constant search for a satisfactory place to live." Concerns about Mount Pleasant's housing stock similarly dated to the early postwar era. In 1950, the City Planning Commission classed the neighborhood as a "conservation area—

corrective action required," although census data from that same year showed that substandard housing in the tract containing the historic black enclave—by then 59 percent African American—stood at just 2 percent. However, while the percentage of substandard housing for the neighborhood as a whole was less than half the city average, its rate of overcrowding was actually slightly higher. Mount Pleasant block clubs also took action to protect housing stock from early on. For example, in 1952 the East 144th Street Improvement Club got the Board of Zoning Appeals to force an absentee owner to reconvert his property back to two-family occupancy, following tenants' complaints of poor maintenance and accumulated rubbish.[25]

Conversion of housing to multifamily occupancy was a prime concern of activists in both neighborhoods. Already ranking high on the GACC's agenda, in 1953 the organization declared "HOME AND NEIGHBORHOOD CONSERVA-TION" to be its "number one emphasis." While questioning the city's assignment of just one housing inspector to the neighborhood, the GACC simultaneously sought a citywide solution to the problem, expressing its concerns to zoning board members and urban redevelopment officials that demolitions in Cedar-Central and industrial projects on vacant land in Lee-Seville were exacerbating overcrowding. As of 1954, however, the organization was still struggling to formulate concrete measures to tackle conversions. That year, its president told the Welfare Federation that the GACC had taken "no action" to correct the problem, and as late as 1956, its Home and Neighborhood Conservation Committee's work remained limited to such events as a slideshow entitled "Blight Can Happen Here." The Housing Committee of the Mount Pleasant Community Council (MPCC) also placed at the top of its 1954 agenda "the prevention and correction of illegal conversions which are generally considered as the first step toward overcrowding and its subsequent result—deterioration" and went further to note that "many remodeling contractors actually encourage and persuade property owners to make illegal conversions," even advising on how to evade existing regulations. Citing the ongoing experiences of Cedar-Central and Hough, the Housing Committee argued that "the inspection staff of the Building Department must be drastically enlarged if it is to do even an acceptable job of code enforcement." Later that year, the MPCC proposed that an ordinance be passed to hold contractors liable for illegal conversions, and that a city housing court be established.[26]

For their part, city officials tended to place the onus of maintaining housing on Glenville and Mount Pleasant residents themselves. Addressing the GACC in 1952, Cleveland Metropolitan Housing Authority head Ernest J. Bohn urged vigilance against any attempts to subvert zoning or building code violations. "Neighborhood conservation is your job as good citizens and members of the area council," Bohn stated. "In many ways it is a bigger job than the rebuilding planned for the Central area," he ventured, because "there will be no public housing here . . . [and] that makes the task of every resident even more important." Along similar lines, L. L. Yancey of the Board of Zoning Appeals commented at a 1953 meeting of the MPCC that "it is up to you to convince the community that you have a sense of responsibility by maintaining your property according to the requirement[s] of the building and zoning laws," which drew the following rebuttal from a member of the organization: "Houses are sold in poor condition to Negroes at inflated prices. . . . After that the new owners haven't the money to fix [them] up and run into the refusal of banks to lend money to Negroes." Two years later, Urban Redevelopment Authority head James T. Yeilding estimated to attendees at another MPCC meeting that they should be spending $3 million per year on home maintenance if they wanted to avoid "becoming a slum." As of 1958, even the Urban League's Arnold Walker, a Mount Pleasant resident, identified housing code violations along with the larger, renting families moving in as situations necessitating "increased activity in the Mt. Pleasant Community Council and a greater awareness of civic responsibilities."[27]

Toward the end of the decade, Mount Pleasant and Glenville residents adopted more proactive strategies to address the issue of conversion as a threat to housing stock; however, against the force of Cleveland's artificial black housing shortage, this was an uphill battle. Around 1957, the MPCC started notifying city officials of housing violations and encouraging members to attend zoning hearings. In 1959 alone, the organization reported that its Housing and Zoning Committee had fought thirty-nine cases before the city's Zoning Board and won thirty-seven. One street club, from East 145th Street, sent twenty-eight members to a hearing that year. Other clubs had circulated petitions, leading the MPCC to remark: "We are indeed very proud of this record. . . . However, we would be even happier if no violations existed which would require the Committee's attention." New information was also uncovered on how conversions were taking place: "Our experience has shown that during the winter months, contractors and carpenters are not able to work on large housing developments and as a result they return to odd jobs doing remodeling work and enlarging third floors and other jobs that can be done on the inside of the house. Our experience has shown that this is their 'Golden Season of Opportunity' to erect numerous additions to houses, kitchens, etc. without permits and without the sanction of the proper city authority." The problem seemed especially urgent that year in light of findings that illegal occupancy ran up to 20 percent in the vicinity of Mount Pleasant's historic black enclave; rates for the neighborhood as a whole were still low, however, compared to Hough and Glenville. In 1960, the MPCC's Housing and Zoning Committee fought twenty-eight more cases in court, winning twenty-five. But by 1964, as grant writers would note in retrospect, the organization had discontinued this proactive approach. "To a large degree this failure resulted from the realization that the Community

Ad for Conversion to Multifamily
Occupancy, 1950. Contractors
advertised in the local black press,
offering to convert attics into rentable
living quarters, in violation of
municipal building codes. Some cash-
strapped African American property
owners took them up on the offer,
while others fought such conversions
via the Board of Zoning Appeals.
(Courtesy of Call & Post Newspapers
of Ohio)

Council [MPCC] was not significantly affecting deterioration within the community," they surmised.[28]

By late 1957, the GACC was also more directly challenging illegal conversions. The chair of its Home and Neighborhood Conservation Committee, lawyer Clarence Gaines, personally attended Board of Zoning Appeals hearings on a weekly basis and successfully fought eighteen out of twenty cases in his first five months. Frequently accompanied by Al Mitchell, a Welfare Federation field representative assigned to the GACC, Gaines told the press, "I believe in this neighborhood. It's a good one and will be a good one in 40 years if we fight every inch of the way against forces that create slums." The GACC subsequently instituted a formal procedure for confronting owners of converted properties and notifying the proper city officials. Following his election to the City Council in 1957, Leo Jackson also pushed the issue, co-sponsoring legislation early the following year to make multifamily conversion punishable by fines and jail time, which brought him into vocal conflict with City Building Commissioner William D. Guion. After three children burned to death in an overcrowded apartment on East 101st Street, Jackson also began advocating on behalf of individual tenants. In early 1959, he reported to the City Council on the results of an inspection he ordered, in the case of an absentee landlord who had evicted a tenant who dared to complain about conditions in her East 105th Street apartment, which found: "1. Cords and open wiring draped over and fastened to woodwork in all 10 suites and entire basement. 2. Insufficient convenient outlets for living rooms, bed rooms, kitchens of all 10 suites. 3. Insufficient electrical outlets provided for laundry and furnace area. 4. Electrical installations constitute a serious hazard . . . [and] the tenants complain that they cannot take baths or wash clothes conveniently because only one small hot water tank is provided for every two suites. The tenant being evicted has medical bills to show that her 7 year old daughter suffered from pneumonia for more than a month this winter because the owner ordered the custodian to keep the heat low." After a 1959 "sidewalk survey" estimated that fully one-quarter of the 2,200 houses in the Miles Standish school district (west of East 105th Street between Superior and Saint Clair Avenues) needed repairs, the GACC focused its battle against overcrowding there. As of 1961, owners were reportedly cooperating and relations with the Board of Zoning Appeals had "greatly improved."[29]

While rehabilitation efforts like those undertaken in the Miles Standish section essentially depended on cooperation from property owners—who by 1961 had spent a combined total of $130,000 in bringing over one hundred properties up to code—an initiative in Mount Pleasant assembled a broader assortment of stakeholders interested in maintaining that neighborhood's living conditions. The Mount Pleasant Housing Improvement Program (HIP) was launched in February 1965 when five residents belonging to the MPCC—apparently with the assistance of Don Mason, a white field worker for the Neighborhood Settlements Association—began organizing tenants in the apartment buildings on East 140th Street north of Kinsman Road, to request that landlords adequately maintain the properties. These volunteer organizers considered the crux of the problem to be a "break in communication," with tenants and landlords blaming each other for maintenance problems and homeowners "perceiving renters as a threat to maintenance of property." After a month's efforts, during which the landlords proved intractable but the tenants responded positively, Mason drafted a proposal for what would become HIP and presented it to the MPCC. The proposal was subsequently passed on to the Businessmen's Interracial Committee on Community Affairs, recently formed in response to local civil rights demands, which in turn referred it to the Greater Cleveland Associated Foundation. In May, the foundation funded HIP with a grant of nearly $40,000, for a two-year demonstration project—said to be "the first of its kind by any area council"—including an office with two full-time staff members and plans to work with existing community groups on a wide-ranging array of programs relating to housing and other quality-of-life concerns.[30]

HIP initially targeted the several dozen four- and six-suite apartments on East 140th Street where the pilot project had been based, because these contained more low-income tenants, were poorly maintained, rarely employed custodians as required by law, and often had absentee owners. When the project got under way in August 1965, thirty-one of the thirty-five buildings lacked valid certificates of occupancy. Just a month later, HIP reported progress not only with tenants but also with owners—excepting one notorious landlord who lived in Cleveland Heights and actually had an outstanding arrest warrant for housing violations and whose case HIP, along with the Urban League, was pressing the city's Housing Department to reopen. In October, HIP resodded lawns on East 140th Street with sod purchased by the apartment building owners, to be installed by resident volunteers; in addition, it was even discussing the feasibility of transforming the apartments into condominiums.

The following month, HIP assigned one of its staff members to another section of the neighborhood earlier identified with blight, the several blocks forming the Kinsman-Union Triangle from East 116th Street to East 119th Street. In early 1966, tenants were "evacuated" from a particularly dilapidated apartment building on East 117th Street; amazingly, within several months HIP successfully convinced the owner of this building not only to fix up the property, but also to let them use one of the basement suites for community programs.[31]

When mere persuasion failed to extract significant concessions from property owners, HIP experimented with more aggressive tactics. After securing a pledge from Mayor Ralph Locher to support code enforcement efforts in March 1966, HIP submitted a detailed report on the extent of the problem and revived the MPCC's tradition of residents attending zoning board hearings. That fall, the local press reported, "The members of HIP have monitored most of the housing court sessions this year," with residents being urged to keep up the pressure. As a result of such efforts, ten additional apartment buildings on East 140th Street got valid certificates of occupancy, the owners of six others were taken to court, and the city levied fines against two others. Against one particularly recalcitrant owner, Fred Jury, HIP organized a petition drive that collected 2,000 signatures as a way to force him to repair his four-suite building and clean up the premises. Jury may not have fit the typical profile of a landlord in the area: he lived in the building and was white, getting up in years, and somewhat eccentric. But in January 1967, HIP's campaign resulted in Jury actually being stripped of his property, said to be the first time this had ever happened to a Cleveland landlord. In a grant application for continued funding it submitted shortly thereafter, HIP could rightly claim that as a result of their efforts, "There has been more housing code enforcement on this stretch of East 140th Street during the past year than during any previous year."[32]

However, HIP did not reserve all blame for apathetic landlords and city officials. Responding to apartment owners' concerns, it initiated work on a "property management" (janitorial) cooperative by early 1967, to provide buildings on East 140th Street with affordable cleaning and maintenance services; although twenty-one of the thirty-five owners had signed on as of September, the co-op was still in the works the following June, with HIP seeking city funds to train janitorial staff for the project. From the start, HIP favored a multicausal explanation for the state of the area's housing stock, as explained by one staff member: "We feel that a combination of the failure to enforce regulations, absentee owners who bleed the property for profits, the owner who has become complacent because of lack of cooperation from tenants[,] and the tenant who is not living up to his responsibility causes the slow deterioration of a neighborhood." HIP's belief that considerable responsibility lay with the tenants reflected the strong middle-class orientation not just of HIP activists, but of the neighborhood as a whole, as reflected in an early pamphlet that exhorted tenants and homeowners alike: "As a resident of Mt. Pleasant, it is your duty to work daily for the BETTERMENT of your community. Be friendly to all new-comers, join and work with the area council. Keep your property, home and apartment in a clean and sanitary condition. Exercise restraint with your children, teach them to respect the rights of others. When you have done all of these things, and find that others are not doing their part, and are making your street deteriorate by not keeping up their property, speak to the street club about the problem. 1) Write letters 2) Get out petitions 3) Call housing, health or police as the case may warrant. The important thing to remember is: DO SOMETHING!" Getting tenants to join street clubs was considered particularly important; in early 1966, HIP reported some progress here, and that there appeared to be "a beginning of the acceptance by homeowners of the fact that a street cannot be maintained if groups of residents are excluded from conservation efforts."[33]

Perhaps the most promising of HIP's endeavors was housing rehabilitation, even if this aspect never achieved its full potential. During its first two years of existence, HIP's efforts had focused on multiple-unit apartment buildings and landlord-tenant issues rather than on maintenance and rehabilitation of houses. However, a December 1966 letter from HIP to the Urban League evidenced a shift, stating that "much housing deterioration occurs because property owners cannot qualify for or afford home improvement loans from banks and savings associations." The letter went on to note that "home improvement monies, however, could be made available at less expense to the borrower if a pool of money was created to serve as a guarantee for the loans or to subsidize the interest charges" and revealed that HIP had approached local industries with the idea for such a fund. By March 1967, a handful of Cleveland companies had declared their support for the initiative, with the intention to "help preserve" their employees' neighborhoods. In August, a "revolving fund" of $150,000 was initiated by six firms, all of whose chief executives sat on the Businessmen's Interracial Committee on Community Affairs. "In most instances, the loan for repairs is granted by a bank with the Cleveland Revolving Fund Inc. acting as a guarantor," explained a Businessmen's Interracial Committee report. "This will make it possible for the $150,000 capital to go much further than if loans were granted directly from the Fund." In effect, the fund would act "sort of like a private FHA," in the words of HIP staffer Donald Mason.[34]

At the outset, thirty-two residents applied for rehabilitation assistance, which HIP considered a good turnout since the project had not yet been actively promoted. HIP identified three general categories among the applicants: young mothers with children, living on poverty-level incomes but not necessarily on welfare; retirees, many of whom had bought houses later in life and were still paying off mortgages; and working couples with children, who had the greatest expectations from the program. Not surprisingly, different motivations were discovered among the groups. Interestingly, of the third and most economically secure group, it was noted that "even those whose income before expenses is quite high tend to have two or three large debts in addition to their mortgage, usually for a car, furniture, and appliances. With the added expense of young children, they have little financial leeway." Even more revealing was that "a few have held off spending money on their Mount Pleasant property because they were considering moving to one of the outlying suburbs." In execution, the rehabilitation program seemed to work well, with the "revolving fund" guaranteeing two of the first six loans. However, HIP did note that "it is too early to guess how much success HIP will have in obtaining loans and whether it can play a pioneering role in altering lending institutions' attitudes. The first signs are positive, in that only one of the four banks contacted has not been cooperative." A more troubling problem was finding black contractors to do the work. "The hope was to use local contractors," HIP noted in 1967, "but they operate with a lack of capital, clerical assistance, and professional habits," thus making "firm" estimates difficult to calculate. The existing evidence suggests that HIP's rehabilitation program was a windfall for those African American contractors who did participate. Meanwhile, larger white-owned firms proved uninterested in these small jobs averaging just $3,000 each. By the end of the year, nineteen HIP rehabilitation projects had been successfully completed.[35]

Despite this promising new approach, the looming end of the grant led HIP to initiate a letter-writing campaign to raise alternative funding. While correspondents included newly elected Mayor Carl B. Stokes, who promised to bolster code enforcement efforts in support of the program, most earnest were the letters of Mount Pleasant residents already helped by HIP. One woman wrote simply: "I had some work done thru the Housing Improvement. Very happy to say they seen to it [that] every thing was done right. To discontinue this program would be bad. . . . Would hate to see this community go down." Another wrote: "I am having my house worked on with the help of HIP. . . . Without HIP I could not have gotten a bank loan to do the work because of my age. There are other people in this neighborhood in the same boat I am in. I will want other improvements on the house at a later time but will need the program if I am to get them." After several months of uncertainty, HIP in early 1968 finally assembled funding from the Cleveland Development Foundation, Businessmen's Interracial Committee, Greater Cleveland Associated Foundation, and the Community Services Center of Mount Pleasant, enough to last through the year. While HIP subsequently looked into the possibility of tapping urban renewal funding for housing code enforcement, the most promising approach instead seemed to be the formation of a nonprofit development corporation eligible for federal grant funding—a previously considered approach, but geared more toward the purchase of properties needing restoration. In July, the Mount Pleasant Community Development Foundation (MPCDF) was formed with both of these objectives in mind. Initially conceived as an "adjunct" of HIP, MPCDF announced plans to buy a condemned house on Luke Avenue for restoration, as well as a community membership drive to begin in September. As of that month, twenty-nine of the original applicants for HIP's rehabilitation project, excepting only the three who had dropped out, had completed renovations through the project.[36]

MPCDF became HIP's successor—anticipating, incidentally, the numerous community development nonprofits that would spring up all over Cleveland and in neighborhoods around the country during the 1980s. But in 1969, MPCDF was ahead of its time; with its future funding uncertain, it struggled. That February, it was continuing to arrange home improvement loans for residents, with the backing of the revolving fund as well as assistance from the Cleveland Bar Association and local architectural student volunteers. MPCDF also hoped to get federal funding through Neighborhood Development Project (NDP) grants, which succeeded urban renewal, and planned to approach the Community Housing Corporation (CHC) connected with Mayor Stokes's new public-private urban development program, "Cleveland: NOW!" In June, however, CHC refused MPCDF's $89,000 request to pay staff salaries. Despite this setback, MPCDF continued to show promise like that of its predecessor HIP. That same month, it hosted an open house in its now-renovated property on Luke Avenue before turning it over to a low-income buyer. In July, MPCDF additionally reported that besides helping a total of forty-eight residents secure home improvement loans—in most of these cases without having to even use the revolving fund—it had recently been awarded federal money from the Department of Housing and Urban Development to purchase and rehabilitate twenty-six housing units on East 119th Street, where the highest concentration of deterioration was evident. Furthermore, it had recruited 604 dues-paying, individual and business memberships and was assisting on a project hatched by CHC to transport to Mount Pleasant about thirty houses displaced by a construction project in the adjacent suburb of Shaker Heights.[37]

Sadly, this innovative approach, which seemed to be getting results, eventually ran out of funds. Despite further letters from Mount Pleasant residents, educators, and others testifying to the efficacy of HIP and its successor, MPCDF, no further support could be garnered from the Greater Cleveland Associated Foundation or any other private source. In his own supporting letter, Director of Community Development Richard R. Green had described MPCDF as an "indigenous group" and emphasized that "they have acted as an effective mechanism for articulating the needs of that community and, contrary to many local groups, *they* have managed to initiate a positive response to those needs." Although MPCDF was still pursuing a federal NDP grant at that point, the city's repeated failure to qualify for such was cited in 1970 as a contributor to MPCDF's demise. Incidentally, some Mount Pleasant residents may not have been so disappointed at the NDP program proposal's failure, since a number of them complained to Leo Jackson, chair of the City Council's Community Development Committee, about the requirement that the neighborhood be designated "blighted" in order to qualify. Indeed, the NDP proposal had declared Mount Pleasant to be 47.4 percent blighted, the lowest rate of any neighborhood included but drastically out of line with any previous estimates.[38]

Certainly the fate of Mount Pleasant's living conditions did not rest upon HIP and its successor MPCDF. As it was, community observers were noting an ongoing "decline" in the western part of the neighborhood by 1971, it being described as a "poverty area" in a grant application of that year. To some, the trajectory seemed irreversible by the later years of the decade. "Mt. Pleasant [once] offered a comfortable, stable lifestyle for a middle class Black community," yet another grant proposal from 1978 began. "Owners have turned their homes into rentals. . . . Lower Mt. Pleasant is physically and psychologically separated from upper Mt. Pleasant, making it increasingly hard for residents to maintain anything but a desperate and isolated stance," the proposal continued, seemingly confirming the realization of HIP activists' worst fears some ten years after the fact.[39]

Scope and Ambition of Reform in Black Middle-Class Neighborhoods

While housing rated highly on the agenda of reform-minded black residents, their vision of how to stem the apparent effects of the unfolding urban crisis extended to a wide variety of quality-of-life issues. The diverse causes they took up were common to most of the city's black middle-class neighborhoods, suggesting a worldview or mind-set held by many who accepted the challenge of improving living conditions in their communities—of addressing the "problems" as they saw them. Looking back over the record, one encounters a vast array of activism around numerous causes, examples of which might seem less significant were each to be considered in isolation; but taken together, they represent a significant collective effort.[40] Unsurprisingly, the issues that activist residents identified and the solutions they proposed exhibited a middle-class bias and sometimes mirrored ideas, current in social work at that time, that black working-class culture had "pathological" aspects. However, reform efforts could also be characterized by a keen and perceptive analysis of underlying structural factors and incorporate elements of pragmatism. Drawn from existing organizations, including churches, the Urban League, the NAACP, and others, reformers enacted the citizenly, associational culture of the 1950s and 1960s on a local level—thereby revealing important continuities to that recognized era of grassroots activism, the 1970s.[41] The various causes around which Cleveland's black middle-class citizen activists mobilized extended almost to the point of being comprehensive, and the approaches adopted ran the gamut from moralistic to sociological. In the end, these residents' efforts proved unable to halt (let alone reverse) the force of urban change, but they did succeed, on their own terms, in maintaining Cleveland's black middle-class neighborhoods as livable to 1980 and beyond.

Some causes were practical as well as cosmetic. Instructive are the house-painting and trash removal "cleanup campaigns" initially coordinated with citywide initiatives in the 1950s, but which local residents expanded, adapted, and continued into subsequent decades. After years of promoting house painting and lawn reseeding through its constituent street clubs, the Glenville Area Community Council (GACC) in 1955 launched "Operation NIP"—short for "Neighborhood Improvement Program" but also intended to "nip in the bud" some of the area's problems, with a particular focus on rat extermination. Ten years later, the neighborhood was still struggling with rat control and cleanup issues like abandoned cars, prompting the GACC to formulate new initiatives such as the "Glenville Action Program" and "Keep Pride in Glenville" campaigns.[42] The MPCC by 1955 had committed itself to a "year round clean up campaign" and even assigned a special committee to the task. In 1961, the MPCC made good on this commitment when it sent delegates to meet with city officials on the matter of a "jungle" of overgrowth north of Kinsman Road between East 143rd and 145th Streets, which was being used as a dumping ground and allegedly sheltered "winos" as well as rats. Long after annual city-sponsored cleanup drives had ceased, the MPCC was still sponsoring these, as in 1966 when 250 truckloads of debris were collected by street clubs as well as Boy Scouts and other youth volunteers. In the Lee-Seville area, trash dumping similarly provided the spark for neighborhood action. The Miles Island Homeowners Association approached Councilman John Pilch in 1967, resulting in a special trash pickup for large junk items. However, dumping on the neighborhood's vacant tracts and especially the city's planned site for public housing—much of it apparently by commercial dumpers—proved difficult to solve. Some observers saw a need for cleanups even in Lee-Harvard by the late 1970s, as revealed in a grant application that called attention to "unpainted homes, bottles and garbage on lawns . . . [which are] on the increase."[43]

An integral part of cleanup efforts was lighting for decorative or security reasons, as revealed by the MPCC's slogan for the 1955 campaign, "CLEAN UP, PAINT UP, FIX UP, AND LIGHT UP." The organization initiated a Christmas lighting contest the following year; in 1958, it was additionally offering porch lights to neighborhood residents at half price. Similar efforts were visible in Glenville, where the Elgin Avenue Street Club won a *Call & Post*-backed Christmas lighting contest in 1963, as well as elsewhere; the Lee-Harvard Community Association (LHCA) started its own such contest by 1966, and the Corlett Area Community Council did by 1968. While these measures on the surface might

Glenville Area Community Council Activist Inspecting Leaf Litter, 1959. Residents lobbied the city to maintain services and improve living conditions in Cleveland's outlying black middle-class neighborhoods. (Courtesy of the *Cleveland Press* Collection, Cleveland State University Library)

seem to contribute only minimally to improving the quality of life in these neighborhoods, events like Christmas lighting contests allowed residents to showcase their community spirit or personal affluence and additionally fostered an atmosphere of friendly competition in which these efforts thrived. More important, they were part of an all-encompassing, middle-class worldview that considered pleasant surroundings an inducement to wholesome sociability and more illumination (in the case of porch lights or streetlights) as contributing to the safety of a neighborhood. Adequate street lighting on East 105th Street was a concern raised by the GACC just months after its founding in 1945; in 1948 the organization joined with other neighborhood groups to request better lighting along Parkwood Drive, and in 1952 it took credit for the installation of new streetlights along nine Glenville streets. The issue's durability was underlined in 1965 when Mrs. Jean Carter, the wife of a newly elected Glenville councilman—and a 1959 purse-snatching victim—promoted a plan for Glenville residents to leave their porch lights on until the city agreed to re-place streetlights.[44]

One of the most militant expressions of community activism in Cleveland's black middle-class neighborhoods, and one also having both moralistic and pragmatic aspects, surrounded the granting of liquor licenses. In 1949, GACC representatives had traveled to Toledo to register a complaint with the state liquor control board, which resulted in the temporary suspension of an East 105th Street bar's permit. In 1950, the MPCC mobilized residents to attend a downtown hearing, with the aim to oppose a bar transfer from Cedar-Central to Mount Pleasant—which was slated to reopen just down the street from a church and school, no less. Their action resulted in the transfer being de-nied, as did the action against a Glenville bar the following year, undertaken in conjunction with the Columbia School PTA. Such efforts were not limited to Glenville and Mount Pleasant; in 1952, citizens in Hough and on the West Side had also opposed bars opening in their neighborhoods, leading state liquor inspectors to undertake a study "to determine whether or not the issuance of new beer and wine permits would be detrimental." In 1955, before being elected councilman, Leo Jackson as head of the GACC's public safety com-mittee became so outraged with a deputy police inspector who signed off on a bar's transfer into Glenville that he circulated a petition condemning the action as "an open invitation to increased lawlessness," which got the inspec-tor dismissed. Voter action in 1958 on "local option" initiatives in Glenville and Hough later restricted the availability of alcohol in those neighborhoods, lead-ing the MPCC to consider a similar ban. According to MPCC president Joseph Fowler, "These bars will try to relocate, and they'll undoubtedly flock to the Mt. Pleasant neighborhood," which in his opinion had enough bars already. How-ever, after some consideration, the MPCC decided not to pursue this strategy, mainly "because the problems incident to the sale of liquor in Mt. Pleasant ap-peared to stem from causes other than the sale of liquor." Lee-Seville residents also had an existing record of opposing alcohol purveyors prior to 1959, when the Lee-Seville Citizens Council clashed with the Broadway YMCA for setting up its "Outpost" facility—directed at area youth in an attempt to provide recre-ation and improve race relations—between two bars. Councilmen represent-ing Glenville, Hough, and Mount Pleasant were concerned enough about the continuing availability of liquor in those neighborhoods to revisit the possi-bility of holding additional local option votes in 1964.[45]

In Lee-Harvard, liquor permit control was a stated function of the LHCA by 1965. In 1967, the organization was embroiled in a fight against the move-ment of bars into the area, recruiting concerned residents to attend city coun-cil hearings on the matter. Two bars in question, both recently shut out of Hough, were opposed on the grounds that one was slated to relocate across from an elementary school—and because their clientele had a notorious reputation. LHCA member Donald Root claimed that these bars had "a long record of arrests of both male and female prostitutes," with Rubie J. McCullough adding: "We don't object to bars per se. But a leopard doesn't change its spots. We are afraid that these bars will bring with them the wrong element." McCullough further described Lee Road as "saturated" with alcohol-serving establishments, adding that "residents are already sensitive to the increase of hoodlumism and vandalism that has occurred as a result of the operations of Shaker-Lee Hall, which caters to teen-age dances." The LHCA enlisted an array of Southeast Cleveland neighborhood organizations in the fight, and even organized a bus trip to Columbus so that activists could protest directly to State Liquor Board officials. In a dramatic show of strength, over one hundred residents, plus three city councilmen, the assistant law director, and two police officers made the trip, more people than could be seated in the small hearing room. Testifying in addition to the councilmen and police officers were two prominent Lee-Harvard residents, Municipal Court judge Lloyd O. Brown and Arnold R. Pinkney, a member of the Cleveland Board of Education. Residents donated sufficient funds to offset the cost of the bus trip and sent more than a hundred telegrams of protest to the state director of liquor control, with 3,000 signing their names to a petition against the bar transfers.[46]

Activists next announced their intention to work with black councilmen George W. White and Clarence Thompson in pursuit of a local option vote to "dry up" the Lee Road business strip, should the transfers be approved. In February 1968, the LHCA was vindicated when the State Liquor Board refused to allow the bars to relocate; and when one of the establishments, the Pullman Bar, decided to appeal the ruling in April, the LHCA chartered another bus trip to Columbus. That summer, following more testimony from local residents and leaders, the Pullman's owners finally decided to desist in their attempts to move into Lee-Harvard. As a preemptive measure, residents led by the LHCA nevertheless went ahead with a successful local option vote to ban bars in the area. The neighborhood's grocery markets were also affected by the measure, reduced to selling lower-alcohol content (3.2 percent) beer—to the consternation of their owners but to the jubilation of those residents opposed to liquor sales, since the new restrictions left only three carryout businesses where alcohol could be legally purchased in the area. Liquor availability in Lee-Harvard would resurface as an issue, notably in 1973 when the LHCA opposed a plan to open a liquor store in the Lee-Harvard Shopping Center because of its close proximity to John F. Kennedy High School. As noted, the struggling commercial development's black owners were none too happy with this outcome.[47]

While activists in middle-class African American neighborhoods took up many of the same issues, particular motivations and outcomes emerged from sometimes quite different local situations. In 1962, Glenville residents organized against plans for an East Boulevard luxury high-rise on the grounds that it would be out of character in the area, circulating petitions and securing Councilman Leo Jackson's assurances that he would oppose the necessary rezoning legislation. While Lee-Seville with its considerable vacant land had a long-standing history of mobilization around zoning, residents of adjacent Lee-Harvard, as a newer and higher-prestige area, expressed similar concerns. In 1961, residents there unsuccessfully opposed a zoning change allowing for a drive-in restaurant on Lee Road, on the grounds that the increased traffic, rodents, and rubbish could make the neighborhood a "less desirable place in which to live." Despite losing this battle, they found an ally in Leo Jackson, who commented, "Negroes have moved to the (Lee-Harvard) area to escape honky-tonks and hamburger joints." In 1967, the LHCA spoke out against a proliferation of gas stations as redundant and unsightly, approaching their councilman about the matter and passing a formal resolution against a rezoning sought by a Clark service station. Interestingly, the organization later moderated its position, in the face of business pullouts in the area; in 1973, when a failed grocery store announced it was planning to sell to a gas station, the LHCA declared that this would be preferable to "an additional boarded up store on Lee Road."[48] In Mount Pleasant, parents of students at Andrew J. Rickoff Elementary School approached the MPCC in 1967 to complain about gas stations for quite a different reason: concern that the associated traffic could potentially endanger children using the crosswalks. Going so far as to organize picketing around this issue, they were placated the following year when one oil company decided to donate flasher signals, to better mark the crosswalks. The GACC also mobilized around the issue of traffic safety as well as that of sufficient parking, lobbying the city for safer pedestrian crossings and improved signage, starting in 1948. Glenville residents also demanded that the city crack down on speeders and better enforce the parking rules, to protect lawns and facilitate street cleaning.[49]

Lee-Seville residents had also been mobilizing around traffic safety and infrastructure improvements for years, but took a more strident approach. After a Beehive Elementary School student was struck and killed on the way home from school in 1961, members of its PTA, along with the Lee-Seville Citizens Council and representatives from area churches and street clubs, approached the city's safety director with 500 signatures demanding a traffic light, school zone signs, and a crossing guard. While traffic surveys were promised, no immediate action was taken on the residents' quite reasonable demands, leading 200 mothers of Beehive pupils to picket the sidewalk-less stretch of South Miles Road where the student had been killed, carrying signs reading "Slow Down," "Let Our Children Live," and "Save Our Children." After three weeks of volunteer patrols by the women and an altercation with a police captain over the legality of their efforts, a paid crossing guard was hired. In another section completely cut off by railroad tracks, the Miles Island Homeowners Association in 1964 similarly recruited volunteer crossing guards for four shifts per day and demanded streetlights, paving, and better sewers in addition to a crosswalk. Clearly, Lee-Seville's quantity of undeveloped land, for which infrastructure was sometimes lacking, motivated residents to seek upgrades. While some improvements were added gradually, much work remained, as the issue resurfaced amid the controversy over proposed public housing for the area in 1968. By then, both the Lee-Seville Area Council and the Lee-Seville Ministerial Alliance were advocating for a railway underpass in order to guarantee police and fire protection to the isolated Miles Island area, and the following year, residents formed the Lee-Seville Citizens for Traffic Improvement after collecting over 3,200 signatures toward this end.[50]

While these active and organized residents had notable successes, other issues they attempted to address proved more intractable. As in the case of housing, the most serious challenges posed by the urban crisis were deeply rooted in metropolitan-wide structural factors that made them difficult to address on the neighborhood level. In the early 1950s, when racial residential transition began in earnest in these outlying black middle-class neighborhoods, the city was already poised for the subsequent economic freefall that accompanied the demise of its traditional heavy industrial base, a loss that proceeded in slow motion through the 1960s but would accelerate dramatically in the 1970s—and which persists today.[51] The accompanying decline in economic stability was experienced first and most severely by working-class African Americans, who were disadvantaged by both continuing racial discrimination and its lingering effects in the form of low seniority. These trends, combined with population displacements from the city's oldest, inner-core neighborhoods and a continuing migration from the South, put pressure on black middle-class Glenville, Mount Pleasant, and, eventually, Lee-Harvard. These interacting factors of course threatened the housing stock; but other effects were manifest in the form of overcrowded schools and a citywide increase in the crime rate. Interestingly, although activist residents of these neighborhoods were often aware of the larger structural dimensions to the problems they faced, many of them were just as likely to fall back on class or culturalist explanations for such symptoms of the urban crisis.

Much as they struggled to avert increasingly crowded conditions in the public schools,[52] activist black middle-class residents encountered adversity in their efforts to maintain thriving business districts. The factors underlying business turnover were complex and akin to racial residential transition. As some scholars have pointed out with regard to "white flight," not only white-owned businesses moving out but also the failure of new ones to move in accounted for their diminishing proportion over time.[53] In addition, the transfer of businesses from white to black ownership could be an exciting prospect for African American entrepreneurs, but unfortunately, this was frequently accompanied by decreased economic stability. As in the case of racial residential transition, larger structural constraints, including "push" factors like access to loans and affordable insurance coverage, as well as "pull" factors, such as the opportunity to conduct potentially more lucrative operations in newer and still-developing suburban areas, similarly played crucial roles in determining whether businesses would be able to persevere in the city. To a considerable degree, too, the small proprietorships occupying these neighborhoods' traditional business strips faced increasing competition from larger corporate enterprises generally located in the suburbs. Business activity in older neighborhoods like Glenville and Mount Pleasant was contracting already prior to racial residential transition. But as seen in the case of the Lee-Harvard Shopping Center, even a business venture benefiting from modern and spacious facilities and situated in a comparatively affluent, outlying area was not guaranteed success. Without losing sight of the overarching structural considerations involved in the decline of urban business districts, the aggravating role played by crime and juvenile delinquency—and equally important, the fear of these whether justified or not—must also be taken into account. In many cases, perception provided the impetus for remedial action, with or without the statistical information necessary to accurately gauge the actual level of risk.

In Glenville and Mount Pleasant, concerns over the state of the neighborhoods' commercial strips dated to the early postwar period. In 1950, GACC volunteers had approached all the business owners on East 105th Street and asked the city to do a better job of street cleaning—requests the organization followed up on in subsequent years when it succeeded in getting new rubbish bins for the strip and formed a special committee that pressured merchants to do a better job of keeping their individual sections of sidewalk clean. In 1955, the GACC assisted in the formation of a Glenville Merchants Civic Association, which in 1958 launched a "SHOP-IN-GLENVILLE" campaign and brainstormed parking improvements for the area. However, for a variety of reasons, it proved difficult to maintain a vibrant business base. Complaints about the quality of grocery offerings in the neighborhood led the GACC to conduct a "Shoppers' Store Check" in 1960, which proposed assigning establishments points on the basis of price, cleanliness, and health regulation compliance. A GACC field worker concluded that local businesses "do not carry the quality and variety of merchandise found in downtown Stores" and found that food items, especially, were bought elsewhere by "discriminating" shoppers. A subsequent study of the residents' shopping habits, for which the City Plan Commission polled over 3,000 Glenville residents in 1961, uncovered that many bought their groceries in suburbs like East Cleveland and Shaker Heights. One of the few quoted who did her shopping within the neighborhood complained, "Unless I get there early the parking lots are always covered with broken glass. Loiterers along the main avenues keep me from walking to the store." Such findings led planners to propose consolidating and upgrading the neighborhood's shopping facilities; no concrete action was taken toward this end, however, and in the meantime observers noted a rising number of vacant storefronts.[54]

Activists in Mount Pleasant pursued a similar approach but went even farther. In conjunction with the 1950 citywide cleanup campaign, the MPCC sent letters to Kinsman Road business owners that read: "Here's a chance for you and the Kinsman community to get into the fight against dirt and uncleanliness and make Kinsman Road a shopping center of which to be proud. . . . We must take steps now to make the neighborhood a better place to live in, work and do business." Apprehension resurfaced in 1958, as the MPCC teamed with local merchants to improve the appearance of the commercial strip in a "fight against the forces of deterioration and decay." Later that year, the organization sponsored a series of meetings with local business owners that continued to place much of the blame with them, as at one luncheon meeting where both the area councilman and an urban renewal staffer exhorted proprietors to maintain standards and keep their premises clean. While one resident participant described the problem as "getting reputable merchants and professional people to fill the void left by departing businesses," the increasing tendency of residents to shop in the suburbs and a lack of parking came up here, too, as major causes for concern. As a result of these meetings, the MPCC and area businesses organized a "giant neighborhood Christmas party" to promote good community relations, purchased several lots for additional parking facilities, and planned to upgrade lighting along the strip. Tragically, these plans were marred by the fatal robbery of a Mount Pleasant store owner at the start of the holiday season. In 1960, the MPCC would again meet with area merchants and vow to seek a permanent increase in beat patrols, following the beating and robbery of a couple who had owned a bakery in the neighborhood for thirty-four years.[55]

By this point, however, strains of pessimism could be heard. A joint committee of the MPCC and Mount Pleasant Community Centers concluded, "Kinsman Rd. tends to give a black eye to adjacent residential streets, most of which are well kept." The committee named traffic congestion, zoning violations, "shoddy" storefronts, loitering and illicit business activity, inadequate policing and street lighting, and unsanitary conditions around eating establishments as conditions needing attention. Likewise, a 1961 report on the neighborhood claimed that "the deterioration of a main route . . . threatens the stability, pride, and standards of the residents." It added: "Deteriorating public highways frequently become social centers for attracting some young people. . . . Criminal elements often infiltrate such areas, [and] introduce illegal and other activities destructive to persons, and neighborhood and community." Later that year, the Mount Pleasant Community Centers organized the Kinsman Conservation Committee to rehabilitate that thoroughfare and Union Avenue to match the neighborhood's generally well-maintained housing stock. Intending to work with city officials and business owners, the committee convinced the City Plan Commission to study conditions in the neighborhood and inspired some local teens to form a "Conservation Club" to help with a survey and assist in litter removal. By fall, the organization had renamed itself the Kinsman-Union Improvement Committee and was attempting to recruit 400 area business owners, of whom about fifty showed up for a subsequent meeting. That these efforts did little to reverse existing trends is suggested by a subsequent grant request from 1963, which repeated earlier evaluations: "Many stores are being converted to businesses which tend to downgrade the neighborhood. On the whole, a sense of drab, demoralizing blight is affecting this important neighborhood commercial strip. . . . The contrast is more marked since this is a community which is generally characterized by pleasant, well-kept homes and gardens."[56]

It is important to sift through these negative assessments carefully, with an eye on the evaluators; for example, "businesses which tend to downgrade the neighborhood" suggests a bias against specialty shops more likely to be black owned and to cater to an African American, often youthful clientele. This is not to imply that no black observers shared such skepticism about the types of businesses setting up shop as the longtime, mostly white merchants moved out. For example, at a 1963 MPCC meeting, social worker George Livingston noted with obvious distaste: "Desperate property owners, with vacant rental space on their hands, will eventually lease to any unsavory, fly-by-night outfit." But the fact that there was a racial dimension attached to business pull-outs comes through in the Union Neighborhood Action Committee's decision, that same year, to approach the Community Relations Board (CRB)—the body that had mediated the city's racial conflicts since 1945—for help in dealing with rising vandalism, shoplifting, and verbal threats against store owners in the vicinity of Kinsman Road and East 116th Street. At the same time, the CRB, after surveying the area, repeated its traditional request that business owners keep their premises and sidewalks clear of litter and cut off the supply of alcoholic beverages to minors.[57]

While the overall trajectory was downward, it is worth noting that some Mount Pleasant business establishments continued to be economically viable in the mid-1960s, including white-owned ones. A 1964 newspaper article featured two businesses that were actually expanding, namely Nathan Sacks's drugstore and gift shop at East 142nd Street and Kinsman and Sam Karp's nearby shoe store—the owners' surnames additionally indicating they were Jewish. Sacks, incidentally, was president of the Mount Pleasant Business and Professional Men's Association, as well as chair of the Fourth District Police Advisory Committee, at the time.[58] But over the course of the 1960s and into the next decade, Mount Pleasant's commercial districts continued their gradual decline. A 1969 economic survey found residents repeating many long-standing complaints about shopping in the area: exorbitant prices, poor selection and shoddy merchandise, shabby-looking establishments, and a dearth of parking space. On the bright side, 223 of the 234 residents interviewed for the study claimed they patronized neighborhood stores, at least to some extent. The most prevalent types of establishments were beauty shops (of which there were 34), groceries and delicatessens (27), barbershops (19), restaurants (17), dry cleaners (16), service stations (13), and variety stores (12)—indicating that small proprietorships were still the norm and hinting at a considerable degree of black ownership. However, the study also recorded an increasing number of vacancies and deteriorated properties, besides noting that many businesses had difficulty obtaining insurance or could obtain only partial coverage. In 1971, the Urban League's Mount Pleasant branch likewise reported that business owners were denied insurance, which it blamed on a high burglary rate. Bemoaning a variety of problems in Mount Pleasant by the late 1970s, particularly in its western half, a 1978 grant application claimed that the "gradual pulling out of business interests, boarded up buildings and burnt out billboards add more fuel to the fear syndrome," which increasingly characterized this once thriving middle-class stronghold.[59]

Observers and residents in Southeast Cleveland neighborhoods besides Mount Pleasant also registered alarm at the deterioration of business thoroughfares. As early as 1962, a "community workshop" sponsored by the LHCA had included a panel discussion asking "Is Lee Road Our Shame or Fame?" By 1967, the LHCA was claiming success in building constructive relationships with area merchants, but less than three years later a grant application would cite symptoms seemingly identical to those faced earlier in Glenville and Mount Pleasant: "Decline of the area is reflected in the increasing number of vacant storefronts, left behind by stable businesses which can not secure adequate insurance protection and the need for iron bars covering windows, not to mention the threat of physical harm to the businessman or his customers." Similar to Mount Pleasant, a Businessmen's Alliance was formed in 1970, and enough Lee-Harvard proprietors expressed optimism in a 1971 "abandonment study" for the Urban League to conclude: "Businessmen interviewed felt the area is stable. They attribute vandalism problems to outsiders and poor police protection." However, many observed that more businesses were leaving the area than were coming in. By 1977, the Harvard Community Services Center was noting "a decrease in the number of retail stores and total service stores in the area" but on a bright note commended the "community pressure" that had motivated a local supermarket to offer better-quality merchandise.[60]

Compared to other areas, Lee-Harvard benefited from the comparative newness of its commercial properties and its greater supply of parking, which helped to slow the rate of business pullouts. Revealingly, merchants operat-

Lee Road Business Strip, 1979. Black middle-class residents of the outlying Lee-Harvard neighborhood were dissatisfied with the appearance and types of businesses lining the main commercial artery, making it a focus of cleanup and quality-control efforts. (Courtesy of the Cleveland Public Library/Official City of Cleveland Photograph)

ing in Corlett's older commercial districts, also interviewed for the aforementioned 1971 study, proved considerably less sanguine. In the aging East 131st Street business strip, a shoe repair shop owner's typical response was summarized: "Party interviewed totally dissatisfied with the area. In response to the question of whether businesses were relocating, interviewed party pointed out the window to the stores closed on his street." The previous year, in fact, the Corlett Area Community Council had held a meeting at the Mount Haven Baptist Church, where more than sixty residents discussed how to keep the neighborhood's storefronts tenanted and resolved to survey area business owners about their intentions. Around 1972, Councilman John Barnes helped form an organization called the Congress of Urban Men, which focused on renovating East 131st Street storefronts. By 1975 Barnes was pointing to some mixed successes, such as the banning of go-go girls from local taverns and the founding of a "neighborhood little theater," which, regrettably, had recently been burglarized. Barnes, like community activists elsewhere, mentioned the tendency of "undesirable" businesses (for example, pawnshops, adult bookstores, and poolrooms) to drive away "more stable" establishments. "If decay is permitted to start here, it will move to Harvard and Lee and Seville," Barnes opined. "Once this area goes, the entire community will follow," he cautioned.

Taking a similar approach, a group of African American businessmen, called the Lee-Seville-Miles Economic Development Corporation, had conducted a 1972 study in the hope of preempting retail losses all along Lee Road, while the following year another business owners' group, Miles Ahead, Inc., was constituted with the intention to upgrade Miles Avenue from Lee Road all the way into the adjacent suburb of Warrensville Heights.[61]

Crime consistently appears as a contributing factor in the decline of business districts in Glenville and the various neighborhoods of Southeast Cleveland, although, as sociologists have found, isolating its specific influence proves incredibly difficult.[62] As previously mentioned, more comprehensive statistical data would establish how much crime rates actually changed over time—but perception takes on special significance in discussing this topic, because fear can be as powerful as actual risk in motivating individuals, whether residents or business owners, to remain in or exit a given area. What follows then, is not a comprehensive analysis of crime in Cleveland's black middle-class neighborhoods following racial residential transition, but rather a look at how residents interpreted the causes and significance of crime, and how perceptions as much as actual crime shaped the reform agendas adopted by these residents.

As with the beginnings of business district deterioration, fears of increased crime in Glenville and Mount Pleasant dated to the early postwar years. Some illicit criminal activity in Glenville took place behind closed doors—whether bootlegging, illegal gambling, or prostitution, all of which were targeted, in one 1952 example, through a leafleting effort by the Earle Avenue Improvement Club inviting residents to report suspicious activities. In a broader version of this approach, in 1953, the GACC's Public Safety Committee circulated questionnaires to neighborhood organizations and individuals seeking "information concerning places and situations known to be public nuisances or in violation of the law." Other crimes in Glenville were more shockingly open, such as the predations of an apparent serial rapist that the *Call & Post* reported on in 1951. Following the revelation that the number of serious crimes—including robberies, burglaries, larcenies, and auto thefts—committed during the month of December 1953 outnumbered those committed over the entire course of 1951, Councilman Harry Jaffe demanded better police protection for the neighborhood. Leo Jackson's subsequent ascent to chairmanship of the GACC's Public Safety Committee in 1954 signaled a more proactive approach, beginning with the issuance of a detailed report compiled from police statistics that documented a one-third rise in the crime rate over the period 1950–55. When the number of reported crimes in the year following the report declined by nearly 20 percent, Jackson and the Public Safety Committee took credit, attributing this to better lines of communication with the Police Department, its actions taken to shut down or closely supervise pool halls and bars, and residents' vigilance in reporting suspicious activities taking place in private homes. A typical memorandum submitted to the Sixth Police District gave the addresses of particular properties with detailed descriptions such as "strong suspicion of organized prostitution. Women have been observed frequenting local bars and returning with men. Automobiles have also been observed to stop frequently at this home." In addition, the GACC's Public Safety Committee went on record in 1955 as supporting police permission to frisk, upon suspicion of concealed weapons, and on one occasion commended an off-duty officer for intervening in a violent dispute between two motorists.[63]

Crime reduction measures continued even after Jackson's election to the City Council forced him to resign as chair of the Public Safety Committee, but in Glenville, as elsewhere, the issue proved tenacious. In 1957, the Public Safety Committee wrote the city's safety director to request more foot patrolmen in dealing with "vagrants, drunks, and loiterers," whose "obscene language and abusive actions" made it "almost impossible for decent people to walk the street." Four block clubs, the Glenville High School PTA, and the 24th Ward Democrats Club joined in calling for more police patrols the following year. In 1960, the beating and robbing of an elderly resident by three youths drew an outcry from the GACC as well as criticism from Councilman Jackson regarding the slow police response time to the incident. GACC Public Safety Committee chair Russell Adrine also emphasized community responsibility, venturing shortly thereafter: "If the community attitude is to pass a problem on the other side of the street because it 'does not concern or affect me immediately' then there is little chance to maintain a high standard for the neighborhood." He concluded that "if the council is to continue to represent the will of the decent people then they must come forth with time, energy and support for the kind of community you want this to be. AT ALL COST this fight must be a never ending ONE." Into the following decade, Glenville activists shifted emphasis toward improving police-community relations, while still encouraging residents to report suspicious or unwholesome activities. However, these traditional middle-class reform strategies were increasingly eclipsed by the appearance of younger-generation militants in Glenville. Most famous, in July 1968, Fred (Ahmed) Evans's Black Nationalists of New Libya engaged in a shoot-out with police that sparked several days of rioting along Superior Avenue. Taking a different approach, neighborhood activists subsequently convened a "people's court" attended by 500 at Cory Methodist Church, to investigate complaints of police brutalizing innocent bystanders in suppressing the disorder. Such activism provides context for aging *Call & Post* editor William O. Walker's insistence that in order to restore the neighborhood's "prosperity," Glenville residents should "eradicate from their midst those irresponsible persons who, despite their protestations about black nationalism and soul brotherhood, are the ones who are destroying the very foundations upon which Negro aspirations rest."[64]

As for Mount Pleasant, the MPCC had expressed concerns about crime as early as 1950, even as the police captain in charge of the district downplayed its prevalence, saying he did "not see any particular problem in the area, in terms of a crime pattern." The Mount Pleasant Community Centers kept their own "confidential statistics" on crime between 1953 and 1957 and concluded that robberies, burglaries, and auto theft were on the increase. Still, what they considered more worrisome was that "information about criminal events or less serious disturbances often spreads rapidly through anxiety-ridden neighborhoods, and frequently can be in highly exaggerated forms. Some white families respond with fear and flight." Overall, crime—as distinguished from juvenile delinquency—did not emerge as a focus of neighborhood reform efforts until the late 1960s, although one grant application did note in retrospect that "major crimes" had nearly doubled between 1964 and 1968. Then, in the summer of 1968, at a time when large numbers of working-class African Americans in Cleveland and around the country were in dramatic rebellion against police brutality and police authority itself, Mount Pleasant resident and MPCC "hotline" founder William Franklin organized a neighborhood-based auxiliary police unit, the Mount Pleasant Citizens of Concern. While Franklin's vision of 300 members—up to one-third of them women—never grew beyond the original thirty, this core group did obtain police training and with much fanfare completed a course in police-community relations. The organization might have expanded had it won the $50,000 in grant funding its founder subsequently sought from the Cleveland Foundation. Franklin was later elected to the City Council, and in 1972 amid reportedly rising crime, he redoubled his efforts for a neighborhood corps of trained police aides. While it is unclear whether such citizen patrols were actually established, three years later Councilman Franklin was still heavily involved in the issue of police protection, having been designated to ride with police serving in the area by the Mount Pleasant Civic and Social Club.[65]

In Lee-Harvard, the LHCA declared its commitment to "citizen-police cooperation" as early as 1965, and by 1967 was reporting improved relations with law enforcement as one of its accomplishments—although at this point such efforts focused on reducing juvenile delinquency over crime per se. By 1971, however, a rash of robberies sparked the formation of a War on Crime Committee out of the Harvard Community Services Center, complete with street lookouts organized through the block clubs, auxiliary police patrols, and a hotline to report suspicious activity. The number of robberies and assaults-to-rob in the area rose from seventeen to sixty-seven between 1966 and 1970, with pharmacies as primary targets—not just for money but also for drugs. By mid-1972, some thirty-five men had been recruited for a police auxiliary, the Harvard Service Patrol, while the block watch program had supposedly prevented an unspecified number of break-ins. Although these efforts were significant,

Patrol commander Billy J. Tanton felt that his organization would need to be doubled in size to be truly effective. Indeed, the Harvard Community Services Center was noting "in the Lee-Harvard area the rate of home break-ins is one of the highest in the city," and in a subsequent grant proposal divulged that the community had been subjected to 779 breaking and entering incidents in 1971 alone. Since a majority of these were perpetrated during daytime working hours, the Center surmised: "it can be assumed that a portion of them were committed by youth who were out of school with no jobs and idle time." Patrol commander Tanton similarly conflated crime and juvenile delinquency, stating: "We think one of the ways we help cut down on crime, and save many potential juvenile delinquents is [that] when they realize their own parents are involved in crime prevention and crime detection, their own inclinations are dampened."[66]

Similar developments were visible in other Southeast Cleveland neighborhoods. In late 1969, the Corlett Area Community Council responded to an increased number of daytime housebreakings by instructing residents to keep a detailed record of their calls to police, in order to counteract—as council president Thomas Sheppard cautioned—"apathy on the part of the police." He also asked residents to contact his organization, as well as their City Council representative. As break-ins and purse-snatchings persisted into 1971, the Union-Miles Civic Association sponsored a meeting of residents, police, and the area councilman at the Avon Baptist Church, where some residents offered to pay a nominal monthly fee for private security patrols. Also in 1971, the breakup of a single burglary ring operating in Lee-Miles (Lee-Seville and Lee-Harvard) was said to have decreased the number of break-ins by nearly 40 percent. In early 1972, the Lee-Seville Citizens Council responded to rising crime rates across Southeast Cleveland by sponsoring a joint meeting with the MPCC, LHCA, Corlett Area Community Council, and several other community organizations. Again, juvenile delinquency and drug use came up, as well as the fact that working wives and mothers left a high proportion of the area's homes unoccupied during the day. Despite these efforts, crime seemed to worsen; in mid-1974, the murder of James P. Christy, a black Lee-Harvard pharmacist who had been active in efforts to establish the auxiliary police patrol, led to widespread community soul-searching and a reward fund to identify the perpetrators of violent crimes. Over the course of 1975, the Urban League's Lee-Harvard branch expressed alarm at several other shootings of local merchants, even as the neighborhood's auxiliary police patrol—renamed the Concerned Citizens Committee of the Southeast Area—expanded to more than a hundred male and female members.[67]

Of all such self-identified problems in black middle-class neighborhoods, so-called juvenile delinquency is the most complicated. As seen, some observers straightforwardly linked delinquent behavior and crime. Some delinquent behaviors could certainly escalate into major crimes; thus, for many residents and observers, delinquency was considered a direct stepping stone to criminality. But judgments about what constitutes delinquency can be notoriously subjective. In general, we may distinguish delinquency from crime as having no apparent economic motive. Youths may engage in delinquent acts for notoriety, to underline group distinctions, as rebellion against authority, or simply for thrills.[68] Youth rebelliousness rose across American society at least from the 1950s onward. But separating such behavior from economic motives is vital to understanding how and why delinquency plagued a relatively affluent community such as Lee-Harvard; indeed, as mentioned, some observers suspected that affluence itself—and especially hard-won affluence—actually fostered and enabled certain delinquent behaviors. While some equated delinquency with criminality, others believed that what youth really needed were recreational outlets, which explains the long-standing emphasis on building such facilities in these neighborhoods.

In Glenville as elsewhere, the earliest attempts to address delinquency were undertaken with the cooperation of schools, social agencies, churches, and parents. Under the slogan "Community Teamwork for Youth," the GACC made juvenile delinquency the theme of its 1952 annual meeting, attended by more than one hundred at Cory Methodist Church. Over the following year, the organization developed its program further, approaching local PTAs and recreational venues, as well as establishing a "delinquency council" and junior police program in the local schools. "Perhaps we are asking too much of the police and not accepting enough of the responsibility ourselves," one participant told the local press. After a 1953 incident in which two nine-year-old boys were beaten, burned with a cigarette, and slashed with a knife by two teenaged bullies, the GACC sent parents on a door-to-door "March on Delinquency" pleading for better supervision of wayward youth. "The responsibility for this brutal act lies with the Glenville community," the organization's secretary declared to the press. The GACC also called for the Police Department's Juvenile Bureau to extend its coverage and to strictly enforce the curfew ordinance. By 1954, the GACC was attempting to address delinquent behavior through a "Teamwork for Youth" committee made possible with $35,000 in grant funding. Lasting into the early 1960s, Teamwork for Youth organized programming at local schools, sought to compile statistics on juvenile delinquency, and lobbied the city for school board supervision, recreational facilities, and improved policing. However, by the late 1960s Glenville reform activists were struggling with the problem of street gangs, as well as blaming black militants for "exciting the young people." In 1967, one United Youth Program worker described Glenville as "in turmoil," with area youth "rapidly losing faith in the old structures which have proved to be empty promises." "These teenagers feel the Y.M.C.A. is too middle class for them," he added.[69]

In Mount Pleasant, the issue of juvenile delinquency came up as early as 1954, when Councilman Joseph Horowitz, with the backing of the MPCC, first demanded city funding for a recreation center to counteract "anti-social tendencies" among local youth. Tellingly, in an MPCC-sponsored forum that year, some participants blamed "complacent" parents for the problem. While the neighborhood had to wait for its recreation center until 1962, concerns with juvenile delinquency mounted. In 1957, the MPCC's Youth Committee first sponsored a program on the topic, and the following year it polled residents on the needs and problems of youth. Girls as well as boys were identified as potential delinquents, as in one group in their late teens whom the Mount Pleasant Community Centers in 1959 reported were "hanging out in a local snack bar and on the street corners" and engaging in "drinking, truancy, sexual promiscuity, association with older men, and hostile and negative behavior."[70] In 1961, residents, school officials, and business owners beseeched the Mount Pleasant Community Centers to do something about the neighborhood's unemployed youth, mostly high school dropouts, who "spend their leisure [time] hanging around corners, in pool rooms, gambling, drinking wine, loitering on the playgrounds and vacant lots in the area, and participating in other forms of anti-social behavior." While these were isolated examples, the juvenile delinquency rate for Mount Pleasant in 1962 was well above the average, and social service providers in the area later claimed it doubled between 1960 and 1965. While much of the work of dealing with juvenile delinquency was left to social workers, some residents began to address the issue themselves. In 1965, members of the East 117th Street Club organized a neighborhood patrol to enforce the curfew ordinance, an approach soon expanded to six more streets in the area. In quite a different approach, Ethel Brock, a lifelong resident, founded the Mount Pleasant Youth Action Council in 1970 with grant funding, through which she offered tutoring and recreation programs to "get the kids off the streets."[71]

While the tendency of both parents having to work was frequently commented upon, the fact that Lee-Harvard as a newer neighborhood initially lacked social service and recreation centers was also considered a cause for concern. As early as 1963 the LHCA's Recreation Committee contacted the Mount Pleasant Community Centers for advice on establishing its own program. Illustrating the extent to which some considered recreation as a panacea for delinquent behavior, LHCA president Rubie J. McCullough told the local press in 1967: "If we had more recreation facilities—if we had any at all—we'd have fewer gangs and maybe it would eliminate some of the vandalism. They promised us something in Kerruish Park years ago. But all they've done is put up a few swings." The Lee-Seville Citizens Council had in fact lobbied for that park's completion at least since 1965; ironically, as illustrated by Glenville and Mount Pleasant, parks and playgrounds actually provided space for youths to dally. The need for more recreational facilities as well as youth job opportunities rated high on the agenda of the combined Southeast area councils meeting called by the LHCA in April 1968 and held, symbolically, at John F. Kennedy High School. Concerns about juvenile delinquency were paramount in the establishment of the Harvard Community Services Center later that year, in which the LHCA took an active role; its opening was preceded by a summer pilot "drop-in center" program offering sports and games, which was co-sponsored by the LHCA and nuns from Saint Henry's convent (out of which it was run). Yet ironically, group discussions in 1970 revealed that some nearby residents were ambivalent about the center. While "several people said they thought one of the main purposes of the center was to take children off the street and find a meeting place for wholesome activities," others complained about the noise it created and the fights that sometimes erupted. In response, "Councilman McCall said the people in the community are not willing to admit that the neighborhood has problems, and the center is a positive response to these problems. . . . It is necessary to have involvement of the community in order to attack problems like juvenile delinquency."[72]

Among the most dismaying instances of juvenile delinquency in Lee-Harvard related to the schools. As mentioned, the LHCA had expressed concern with the conduct of children on the way home from school as early as 1967, and, even earlier, resident Ancusto Butler had organized a 1965 sidewalk "stand-in" along Harvard Avenue to discourage John F. Kennedy High School students from tossing litter onto lawns. In 1975, the Lee-Harvard Urban League was still pondering what to do about junior high and high school students "congregating" along the business strip after school, which prompted school officials to ask that the neighborhood's auxiliary police volunteers be deployed during school dismissal. More sensational yet were several firearm-related incidents that occurred in and on the premises of John F. Kennedy High School. In 1970, one student shot and wounded another in a school hallway, following an argument. In late 1973, another Kennedy student was shot in the parking lot, although observers noted that in the same week there was also a shooting in the affluent Shaker Heights schools. Early the next year, police arrested a student for drawing an unloaded gun during an argument, and the following week, youths fired shots at a teacher in the school parking lot after he attempted to expel them from the school grounds.[73]

As a result of this last incident, Kennedy principal George E. Mills called a meeting with parents, for which 1,500 showed up to hear him announce that six guns had recently been confiscated and that he was instituting strict new security measures. Students were henceforth barred from using the parking lot, a remedy some parents had previously opposed because it would prevent their children from driving to school. By way of explanation, several school officials as well as a former PTA officer expressed their belief that a lack of parental involvement and poor discipline underlay the problem. Kennedy students felt these were instances where bluffing got out of hand and also ascribed some influence to macho imagery from popular movies like *Shaft* and *Superfly*. Similar cases were noted at John Adams High School; the hiring of security guards there in 1970 did not prevent a student from being robbed of his coat at gunpoint in a hallway that year. Such gun-related incidents occasionally occurred even at the junior high school level, as when three boys were wounded by gunfire exchanged in the course of an after-school fight at Corlett's Robert Jamison Junior High in 1975.[74] All these incidents are noteworthy because they fit into a larger pattern of community concern and an agenda around which black middle-class activists had been mobilizing for years.

Some observers had always regarded Lee-Harvard's comparative affluence as a potential factor in juvenile misbehavior—a judgment often accompanied by charges of poor parental discipline. Revealingly, among those problems that led the LHCA to meet with police in 1966 was drag racing, further underlining that some Lee-Harvard youth had cars at their disposal. Those present at a 1973 Urban League meeting complained that "the youth contribute to these problems on their own since they feel they can do anything they want to do. They also do these things to keep up with their friends or to stay in the group. Also, they do things to spite their parents." One participant opined that "problems are caused when the parents give their children, as young as 14 years of age, their own cars to keep them busy so they don't bother them. Their parents have a tendency to want to show off their own houses and cars and give their children lots of things that show [status], rather [than] to discipline them, and get involved in their activities." Following the crisis precipitated by the slaying of pharmacist James P. Christy in 1974, one resident told the press: "Total community cooperation is necessary as far as these kids go. Maybe there should be beat policemen with radios, but there should be more parental concern." That this theme would continue beyond the decade comes through in the community's furor over the 1981 beating death of a seventeen-year-old by gang members at the Lee-Harvard intersection. At a meeting attended by 250 people, angry residents exhorted parents to rein in their children and demanded that police enforce curfew violations in the neighborhood. "You must tighten up your laws at home," commented one resident present. "If laws at home are broken, you can be sure laws on the street will be broken."[75]

■

The black neighborhoods discussed in this chapter, and particularly Lee-Harvard, retained middle-class residents into the 1980s and beyond. In fact, the 1980 census estimated Lee-Harvard's and Lee-Seville's combined median income at $21,000, dramatically higher than the city's at $12,300 and higher even than the county's at $18,000. The houses there, pricing in at a median of $37,000, were among Cleveland's most expensive. Even in hardest-hit Glenville, organizations like the East 111th Street Club were as of 1981 keeping alive the traditional reform agenda of beautifying yards, lobbying the city to maintain vacant lots, and reporting "suspicious" activities. "People want to say it's a dead section, but it's alive," one resident of the former "Gold Coast" section along East Boulevard asserted in 1985. "The neighborhood is growing. People want to live in this section," she insisted. A 1979 newspaper feature on Southeast Cleveland encapsulated the theme of upwardly mobile African American residents having come in search of better housing and schools, stating that for many, "the move [there] represented the end of a struggle to lift themselves from the squalor of the inner-city and give their children a better chance in life." Though focused mainly on Lee-Harvard, the feature mentioned Mount Pleasant's "stately, older homes" and "small, neat front lawns," and that Lee-Seville "resembles a suburban subdivision, with rows of small, box-like homes lining its quiet streets." While many of Lee-Harvard's original, highest-status African American pioneers had since moved to the suburbs, the neighborhood had supposedly "become the home for countless black families moving into the middle-class and seeking the good life." A wide mix of socio-economic levels characterized the area, including "retirees and newlyweds, laborers and doctors, people who rely on food stamps to buy their groceries and those who have maids to do the shopping." Some residents hired professional landscaping companies to do their yard work, while on the other hand, according to one longtime resident, "there are some [families] that may be living over their heads out here, but they moved here to provide their kids with the good things and they're willing to work hard to be here."[76]

But while this particular article expressed a nearly boundless exuberance at hard-striving black families, other renditions were just as likely to revisit the traditional fears that upward mobility came with insecurities. "It looks like the suburbs—but again, appearances are deceiving," went a 1985 newspaper article on Lee-Harvard that continued on to say: "The houses around Charles W. Eliot Junior High School are especially well-maintained, which makes it hard to believe the playground and athletic fields near the school . . . have been hangouts for street gangs that have harassed schoolchildren." Rubie J. McCullough, still the director of the Harvard Community Services Center and interviewed for the article, continued to emphasize the widespread phenomenon of both parents working, which in her view negatively impacted children. "They write about us being middle-class, but if that were true, we'd have much more parental participation in the schools," commented McCullough, adding that despite calls for more police in the area, what Lee-Harvard really needed was "more community involvement."[77] Upwardly mobile black Clevelanders in 1980 had many accomplishments of which to be proud, but for many who chose to remain in these city neighborhoods, the same old fears and insecurities about maintaining a reasonable quality of life remained. Cultural and even moral explanations for the symptoms of the urban crisis continued to carry weight, even as large-scale structural factors like the final collapse of the city's industrial economy demonstrably shaped the lives of many Clevelanders, and particularly those disproportionately black residents mired in poverty—more and more of whom would eventually make their way into these former preserves of the black middle class.

Epilogue

The trees are full-grown now, but otherwise the trim brick bunga-lows on Myrtle Avenue in Cleveland's southeastern corner look much the same as when African American contractor Arthur Bus-sey built them in 1959.[1] Sitting on well-groomed lawns, they are still recognizable by the distinctive "B" incorporated into their decorative front screen doors, but they are otherwise virtually indistinguishable from the typi-cal brick, single-family homes lining the residential streets of nearby Maple Heights and Garfield Heights, or Euclid to the northeast of the city—suburbs to which upwardly mobile, middle-class blacks were moving in increasing numbers by the 1980s. Whereas most of the homeowners on Myrtle Avenue are elderly, the housing on Sunny Glenn Avenue just two blocks to the north was built with a different clientele in mind: young African American profes-sionals. Here, townhouses constructed in the late 1990s resemble those found in the farthest-outlying suburbs like Solon and Aurora. Some have sold for over $200,000—four times the city's current median home value, and nearly double that for the metropolitan area as a whole, which currently stands at around $125,000. Even in Glenville, where poverty spiked as early as the 1960s, long-time homeowners have admirably maintained their sumptuous homes on East Boulevard and Wade Park Avenue, while younger buyers with more means move into the newly restored "Heritage Lane" houses on East 105th Street or purchase New Urbanist properties built as part of Cleveland's postindustrial "renaissance." Long after most upwardly mobile African Americans departed for the suburbs, then, some continue to choose the city as a place to enact their dreams of a better life. Yet, especially since the Great Recession hit in 2008, all has not been well with the black middle class, whether in Cleveland, in its sub-urbs, or in other metropolitan areas around the country.

Although an in-depth examination is beyond the scope of this book, an overview of Cleveland's black suburbanization aids in understanding how pat-terns of geographic mobility played out beyond the neighborhoods discussed here and offers useful perspective on the post-1980 situation faced by the former "surrogate suburbs" of Glenville, Mount Pleasant, and Lee-Miles. The exodus of upwardly mobile African Americans out of the city has followed two main vectors. One points to the northeast, with black families moving into East

Cleveland by the mid-1960s and Cleveland Heights by the 1970s, followed by Euclid in the 1980s, and then South Euclid and Richmond Heights in the 1990s. This vector is currently crossing the Cuyahoga County line into adjacent Lake County, as black families move beyond Euclid into Wickliffe and Willoughby Hills. The other vector extends to the southeast, where African Americans gained access to portions of Shaker Heights and Garfield Heights as early as the late 1950s, before moving into Warrensville Heights in the late 1960s, Maple Heights in the late 1970s, and Bedford and Bedford Heights in the 1980s.[2] Upwardly mobile black families have in recent years been buying in Solon, the southeasternmost Cuyahoga County suburb, which has experienced rapid growth since the 1990s. Preexisting black suburban enclaves, a historic pattern explored by Andrew Wiese, also characterized the Cleveland area, with significant clusters in Woodmere, Chagrin Falls, Maple Heights, Oakwood, and Berea influencing postwar population dynamics in the surrounding areas. And in a continuation of the observable pattern in the neighborhoods covered here, African Americans gravitated toward suburbs with substantial Jewish populations, notably Cleveland Heights and Shaker Heights, and to a somewhat lesser extent, University Heights and Beachwood. In 1965, only about 1 percent of all African Americans in Greater Cleveland were suburban residents, whereas in 2010, approximately half were. Yet despite this shift, the metropolitan area remains highly segregated today—among the most segregated in the country—with substantial portions in the east, and especially the west and south, exhibiting a black population share well below 10 percent.[3]

While the explicitly racialized, "dual" housing market of the previous century has evolved into one that presently reproduces racial inequality in a subtler fashion, upwardly mobile African Americans clearly still feel the desire to expand their living options by relocating to the metropolitan periphery. Overcrowding in city neighborhoods may no longer be an issue in the post–Great Migration era, but older housing stock with a weightier maintenance burden, limited or poor-quality shopping options, and unsatisfactory public schools remain prime motivating factors, not to mention fear of crime or—with the stagnation of Cleveland's economy—proximity to jobs. Although a remnant of the black middle class continues to call the outer city home, it should come as no surprise that in recent decades, the neighborhoods discussed in this book declined in prestige as many higher income earners extended the historic strategy of geographic mobility to more distant destinations, their places taken by less-affluent individuals. Indeed, the above-listed concerns, based to a considerable extent on large-scale structural factors, were issues around which black middle-class activists mobilized as early as the 1950s. The signal strength of the "second ghetto" literature expounded by historians following Arnold Hirsch has been to underline the enormity of economic and political structures that have historically buttressed racial segregation by impeding

African American access to resources like housing, with the implication that nothing short of a thoroughgoing overhaul of the racial status quo can possibly halt the cycle of re-segregation and disinvestment that has so often followed in the wake of racial residential transition. However, this historiography has fallen short in underestimating black agency, the ability of African Americans—and especially those with comparatively greater economic resources—to push against and reshape the manifold barriers placed in their way. The particular "middling sort" profiled in this study changed neighborhoods, and in the process they changed the city, creating lifeworlds at the urban periphery that fulfilled their expectations, at least temporarily. When their situation grew too burdensome, they took this quest elsewhere, and are now changing the suburbs as well.

Upwardly mobile African Americans have had to confront new residential challenges since 1980. In Cleveland, the contemporary foreclosure crisis began earlier than elsewhere, with predatory lending becoming a public issue already in the mid-1990s. City officials actually passed legislation regulating loan terms, which was blocked by the Republican-led state legislature in 2002, and in 2008 attempted to sue several dozen mortgage companies for creating a public nuisance through their securitization of subprime loans.[4] Despite being among the metropolitan areas hardest hit by the onset of recession,[5] Cleveland's experience was not characterized by overinflation in the form of a housing bubble. However, in keeping with the nationwide pattern that saw already disparate black household wealth even further eroded by the downturn,[6] African American homeowners, not just in Cleveland, but also in suburbs such as Euclid, Shaker Heights, Garfield Heights, Maple Heights, and even Solon, were more severely impacted by the economic crisis. Indeed, researchers mapping the incidence of foreclosures have documented the heaviest concentrations along the two vectors described earlier.[7] But even though African American populations have grown mainly in areas to Cleveland's northeast and southeast, all of the "inner ring" suburbs bordering the city are having to devote increased attention to the issues of aging housing stock and infrastructure, struggling traditional commercial strips, and job loss.[8] These concerns will only become more acute in the near future. Virtually all of Cleveland's historic East Side black neighborhoods experienced precipitous population declines over the past decade, with Glenville and Mount Pleasant among the hardest hit. Not only are African American families increasingly seeking accommodations on the city's West Side where the black population was until quite recently limited to a single settlement; ironically, the rash of suburban foreclosures and accompanying decline in house prices and rents have improved many African American home seekers' chances of gaining access there.[9]

Like metropolitan areas across the country, Greater Cleveland continues to undergo a process of urban sprawl—whereby suburbia is being extended to "exurbia" in a push-pull dynamic driving population to ever-farther out-lying areas, and in which race continues to play a significant but too often un-acknowledged role.[10] Especially in the wake of the Great Recession, to what degree this process is sustainable is an open question—as is what the future will hold for those areas with fewer resources, lying closer to the urban core. But if the findings in this study provide any indication, upwardly mobile African Americans, like the "pioneers" of an earlier era, will continue to strive—despite challenges, resistance, and adversity—after opportunities to improve their living conditions, even to the outermost metropolitan limits.

Notes

Abbreviations

ADC   Archives, Diocese of Cleveland

AJC   Anthony J. Celebrezze Papers, WRHS

ARC   Amistad Research Center, Tulane University, New Orleans

ASS   Alta Social Settlement Records, WRHS

C&P   *Cleveland Call & Post*

CBP   Casimir Bielen Papers, WRHS

CBS   Carl B. Stokes Papers, WRHS

CCC   Council of Churches of Christ of Greater Cleveland Records, WRHS

CCCA   Cleveland City Council Archives

CCRO   Cuyahoga County Recorder's Office, Cleveland

CDF   Cleveland Development Foundation Records, WRHS

CG   *Cleveland Gazette*

CHR   Council on Human Relations Records, WRHS

CMHA   Cleveland Metropolitan Housing Authority

CMP   Cleveland Mayoral Papers, WRHS

CN   *Cleveland News*

CP   *Cleveland Press*

CPC   *Cleveland Press* Collection, Special Collections, Michael Schwartz Library, Cleveland State University

CPL   Cleveland Public Library

CWRU   Case Western Reserve University, Cleveland

EENH   East End Neighborhood House Records, WRHS

EJB   Ernest J. Bohn Papers, Special Collections, Kelvin Smith Library, CWRU

FCP   Federation for Community Planning Records, WRHS

FHLBB   Records of the Federal Home Loan Bank Board (RG 195), National Archives II, College Park, Md.

FLP   Frank Lyons Papers, WRHS

FSH   Frank Smith Horne Papers, ARC

GCCUC   Greater Cleveland Clean Up Campaign Records, WRHS

GCNCA   Greater Cleveland Neighborhood Centers Association Records, WRHS

GGF   George Gund Foundation Records, WRHS

JCC   Jewish Community Center of Cleveland Records, WRHS

JCF	Jewish Community Federation of Cleveland Records, WRHS
JKP	Julian Krawcheck Papers (unprocessed collection), WRHS
KTNC	Kathryn Tyler Neighborhood Center Records, WRHS
LAJ	Leo A. Jackson Papers (unprocessed collection), WRHS
LCM	Library of Congress, Manuscripts Division, Washington, D.C.
LHR	League for Human Rights Records, WRHS
MKP	Maurice Klain Research Papers, WRHS
NAACP-CB	NAACP (Cleveland Branch) Records, WRHS
NAACP-LC	NAACP Records, LCM
NSC	Nationalities Services Center Records, WRHS
NUL	National Urban League Records, LCM
OHS	Ohio Historical Society, Columbus
PD	*Cleveland Plain Dealer*
RCPO	Regional Church Planning Office Records, WRHS
RJM	Rubie J. McCullough Papers (unprocessed collection), WRHS
RJP	Ralph J. Perk Papers, WRHS
TAB	Thomas A. Burke Papers, WRHS
TCF	The Cleveland Foundation Records, WRHS
ULC	Urban League of Cleveland Records, WRHS
USR	University Settlement Records, WRHS
WCS	Warrensville Center Synagogue Records, WRHS
WRHS	Western Reserve Historical Society, Cleveland
YMCA	YMCA of Cleveland Records, WRHS

Introduction

1. *C&P*, July 18, 1953.

2. Loeb obituary, *C&P*, August 26, 1978; Charles H. Loeb, *The Future Is Yours: A History of the Future Outlook League* (Cleveland, 1947), [5]; *C&P*, January 10, 1953.

3. See Will Cooley, "Moving On Out: Black Pioneering in Chicago, 1915–1950," *Journal of Urban History* 36 (July 2010): 485–506; and Andrew Wiese, *Places of Their Own: African American Suburbanization in the Twentieth Century* (Chicago, 2004), 129–32. On the most famous black "pioneer," Detroit physician Ossian Sweet, see Kevin Boyle, *Arc of Justice: A Saga of Race, Civil Rights, and Murder in the Jazz Age* (New York, 2004).

4. On controversy surrounding this term, see Thomas J. Sugrue, "Revisiting the Second Ghetto," *Journal of Urban History* 29 (March 2003): 283. I use "ghetto" rarely and only with reference to the Cedar-Central district.

5. For a recent study centering black agency that treats moving around the city as a form of resistance, see Marcus Anthony Hunter, *Black Citymakers: How the Philadelphia Negro Changed Urban America* (New York, 2013), esp. 14–15, 84, 102, 109, 156, 163, 212–14.

6. For a similar emphasis, see Wiese, *Places of Their Own*, 6–7, 290.

7. See Arnold R. Hirsch, *Making the Second Ghetto: Race and Housing in Chicago, 1940–1960*, reprint ed. (Chicago, 1998); Thomas J. Sugrue, *The Origins of the Urban Crisis:*

Race and Inequality in Postwar Detroit (Princeton, N.J., 1996); and David M. P. Freund, Colored Property: State Policy and White Racial Politics in Suburban America (Chicago, 2007). Similar studies include Kevin Fox Gotham, Race, Real Estate, and Uneven Development: The Kansas City Experience, 1900–2000 (Albany, N.Y., 2002); LeeAnn Lands, The Culture of Property: Race, Class, and Housing Landscapes in Atlanta, 1880–1950 (Athens, Ga., 2009); and Colin Gordon, Mapping Decline: St. Louis and the Fate of the American City (Philadelphia, 2008). Important works emphasizing structure but acknowledging some degree of black agency are Henry Louis Taylor Jr., "City Building, Public Policy, the Rise of the Industrial City, and Black Ghetto-Slum Formation in Cincinnati, 1850–1940," in Race and the City: Work, Community, and Protest in Cincinnati, 1820–1970, ed. Henry Louis Taylor Jr. (Urbana, Ill., 1993), 156–92; Raymond A. Mohl, "Making the Second Ghetto in Metropolitan Miami, 1940–1960," Journal of Urban History 21 (March 1995): 395–427; Ronald H. Bayor, Race and the Shaping of Twentieth Century Atlanta (Chapel Hill, N.C., 1996); Robert O. Self, American Babylon: Race and the Struggle for Postwar Oakland (Princeton, N.J., 2003); and Charles E. Connerly, "The Most Segregated City in America": City Planning and Civil Rights in Birmingham, 1920–1980 (Charlottesville, Va., 2005).

8. From the "Symposium on Thomas J. Sugrue: The Origins of the Urban Crisis," Labor History 39 (February 1998): 43–69, see especially the contributions by Eric Arnesen, Nancy Gabin, and Joe W. Trotter and Sugrue's rebuttal; in the symposium on the twenty-year anniversary of Arnold Hirsch's Making the Second Ghetto, in Journal of Urban History 29 (March 2003): 233–309, see especially those by Amanda Irene Seligman, Thomas Sugrue, Heather Ann Thompson, and Hirsch's rebuttal.

9. In a literal illustration of this formulation, Cleveland's main black newspaper for a while carried a "Suburban Chatterbox" column on happenings in outlying city neighborhoods like "Miles Heights" (Lee-Seville), Mount Pleasant, and Collinwood; see C&P, January 28, 1950.

10. Joe William Trotter Jr., Black Milwaukee: The Making of an Industrial Proletariat, 1915–1945 (Urbana, Ill., 1985); James R. Grossman, Land of Hope: Chicago, Black Southerners, and the Great Migration (Chicago, 1989); Earl Lewis, In Their Own Interests: Race, Class, and Power in 20th Century Norfolk, Virginia (Los Angeles, 1991); Richard W. Thomas, Life for Us Is What We Make It: Building Black Community in Detroit, 1915–1945 (Bloomington, Ind., 1992); Robin D. G. Kelley, Race Rebels: Culture, Politics, and the Black Working Class (New York, 1994); Tera W. Hunter, To 'Joy My Freedom: Southern Black Women's Lives and Labors after the Civil War (Cambridge, Mass., 1997); Shirley Ann Wilson Moore, To Place Our Deeds: The African American Community in Richmond, California, 1910–1963 (Berkeley, Calif., 2000); Luther Adams, Way Up North in Louisville: African American Migration in the Urban South, 1930–1970 (Chapel Hill, N.C., 2010).

11. Wiese, Places of Their Own; see also Richard Harris, "Chicago's Other Suburbs," Geographical Review 84 (October 1994): 394–410; Richard Harris and Robert Lewis, "The Geography of North American Cities and Suburbs, 1900–1950: A New Synthesis," Journal of Urban History 27 (March 2001): 262–92; Becky M. Nicolaides, My Blue Heaven: Life and Politics in the Working-Class Suburbs of Los Angeles, 1920–1965 (Chicago, 2002); and Elaine

Lewinnek, *The Working Man's Reward: Chicago's Early Suburbs and the Roots of American Sprawl* (New York, 2014).

12. For context, see Jon C. Teaford, *Cities of the Heartland: The Rise and Fall of the Industrial Midwest* (Bloomington, Ind., 1994).

13. This pattern has been noted but not much examined, with focus remaining on central-city districts. See T. J. Woofter Jr., *Negro Problems in Cities* (Garden City, N.Y., 1928), 106–9; Olivier Zunz, *The Changing Face of Inequality: Urbanization, Industrial Development, and Immigrants in Detroit, 1880–1920* (Chicago, 1982), 352–53; Thomas L. Philpott, *The Slum and the Ghetto: Neighborhood Deterioration and Middle-Class Reform, 1880–1930* (Belmont, Calif., 1991), 120–29, 142, 150, 183–202; and Taylor, "City Building," 159. Somewhat deeper discussions are Sugrue, *Origins of the Urban Crisis,* 37–41, 63–71; and Sherry Lamb Schirmer, *A City Divided: The Racial Landscape of Kansas City, 1900–1960* (Columbia, Mo., 2002), 32–39.

14. See Wiese, *Places of Their Own,* 160–61, 254, 263–64; and E. Franklin Frazier, "Occupational Classes among Negroes in Cities," *American Journal of Sociology* 35 (March 1930): 718–38. Earl Lewis downplays social distancing by upwardly mobile African Americans, suggesting that "class in the black community must be viewed as part of an intraracial discourse." Lewis, "Connecting Memory, Self, and the Power of Place in African American Urban History," *Journal of Urban History* 21 (March 1995): 358.

15. For a discussion of suburbanization in terms of "spatial advantage" for African Americans, see Wiese, *Places of Their Own,* 141–63.

16. Hirsch, *Making the Second Ghetto,* 40–99; Steven Grant Meyer, *As Long as They Don't Live Next Door: Segregation and Racial Conflict in American Neighborhoods* (Lanham, Md., 2000). See also William M. Tuttle Jr., "Contested Neighborhoods and Racial Violence: Prelude to the Chicago Riot of 1919," *Journal of Negro History* 55 (October 1970): 266–88; Vincent P. Franklin, "The Philadelphia Race Riot of 1918," *Pennsylvania Magazine of History and Biography* 99 (July 1975): 336–50; David Allen Levine, *Internal Combustion: The Races in Detroit, 1915–1926* (Westport, Conn., 1976); Thomas L. Philpott, *The Slum and the Ghetto: Immigrants, Blacks, and Reformers in Chicago, 1880–1930* (New York, 1978), 152–79; Sugrue, *Origins of the Urban Crisis,* 231–41, 246–58; Glenn T. Eskew, *But for Birmingham: The Local and National Movements in the Civil Rights Struggle* (Chapel Hill, N.C., 1997), 53–83; Schirmer, *City Divided,* 42, 74, 104–7; David Jason Leonard, "'No Jews and No Coloreds Are Welcome in This Town': Constructing Coalitions in Postwar Los Angeles" (Ph.D. diss., University of California, Berkeley, 2002), 243–51; Josh Sides, *L.A. City Limits: African American Los Angeles from the Great Depression to the Present* (Berkeley, Calif., 2004), 102–27; Douglas Flamming, *Bound for Freedom: Black Los Angeles in Jim Crow America* (Berkeley, Calif., 2005), 67, 140–41, 261; Connerly, *"Most Segregated City,"* 69–101; Kevin M. Kruse, *White Flight: Atlanta and the Making of Modern Conservatism* (Princeton, N.J., 2005), 42–48, 89–90, 102–3; James Wolfinger, *Philadelphia Divided: Race and Politics in the City of Brotherly Love* (Chapel Hill, N.C., 2007), 85–112; Dennis P. Halpin, "'The Struggle for Land and Liberty': Segregation, Violence, and African American Resis-

tance in Baltimore, 1898–1919," *Journal of Urban History* (forthcoming); Wiese, *Places of Their Own*, 155, 198–201, 213, 229; and Cooley, "Moving On Out."

17. John C. Ransom, "The 'Best Location in the Nation' to 'The Mistake on the Lake': The Image and Reality of Cleveland, 1920s–1970s" (M.A. thesis, Case Western Reserve University, 1992), 24–29. For black agreement on this point, see Horace Cayton, "America's Ten Best Cities for Negroes," *Negro Digest* 5 (October 1947): 4–10; and "Cleveland: The Friendly City to Negroes," *Jet* 7 (November 25, 1954): 10–13. However, see *C&P*, December 19, 1953; a stinging, off-the-record critique is "The Product Cleveland," ca. February 14, 1947, NUL, box I:F91, "Affiliates File, Cleveland, 1943–1950" folder.

18. Arnold R. Hirsch, "Massive Resistance in the Urban North: Trumbull Park, Chicago, 1953–1966," *Journal of American History* 82 (September 1995): 522–50. Cleveland nevertheless had a number of white working-class neighborhoods where conflicts developed periodically; on the most notorious, see Todd M. Michney, "Race, Violence, and Urban Territoriality: Cleveland's Little Italy and the 1966 Hough Uprising," *Journal of Urban History* 32 (March 2006): 404–28.

19. Sugrue, *Origins of the Urban Crisis*, 241–46.

20. Kenneth Wayne Rose, "The Politics of Social Reform in Cleveland, 1945–1967: Civil Rights, Welfare Rights, and the Response of Civic Leaders" (Ph.D. diss., Case Western Reserve University, 1988); Leonard N. Moore, *Carl B. Stokes and the Rise of Black Political Power* (Urbana, Ill., 2002), esp. 19–20; Carl B. Stokes, *Promises of Power: A Political Autobiography* (New York, 1973), 48–49, 93–94, 131–32, 148.

21. Sugrue, *Origins of the Urban Crisis*, 224–25; Hirsch, *Making the Second Ghetto*, 245–46. For the assessment that "in general the climate of racial relations is good in Cleveland and does not have the tensions which in some cities have boiled over into riots," see *New York Times*, November 3, 1957.

22. See John J. Grabowski, "Social Reform and Philanthropic Order in Cleveland, 1896–1920," in *Cleveland: A Tradition of Reform*, ed. David D. Van Tassel and John J. Grabowski (Kent, Ohio, 1986), 44–49.

23. Hirsch, *Making the Second Ghetto*, 68–99; David R. Roediger, *Working Toward Whiteness: How America's Immigrants Became White* (New York, 2005), 157–77, 224–34; Freund, *Colored Property*, 243–381.

24. For more extensive treatments of such areas, but which focus mainly on the experience of white residents, see Wendell Pritchett, *Brownsville, Brooklyn: Blacks, Jews, and the Changing Face of the Ghetto* (Chicago, 2002); Amanda I. Seligman, *Block by Block: Neighborhoods and Public Policy on Chicago's West Side* (Chicago, 2005); and Gerald Gamm, *Urban Exodus: Why the Jews Left Boston and the Catholics Stayed* (Cambridge, Mass., 1999).

25. "Statistics of Jews," *American Jewish Year Book* 22 (1920–21): 372. On Cleveland's Jews, see Lloyd P. Gartner, *History of the Jews of Cleveland* (Cleveland, 1978, 1987); and Judah Rubenstein with Jane Avner, *Merging Traditions: Jewish Life in Cleveland*, rev. ed. (Cleveland, 2004).

26. Gamm, *Urban Exodus*; John T. McGreevy, *Parish Boundaries: The Catholic Encounter with Race in the Twentieth-Century Urban North* (Chicago, 1996); Pritchett, *Brownsville*. In explaining Baltimore's experience, Kenneth D. Durr and Antero Pietila similarly impute significance to Jewish neighborhoods; see Durr, *Behind the Backlash: White Working-Class Politics in Baltimore, 1940–1980* (Chapel Hill, N.C., 2003), 102–3; and Pietila, *Not in My Neighborhood: How Bigotry Shaped a Great American City* (Chicago, 2010), esp. 108–15.

27. John Bracey and August Meier, "Towards a Research Agenda on Blacks and Jews in United States History," *Journal of American Ethnic History* 12 (Spring 1993): 60–67; Joe William Trotter Jr., "African Americans, Jews, and the City: Perspectives from the Industrial Era, 1900–1950," in *African Americans and Jews in the Twentieth Century: Studies in Convergence and Conflict*, ed. V. P. Franklin et al. (Columbia, Mo., 1998), 193–207. See also the frank, probing analysis in Robert G. Weisbord and Arthur Stein, "Negro Perceptions of Jews between the World Wars," *Judaism* 18 (Fall 1969): 428–47; and Hasia Diner, "Between Words and Deeds: Jews and Blacks in America, 1880–1935," in *Struggles in the Promised Land*, ed. Jack Salzman and Cornel West (New York, 1997), 87–106.

28. Paralleling this study's findings are Cheryl Lynn Greenberg, "Liberal NIMBY: Jews and Civil Rights," *Journal of Urban History* 38 (May 2012): 452–66; and Lila Corwin Berman, "Jewish Urban Politics in the City and Beyond," *Journal of American History* 99 (September 2012): 492–519.

29. For African Americans ranking service work, see Charles Pete T. Banner-Haley, *To Do Good and To Do Well: Middle-Class Blacks and the Depression, Philadelphia, 1929–1941* (New York, 1993), 52–53. On dual-income earning, see Bart Landry, *Black Working Wives: Pioneers of the American Family Revolution* (Berkeley, Calif., 2002). On post-1964 developments, see Bart Landry, *The New Black Middle Class* (Berkeley, Calif., 1987); and Charles T. Banner-Haley, *The Fruits of Integration: Black Middle Class Ideology and Culture, 1960–1990* (Jackson, Miss., 1994).

30. Burton J. Bledstein, "Introduction: Storytellers to the Middle Class," in *The Middling Sorts: Explorations in the History of the American Middle Class*, ed. Burton J. Bledstein and Robert D. Johnston (New York, 2001). Michelle Mitchell prefers "aspiring classes," following Glenda Gilmore's observation that African Americans did not self-identify as "middle class" before the Great Migration; see Mitchell, *Righteous Propagation: African Americans and the Politics of Racial Destiny after Reconstruction* (Chapel Hill, N.C., 2004), 9–10, 253n25.

31. Richard Harris, "The Rise of Filtering Down: The American Housing Market Transformed, 1915–1929," *Social Science History* 37 (Winter 2013): 515–49; Clifford E. Clark Jr., *The American Family Home, 1800–1960* (Chapel Hill, N.C., 1986); Robert M. Fogelson, *Bourgeois Nightmares: Suburbia, 1870–1930* (New Haven, Conn., 2005); Jeffrey M. Hornstein, *A Nation of Realtors®: A Cultural History of the Twentieth-Century American Middle Class* (Durham, N.C., 2005); Freund, *Colored Property*. On housing trends prior to the Great Depression, see Michael J. Doucet and John C. Weaver, "Material Culture and the North American House: The Era of the Common Man, 1870–1920," *Journal of American History*

72 (September 1985): 560–84; and Robert G. Barrows, "Beyond the Tenement: Patterns of American Urban Housing, 1870–1930," *Journal of Urban History* 9 (August 1983): 395–420.

32. Margaret Garb, *City of American Dreams: A History of Home Ownership and Housing Reform in Chicago, 1871–1919* (Chicago, 2005), 2, 38–39, 187. Those of lesser means also aspired to own property; see Monroe Nathan Work, "Negro Real Estate Holders of Chicago" (M.A. thesis, University of Chicago, 1903), 23–24; and Wiese, *Places of Their Own,* 82–87, 145.

33. On Cedar-Central, see Kenneth L. Kusmer, *A Ghetto Takes Shape: Black Cleveland, 1870–1930* (Urbana, Ill., 1976); and Kimberley L. Phillips, *AlabamaNorth: African-American Migrants, Community, and Working-Class Activism in Cleveland, 1915–1945* (Urbana, Ill., 1999).

34. Christopher G. Wye, "The New Deal and the Negro Community: Toward a Broader Conceptualization," *Journal of American History* 59 (December 1972): 621–39; "Area Descriptions—Security Map of Cuyahoga County," Cleveland, Area D-21, [1939,] HOLC City Survey File, FHLBB, box 87, "Greater Cleveland, OH" folder.

35. On pre–New Deal African American homeownership, see Woofter, *Negro Problems,* 137–51; and Charles S. Johnson, prep., *Negro Housing: Report of the Committee on Negro Housing,* ed. John M. Gries and James Ford (Washington, D.C., 1932, reprint 1969), 79–91. For context, see William J. Collins and Robert A. Margo, "Race and Home Ownership: A Century-Long View," *Explorations in Economic History* 38 (January 2001): 68–92.

36. Earl Lewis, *In Their Own Interests: Race, Class and Power in 20th Century Norfolk, Virginia* (Los Angeles, 1991); Virginia W. Wolcott, *Remaking Respectability: African American Women in Interwar Detroit* (Chapel Hill, N.C., 2001). On respectability and "uplift," see also Evelyn Brooks Higginbotham, *Righteous Discontent: The Women's Movement in the Black Baptist Church, 1880–1920* (Cambridge, Mass., 1993); Kevin Gaines, *Uplifting the Race: Black Leadership, Politics, and Culture in the Twentieth Century* (Chapel Hill, N.C., 1996); Stephanie Shaw, *What a Woman Ought to Be and Do: Black Professional Women Workers during the Jim Crow Era* (Chicago, 1996); and Touré F. Reed, *Not Alms but Opportunity: The Urban League and the Politics of Racial Uplift, 1910–1950* (Chapel Hill, N.C., 2008).

37. Noteworthy studies treating black middle-class neighborhoods include Lynne B. Feldman, *A Sense of Place: Birmingham's Black Middle-Class Community, 1890–1930* (Tuscaloosa, Ala., 1999); Banner-Haley, *To Do Good and to Do Well*; Georgina Hickey, "From Auburn Avenue to Buttermilk Bottom: Class and Community Dynamics among Atlanta's Blacks," in *Historical Roots of the Urban Crisis: African Americans in the Industrial City, 1900–1950,* ed. Henry Louis Taylor Jr. and Walter Hill (New York, 2000), 109–43; and Bruce D. Haynes, *Red Lines, Black Spaces: The Politics of Race and Space in a Black Middle-Class Suburb* (New Haven, Conn., 2001). On the relevant sociological literature, see Mary E. Pattillo, "Black Middle Class Neighborhoods," *Annual Review of Sociology* 31 (2005): 305–29.

38. Lewis, *In Their Own Interests*. For initial yet limited treatments of neighborhood-based, quality-of-life activism, see Steven Gregory, *Black Corona: Race and the Politics*

of Race in an Urban Community (Princeton, N.J., 1998), esp. 146–56; Sylvia Hood Washington, *Packing Them In: An Archaeology of Environmental Racism in Chicago, 1865–1954* (Lanham, Md., 2005), 158–92; and Connerly, *"Most Segregated City,"* 217–30.

Chapter 1

1. Traceability in Cleveland land records is complicated by incomplete mortgagor-mortgagee indexes. Three exciting recent studies touching on the topic of African American property holding are Andrew W. Kahrl, *The Land Was Ours: African American Beaches from Jim Crow to the Sunbelt South* (Cambridge, Mass., 2012); N. D. B. Connolly, *A World More Concrete: Real Estate and the Making of Jim Crow South Florida* (Chicago, 2014); and Kevin McGruder, *Race and Real Estate: Conflict and Cooperation in Harlem, 1890–1920* (New York, 2015).

2. 1920 Manuscript Census, Enumeration District 340, p. 29A; City of Cleveland, Building Permit No. 12535-B, September 5, 1916, Department of Building and Housing, City Hall; Cleveland City Directories, 1916–29 (Cleveland: Cleveland Directory Co.); 1930 Manuscript Census, Enumeration District 775, p. 4A.

3. 1920 Manuscript Census, Enumeration District 340, p. 3B; City of Cleveland, Building Permit No. 13671-B, January 9, 1917, Department of Building and Housing; Cleveland City Directories, 1918–22, 1925–26; 1930 Manuscript Census, Enumeration District 803, p. 9B.

4. 1930 Manuscript Census, Enumeration District 803, p. 9A; Property Deed, January 22, 1923, vol. 2739, p. 520, CCRO; City of Cleveland, Building Permit No. 32745-A, May 31, 1923, Department of Building and Housing; Property Deed, April 15, 1924, vol. 3045, p. 438, CCRO; City of Cleveland, Building Permit No. 34927-A, November 20, 1923, Department of Building and Housing; Cleveland City Directory, 1916–17; 1920 Manuscript Census, Enumeration District 390, p. 13A; Cleveland City Directories, 1925–29.

5. Mortgage, April 29, 1915, vol. 1648, p. 265, CCRO; Property Deed, April 30, 1915, vol. 1674, p. 85, CCRO; 1920 Manuscript Census, Enumeration District 259, p. 3B; Cleveland City Directory, 1915; Marriage Record, License 73565, May 29, 1911, vol. 78, p. 142, Cuyahoga County; Mortgage, August 23, 1916, vol. 1825, p. 190, CCRO; Mortgage, January 25, 1924, vol. 2933, p. 618, CCRO.

6. Mortgage, November 12, 1917, vol. 1912, p. 426, CCRO; Property Deed, November 13, 1917, vol. 1976, p. 631, CCRO; Mortgage, March 18, 1924, vol. 2913, p. 212, CCRO; Mortgage, March 12, 1925, vol. 3163, p. 139, CCRO; Mortgage, January 20, 1927, vol. 3458, p. 360, CCRO; Mortgage, January 3, 1930, vol. 3796, p. 31, CCRO; Mortgage, October 16, 1917, vol. 1967, p. 259, CCRO.

7. Mortgage, June 27, 1923, vol. 2796, p. 46, CCRO; Mortgage, September 6, 1923, vol. 2797, p. 90, CCRO; Mortgage, June 11, 1925, vol. 3186, p. 557, CCRO; Property Deed, June 12, 1925, vol. 3119, p. 473, CCRO; Property Deed, April 6, 1928, vol. 3590, p. 617, CCRO; Mortgage, April 27, 1926, vol. 3422, p. 605, CCRO; Mortgage, July 1, 1927, vol. 3619, p. 507, CCRO.

8. Property Deed, July 1, 1926, vol. 3393, p. 504; *C&P*, March 5, 1936.

9. Welfare Federation of Cleveland, "Study of Cleveland's Negro Areas," February 22,

1940, at CPL, Public Administration Library, City Hall. On Cedar-Central, see Kenneth L. Kusmer, *A Ghetto Takes Shape: Black Cleveland, 1870–1930* (Urbana, Ill., 1976).

10. *CP*, August 9, 1941; Real Property Inventory of Metropolitan Cleveland, *A Sheet-a-Week* (September 22, 1938); "Mt. Pleasant [Branch], 14000 Kinsman Road," [ca. 1938], on file at CPL, Mount Pleasant Branch; "Annual Report of the Executive Director," April 25, 1927, JCC, container 3, folder 41; *PD*, January 4, 1932; Todd M. Michney, "Changing Neighborhoods: Race and Upward Mobility in Southeast Cleveland, 1930–1980" (Ph.D. diss., University of Minnesota, 2004), 28–32.

11. *PD*, September 12, 1930; 1900 Manuscript Census, Newburgh Township, Enumeration District 225; *Cleveland Journal*, July 27, 1907. Blue's promotion methods were fairly typical; see Andrew Wiese, *Places of Their Own: African American Suburbanization in the Twentieth Century* (Chicago, 2004), 68–72.

12. 1910 Manuscript Census, Newburgh Township, Enumeration District 28; Property Deeds, CCRO, black families identified using 1920 and 1930 Manuscript Census; *CP*, March 25, 1946; 1920 Manuscript Census, Enumeration Districts 339–40.

13. Becky M. Nicolaides, *My Blue Heaven: Life and Politics in the Working-Class Suburbs of Los Angeles, 1920–1965* (Chicago, 2002), 33–34; Andrew Wiese, "Black Housing, White Finance: African American Housing and Homeownership in Evanston, Illinois, before 1940," *Journal of Social History* 33 (Winter 1999), 435–36; Wiese, *Places of Their Own*, 77.

14. Natalie Middleton, interview transcript, December 20, 1986, St. James AME Church Oral History Project Interviews, WRHS, container 2, folder 26; *C&P*, June 26, 1948; "Study of Cleveland's Negro Areas."

15. "Area Descriptions—Security Map of Cuyahoga County," Cleveland, Area D-12, September 13, 1939, HOLC City Survey File, FHLBB, box 87, "Greater Cleveland, OH" folder. For context, see Richard Harris, "Self-Building in the Urban Housing Market," *Economic Geography* 67 (January 1991): 1–21; Richard Harris, "Reading Sanborns for the Spoor of the Owner Builder, 1890s–1950s," in *Exploring Everyday Landscapes: Perspectives on Vernacular Architecture VII*, ed. Annemarie Adams and Sally McMurry (Knoxville, Tenn., 1997), 251–67; Henry Louis Taylor Jr., "Creating the Metropolis in Black and White: Black Suburbanization and the Planning Movement in Cincinnati, 1900–1950," in *Historical Roots of the Urban Crisis*, ed. Henry Louis Taylor Jr. and Walter Hill (New York, 2000), 51–71; and Nicolaides, *My Blue Heaven*, 28–33. Self-building by African Americans was noted early on, all over the country. See T. J. Woofter Jr., *Negro Problems in Cities* (Garden City, N.Y., 1928), 108; Wiese, "The Other Suburbanites"; Wiese, "Black Housing," 442–44; Wiese, *Places of Their Own*; Shirley Ann Wilson Moore, *To Place Our Deeds: The African American Community in Richmond, California, 1910–1963* (Berkeley, Calif., 2000); and Lynne B. Feldman, *A Sense of Place: Birmingham's Black Middle Class Community, 1890–1930* (Tuscaloosa, Ala., 1999), 60–67.

16. Property Deeds, CCRO, and Building Permits, City of Cleveland, Department of Building and Housing, identified using index at CCCA, for black owners listed in 1920 Manuscript Census, Enumeration Districts 339 and 340, and 1930 Manuscript Census, Enumeration Districts 503, 508, 511, 775, 801–3, 808; Building Permit No. 11088-A, March

29, 1916; 1920 Manuscript Census, Enumeration District 340, p. 4A; Building Permits Nos. 13270-A, 29757-C, and 41089-A, dated November 9, 1916, September 26, 1922, and March 5, 1925; Building Permits Nos. 12535-B, 14288-A, 14841-A, and 15071-B, dated September 5, 1916, April 23, 1917, July 11, 1917, and August 15, 1917; 1920 Manuscript Census, Enumeration District 340, p. 28B. Meade's Building Permit No. 17459-C, dated February 17, 1919, is missing but listed in the permit index.

17. Mildred Foster, taped interview with author, November 12, 2003; "Area Descriptions—Security Map of Cuyahoga County," Cleveland, Area C-49, September 13, 1939, and Area C-50, September 19, 1939, HOLC City Survey File, FHLBB, box 87, "Greater Cleveland, OH" folder; U.S. Bureau of the Census, *Housing: Supplement to the First Series, Housing Bulletin for Ohio, Cleveland Block Statistics* (Washington, D.C., 1942), 55, 57–58. The earliest deed located for "Kinsman Heights" was to Edna Lee (wife of Henry), Property Deed, September 18, 1919, vol. 2278, p. 215, CCRO.

18. 1930 Manuscript Census, Enumeration Districts 503, 508, 511, 775, 801, 802, 803, 808. For examples of pre–World War I migrants to Mount Pleasant, see *C&P*, May 8, 1943 (Horace Franklin obituary); and *C&P*, January 21, 1950 (Simon Stanard).

19. Kusmer, *Ghetto Takes Shape*, 227n32; Kimberley L. Phillips, *AlabamaNorth: African-American Migrants, Community, and Working-Class Activism in Cleveland, 1915–1945* (Urbana, Ill., 1999), 136–37.

20. Kusmer, *Ghetto Takes Shape*, 211. Andrew Wiese has stressed the importance homeownership held for Southern-born residents; Wiese, "Other Suburbanites," 1515.

21. For a community outside Baltimore with a similarly diverse occupational structure, see Calinda Nivel Lee, "Creating the Pleasant View: The Impact of Gender, Race, and Class on African American Suburbanization, 1837–1999" (Ph.D. diss., Emory University, 2002). For members of a blue-collar Dallas black community that "saw themselves rising into the middle class," see Wiese, *Places of Their Own*, 204.

22. Russell H. Davis, *Black Americans in Cleveland from George Peake to Carl B. Stokes* (Washington, D.C., 1972), 251, 276, 300. On the significance of postal work, see Philip F. Rubio, "'There's Always Work at the Post Office': African Americans Fight for Jobs, Justice, and Equality at the United States Post Office, 1940–71" (Ph.D. diss., Duke University, 2006), 7n20. On labor organizing among black postal and service workers, see Christopher G. Wye, "Midwest Ghetto: Patterns of Negro Life and Thought in Cleveland, Ohio, 1929–1945" (Ph.D. diss., Kent State University, 1973), 177–88.

23. Herbert R. Northrup, *Organized Labor and the Negro* (1944; New York, 1971), 38–41; Herman D. Bloch, "Craft Unions and the Negro in Historical Perspective," *Journal of Negro History* 43 (January 1958): 10–33. On the nuances of racial discrimination in the Cleveland building trades, see Phillips, *AlabamaNorth*, 115–18; and "Progress Report . . . Building Trades," October 1, 1947, NUL, box I:F91, "Affiliates File, Cleveland, 1943, 1947, 1950" folder.

24. Davis, *Black Americans*, 156.

25. Hawkins obituary, *C&P*, April 20, 1957. On transport workers, see Phillips, *AlabamaNorth*, 82–83. On chauffeuring's significance for black Angelinos, see Douglas Flamming, *Bound for Freedom: Black Los Angeles in Jim Crow America* (Berkeley, Calif., 2005), 75–76.

26. Another estimate found 45 percent of black men doing unskilled work that year; Kusmer, *Ghetto Takes Shape*, 201. For the present study, occupational categories follow U.S. Bureau of the Census, *Alphabetical Index of Occupations and Industries: 1950* (Washington, D.C., 1950).

27. On black access to industrial work, see Phillips, *AlabamaNorth*, 57–72, 78–82.

28. *C&P*, October 28, 1937. Parham received an additional $1,000 bonus after twenty-five years' service; *C&P*, January 21, 1956. On Pullman porters as vital information passers, see Larry Tye, *Rising from the Rails: Pullman Porters and the Making of the Black Middle Class* (New York, 2004). On black Clevelanders in service, see Phillips, *AlabamaNorth*, 83–86.

29. On black women working as domestics and in commercial laundries, see Phillips, *AlabamaNorth*, 75–76, 88–92.

30. 1930 Manuscript Census, Enumeration Districts 513, 812; Donna Whyte and Dianne McIntyre, taped interview with author, January 28, 2003. For an analogous example of patronage, see Feldman, *Sense of Place*, 51.

31. *CP*, February 20, 22–24, 1940 (series on Glenville); Deming Realty Co., "Home Sweet Home," [ca. 1909], WRHS.

32. "Jewish Population Study, Greater Cleveland, 1925–1926," JCF, container 11, folder 182; "Annual Report of the Executive Director," April 25, 1927, JCC, container 3, folder 41; "Area Descriptions—Security Map of Cuyahoga County," Cleveland, Area D-23, October 19, 1939, HOLC City Survey File, FHLBB, box 87, "Greater Cleveland, OH" folder.

33. National Jewish Welfare Board, "General Summary of the Survey of the Group Work Resources Available," [1945], JCC, container 26, folder 112; "Area Descriptions—Security Map of Cuyahoga County," Cleveland, Area C-56, September 15, 1939, HOLC City Survey File, FHLBB, box 87, "Greater Cleveland, OH" folder; David Mayo Austin et al., "Community Council: Test Tube for Democracy; A Case Study of the Glenville Area Community Council" (M.S. thesis, School of Applied Social Sciences, Western Reserve University, 1948), 23–24; "Historical Report of the Parish of St. Thomas Aquinas Church," [1945], and "Historical Report of the Parish of St. Aloysius," [1945], both in ADC.

34. "Area Descriptions—Security Map of Cuyahoga County," Cleveland, Area D-23, October 19, 1939, HOLC City Survey File, FHLBB, box 87, "Greater Cleveland, OH" folder; 1910 Manuscript Census, Enumeration District 406, p. 3A; "Study of Cleveland's Negro Areas"; Austin et al., "Community Council," 31–32.

35. "Report on Negro Migration and Its Effects," [ca. 1925?], Charles Waddell Chesnutt Papers, microfilm ed., frames 1130–48, WRHS; Property Deeds (CCRO) of black residents from 1920 Manuscript Census, Enumeration Districts 462, 465, 467–68, 473, 619, and 1930 Manuscript Census, Enumeration Districts 443, 451; *C&P*, May 10, 1952; *Cleveland Herald*, October 6, 1944. On Myers, see Kusmer, *Ghetto Takes Shape*, 122–26.

36. Mortgage, May 24, 1916, vol. 1757, p. 471, CCRO; Mortgage, December 16, 1915, vol. 1729, p. 494, CCRO; *C&P*, May 30, 1953. By 1940, the paper was reporting, "In almost every case where a Negro owns a home in the so-called white sections they have succeeded in securing mortgages only through the intervention of some white party, who effected the actual loan." *C&P*, February 22, 1940.

37. "United States Post Office, Cleveland, Ohio," February 7 and 14, 1940, HOLC City Survey File, FHLBB, box 87, "Cleveland, OH [#2]" folder. An even higher 350 dwelling units were black-occupied according to that year's census; U.S. Bureau of the Census, *Housing . . . Cleveland Block Statistics*, 33–34, 43–46, 50–52.

38. 1930 Manuscript Census, Enumeration Districts 433, 435, 438–41, 443–44, 446–47, 449, 451–53, 458, 460, 466, 476–77, 479, 759–61, 798.

39. Davis, *Black Americans*, 232, 234, 237, 239, 244, 250, 291; Kusmer, *Ghetto Takes Shape*, 268, 271–72; Glenn obituary, *C&P*, April 28, 1951. On the careers of Davis and Green, see Kusmer, *Ghetto Takes Shape*, 118–21, 248–49.

40. Davis, *Black Americans*, 227, 241, 244, 276; Kusmer, *Ghetto Takes Shape*, 194–95; Boyd obituary, *C&P*, February 19, 1944; *C&P*, July 1, 1937.

41. Glenn obituary, *C&P*, December 31, 1960; Fairfax obituary, *C&P*, October 19, 1939; *C&P*, May 8, 1948; Phillips, *AlabamaNorth*, 112.

42. On the significance of black beauty culture, see Victoria W. Wolcott, *Remaking Respectability: African American Women in Interwar Detroit* (Chapel Hill, N.C., 2001), 30–31, 89–90.

43. "Baptist Churches," [late 1930s], FLP, container 1, folder 12; Foster interview; Area Descriptions," Area D-23. On Cleveland black churches, see Phillips, *AlabamaNorth*, 166–76.

44. *C&P*, February 10, 1934; *C&P*, July 1, 1937; *CP*, April 12, 1958; *CP*, August 9, 1941; *C&P*, April 19, 1958; unidentified clipping, "Mt. Pleasant Mothers Give $5,000," ca. April 12, 1958, Perry Brooks Jackson Papers, WRHS, container 19, folder 4; *C&P*, September 7, 1939; "Forest City Garden Club," [1950], Henry Lee Moon Family Papers, WRHS, container 2, folder 1.

45. Adrienne Kennedy, *People Who Led to My Plays* (New York, 1987), 47–48. On middle-class social clubs in Cedar-Central, see Phillips, *AlabamaNorth*, 182.

46. Allan Spear, *Black Chicago: The Making of a Negro Ghetto, 1890–1920* (Chicago, 1967); William M. Tuttle Jr., "Contested Neighborhoods and Racial Violence: Prelude to the Chicago Riot of 1919," *Journal of Negro History* 55 (October 1970): 266–88; Thomas L. Philpott, *The Slum and the Ghetto: Neighborhood Deterioration and Middle-Class Reform, 1880–1930* (Belmont, Calif., 1991).

47. See especially Thomas A. Guglielmo, *White on Arrival: Italians, Race, Color, and Power in Chicago, 1890–1945* (New York, 2003), 146–71; and David R. Roediger, *Working Toward Whiteness: How America's Immigrants Became White* (New York, 2005), 157–77. On the significance of newer neighborhoods for Southern and Eastern Europeans, see Thomas Kessner, *The Golden Door: Italian and Jewish Mobility in New York City, 1880–1915* (New York, 1977); Joseph Bigott, *From Cottage to Bungalow: Houses and the Working Classes in Metropolitan Chicago, 1869–1929* (Chicago, 2001); and Will Cooley, "Moving Up, Moving Out: Social Mobility in Chicago, 1914–1972" (Ph.D. diss., University of Illinois, 2008), 46–64.

48. Kusmer, *Ghetto Takes Shape*, 171.

49. Andrew Wiese has noted this phenomenon; Wiese, "Black Housing," 430–31.

50. John Palasics, taped interview with author, October 20, 2001; Pauline Leber, taped

interview with author, December 6, 2001; Whyte and McIntyre interview. For instances of individual black families accepted by white residents, see Paul Frederick Cressey, "The Succession of Cultural Groups in the City of Chicago" (Ph.D. diss., University of Chicago, 1930), 232; and St. Clair Drake and Horace R. Cayton, *Black Metropolis: A Study of Negro Life in a Northern City* (New York, 1945), 176–77, 182.

51. Wiese claims that banks did not lend to blacks in Evanston, Illinois, despite mentioning several instances in which they did; "Black Housing," 438, 446–47. Woofter reported falling interest rates for black borrowers as of 1928 but noted that "it is probable that Negroes still pay a higher rate, distributed in fees, searches of abstracts, renewal commissions and other additions to the legal rates, than do white buyers." Woofter Jr., *Negro Problems*, 146.

52. Wiese asserts that whites lent to blacks with profits in mind, or sometimes paternalistically; "Black Housing," 439–41. Individuals still held nearly a fifth of mortgages in the Cleveland market after the New Deal policy changes; HOLC, Division of Research and Statistics, "Confidential Report of a Resurvey [of] Greater Cleveland, Ohio," March 15, 1940, p. 75, HOLC City Survey File, FHLBB, box 87, "Cleveland, Ohio Re-Survey #1" folder.

53. Cleveland City Directories, 1914–30; 1920 and 1930 Manuscript Censuses; Cuyahoga County Marriage Records; Mortgage, March 5, 1926, vol. 3441, p. 287, CCRO; Mortgage, October 17, 1927, vol. 3682, p. 122, CCRO; Mortgage, September 24, 1929, vol. 3971, p. 63, CCRO; Mortgage, June 27, 1919, vol. 2045, p. 578, CCRO.

54. Mortgage, July 16, 1915, vol. 1722, p. 4, CCRO; Mortgage, February 5, 1916, vol. 1722, p. 316, CCRO; Mortgage, May 8, 1917, vol. 1837, p. 611, CCRO; Mortgage, March 7, 1928, vol. 3689, p. 227, CCRO; Mortgage, May 27, 1929, vol. 3915, p. 181, CCRO; Mortgage, January 13, 1928, vol. 3688, p. 393, CCRO; Mortgage, September 25, 1923, vol. 2714, p. 252, CCRO; Mortgage, May 8, 1916, vol. 1752, p. 250, CCRO; Mortgage, November 19, 1919, vol. 2096, p. 567, CCRO; Mortgage, September 26, 1925, vol. 3137, p. 254, CCRO; Mortgage, May 8, 1930, vol. 4049, p. 231, CCRO.

55. Gerald Lander, taped interview with author, December 13, 2002; Adeline Davis, taped interview with author, October 9, 2001; David Krieger, taped interview with author, October 7, 2001; *CG*, April 27, 1935; *C&P*, April 6, 1939; *C&P*, June 17, 1937.

56. Kusmer, *Ghetto Takes Shape*, 168–69; *C&P*, October 26, 1940. On efforts to put a restrictive covenant in place, see Wade Park Committee Records, WRHS. On covenants' early use and legality, see Ewen McKenzie, *Privatopia: Homeowner Associations and the Rise of Residential Private Government* (New Haven, Conn., 1994), 29–55; Robert M. Fogelson, *Bourgeois Nightmares: Suburbia, 1870–1930* (New Haven, Conn., 2005), esp. 95–131; and Wendy Plotkin, "Deeds of Mistrust: Race, Housing, and Restrictive Covenants in Chicago, 1900–1953" (Ph.D. diss., University of Illinois at Chicago, 1999). Though rarely enforced in court, covenants sent a powerful signal that nonwhites were unwelcome; see Richard R. W. Brooks and Carol M. Rose, *Saving the Neighborhood: Racially Restrictive Covenants, Law, and Social Norms* (Cambridge, Mass., 2013).

57. *CG*, July 23, 1927; Minutes, Executive Committee, October 6, 1938, Jewish Community Council of Cleveland Records (microfilm collection), WRHS. On Smith, see Kus-

mer, *Ghetto Takes Shape*, 130–34. In Chicago, Jews as well as Catholics apparently joined restrictive associations, even serving in positions of leadership; Philpott, *Slum and the Ghetto*, 162–68, 197–98.

58. "From Mrs. Jacob Amster," [1956], JKP; "From Allen E. Reublin," [1956], JKP; "Area Descriptions," Area D-23; "From Mr. and Mrs. Malcolm Grayson," [1956], JKP; "From Dr. Charles Garvin," [1956], JKP; *Philadelphia Tribune*, September 1, 1938.

59. See Michney, "Changing Neighborhoods," 55–61.

60. Gloria C. Ferguson, taped interview with author, September 6, 2003; anonymous interview with author, September 16, 2003; Paul Glenn, taped interview with author, July 16, 2001.

61. Palasics interview; Paul Simpson, taped interview with author, November 26, 2002. For more African Americans acquiring fluency in European languages, see Phillips, *AlabamaNorth*, 146.

62. Kennedy, *People*, 30, 31; Foster interview; Beni Giterman, taped interview with author, December 3, 2002; Phil Lipton, taped interview with author, December 2, 2002.

63. Glenn interview; Mildred Lipton, taped interview with author, December 2, 2002; Stanley Kutler, taped telephone interview with author, October 23, 2001.

64. Ferguson interview; Collins Munns, taped telephone interview, July 12, 2001; "From Rudolph D. Henderson, Jr.," [1956], JKP; anonymous interview with author, September 16, 2003; "From Mr. and Mrs. Malcolm Grayson"; Louis Barracato, taped interview with author, November 20, 2002.

65. Harold Bilsky, taped interview with author, November 26, 2002; James H. Jefferson Sr. obituary, *PD*, December 29, 2000. Other Jewish residents owned businesses in Cedar-Central; see Sanford Watzman, *All the Way to Y2K: Life of a Jewish American in the Last Three Quarters of the 20th Century* (Silver Spring, Md., 2000), 265–74.

66. Ferguson interview; Simpson interview; Foster interview; 1930 Manuscript Census, Enumeration District 808, p. 3B.

67. According to a former Mount Pleasant Jewish resident, "The Italians tended not to have maids"; Watzman, *All the Way*, 61. One interviewee estimated that one-third of the Jewish families in the neighborhood employed domestic servants; Erwin Edelman, taped interview with author, November 23, 2002.

68. Bilsky interview; Stanley Lasky, written response to interview questions, April 25, 2001; Munns interview; Phillips, *AlabamaNorth*, 144; Watzman, *All the Way*, 58–62. On Jewish wives working at family businesses, see Elizabeth Ewen, *Immigrant Women in the Land of Dollars: Life and Culture on the Lower East Side, 1890–1925* (New York, 1985), 167–68; Kathie Friedman-Kasaba, *Memories of Migration: Gender, Ethnicity, and Work in the Lives of Jewish and Italian Women of New York, 1870–1924* (Albany, N.Y., 1996), 127–29; and Sidney Stahl Weinberg, *The World of Our Mothers: Lives of Jewish Immigrant Women* (Chapel Hill, N.C., 1998), 238–40.

69. Victoria W. Wolcott, *Race, Riots, and Roller Coasters: The Struggle over Segregated Recreation in America* (Philadelphia, 2012); Jeff Wiltse, *Contested Waters: A Social History of Swimming Pools in America* (Chapel Hill, N.C., 2007), esp. 121–80. On such incidents in

Chicago, see Philpott, *Slum and the Ghetto*, 170; and Drake and Cayton, *Black Metropolis*, 104–6. On the contemporaneous campaign to desegregate beaches and swimming pools in Los Angeles, see Flamming, *Bound for Freedom*, 216–18, 271–75, 289–91.

70. *CG*, July 30, 1927; *CG*, July 28, 1928; "Statement of Mrs. C. E. Persons," July 20, 1928, William R. Hopkins Papers, WRHS, container 4, folder 2; *CG*, July 12, 1930.

71. *CG*, January 14, 1928. On Meade, see Davis, *Black Americans*, 156–57; on the 1884 Act and Smith's role in getting it passed, see Marilyn Kaye Howard, "Black Lynching in the Promised Land: Mob Violence in Ohio, 1876–1916" (Ph.D. diss., Ohio State University, 1999).

72. *CG*, August 27, 1927; Thomas Fleming to George Myers, August 11, 1927, George A. Myers Papers, OHS, microfilm roll 18; Edwin Barry to George Myers, April 20, 1928, and Clayborne George to George Myers, May 25, 1928, both in ibid.; *CG*, July 28, 1928.

73. *CG*, July 28, 1928; "Statement of Mrs. C. E. Persons"; *CG*, August 27, 1927.

74. In 1930, the total number of African American households in Wards 28 and 29, to the southwest and northeast of the park, respectively, was fifty-six; 1930 Manuscript Census, Enumeration Districts 493, 827.

75. Margie Glass, interview transcript, December 12, 1986, St. James Oral History Project, container 1, folder 16; Phillips, *AlabamaNorth*, 145–46; John J. Grabowski, "A Social Settlement in a Neighborhood in Transition: Hiram House, Cleveland, Ohio" (Ph.D. diss., Case Western Reserve University, 1977), 160.

76. *CG*, July 14, 1934; *C&P*, July 21, 1934; *C&P*, August 4, 1934.

77. Mark Naison, "Remaking America: Communists and Liberals in the Popular Front," in *New Studies in the Politics and Culture of U.S. Communism*, ed. Michael E. Brown et al. (New York, 1993), 45–73. On the Communist Party's civil rights record, see Gerald Horne, "The Red and the Black: The Communist Party and African-Americans in Historical Perspective," in ibid., 199–237; and Nelson Lichtenstein, "Opportunities Found and Lost: Labor, Radicals, and the Early Civil Rights Movement," *Journal of American History* 75 (December 1988): 786–811.

78. *C&P*, April 13, 1935; Wye, "Midwest Ghetto," 413–15; *CG*, April 20, 1935; *C&P*, April 27, 1935; *C&P*, June 6, 1935; *C&P*, July 25, 1935; *C&P*, August 22, 1935. On Maude White and local Communist Party involvement with blacks, see Phillips, *AlabamaNorth*, 200–203; on Communist support among Mount Pleasant's ethnics, see Watzman, *All the Way*, 174–76; and Michney, "Changing Neighborhoods," 48–49.

79. *C&P*, May 28, 1936; *C&P*, June 18, 1936; *C&P*, July 9, 1936; *PD*, July 10, 1936; *C&P*, July 16, 1936; *C&P*, July 23, 1936. On NAACP-Communist Party cooperation during this era, see "A New Crowd Challenges the Old Guard in the NAACP, 1933–1941," *American Historical Review* 102 (April 1997): 340–77.

80. Harold Ticktin, taped interview with author, February 11, 2002; *C&P*, July 21, 1938; *C&P*, July 14, 1938; *C&P*, August 11, 1938.

81. *C&P*, August 11, 1938.

82. Ibid.; *CG*, August 27, 1938; *CG*, August 13, 1938; *C&P*, August 25, 1938; *CG*, August 20, 1938; *C&P*, September 1, 1938; *CG*, September 3, 1938.

83. *C&P*, September 8, 1938; *CG*, September 10, 1938; *C&P*, September 15, 1938; *CG*, September 17, 1938; *C&P*, September 22, 1938; *CG*, October 1, 1938; *PD*, October 3, 1938; *CG*, October 8, 1938; *C&P*, October 13, 1938; *CG*, October 15, 1938.

84. *C&P*, August 10, 1939; *C&P*, July 13, 1939; *C&P*, July 20, 1939; *C&P*, August 3, 1939; *C&P*, August 31, 1939; *C&P*, October 12, 1939; *C&P*, October 19, 1939.

85. Davis, *Black Americans*, 274; Arnold R. Hirsch, *Making the Second Ghetto: Race and Housing in Chicago, 1940-1960*, reprint ed. (Chicago, 1998), 63-66.

86. Wye, "Midwest Ghetto," 118-24 (quote from 124); Davis, *Black Americans*, 272; Christopher G. Wye, "The New Deal and the Negro Community: Toward a Broader Conceptualization," *Journal of American History* 59 (December 1972), 631, 634, 636; Phillips, *AlabamaNorth*, 149, 185, 194, 196-97. On black Detroiters' Depression-era survival strategies, see Wolcott, *Remaking Respectability*, 169-205.

87. Wye, "Midwest Ghetto," 120-21, 235-45; Phillips, *AlabamaNorth*, 193-95, 197; Wye, "New Deal," 634-36; Davis, *Black Americans*, 296-97.

88. Wye, "Midwest Ghetto," 23, 231-32, 244-47; Charles W. Chesnutt, "The Negro in Cleveland," *Clevelander* 5 (November 1930): 26; Kusmer, *Ghetto Takes Shape*, 194-95; Davis, *Black Americans*, 290.

89. Wye, "New Deal"; Real Property Inventory of Metropolitan Cleveland, *A Sheet-a-Week* (December 9, 1937); *Atlanta Daily World*, July 15, 1937; *C&P*, May 26, 1938; *C&P*, October 13, 1938; *C&P*, April 27, 1939. For the fullest exposition to date of racialized New Deal housing policies, see David M. P. Freund, *Colored Property: State Policy and White Racial Politics in Suburban America* (Chicago, 2007).

90. Wye, "Midwest Ghetto," 74-77, 81-82, 86-88 (quote from 88); "Study of Cleveland's Negro Areas"; "Area Descriptions," Areas D-12 and D-23. The Depression opened opportunities for African Americans elsewhere; see Annette Fishbein, "The Expansion of Negro Residential Areas in Chicago, 1950-60" (M.A. thesis, University of Chicago, 1962), 6.

91. For this conclusion, compare U.S. Bureau of the Census, *Housing . . . Cleveland Block Statistics*, 55; and U.S. Bureau of the Census, *Housing—Analytical Maps: Cleveland, Ohio Block Statistics*, 133.

92. 1930 Manuscript Census; Cuyahoga County Land Records; Cleveland City Directories, 1930, 1940; Cleveland Necrology File, CPL; Howard Whipple Green, *Planes of Living in Cuyahoga County*, Part I (Cleveland, 1941), Map 41.

93. Ronald Ferguson, taped telephone interview with author, August 29, 2003; Simpson interview; *C&P*, May 29, 1948; Michney, "Changing Neighborhoods," 67-70.

Chapter 2

1. "Report of Mass Meeting," ca. April 8, 1945, JCC, Series II, container 5, folder 103; Property Deed, July 18, 1944, vol. 5692, p. 253, CCRO. On Gillespie's civil rights activities, see Russell H. Davis, *Black Americans in Cleveland from George Peake to Carl B. Stokes* (Washington, D.C., 1972), 273; and Kenneth L. Kusmer, *A Ghetto Takes Shape: Black Cleveland, 1870-1930* (Urbana, Ill., 1976), 249-50.

2. "Report of Mass Meeting"; Frank T. Suhadolnik to Thomas A. Burke, April 10, 1945, CMP, container 1, folder 23; Chester K. Gillespie to Thomas A. Burke, April 9, 1945, in ibid.

3. Joseph L. Arnold, "The Neighborhood and City Hall: The Origins of Neighborhood Associations in Baltimore, 1880–1911," *Journal of Urban History* 6 (November 1979): 3–30; Patricia Mooney-Melvin, "Before the Neighborhood Organization Revolution: Cincinnati's Neighborhood Improvement Associations, 1890–1940," in *Making Sense of the City: Local Government, Civic Culture, and Community Life in Urban America*, ed. Robert B. Fairbanks and Patricia Mooney-Melvin (Columbus, Ohio, 2001), 95–118; Robert Fisher, *Let the People Decide: Neighborhood Organizing in America* (Boston, 1994), 66–97; Ewen McKenzie, *Privatopia: Homeowner Associations and the Rise of Residential Private Government* (New Haven, Conn., 1994), 71–78; Zorita Wise Mikva, "The Neighborhood Improvement Association: A Counterforce to the Expansion of Chicago's Negro Population" (M.A. thesis, University of Chicago, 1951).

4. "Report of Mass Meeting"; Suhadolnik to Burke.

5. "Recreation Resources and Needs in the Glenville Area," September 1945, FCP, container 28, folder 693; U.S. Bureau of the Census, *Housing: Supplement to the First Series, Housing Bulletin for Ohio, Cleveland Block Statistics* (Washington, D.C., 1942), 33, 43–44; Howard Whipple Green, *Jewish Families in Greater Cleveland* (Cleveland, 1939).

6. Suhadolnik to Burke; "Report of Mass Meeting"; "Memo for Mayor," May 17, 1945, CMP, container 1, folder 23; *CP*, May 17, 1945. Beebe responded to charges of anti-Semitism by announcing his group had forty Jewish members.

7. An important exception is Wendell Pritchett, *Brownsville, Brooklyn: Blacks, Jews, and the Changing Face of the Ghetto* (Chicago, 2002). For a look at an "undefended" neighborhood undergoing transition, see Egbert F. Schietinger, "Real Estate Transfers during Negro Invasion: A Case Study" (M.A. thesis, University of Chicago, 1948).

8. *CN*, April 2, 1945; "Report of Mass Meeting"; "Minutes for the Exploratory Meeting for the Glenville Area Community Council," January 10, 1945, JCC, Series II, container 5, folder 103; "Minutes of the Temporary Executive Committee, Glenville Area Community Council," January 29, 1945, in ibid.; "Minutes of the Temporary Executive Committee, Glenville Area Community Council," February 2, 1945, in ibid.; *PD*, April 1, 1945; *CP*, April 2, 1945; *CP*, April 23, 1945.

9. *CP*, April 25, 1945; *PD*, April 25, 1945; *CP*, April 27, 1945.

10. *CP*, April 2, 1945; "Glenville Area Community Council, Minutes of the Temporary Executive Committee," April 5, 1945, JCC, Series II, container 5, folder 103; "Press Release," [ca. April 3, 1945], NAACP-CB, container 36, folder 4.

11. Memo, "Mr. Russell Davis: Recommendations," April 5, 1945," NAACP-CB, container 36, folder 4; GACC, "Statement to the Cleveland Board of Education," December 1945, in ibid.; Ruth Ackerman and Netta Siegel, "The Glenville Area Community Council: A Case Study," May 31, 1945, pp. 5–6, 21, JCC, container 2, folder 26; H. S. Beebe to Sanford Solender, April 27, 1945, JCC, Series II, container 5, folder 103; L. L. Yancey to Francis Payne Bolton, May 7, 1945, Francis Payne Bolton Papers, WRHS, container 135, folder 2391; "Glen-

ville Area Community Council, Minutes of the Temporary Executive Committee," April 19, 1945, JCC, Series II, container 5, folder 103; *PD*, May 23, 1945; Minutes, Community Relations Board, July 17, 1945, CMP, container 1, folder 23; D. R. Sharpe to Chief Matowitz, July 19, 1945, in ibid.

12. Christopher G. Wye, "Midwest Ghetto: Patterns of Negro Life and Thought in Cleveland, Ohio, 1929–1945" (Ph.D. diss., Kent State University, 1973), 91–93, 99–102; Todd M. Michney, "Constrained Communities: Black Cleveland's Experience with World War II Public Housing," *Journal of Social History* 40 (Summer 2007): 933–56.

13. Michney, "Constrained Communities," 937–38; Wye, "Midwest Ghetto," 94–96, 142–63, 273–95, 383, 431–33; *C&P*, July 13, 1939; Kimberley L. Phillips, *AlabamaNorth: African-American Migrants, Community, and Working-Class Activism in Cleveland, 1915–45* (Urbana, Ill., 1999), 226–52.

14. Mrs. Harry Mendelsohn to "Dear President [Roosevelt]," January 1, 1943, EJB, U.S. War Housing, container 1, folder 4; Memo, Katharine Patch to Mr. D. E. Mackelmann, January 9, 1943, in ibid.; *C&P*, August 5, 1944; *C&P*, May 5, 1945; Davis, *Black Americans*, 308.

15. Langston Hughes, "Here to Yonder; Cleveland—A Good Town," 1946, in Manuscript Vertical File, WRHS; *C&P*, September 26, 1942; Adrienne Kennedy, *People Who Led to My Plays* (New York, 1987), 57; "From Wm. T. McKnight," [1956], JKP. On Myers, Payne, and Boyd, see Davis, *Black Americans*, 241, 291, 288; and Kusmer, *Ghetto Takes Shape*, 272–73.

16. *CP*, October 5, 1944; *C&P*, April 1, 1944; *C&P*, June 24, 1944.

17. "From James C. Weaver," [1956], JKP; Ackerman and Siegel, "Glenville Area Community Council," 3; Minutes, Board of Trustees, CEA, November 15, 1944, JCC, container 5, folder 32; "Jewish Suburban Population Movement in Cleveland and Its Impact on Communal Institutions," May 1957, JCF, container 11, folder 184.

18. See Pritchett, *Brownsville*; Thomas J. Sugrue, *The Origins of the Urban Crisis: Race and Inequality in Postwar Detroit* (Princeton, N.J., 1996), 242–45; and Arnold R. Hirsch, *Making the Second Ghetto: Race and Housing in Chicago, 1940–1960*, reprint ed. (Chicago, 1998), 193–94. On institutions, see Gerald Gamm, *Urban Exodus: Why the Jews Left Boston and the Catholics Stayed* (Cambridge, Mass., 1999); and John T. McGreevy, *Parish Boundaries: The Catholic Encounter with Race in the Twentieth Century Urban North* (Chicago, 1996). For early discussions of Jewish upward mobility, see Marshall Sklare, ed., *The Jews: Social Patterns of an American Group* (Glencoe, Ill., 1958); for critique, see Stephen Steinberg, "The Rise of the Jewish Professional: Case Studies of Intergenerational Mobility," *Ethnic and Racial Studies* 9 (October 1986): 502–13.

19. "From James C. Weaver"; handwritten notes, "Glenville Area," November 1945, JCC, Series II, container 5, folder 103.

20. Mary Gilbert to Fred Rogers, March 29, 1945, Hiram House Records, WRHS, container 26, folder 3; "Mt. Pleasant Area: A Study of Recreational Needs," 3, 12; U.S. Bureau of the Census, *United States Census of Housing: 1950 Block Statistics*; U.S. Bureau of the Census, *Housing: Supplement . . . Cleveland Block Statistics* (Washington, D.C., 1942).

21. "Digest of 'Jewish Families in Greater Cleveland,'" 1937, JCF, container 11, folder 182; "Comments Regarding Population of Children in the Mt. Pleasant Neighborhood," [1941?], JCC, container 3, folder 45; Todd M. Michney, "Changing Neighborhoods: Race and Upward Mobility in Southeast Cleveland, 1930–1980" (Ph.D. diss., University of Minnesota, 2004), 219–25; "1943–1944 Annual Report H. Okilman," 10, 13–14, JCC, container 3, folder 49.

22. "Minutes for the Exploratory Meeting for the Glenville Community Council"; Ackerman and Siegel, "Glenville Area Community Council," 7; "Annual Report—Junior Division 1941–1942," JCC, container 3, folder 48; Minutes, Race Relations Committee, March 1, 1945, FCP, container 36, folder 882; Minutes, "Special Committee on the Young Adult Program," December 18, 1945, JCC, container 5, folder 32; "Minutes of the Temporary Executive Committee," January 29, 1945; *PD*, July 8, 1945; Minutes, GACC, Executive Board, October 1, 1945, JCC, Series II, container 5, folder 103.

23. Beebe to Solender; Memo, "Mr. Russell Davis: Recommendations"; *C&P*, May 26, 1945; "Report of Mass Meeting"; Ackerman and Siegel, "Glenville Area Community Council," 4.

24. "Recreation Resources and Needs in the Glenville Area"; Ackerman and Siegel, "Glenville Area Community Council," 4; Z. A. Buzek to "Your Excellency," June 20, 1945, St. Agatha Parish correspondence, ADC. On wartime conversion policy, see Michney, "Constrained Communities."

25. Austin et al., "Community Council," 35; *CP*, December 11, 1944; Homer W. Sheffield, Olee Sheffield, and Jean Dorgham, taped interview with author, November 3, 2001.

26. Formed as early as World War I in New York City, community councils were not used to address racial residential transition in Detroit until 1947, in Chicago until 1949, in Cincinnati until 1956, or in Louisville until 1963. See Patricia Mooney-Melvin, *The Organic City: Urban Definition and Neighborhood Organization, 1880–1920* (Lexington, Ky., 1987), 160–71; Lila Corwin Berman, *Metropolitan Jews: Politics, Race, and Religion in Postwar Detroit* (Chicago, 2015), 65–70; Philip A. Johnson, *Call Me Neighbor, Call Me Friend* (Garden City, N.Y., 1965), 73, 76; John Clayton Thomas, *Between Citizen and City: Neighborhood Organizations and Urban Politics in Cincinnati* (Lawrence, Kans., 1986), 22–42; and Tracy E. K'Meyer, *Civil Rights in the Gateway to the South: Louisville, Kentucky, 1945–1980* (Lexington, Ky., 2009), 114–16.

27. Welfare Federation, Committee on Inter-racial Code, May 1, 1945, FCP, container 2, folder 34. On White, see Kusmer, *Ghetto Takes Shape*, 283.

28. Memo, George Edmund Haynes et al. to Cleveland Church Federation, January 1942 (preliminary draft dated May 13, 1941), 13–14, CCC, container 6, folder 249; Report attached to David Baylor to Mr. Douglas Coulter, July 22, 1943, NAACP-LC, Group II, container A507, folder 1; Memo, Henry Ollendorff to "Headworkers of the Cleveland Settlements," ca. January 28, 1943, JCC, container 8, folder 97; *CP*, July 30, 1943.

29. *CP*, August 7, 1943; "Confidential Memorandum to the Board of Trustees of the Young Men's Christian Association," July 26, 1943, NAACP-LC, Group II, box A507, folder 1; *CP*, August 25, 1944; "The Group Work Council of the Welfare Federation of Cleveland,

1935–1945," January 18, 1945, p. 22, EENH, container 4, folder 1; Cuyahoga County Council for Civilian Defense, Minutes, February 12, 1945, EJB, U.S. War Housing, container 1, folder 49.

30. Minutes, Jewish Community Council, February 7, 1945, JCC, container 6, folder 55; *CP*, November 9, 1945. See also *To Promote Amicable Relations: Thirty-Year History of the Cleveland Community Relations Board* (Cleveland, 1975); and Kenneth Wayne Rose, "The Politics of Social Reform in Cleveland, 1945–1967: Civil Rights, Welfare Rights, and the Response of Civic Leaders" (Ph.D. diss., Case Western Reserve University, 1988), 15–67. On analogous bodies, see Hirsch, *Making the Second Ghetto*, 44, 177; Robert A. Burnham, "The Mayor's Friendly Relations Committee: Cultural Pluralism and the Struggle for Black Advancement," in *Race and the City: Work, Community, and Protest in Cincinnati, 1820–1970*, ed. Henry Louis Taylor (Urbana, Ill., 1993), 258–79; and Kevin Allen Leonard, "'In the Interest of All Races': African Americans and Interracial Cooperation in Los Angeles during and after World War II," in *Seeking El Dorado: African Americans in California*, ed. Lawrence de Graf, Kevin Mulroy, and Quintard Taylor (Seattle, 2001), 309–40.

31. Austin et al., "Community Council," 57–58; Ackerman and Siegel, "Glenville Area Community Council," 8, 18, 20; W. T. McCullough to Thomas Burke, April 10, 1945, CMP, container 1, folder 23; Sanford Solender to H. S. Beebe, May 7, 1945, JCC, Series II, container 5, folder 103.

32. Minutes, CEA Staff, March 1, 1946, JCC, container 3, folder 50; "Evaluation of Staff Meetings—1946," JCC, container 3, folder 51; *CP*, June 5, 1946; *PD*, June 7, 1946.

33. See Judith Ann Trolander, *Settlement Houses and the Great Depression* (Detroit, 1975), 134–37; Anne-Lise Halvorsen and Jeffrey E. Mirel, "Intercultural Education in Detroit, 1943–1954," *Paedagogica Historica* 49, no. 3 (2013): 361–81; and Stuart G. Svonkin, *Jews against Prejudice: American Jews and the Fight for Civil Liberties* (New York, 1997), esp. 62–78.

34. *PD*, September 3, 1942; "Report of Intersettlement League of Mothers Clubs," June 16, 1938, and unidentified clipping, "Heads League," 1937, EENH, container 16, folder 2; "Headworker's Report," ca. March 1938, EENH, container 4, folder 4; "Radio Script, WHK," November 3, 1942, EENH, container 4, folder 1; "Presentation of Adult Activities," October 29, 1943, JCC, container 3, folder 49.

35. Bertha Park to Mr. and Mrs. Lyons, February 2, 1939, FLP, container 1, folder 12; Minutes, Race Relations Committee, Cleveland Church Federation, June 3, 1942, CCC, container 6, folder 249; "Race Relations Clinic," February 9, 1945, CCC, container 6, folder 251; *CP*, February 17, 1951; *PD*, February 22, 1941; *CP*, February 16, 1946; C. L. Sharpe and Grace Meyette to "Dear Friend," February 6, 1943, LHR, container 3, folder 1; *CP*, February 15, 1943; *PD*, February 15, 1943.

36. "Statement of Principles for Interracial and Intercultural Relations," ca. April 5, 1946, EENH, container 26, folder 1; Frank Baldau to "All Board Members," July 9, 1946, CMP, container 1, folder 22; "Head Worker's Report for June 1946," EENH, container 4, folder 5; "Head Workers' Report for Last Half of Summer 1946," in ibid.

37. *CP*, February 15, 1943; unidentified draft, "After spending part . . ." [ca. 1944–45],

LHR, container 5, folder 4; Frank Brosta to Thomas Burke, March 15, 1945, CMP, container 1, folder 17; Telegram, Brotherhood Rally of the 30th Ward to Thomas Burke, March 18, 1946, and related materials, CMP, container 1, folder 22; Community Relations Board, "Report of the Executive Director," October 16, 1945, CMP, container 1, folder 21; Community Relations Board, "Report of the Executive Director," April 18, 1946, in ibid. For similar black-Jewish activism, see David Jason Leonard, "'No Jews and No Coloreds Are Welcome in This Town': Constructing Coalitions in Post-war Los Angeles" (Ph.D. diss., University of California, Berkeley, 2002).

38. Minutes, Committee on Negro-Jewish Relations, August 14, 1941, Jewish Community Council Minutes and Reports (microfilm collection), WRHS; Minutes, Negro-Jewish Relations Committee, May 16, 1944, in ibid.; Jewish Community Council, "Minutes of a Meeting Held October 11, 1944," JCF, container 6, folder 88. For similar patterns, see Dominic J. Capeci Jr., "Black-Jewish Relations in Wartime Detroit: The Marsh, Loving, Wolf Surveys and the Race Riot of 1943," *Jewish Social Studies* 47 (Summer/Autumn 1985): 221–42.

39. Austin et al., "Community Council," 41–54; *CP*, January 19, 1940; *PD*, January 19, 1940; A. H. Murray, Secretary, "The Glenville Community Council," [1940], JCC, Series II, container 5, folder 103; "The Negro Welfare Association Program 1937," FCP, container 36, folder 892; "Annual Report for the Year 1934 of the Negro Welfare Association," NUL, box I:N8, "Cleveland, Ohio, Annual Reports, 1934–1953" folder.

40. *C&P*, July 21, 1945; "Annual Report of the 105th Street Branch, Council Educational Alliance, September 1945 to June 1946," JCC, Series II, container 5, folder 97; *C&P*, June 15, 1946; *CP*, January 19, 1948; *C&P*, June 8, 1946; *C&P*, August 9, 1947.

41. "Community Meeting," ca. November 7, 1945, JCC, Series II, container 5, folder 103; "Mass Meeting," ca. March 22, [1946?], NAACP-CB, container 36, folder 4.

42. *Glenville Bulletin* (December 6, 1946), NAACP-CB, container 36, folder 4; "Do You Want Bilboism Here?" ca. January 15, 1947, ULC, container 41, folder 2; William Haber to Charles Lucas, July 14, 1948, NAACP-CB, container 24, folder 1; GACC, "Toward a Better Glenville—4th Annual Report," June 1949, FCP, container 28, folder 693; Minutes, GACC, Executive Committee, August 5, 1946, JCC, Series II, container 5, folder 103; GACC, "5th Annual Report," May 1950, in ibid.; *C&P*, January 21, 1950; *Glenville Area Community Council Bulletin* (March–April 1951), NAACP-CB, container 36, folder 4. For more on the Euclid Beach campaign, see Victoria W. Wolcott, *Race, Riots, and Roller Coasters: The Struggle over Segregated Recreation in America* (Philadelphia, 2012), 57–59.

43. "Glenville Area Community Council, Minutes of the Temporary Executive Committee," April 19, 1945; GACC to Board of Education, May 22, 1945, JCC, Series II, container 5, folder 103; *CP*, August 27, 1945; *CP*, August 28, 1945; "Report of the Recreation Committee," October 1, 1945, JCC, Series II, container 5, folder 103; GACC, "Summary of the First Annual Report," June 11, 1946, in ibid.; Austin et al., "Community Council," 66–67.

44. Minutes, GACC, Executive Board, October 1, 1945, JCC, Series II, container 5, folder 103; Minutes, GACC, Executive Board, November 12, 1945, in ibid.; Austin et al., "Community Council," 67; Memo to Chester Zmudzinski, January 8, 1946, JCC, Series II, con-

tainer 5, folder 103; Sanford Solender to Russell Davis, January 14, 1946, in ibid.; Minutes, GACC, Executive Board, February 7, 1946, in ibid.; Minutes, GACC, Executive Board, December 20, 1945, in ibid.

45. Minutes, GACC, Executive Board, February 7, 1946; "Summary of the First Annual Report"; Minutes, GACC, Executive Committee, August 5, 1946; "Annual Report of the 105th Street Branch, Council Educational Alliance, September 1945 to June 1946," JCC, Series II, container 5, folder 97; Austin et al., "Community Council," 68.

46. Unidentified newspaper clipping, "Glenville Group Meets Tuesday," [ca. June 11, 1946], in "Glenville Area and Community Council" (microfiche), CPC; *CP*, June 12, 1946; *Glenville Bulletin* (September 26, 1946), JCC, Series II, container 5, folder 103; *Glenville Bulletin* (December 6, 1946), in ibid.; *PD*, May 15, 1947.

47. Austin et al., "Community Council," 70–90 (quotes from 87, 89).

48. *CP*, June 5, 1947; Flyer, "Citizens Court," ca. June 11, 1947, FCP, container 28, folder 693; *PD*, June 12, 1947; *CP*, June 12, 1947.

49. Austin et al., "Community Council," 179–234 (quote from 228); *Glenville Bulletin* (December 30, 1947), NAACP-CB, container 36, folder 4; Minutes, GACC, Executive Committee Meeting, January 13, 1947, JCC, Series II, container 5, folder 103.

50. "The Glenville Area Community Council Presents the Cleveland Women's Orchestra," April 7, 1948, NAACP-CB, container 36, folder 4; *CP*, June 11, 1948; Minutes, GACC, January 31, 1949, NAACP-CB, container 36, folder 4; *CN*, June 14, 1949; *PD*, June 15, 1949; GACC, "Toward a Better Glenville."

51. "Improvement Board Aim of Mt. Pleasant Council," *CP*, [November 1947], in "Mt. Pleasant Community Council," CPC; Minutes, CEA General Staff Meeting, March 7, 1947, JCC, container 3, folder 51; MPCC to Charles Lucas, March 31, 1947, NAACP-CB, container 38, folder 3; Minutes, Area Councils Committee, Welfare Federation, April 24, 1947, FCP, container 28, folder 674; Minutes, Area Councils Committee, Welfare Federation, November 24, 1947, in ibid.; Minutes, Mt. Pleasant Advisory Board Meeting, February 23, 1948, JCC, Series II, container 5, folder 100.

52. "The Mount Pleasant Area Study," May 16, 1950, FCP, container 49, folder 1175; Minutes, Area Councils Committee, November 3, 1950, FCP, container 28, folder 674; Lowell Henry to Sidney Jackson Jr., January 29, 1952, FCP, Field Service Advisory Committee, microfilm roll 10.

53. U.S. Bureau of the Census, *16th Census of the United States, 1940: Population and Housing—Statistics for Census Tracts: Cleveland, Ohio, and Adjacent Area* (Washington, D.C., 1942), 5; U.S. Bureau of the Census, *United States Census of Population: 1950—Census Tract Statistics, Cleveland, Ohio, and Adjacent Area* (Washington, D.C., 1952), 12, 13, 15, 16.

54. Minutes, Intercultural and Interracial Relations Committee, Group Work Council, October 4, 1956, FCP, container 36, folder 877; Ann Werneke, "The Church in the Changing City: A Study in Contrasts," [1961], 17, RCPO, container 2, folder 7; Austin et al., "Community Council," 24, 36; "Area Characteristics, Mount Pleasant [1950]," FCP, container 9, folder 225; "Mount Pleasant Area Study"; "Evaluation of the Present and Future Location

of Mt. Pleasant Facilities," [May 1949], JCC, container 30, folder 1; "Enrollment of Children in Mt. Pleasant-Kinsman-Shaker-Extension for 1944–1948," in ibid.

55. U.S. Bureau of the Census, *United States Census of Housing: 1950 Block Statistics, Cleveland, Ohio* (Washington, D.C., 1952), 47; U.S. Bureau of the Census, *Housing: Supplement to the First Series, Housing Bulletin for Ohio, Cleveland Block Statistics* (Washington, D.C., 1942), 44; Cleveland City Directories, 1940–44, 1947, 1951 (Cleveland: Cleveland Directory Co.); Property Deeds, CCRO.

56. "Did You Know?" [ca. 1950], NAACP-CB, container 36, folder 4; *C&P*, July 21, 1945; *C&P*, January 25, 1947; *C&P*, November 29, 1947; *PD*, May 15, 1947; *C&P*, August 19, 1950; Burks obituary, *PD*, July 28, 2001.

57. *C&P*, July 14, 1945; *C&P*, June 15, 1946; Minutes, GACC, Executive Board Meeting, February 7, 1946, JCC, Series II, container 5, folder 103; *C&P*, November 23, 1946; *C&P*, May 3, 1952; *C&P*, October 13, 1945; *C&P*, April 7, 1945; *C&P*, June 1, 1946; *C&P*, March 1, 1947; Regional Church Planning Office, "The Church in a Changing Neighborhood," October 30, 1961, pp. 28–31, WRHS; *C&P*, September 2, 1950.

58. *C&P*, July 20, 1946; *C&P*, November 15, 1947; *C&P*, November 22, 1947; Group Work Council, "Mt. Pleasant Area: A Study of Recreational Needs in a Changing Community," April 9, 1952, p. 12, GCNCA, container 4, folder 56; "Mount Pleasant Area Study"; *CP*, March 23, 1951.

59. *C&P*, January 3, 1948; *C&P*, January 31, 1948; *C&P*, December 27, 1947; *C&P*, February 14, 1948; *C&P*, April 2, 1949; *C&P*, October 16, 1948.

60. *C&P*, February 14, 1948; *C&P*, March 13, 1948; *C&P*, April 24, 1948; *C&P*, December 18, 1948; *C&P*, November 4, 1950.

61. *C&P*, December 13, 1947; *C&P*, August 14, 1948. On African American landlords elsewhere defending their interests, see Josh Sides, *L.A. City Limits: African American Los Angeles from the Great Depression to the Present* (Berkeley, Calif., 2004), 123; Will Cooley, "Moving Up, Moving Out: Race and Social Mobility in Chicago, 1914–1972" (Ph.D. diss., University of Illinois, Urbana-Champaign, 2008), 115–21; and N. D. B. Connolly, *A World More Concrete: Real Estate and the Making of Jim Crow South Florida* (Chicago, 2014).

62. Minutes, Community Relations Board, June 25, 1946, CMP, container 1, folder 22; *C&P*, July 13, 1946; GACC, "Toward a Better Glenville"; Memo, Area Councils Joint Committee on Recreation to Finance Committee of City Council, March 1, 1949, FCP, Joint Recreation Committee with Area Council, microfilm roll 10; "Securing These Rights: A Report on the Work of the Community Relations Board," January 1950, CMP, container 1, folder 22.

63. GACC, "Statement to the Cleveland Board of Education"; *CP*, December 4, 1945; "Glenville Area Community Council Progress Report," February 1946, JCC, Series II, container 5, folder 103; Minutes, GACC, Executive Committee Meeting, August 5, 1946; Minutes, Community Relations Board, June 25, 1946; *C&P*, July 6, 1946; *C&P*, October 12, 1946; Henry to Jackson Jr.

64. "Glenville Area Community Council, Minutes of the Temporary Executive Com-

mittee," April 5, 1945; Minutes, GACC, Executive Board, October 1, 1945; Minutes, GACC, Executive Committee Meeting, February 19, 1947, JCC, Series II, container 5, folder 103; *CP*, July 23, 1947; "Mount Pleasant Area Study"; *C&P*, March 17, 1938; "Boys Work Activities," [ca. January 1937], YMCA, Series II, container 1, folder 11; Jane Hunter to Group Work Council, June 18, 1945, Phillis Wheatley Association Records, WRHS, container 12, folder 6.

65. Minutes, GACC, Executive Committee Meeting, January 13, 1947; Austin et al., "Community Council," 30; *C&P*, October 25, 1947; "Annual Staff Report—1946-1947," JCC, Series II, container 5, folder 97; Minutes, Area Councils Committee, April 12, 1950, FCP, container 28, folder 674; *C&P*, February 28, 1948; *C&P*, December 25, 1948; *C&P*, December 18, 1948; *C&P*, September 11, 1948.

66. Austin et al., "Community Council," 150-68 (quotes from 167).

67. Ibid., 168-70.

68. Ibid., 126-39, 140-41 (quotes).

69. Ibid., 140-42.

70. "Report on the Senior Division—1939-1940," JCC, container 3, folder 47; "Annual Report—1944-1945," JCC, Series II, container 5, folder 96; "1943-1944 Annual Report H. Okilman," 7, 9-11, 13-14; "Council Educational Alliance Planning Staff Meetings, September 23-26, 1945," 13-15, JCC, container 3, folder 50.

71. Minutes, CEA Staff Meeting, October 27, 1945, JCC, container 3, folder 50; "CEA Staff Meeting, December 7, 1945," in ibid.; "Annual Report of the 105th Street Branch, Council Educational Alliance, September 1945 to June 1946," JCC, Series II, container 5, folder 97; "Evaluation of Staff Meetings—1946," 25-27, JCC, container 3, folder 51.

72. "Evaluation of Staff Meetings—1946," 22-23, JCC, container 3, folder 51; "Annual Staff Report—1946-1947," JCC, Series II, container 5, folder 97; Saul Farber, "The Experience of the Council Educational Alliance with Teen-Age Councils," 1947, JCC, container 5, folder 100.

73. "Summary of Study Concerning East 105th Street House," June 1947, JCC, container 27, folder 3; Minutes, Mt. Pleasant Branch Staff Meeting, December 19, 1947, JCC, container 32, folder 32; Minutes, Mt. Pleasant Staff Meeting, January 23, 1948, in ibid.; Minutes, Board of Trustees, CEA, May 27, 1948, JCC, container 5, folder 33.

74. Minutes, Mt. Pleasant Advisory Board, May 2, 1949, JCC, container 30, folder 3; "Report of the Mt. Pleasant Advisory Committee to Board of Trustees," December 12, 1949, JCC, container 30, folder 1; Minutes, CEA Staff Meeting, October 2, 1945, in ibid.; Austin et al., "Community Council," 103; "Council Educational Alliance Planning Staff Meetings, September 23-26, 1945," JCC, container 3, folder 50.

75. CEA, "Annual Report of Northeast Branch, September 1947-June 1948," JCC, Series II, container 5, folder 97; "Minutes of Membership Committee of Northeast Advisory Committee," April 26, 1950, JCC, container 27, folder 1; "Shaker-Lee Branch Report—1950-51," JCC, Series II, container 5, folder 108; "Report of the Mt. Pleasant Advisory Committee to Board of Trustees," December 12, 1949, JCC, container 30, folder 1; Harold Arian to John Jones, April 8, 1952, JCC, container 27, folder 119.

76. "They Came[,] They Talked[,] and Here Is What They Said," March 27, 1949, JCF,

container 6, folder 90; CEA, "Service Commentary: Budget Analysis, 1947–1948," JCC, container 5, folder 33; Minutes, Shaker-Lee Advisory Committee, April 16, 1951, JCC, container 30, folder 1.

Chapter 3

1. *C&P*, January 10, 1953.

2. Ibid.; *C&P*, January 17, 1953; *C&P*, September 6, 1952.

3. "Proposal, Cleveland Urban League Special Housing Program," [ca. April 17, 1959], CDF, container 60, folder 11; "Temporary War Housing," January 1, 1945, EJB, CMHA Records, container 2, folder 17.

4. *C&P*, January 17, 1953; *C&P*, January 10, 1953. For a man who singlehandedly dug the foundation and built his brick home over five years, see *C&P*, January 25, 1958.

5. Cleveland Urban League, Research Department, "The Negro in Cleveland, 1950–1963: An Analysis of the Social and Economic Characteristics of the Negro Population" (June 1964), 16–17, 25, WRHS.

6. See Arnold R. Hirsch, *Making the Second Ghetto: Race and Housing in Chicago, 1940–1960*, reprint ed. (Chicago, 1998), 100–170, 212–58; Thomas J. Sugrue, *The Origins of the Urban Crisis: Race and Inequality in Postwar Detroit* (Princeton, N.J., 1996), 76–88, 209–29; and Christopher Silver, "The Racial Origins of Zoning in American Cities," in *Urban Planning and the African American Community: In the Shadows*, ed. June Manning Thomas and Marsha Ritzdorf (Thousand Oaks, Calif., 1997), 23–42.

7. For comments to this effect, see *C&P*, July 5, 1952; and *PD*, February 10, 1953.

8. See Becky M. Nicolaides, *By Blue Heaven: Life and Politics in the Working-Class Suburbs of Los Angeles, 1920–1965* (Chicago, 2002), 2.

9. *Pittsburgh Courier*, July 30, 1927; Christopher G. Wye, "Midwest Ghetto: Patterns of Negro Life and Thought in Cleveland, Ohio, 1929–1945" (Ph.D. diss., Kent State University, 1973), 244. For additional context, see "Area Descriptions—Security Map of Cuyahoga County," Cleveland, Area D-10, September 9, 1939, HOLC City Survey File, FHLBB, box 87, "Greater Cleveland, OH" folder.

10. "Miles Heights Vice Cleanup Started," *CP*, ca. March 1932, in "Miles Heights" (microfiche), CPC; "Miles Heights Village," *Cleveland Historical*, http://clevelandhistorical.org/items/show/297 (May 15, 2014); *Pittsburgh Courier*, February 9, 1929; *Baltimore Afro-American*, November 16, 1929; *New Journal and Guide* [Norfolk, Va.], December 27, 1930; *Pittsburgh Courier*, March 21, 1931; Welfare Federation of Cleveland, "Study of Cleveland's Negro Areas," February 22, 1940, CPL, Public Administration Library, City Hall. On Miles Heights' history, see *CP*, August 1 and 2, 1962; and *CP*, April 4, 1969.

11. See Wilbur H. Watson, *The Village: An Oral Historical and Ethnographic Study of a Black Community* (Atlanta, 1989); for context, see Andrew Wiese, "The Other Suburbanites: African American Suburbanization in the North before 1950," *Journal of American History* 85 (March 1999): 1502–14.

12. "Area Descriptions," Area D-10; "Area Descriptions—Security Map of Cuyahoga County," Garfield Heights, Area D-9, [1939], HOLC City Survey File, FHLBB, box 87,

"Greater Cleveland, OH" folder; U.S. Bureau of the Census, *Housing: Supplement to the First Series, Housing Bulletin for Ohio, Cleveland Block Statistics* (Washington, D.C., 1942), 61–62. For "Negro slum," see *CP*, April 9, 1943.

13. CMHA, "Annual Report 1943," [14]; *CP*, November 16, 1943; *PD*, November 16, 1943; *C&P*, November 27, 1943; *CP*, January 3, 1944; *PD*, January 3, 1944; *C&P*, January 15, 1944.

14. On race-related, wartime public housing opposition, see Sugrue, *Origins of the Urban Crisis*, 72–81; William R. Barnes, "A National Controversy in Miniature: The District of Columbia Struggle over Public Housing and Redevelopment, 1943–1946," *Prologue* 9 (Summer 1977): 91–104; Kenneth D. Durr, *Behind the Backlash: White Working-Class Politics in Baltimore, 1940–1980* (Chapel Hill, N.C., 2003), 23–25; and Delores Nason Mc-Broome, "Catalyst for Change: Wartime Housing and African Americans in California's East Bay," in *American Labor in the Era of World War II*, ed. Sally M. Miller and Daniel A. Carnford (Westport, Conn., 1995), 195–96. On *black* residents opposing temporary war housing, see Preston H. Smith II, "The Quest for Racial Democracy: Black Civic Ideology and Housing Interests in Postwar Chicago," *Journal of Urban History* 26 (January 2000): 136–43. Andrew Wiese emphasizes how such housing facilitated African American access to the urban periphery; see Andrew Wiese, *Places of Their Own: African American Suburbanization in the Twentieth Century* (Chicago, 2004), 135–38.

15. *C&P*, February 18, 1945; *PD*, May 16, 1945; "Special Meeting of the Cleveland Community Relations Board," June 5, 1945, CMP, container 1, folder 23; John Fisher to Mayor Burke, April 9, 1945, in ibid.; *Cleveland Union Leader*, July 27, 1945; *C&P*, July 28, 1945; *Cleveland Union Leader*, October 15, 1945. On Seville Homes outlasting the war, see Todd M. Michney, "Constrained Communities: Black Cleveland's Experience with World War II Public Housing," *Journal of Social History* 40 (Summer 2007): 947–49.

16. *CN*, September 20, 1945; *C&P*, September 29, 1945; *C&P*, July 26, 1947; *C&P*, August 2, 1947; *C&P*, November 1, 1947; *C&P*, March 6, 1948; *C&P*, October 23, 1948; *C&P*, November 6, 1948; Watson, *The Village*, 124; *C&P*, June 27, 1953. On lack of services as municipal neglect and a spur to black activism, see Wiese, *Places of Their Own*, 75–77, 205.

17. On zoning as white resistance, from establishing "buffer zones" to condemning existing black settlements ("expulsive" zoning), see especially Wiese, *Places of Their Own*, 91, 97, 104–8, 117, 227–29, 291; and Yale Rubin, "The Roots of Segregation in the Eighties: The Role of Local Government," in *Divided Neighborhoods: Changing Patterns of Racial Segregation*, ed. Gary A. Tobin (Newbury Park, Calif., 1987), 208–26.

18. *CN*, March 19, 1948; *CP*, May 11, 1948; *CP*, October 12, 1951; *PD*, October 12, 1951; *CN*, November 8, 1951; "Report to City Council by the City Planning Commission on Ordinance No. 1092-51," September 7, 1951, in Legislative Files, CCCA; *CN*, November 9, 1951.

19. *C&P*, October 13, 1951; *C&P*, November 17, 1951; *CP*, October 12, 1951; Sylvia Hood Washington, "Packing Them In: A Twentieth Century Working Class Environmental History" (Ph.D. diss., Case Western Reserve University, 2000), 24n31; "Fact Sheet—Lee-Seville Rezoning," January 10, 1952, NAACP-CB, container 37, folder 5; *C&P*, April 22, 1950; *C&P*, May 13, 1950.

20. *CN*, November 13, 1951; *CN*, November 23, 1951. On the rezoning fight as an attempt

"to prevent this thing from becoming just another across the railroad tracks [Negro] area,"
see "Cook, Carriebell J. (Mrs.) Jan. 10; Febr. 8; March [1962]," 184–86, MKP, container 3,
folder 108.

21. "Western Union," ca. November 1951, NAACP-CB, container 37, folder 5; *C&P*,
December 22, 1951; "Minutes of Meeting Held January 4, 1952," NAACP-CB, container 32,
folder 6; Ralph Findley and Fred Moore to Thad Fusco, January 5, 1952, NAACP-CB, container 37, folder 5; "Lee-Seville Rezoning Conference Attendance," January 10, 1952, in
ibid.; Memo, Donald Stier to Charles Lucas, February 6, 1952, in ibid.; *CP*, February 2, 1952;
CP, February 29, 1952; *PD*, February 29, 1952.

22. Mary Spivey et al. to "Dear Minister," January 31, 1952, NAACP-CB, container 37,
folder 5; Mary Spivey and Fred Moore to "Dear Sirs," February 1, 1952, in ibid.; "Script for
Sound Truck," ca. February 4, 1952, in ibid.; "Fact Sheet—Lee-Seville Rezoning," January
10, 1952, in ibid.; Typewritten draft, "The area involved . . . ," ca. February 1952, in ibid.;
C&P, January 19, 1952; "Information for PD," ca. February 4, 1952, NAACP-CB, container
37, folder 5.

23. Quincella Pulley to Charles Lucas, February 26, 1952, NAACP-CB, container 37,
folder 5; C. L. Sharpe et al. to Joseph Crowley, March 4, 1952, in ibid.; Joseph Crowley to
C. L. Sharpe, March 7, 1952, in ibid.; *C&P*, March 1, 1952; Minutes, Cleveland Clearinghouse
on Civil Liberties, March 7, 1952, NAACP-CB, container 32, folder 6; Mary Spivey et al. to
"Dear Reverend," March 11, 1952, NAACP-CB, container 37, folder 5; Mary Spivey et al. to
"Dear Circulator," March 11, 1952, in ibid.; Mary Spivey et al. to "Dear Leader," March 11,
1952, in ibid.; "Homes—Not Factories," ca. March 19, 1952, in ibid.

24. *CN*, March 19, 1952; *CP*, March 19, 1952; "Speakers: Hearing—3/19/52," NAACP-CB,
container 37, folder 5; *CP*, March 20, 1952; *PD*, March 20, 1952.

25. "Statement of the Electric Controller & Manufacturing Company's Position" and
"Notes on Lee-Seville Re-Zoning," ca. March 19, 1952, NAACP-CB, container 37, folder 5;
"YOU CAN WIN!," ca. April 2, 1952, in ibid.; *PD*, April 3, 1952; undated clipping, "Lee-Seville
Settlement Hopes Fade," *CP*, April 1952, in EJB, Scrapbooks, vol. 11; *C&P*, April 26, 1952;
PD, May 16, 1952; Minutes, "American Civil Liberties Union Clearing House Committee,"
April 4, 1952, ULC, container 39, folder 9.

26. On postwar opposition to public housing proposed for outlying areas, see Hirsch,
Second Ghetto, 223–29; Sugrue, *Origins of the Urban Crisis*, 81–86; John F. Bauman, *Public Housing, Race, and Renewal: Urban Planning in Philadelphia, 1920–1974* (Philadelphia, 1987), 160–66; James Wolfinger, *Philadelphia Divided: Race and Politics in the City of Brotherly Love* (Chapel Hill, N.C., 2007), 197–202; Eric Fure-Slocum, *Contesting the Postwar City: Working-Class and Growth Politics in 1940s Milwaukee* (New York, 2013), 320–64;
Don Parson, "The Decline of Public Housing and the Politics of the Red Scare: The Significance of the Los Angeles Housing War," *Journal of Urban History* 33 (March 2007):
400–417; and Deirdre L. Sullivan, "'Letting Down the Bars': Race, Space, and Democracy
in San Francisco, 1936–1964" (Ph.D. diss., University of Pennsylvania, 2003), 152–56. For a
detailed study, see Martin Meyerson and Edward C. Banfield, *Politics, Planning, and the
Public Interest: The Case of Public Housing in Chicago* (New York, 1955).

27. *PD*, June 18, 1952; *CP*, June 18, 1952; *CP*, June 19, 1952; *Maple Heights Press*, June 19, 1952; *PD*, June 19, 1952; *C&P*, July 5, 1952; *CN*, June 18, 1952.

28. *CP*, June 19, 1952; *Maple Heights Press*, June 26, 1952; *CP*, June 25, 1952; *CN*, June 25, 1952; *CN*, June 23, 1952; *PD*, June 23, 1952; *CP*, June 23, 1952; *CP*, June 27, 1952.

29. *CN*, June 25, 1952; *CP*, June 24, 1952; *PD*, July 3, 1952; *Neighborhood News*, July 31, 1952; *C&P*, July 19, 1952.

30. *CP*, August 5, 1952; *CN*, August 5, 1952; *PD*, August 7, 1952; *CN*, August 28, 1952; "Petition for Initiated Ordinance" [September 1952], Petitions, Lee-Seville (432–52)/Public Housing-Low Rent (2017–52), CCCA; *CP*, September 4, 1952.

31. *CP*, September 29, 1952; *PD*, October 18, 1952; *CP*, October 21, 1952; undated clipping, "OK's Housing Project Protest," *CN* [ca. October 1952], in EJB, Scrapbooks, vol. 11; *CP*, November 28, 1952; "The Vote on the Bond Issue for Urban Redevelopment," ca. November 4, 1952, EJB, General Files, container 4, folder 28.

32. *CP*, December 11, 1952; *CP*, December 17, 1952; *CP*, December 16, 1952; *PD*, December 18, 1952; *CP*, January 5, 1953; *PD*, January 6, 1953; *CP*, January 6, 1953.

33. *C&P*, January 31, 1953; *PD*, February 3, 1953; *CP*, February 3, 1953; *PD*, February 4, 1953; *C&P*, February 7, 1953; *CP*, February 6, 1953; *PD*, February 7, 1953; *CN*, February 10, 1953; *CP*, February 10, 1953; *CP*, February 12, 1953; *PD*, February 18, 1953. Site selection similarly came to rest with Chicago's city council, while in Detroit, Mayor Albert Cobo won a ban on outlying projects. See Hirsch, *Second Ghetto*, 219, 240; and Sugrue, *Origins of the Urban Crisis*, 84–86.

34. Memo, William Divers to Katharine Patch, November 13, 1944, EJB, U.S. War Housing, container 1, folder 25; Howard Whipple Green, "How Many Negroes in Cuyahoga County Can Pay $40.00 or More per Month for Rent?" ca. November 9, 1944, in ibid.; *C&P*, May 15, 1948; *CP*, March 22, 1952; *CP*, April 22, 1952; *CP*, June 19, 1952; *CN*, July 1, 1952; *PD*, July 1, 1952; *CP*, July 1, 1952; *C&P*, July 12, 1952; *CP*, July 12, 1952.

35. "Relocation Plan—Project Nos. 1-B and 1-K," August 18, 1952, EJB, CMHA Records, container 1, folder 20; Memo, Richard Hopkins to Thomas Burke, October 8, 1952, TAB, container 3, folder 105; *CN*, October 21, 1952; R. V. Hopkins to Thomas Burke, October 22, 1952, EJB, General Files, container 4, folder 28; George Goudreau to Mayor [Burke] and attached memo, January 19, 1953, TAB, container 3, folder 81; *PD*, February 28, 1953; *CN*, March 11, 1953; *CP*, March 11, 1953.

36. *PD*, July 3, 1952; *PD*, August 7, 1952; *PD*, January 16, 1953; *PD*, January 9, 1953; Minutes, Cleveland Clearinghouse on Civil Liberties, January 20, 1953, NAACP-CB, container 32, folder 6; *CN*, March 12, 1953; *CP*, March 12, 1953; *C&P*, September 5, 1953; *CP*, September 28, 1953.

37. *C&P*, November 9, 1957; "Percent Nonwhite for Statistical Areas, 1960–1980," n.d., CBP, Series II, container 1, folder 4; *CP*, March 6, 1961; *CP*, March 21, 1961; *CP*, March 14, 1961; *CP*, March 31, 1961; *CP*, March 20, 1961; *CP*, March 30, 1961.

38. *CP*, April 21, 1961; *CP*, April 22, 1961; *C&P*, April 29, 1961; *CP*, May 6, 1961; *PD*, May 6, 1961; *CP*, May 10, 1961; *C&P*, May 20, 1961; *C&P*, May 13, 1961; *CP*, May 12, 1961; *CP*, May

22, 1961; *C&P*, May 27, 1961; *CP*, May 26, 1961; *CP*, May 31, 1961; *CP*, June 26, 1961; *CP*, June 12, 1961; *CP*, July 21, 1961; *CP*, July 24, 1961.

39. *CP*, December 4, 1961; *CP*, January 16, 1962; *CP*, January 16, 1962; *CP*, April 18, 1966; *CP*, May 16, 1966. On the 1968–69 controversy under Stokes, see Leonard N. Moore, "Class Conflicts over Residential Space in an African-American Community: Cleveland's Lee-Seville Public Housing Controversy," *Ohio History* 111 (Winter–Spring 2002): 1–19; and Washington, "Packing Them In."

40. Minutes, Community Relations Board, November 6, 1953, AJC, container 1, folder 11; Telegram, James Levy and Charles Lucas to Thomas Burke, October 22, 1953, TAB, container 3, folder 105; Telegram, Isaac Jackson and Stanley Tolliver to Burke, October 22, 1953, in ibid.; Edwin Brown to Burke, October 23, 1953, in ibid.; Telegram, Paul Klein to Burke, October 22, 1953, in ibid.; Alfred Granakis to Burke, October 23, 1953, in ibid.

41. "Cleveland, Ohio," ca. 1954, NAACP-LC, Group II, container C147, folder 2; *C&P*, October 31, 1953.

42. Wiese, *Places of Their Own*, 170–71. On Atlanta's Walter Aiken, the nation's foremost black developer, see ibid., 177–80. On Chicago's black building tradesmen, including one who supplied 700 brick single-family homes in an outlying neighborhood, see Jeffrey Helgeson, *Crucibles of Black Empowerment: Chicago's Neighborhood Politics from the New Deal to Harold Washington* (Chicago, 2014), 62–70, 113–14, 151–58.

43. This conclusion comes from looking in the 1940 city directory for the occupations of those named in Home Builders Association of Greater Cleveland, "Builder Membership Directory for 1954," CDF, container 31, folder 6. Jews were notably represented; see "Builders Division, Contractors and Suppliers Unit," February 16, 1959, JCF, container 22, folder 335.

44. *C&P*, May 7, 1949; Bussey obituary, *C&P*, February 28, 1972; *C&P*, June 21, 1958. See *C&P*, August 18, 1938, for prior outrage at St. James AME's awarding a contract to a white firm; for a church built by black tradesmen, see *C&P*, November 16, 1939.

45. "From Eugene Howard," [1959?], JKP; *C&P*, May 7, 1949; Bussey obituary; *C&P*, October 22, 1949; Morgan obituary, *C&P*, August 7, 1982; *CP*, April 2, 1959; Fagan obituary, *C&P*, October 17, 1970; *C&P*, March 17, 1956. For a sense of black access locally, see "Progress Report . . . Building Trades," October 1, 1947, NUL, box I:F91, "Affiliates File, Cleveland, 1943, 1947, 1950" folder.

46. *C&P*, August 15, 1953; *C&P*, August 7, 1954; Memo, Arnold Walker to Albert Cole, October 2, [1953?], NUL, box I:E40, "Affiliates File, Cleveland, Ohio, 1947–1954" folder; Interview transcript, "[K. C.] Jones—1a," July 8, 1958, pp. 62–64, MKP, container 7, folder 331.

47. *C&P*, August 22, 1953; *C&P*, May 1, 1954; *CP*, June 3, 1954; *CP*, July 16, 1954; *CP*, July 17, 1954; Community Relations Board, "Report of the Executive Director, June-July-August 1954," AJC, container 1, folder 11; *C&P*, July 24, 1954.

48. *C&P*, September 27, 1952; *C&P*, August 22, 1953; *C&P*, August 15, 1953; *C&P*, July 24, 1954; *C&P*, July 7, 1954.

49. "'53 Housing," June 3, 1953, NUL, box I:C52, "Affiliates File, Cleveland, Ohio, 1952–

1953" folder; *C&P*, February 13, 1954; *C&P*, March 10, 1956; *PD*, November 16, 1954; *C&P*, December 4, 1954; *C&P*, January 29, 1955; *C&P*, April 2, 1955.

50. *PD*, April 8, 1955; *PD*, April 15, 1955; *C&P*, March 10, 1956; *PD*, November 23, 1955; *PD*, March 3, 1956; *PD*, March 6, 1956.

51. *C&P*, September 20, 1952; *C&P*, May 2, 1953; *C&P*, March 28, 1953; *C&P*, August 15, 1953; *C&P*, April 10, 1954.

52. *C&P*, May 17, 1958; *C&P*, June 20, 1953; *C&P*, July 3, 1954; *C&P*, April 3, 1954; *C&P*, January 15, 1955; *C&P*, January 29, 1955.

53. *C&P*, March 3, 1956; *C&P*, May 17, 1958; *C&P*, May 9, 1959; *C&P*, March 5, 1955; *CP*, April 2, 1959.

54. For a more successful wartime effort, see Henry Louis Taylor Jr., "Creating the Metropolis in Black and White: Black Suburbanization and the Planning Movement in Cincinnati, 1900–1950," in *Historical Roots of the Urban Crisis*, ed. Henry Louis Taylor Jr. and Walter Hill (New York, 2000), 62–63. Private builders supplied just seventy-four new houses for black Philadelphians during World War II; see Bauman, *Redevelopment, Race, and Renewal*, 58. For more white firms building black suburban housing, see Wiese, *Places of Their Own*, 121–22, 203–6.

55. Katharine Patch to William Divers, November 21, 1944, EJB, U.S. War Housing, container 1, folder 32; *CP*, November 16, 1944; *C&P*, December 16, 1944; *PD*, May 11, 1945; *C&P*, September 1, 1945; *C&P*, November 1, 1947.

56. *C&P*, August 2, 1947; *C&P*, August 9, 1947; Community Relations Board, "Report of the Executive Director, June-July-August 1954"; Minutes, Community Relations Board, February 4, 1955, AJC, container 1, folder 12.

57. *PD*, April 9, 1955; *C&P*, April 16, 1955; Minutes, Community Relations Board, May 5, 1955, AJC, container 1, folder 11; *PD*, April 30, 1955; *CP*, July 26, 1955; *C&P*, July 30, 1955; Cranbrook Builders, Inc., to J. Stanley Baughman, April 7, 1956, CDF, container 43, folder 3; Cranbrook Builders, Inc., to Cleveland Development Foundation, April 30, 1956, in ibid.; *C&P*, January 21 and February 4, 1956; Minutes, Community Relations Board, April 9, 1956, AJC, container 1, folder 13.

58. *CP*, May 11, 1957; *C&P*, June 22, 1957; *CP*, August 5, 1960; "[K. C.] Jones—1a," 51–52; Cleveland Development Foundation, "Progress: East Side–West Side, All Around the Town!," 1958, ULC, container 39, folder 9; *CP*, April 2, 1959; "From George Dubin," [1959], JKP; "Revised Long Range Plan and Program," January 16, 1962, CDF, container 43, folder 12. On Dubin's earlier reputation, see *PD*, December 28, 1948; and *CP*, December 29, 1948. In the Urban League housing director's assessment: "I am not sure he [Dubin] fits the category of . . . able and reputable, but he is at least one man who is building a lot of homes and making them available to Negroes." "[K. C.] Jones—1a," 62.

59. *C&P*, April 18, 1959; *CP*, April 17, 1959; *PD*, March 3, 1955; *C&P*, May 14, 1960; *C&P*, December 10, 1960; *C&P*, April 22, 1961; *C&P*, July 20, 1963; *C&P*, June 29, 1963; *C&P*, July 6, 1963; *C&P*, November 7, 1964.

60. "The Church on Lee Road," Regional Church Planning Office Report No. 21 (January 1964), 6, WRHS; Hirsch, *Second Ghetto*, 28.

61. On the Supreme Court cases from 1940 to 1953 that overturned restrictive covenants, see especially Wendy Plotkin, "Deeds of Mistrust: Race, Housing, and Restrictive Covenants in Chicago, 1900–1953" (Ph.D. diss., University of Illinois at Chicago, 1999), 139–252.

62. Howard Whipple Green, *Family and Housing Characteristics, 1949 Edition*, Part I, Report #26 (Cleveland, 1949), Map 7; "Area Descriptions—Security Map of Cuyahoga County," Cleveland [East Side], Area A-19, October 10, 1939, HOLC City Survey File, FHLBB, box 87, "Greater Cleveland, OH" folder; "Area Descriptions—Security Map of Cuyahoga County," Cleveland [East Side], Area B-33, October 10, 1939, in ibid.; "Area Descriptions—Security Map of Cuyahoga County," Cleveland, Area C-48, September 12, 1939, in ibid.; *PD*, October 23, 1949; *CP*, June 13, 1951.

63. For 1949 and 1954 incidents that were similarly resolved, see Wolfinger, *Philadelphia Divided*, 178, 183–85.

64. "Memorandum on Housing Situation, Lee-Harvard Area," [July 23, 1953], NAACP-LC, Group II, container A314, folder 7; *C&P*, November 21, 1953; *C&P*, July 18, 1953; Stewart obituary, *C&P*, July 25, 1981; "Emergency Community Relations Board Meeting Called 7/14/53," TAB, container 1, folder 22; *CP*, July 15, 1953; "Jackson, Perry B., 8/11," MKP, container 6, folder 321; "CRB Meeting Called for Wednesday Evening, 7-15-53," TAB, container 1, folder 22; *Pittsburgh Courier*, July 25, 1953; [L.] Pearl [Mitchell] to Roy [Wilkins], August 8, 1953, NAACP-LC, Group II, container A314, folder 7.

65. *PD*, July 11, 1953; *CP*, July 13, 1953; "Memorandum on Housing Situation"; Charles Lucas to Roy [Wilkins], August 8, 1953, NAACP-LC, Group II, container A314, folder 7. The neighborhood was estimated to be 70 percent Catholic, 20 percent Jewish, and 10 percent Protestant. For over a decade, a few African American families had belonged to Saint Cecelia's and had sent their children to the parish school; E. A. Kirby to Rev. V. B. Balamat, January 3, 1940, "Nationalities—Blacks, 1921–1940" file, Bishop Schrembs Papers, ADC. On tolerance efforts there, see Dorothy Ann Blatnica, *"At the Altar of Their God": African American Catholics in Cleveland, 1922–1961* (New York, 1995), 151, 158, 173.

66. "Memorandum on Housing Situation"; Memo, Paul Klein to Madison Jones, December 29, 1955, NAACP-LC, Group II, container A314, folder 7; "Emergency Community Relations Board Meeting Called 7/14/53"; *CP*, July 14, 1953; *PD*, July 14, 1953; *CN*, July 14, 1953; *CP*, July 15, 1953; Eleanor Ryder to Frank Baldau, July 14, 1953, FCP, container 28, folder 693; "Resolution of Antioch Baptist Church," July 12, 1953, TAB, container 3, folder 83; *CN*, July 15, 1953.

67. *CP*, June 16, 1950; *CP*, January 8, 1958; *CP*, December 6, 1951; Busa obituary, *PD*, May 12, 2006. Last names from the 1953 city directory indicate that well over half of the Talford Avenue residents were of Southern or Eastern European ancestry, with Czechs, Italians, and Hungarians most prominently represented. Skilled workers made up approximately 43 percent of the household heads. For helpful context, see Thomas J. Sugrue's discussion of Detroit's "intensely communal" white working-class neighborhoods; *Origins of the Urban Crisis*, 213–18.

68. *CP*, July 14, 1953; *PD*, July 14, 1953; "Emergency Community Relations Board Meet-

ing Called 7/14/53"; *CP*, July 15, 1953; *CP*, July 15, 1953; "CRB Meeting Called for Wednesday Evening."

69. "CRB Meeting Called for Wednesday Evening"; "CRB Meeting Called for Monday Evening, 7–20–53," TAB, container 1, folder 22.

70. "CRB Meeting Called for Wednesday Evening"; "CRB Meeting Called for Monday Evening"; *PD*, July 17, 1953; Eleanor Ryder to Frank Baldau, July 21, 1953, FCP, container 28, folder 693; "Memorandum on Housing Situation."

71. "A Neighbor" to Wendell Stewart, July 16, 1953, TAB, container 3, folder 83; "Many Oldtime Clevelanders" to Mayor Burke, July 21, 1953, in ibid.; *C&P*, July 18, 1953.

72. "CRB Meeting Called for Monday Evening"; *CP*, July 21, 1953; *PD*, July 21, 1953.

73. "Memorandum on Housing Situation"; *C&P*, July 25, 1953; *PD*, July 22, 1953; *CP*, July 22, 1953; *CP*, July 31, 1953.

74. *Catholic Universe Bulletin*, November 13, 1953; Minutes, Community Relations Board, December 4, 1953, AJC, container 1, folder 11; *CP*, November 7, 1953; *C&P*, November 14, 1953; Minutes, Cleveland Clearinghouse on Civil Liberties, November 20, 1953, NAACP-CB, container 32, folder 6; *C&P*, November 21, 1953.

75. Minutes, Cleveland Clearinghouse on Civil Liberties, November 20, 1953, December 18, 1953, ULC, container 39, folder 9; *C&P*, November 14, 1953; Minutes, Community Relations Board, May 7, 1954, AJC, container 1, folder 11; Memo, Klein to Jones, December 29, 1955. Black pioneers frequently bore psychological burdens; see Wiese, *Places of Their Own*, 155.

76. Community Relations Board, "Report of the Executive Director," May 1953, TAB, container 1, folder 22.

77. *C&P*, October 6, 1951; *C&P*, February 16, 1952; *C&P*, August 8, 1953; *C&P*, January 2, 1954.

78. *C&P*, April 10, 1954; *C&P*, July 24, 1954; Stanford P. M. Berry II to Anthony Celebrezze, August 3, 1954, AJC, container 1, folder 7; Community Relations Board, "Report of the Executive Director," December 1954, AJC, container 1, folder 12; *C&P*, March 26, 1955.

79. *C&P*, January 7, 1956; *C&P*, January 14, 1956; *PD*, January 5, 1956; *CP*, September 23, 1955; *C&P*, October 1, 1955; *CP*, September 6, 1956. Making it even more attractive, the Ludlow area fell within the Shaker Heights school district.

Chapter 4

1. Murtis Taylor, interview transcript, October 17, 1986, pp. 41–42, St. James AME Church Oral History Project Interviews, WRHS, container 2, folder 36; *CP*, June 2, 1976. On Karamu House, see Andrew M. Fearnley, "Writing the History of Karamu House: Philanthropy, Welfare, and Race in Wartime Cleveland," *Ohio History* 115 (2008): 80–100. For a critical assessment of teen conduct at the weekly dances, which contributed to their discontinuation, see *C&P*, October 28, 1950.

2. Taylor, interview transcript, 42–46; Collins Munns, taped telephone interview with author, July 12, 2001.

3. For a key example of disproportionate focus on "defended" neighborhoods, see

Thomas J. Sugrue, *The Origins of the Urban Crisis: Race and Inequality in Postwar Detroit* (Princeton, N.J., 1996), 231–58.

4. On urban Catholics facing racial integration, see especially John T. McGreevy, *Parish Boundaries: The Catholic Encounter with Race in the Twentieth Century* (Chicago, 1996).

5. On the concept of a "tipping point," first hypothesized in 1958, see John M. Goering, "Neighborhood Tipping and Racial Transition: A Review of the Social Science Evidence," *Journal of the American Institute of Planners* 44 (January 1978): 68–78; see also Barrett A. Lee and Peter B. Wood, "Is Neighborhood Racial Succession Place Specific?" *Demography* 28 (February 1991): 21–40.

6. Regional Church Planning Office, "The Church in a Changing Neighborhood," October 30, 1961, WRHS; "Report on Arlington Branch and the Effect of Population Shifts," December 1955, JCC, Series II, container 5, folder 102; "Review of F.S.A. Participation in the Glenville Area Community Council," June 16, 1954, FCP, container 28, folder 693; Group Work Council, Unmet and New Needs Committee, "East Glenville Area Report," January 1958, in ibid.

7. "From Dr. Charles Garvin," [1956], JKP; Minutes, Arlington Branch Advisory Committee, March 14, 1955, JCC, container 27, folder 3; RCPO, "Church in a Changing Neighborhood," 4, 7; "From J. W. Carmack," [1956], JKP.

8. Jewish Welfare Federation, "Report of the Group Work Study Committee," September 1947, JCC, container 6, folder 63; "Jewish Community Centers of Cleveland Facilities Inventory," [1952], JCF, container 21, folder 315; "Progress Report, Cleveland Jewish Community Center's New Building," December 1954, JCF, container 20, folder 314; RCPO, "Church in a Changing Neighborhood," 6; "Report on Arlington Branch and the Effect of Population Shifts."

9. "Review of F.S.A. Participation"; "Opinions Regarding Movement of Jewish Population during Next Five Years," February 15, 1955, JCF, container 20, folder 314; "Arlington Branch Report," [ca. January 1958], JCC, container 27, folder 5.

10. "Review of Trends & Accomplishments during the 1948–49 & 1949–50 Periods," JCC, Series II, container 5, folder 102; "Annual Report 1950–51," in ibid.; "Group Analysis—Group Work II," May 1953, pp. 21–45, JCC, container 28, folder 16; "Quarterly Report, Arlington Branch, Jewish Community Centers," [November 1954], JCC, Series II, container 5, folder 102; Minutes, Arlington Branch Advisory Committee, December 13, 1954, JCC, container 27, folder 4.

11. Minutes, Arlington Branch Advisory Committee, February 14, 1955, JCC, container 27, folder 3; Minutes, Group Work Council, Intercultural and Interracial Relations Committee, June 2, 1955, FCP, container 36, folder 877; Minutes, Intercultural and Interracial Relations Committee, Group Work Council, October 6, 1955, in ibid.; Memo, Howard Robbins to Herman Eigen, "Arlington Branch 1955 and the Effect of Population Shifts," JCC, container 27, folder 5; Minutes, Arlington Branch Advisory Committee, January 9, 1956, JCC, container 27, folder 3.

12. "A Brief History of the Arlington Branch," [ca. 1959], JCC, container 27, folder 5; "Annual Report, Prep and Pre-Prep Divisions—1956–1957," in ibid.; "Report on Arling-

ton Branch and the Effect of Population Shifts"; *C&P*, March 14, 1953; RCPO, "Church in a Changing Neighborhood," 31–32; John Baden, "Residual Neighbors: Jewish–African American Interactions in Cleveland from 1900 to 1970" (M.A. thesis, Case Western Reserve University, 2011), 48, 73–74. Into the present, one Jewish-owned business remained, Gordon Cycle & Supply, Inc.; *PD*, September 26, 2006.

13. *C&P*, May 27, 1950; *C&P*, June 17, 1950; *Glenville YMCA News* (March 15, 1952), NAACP-CB, container 36, folder 4; "Meeting to Discuss Non-affiliated Youth Gangs in the Glenville Area," June 24, 1952, JCC, container 28, folder 16; Minutes, Group Work Council, Intercultural and Interracial Relations Committee, June 2, 1955, FCP, container 36, folder 877; Minutes, Group Work Council, Intercultural and Interracial Relations Committee, May 5, 1955, in ibid.; Minutes, Group Work Council, Committee on Intercultural and Interracial Relations, November 4, 1954, in ibid. On planning for a Glenville YMCA, see "Second Report of the Glenville Area Extension Committee," November 25, 1947, YMCA, Series II, container 1, folder 14. For similar challenges elsewhere, see Judith Ann Trolander, *Professionalism and Social Change: From the Settlement House Movement to Neighborhood Centers, 1886 to the Present* (New York, 1987), 100–105.

14. *Glenville Area Community Council Bulletin* (March–April 1951), NAACP-CB, container 36, folder 4; GACC, 6th Annual Report (1951), FCP, container 28, folder 693; *CP*, February 20, 1952; *Glenville Area Community Council Bulletin* (March 1953), NAACP-CB, container 36, folder 4; GACC, 8th Annual Report, May 1953, in ibid.; GACC, "1957–58 Committee Reports in Brief," FCP, container 28, folder 693; "Minutes of Arlington Advisory Committee," January 12, 1953, JCC, container 27, folder 2; Minutes, Intercultural and Interracial Relations Committee, June 2, 1955; "Minutes of the Arlington Branch Advisory Committee," December 9, 1957, JCC, container 27, folder 3.

15. *C&P*, May 30, 1953; *C&P*, June 6, 1953; *C&P*, June 20, 1953; Minutes, Community Relations Board, June 5, 1953, TAB, container 1, folder 22.

16. *C&P*, April 3, 1954; *C&P*, March 27, 1954; Minutes, Community Relations Board, April 9, 1954, AJC, container 1, folder 11; Minutes, Community Relations Board, June 4, 1954, in ibid.; *C&P*, April 10, 1954.

17. *C&P*, June 5, 1954; Minutes, Community Relations Board, June 4, 1954; *C&P*, June 12, 1954; *C&P*, June 19, 1954; "Christian Social Action in Action," [July?] 1954, AJC, container 1, folder 7; *C&P*, July 10, 1954; *C&P*, June 26, 1954; Community Relations Board, "Report of the Executive Director, June-July-August 1954," AJC, container 1, folder 11.

18. "Report of the Executive Director, June-July-August 1954"; Minutes, Community Relations Board, November 5, 1954, AJC, container 1, folder 11; *C&P*, December 25, 1954; *C&P*, July 9, 1955; Community Relations Board, "Report of the Executive Director, June-July-August 1955," AJC, container 1, folder 12; *C&P*, October 29, 1955.

19. Community Relations Board, "Report of the Executive Director," March 1956, AJC, container 1, folder 13; *C&P*, April 7, 1956; Community Relations Board, "Report of the Executive Director," June 1957, AJC, container 1, folder 14; Minutes, Community Relations Board, September 5, 1957, in ibid.; *C&P*, July 20, 1957; Community Relations Board, "Report of the Executive Director, July–August 1957," AJC, container 1, folder 14.

20. *C&P*, August 22, 1959; "Housing Crisis: Presented . . . at the Intergroup Relations Workshop, Western Reserve University, November 6–7, 1959," NUL, box I:C52, "Affiliates File, Cleveland, Ohio, 1959–1960" folder; *C&P*, August 29, 1959. The city directory for that year indicates that many Lithuanians, Italians, and Slavs lived on the block.

21. "Housing Crisis"; *C&P*, August 29, 1959; *C&P*, September 19, 1959; Minutes, Community Relations Board, November 12, 1959, AJC, container 1, folder 15; "Report of the Department of Civil Rights and Housing for April 1960," AJC, container 1, folder 16; Minutes, Community Relations Board, May 5, 1960, in ibid.

22. Minutes, GACC, Executive Board, October 1, 1945, JCC, Series II, container 5, folder 103; Minutes, Community Relations Board, November 5, 1954; *C&P*, July 20, 1957; Minutes, Glenville Rehabilitation-Conservation Steering Committee, July 22, 1959, September 23, 1959, LAJ.

23. Memo, "CRB Executive Director [William Gremley] to CRB Members," ca. May 10, 1960, AJC, container 1, folder 16; *C&P*, May 14, 1960; "Corlett Homeowners Improvement Assn. Inc.," [ca. August 1961], JKP; Ann Werneke, "The Church in the Changing City: A Study in Contrasts," [1961], 20–21, RCPO, container 2, folder 7; *CP*, June 12, 1963.

24. On blockbusting generally, see W. Edward Orser, *Blockbusting in Baltimore: The Edmondson Village Story* (Lexington, Ky., 1994); Kevin Fox Gotham, *Race, Real Estate, and Uneven Development: The Kansas City Experience, 1900–2000* (Albany, N.Y., 2002), 103–16; and Amanda I. Seligman, *Block by Block: Neighborhoods and Public Policy on Chicago's West Side* (Chicago, 2005), 151–62.

25. "From Wm. T. McKnight," [1956], JKP; Memo, "CRB Testimony at Public Hearings," May 31, 1960, AJC, Series II, container 4, folder 71; "From G. W. Jones," ca. September 1960, JKP; "From Councilman Leo Jackson," June 1961, JKP.

26. "From K. C. Jones," March 1961, JKP; "From Councilman Leo Jackson"; "From Ronald Lewis," ca. September 1960, JKP; "Mrs. Betty Hansen," ca. August 1961, JKP. For more on tactics, see Amanda I. Seligman, "'Apologies to Dracula, Werewolf, Frankenstein': White Homeowners and Blockbusters in Chicago," *Journal of the Illinois State Historical Society* 94 (2001): 70–95.

27. "From Dr. David Barr," [1956], JKP; "From Wm. T. McKnight"; *C&P*, April 7, 1956; Sigmund Weintraub to Thomas A. Burke, January 19, 1953, TAB, container 3, folder 105.

28. "From John T. Hefner," [1956], JKP; "From Ernest Weber," [1956], JKP; "From Dr. David Barr," [1956], JKP; "From Mr. and Mrs. Joe (Beatrice) Hunt," [1956], JKP.

29. "From John T. Hefner"; "From Mrs. Jeanette Gray," [1956], JKP; undated clipping, "Illogical Fears Persist," *CP* [1961], JKP; M. Harden to "Dear Sir," August 15, 1961, JKP.

30. "Meeting to Discuss Non-Affiliated Youth Gangs"; "Swimming Pool Situation, June–July 1954," AJC, container 1, folder 7; *C&P*, July 31, 1954; Gerard Anderson Jr. to Anthony Celebrezze, June 21, 1955, NAACP-CB, container 32, folder 2; "Mayor" to Gerard Anderson Jr., June 28, 1955, in ibid.; Community Relations Board, "Report of the Executive Director, June-July-August 1955," AJC, container 1, folder 12. On the NAACP's post-1948 shift, see Manfred Berg, "Black Civil Rights and Liberal Anticommunism: The NAACP in the Early Cold War," *Journal of American History* 94 (June 2007): 75–96.

31. *C&P*, November 18, 1950; *C&P*, October 13, 1951; *C&P*, October 20, 1951.

32. "Meeting of the Glenville Branch [YMCA] Board of Managers," November 14, 1951, NAACP-CB, container 36, folder 4; Community Relations Board, "Report of the Executive Director, September–October 1953," AJC, container 1, folder 11; "Report on Addison Jr. High School and Patrick Henry Jr. High School," October 13, 1954, AJC, container 1, folder 7; "Second Report, Patrick Henry Jr. High School," October 20, 1954, in ibid.; Minutes, Arlington Branch Advisory Committee, November 8, 1954, JCC, container 27, folder 2.

33. *CP*, June 12, 1963; Cleveland Community Relations Board, "Report for 1963," CHR, container 3, folder 64; Werneke, "Church in the Changing City," 24, 27, 31; RCPO, "Church in a Changing Neighborhood," 28–33; "Glenville Area Analysis," [ca. 1960?], FCP, container 28, folder 694; *Catholic Universe Bulletin*, September 30, 1960; *Catholic Universe Bulletin*, February 15, 1963.

34. "Area Characteristics: Mount Pleasant [1950]," FCP, container 9, folder 225; "The Mount Pleasant Area Study," May 16, 1950, FCP, container 49, folder 1175; "From J. W. Carmack"; "Non-white Residential Patterns," December 1959, p. 11, AJC, container 1, folder 9; "Area Characteristics; Mount Pleasant [1960/1965]," FCP, container 9, folder 225; Leah Milkman Rich, "The Mount Pleasant Community Centers of the Neighborhood Settlement Association of Cleveland," February 1961, GCNCA, container 4, folder 57.

35. Sanford Watzman, *All the Way to Y2K: Life of a Jewish American in the Last Three Quarters of the 20th Century* (Silver Spring, Md., 2000), 446; "Evaluation of the Present and Future Location of Mt. Pleasant Facilities," [May 1949], JCC, container 30, folder 1; Minutes, Shaker-Lee Advisory Committee, October 18, 1951, in ibid.; "Progress Report, Cleveland Jewish Community Center's New Building," December 1954, JCF, container 20, folder 314; Map, "Distribution of Cleveland Jewish Population Based on 1958 Day of Atonement Census," JCF, container 11, folder 184.

36. I. Jaffe to Irving Rabinsky, December 25, 1949, Bureau of Jewish Education Records, WRHS, container 14, folder 380; Nathan Brilliant to Lloyd Schwenger, October 22, 1953, WRHS, container 14, folder 378; *Twentieth Jubilee Banquet* (January 22, 1950), WCS, container 1, folder 1; *K.J.C. Newsletter* (October 1952), WCS, container 1, folder 2; Rabbi Jacob Muskin to Herman Eigen, September 17, 1956, JCC, Series II, container 5, folder 107; *Kinsman-Shaker Courier* (September 1956), WCS, container 1, folder 2; N'vai Zedek Congregation to "Dear Member," March 22, 1959, Jacob Muskin Papers, WRHS, container 1, folder 12; *It's Happening Here: The Story of the Jewish Community Federation of Cleveland and Its Agencies* (ca. 1967), 22, JCF, container 8, folder 122.

37. Eugene Brudno, taped interview with author, January 6, 2003; see also Phillip Timothy Gay, "Eugene the Egg Man: He Was Friend and Mentor to Neighborhood Kids," *PD Magazine*, August 28, 1983, 14–22. A "Russian-Turkish Bath" (*schvitz*) established in 1927 still operates in the neighborhood; see *PD*, August 6, 1961; and *Cleveland Jewish News*, January 31, 2002.

38. "City's Area Councils Make Flank Attack on Race Tension," *PD* [ca. September 1951], EJB, Scrapbooks, vol. 11 (1951–52); *CP*, March 14, 1953; *PD*, March 17, 1953; *CP*, March 17, 1953.

39. *PD*, February 17, 1957; "Fact Sheet," [1957], NSC, container 23, folder 2; *Mt. Pleasant Community Council Bulletin* (February 1958), NAACP-CB, container 38, folder 3; "Brotherhood in Our Neighborhood" (program), ca. February 12, 1958, in ibid.; Jacob Muskin, John Tivenan, and Perry Jackson to Sol Green, March 11, 1957, JCC, container 31, folder 19; Minutes, Shaker-Lee Branch Advisory Committee, January 19, 1959, JCC, container 30, folder 2; "Joseph Sokol Memorial Program," January 15, 1961, JCC, Series II, container 7, folder 146. On Jews' continuing involvement after moving to the suburbs, see Jordan Stanger-Ross, "Neither Fight Nor Flight: Urban Synagogues in Postwar Philadelphia," *Journal of Urban History* 32 (September 2006): 791–812; and Lila Corwin Berman, "Jewish Urban Politics in the City and Beyond," *Journal of American History* 99 (September 2012): 492–519.

40. "Preliminary Request for Construction Assistance," [1968?], TCF, Series II, container 37, folder 888; "Summary of Mt. Pleasant Human Relations Workshop," ca. March 1953, NAACP-CB, container 38, folder 3; Minutes, Group Work Council, Committee on Intercultural and Interracial Relations, June 10, 1954, FCP, container 36, folder 877; Taylor interview transcript, 44–47.

41. Minutes, Intergroup Relations Committee, Group Work Council, January 8, 1959, and May 7, 1959, FCP, container 36, folder 878; newspaper clipping, "Five Year Move for Mt. Pleasant Unity Is Planned," *CP*, [ca. November 1959], in "Mt. Pleasant Community Services Center," CPC; *CP*, December 10, 1959; Minutes, Intergroup Relations Committee, Group Work Council, February 4, 1960, FCP, container 36, folder 878; Minutes, Board of Trustees, Mount Pleasant Community Centers, September 17, 1962, and January 21, 1963, GCNA, container 4, folder 56; Irving Lerner to "Dear Parents," March 15, 1963, JCC, Series II, container 7, folder 146; Memo, Irv Lerner to Julian Kolby, May 10, 1967, in ibid.; *CP*, August 8, 1966.

42. "Community Holiday Program," [ca. December 23, 1948], CPL, Mt. Pleasant Branch; *CN*, December 8, 1956; *C&P*, December 8, 1962; *CP*, December 17, 1957; *Mt. Pleasant Community Council Bulletin* (November 1955), NAACP-CB, container 38, folder 3; *Mt. Pleasant Community Council Bulletin* (February 1956), in ibid.; *CP*, February 16, 1953; *C&P*, February 27, 1960; *CP*, February 12, 1955; Henry Ollendorff to J. Kimball Johnson, April 25, 1955, TCF, container 6, folder 1; "Evaluation of Special Projects," [ca. June 22, 1956], in ibid.; *CP*, June 18, 1959; *CP*, June 20, 1959. For additional context, see "Events Leading Up to the Formation of the Council on Human Relations," [1955?], NAACP-CB, container 34, folder 4; and the clippings in "Council on Human Relations," CPC.

43. *C&P*, July 17, 1954; *C&P*, August 7, 1954; *C&P*, July 24, 1954.

44. *C&P*, September 18, 1954; *C&P*, September 25, 1954; *C&P*, October 30, 1954; *C&P*, November 6, 1954; *C&P*, July 30, 1960; *C&P*, June 13, 1964.

45. *CP*, March 24, 1953; Stanley Lasky, written response to interview questions, received April 25, 2001; Bernard Levine, taped interview with author, December 9, 2002; Ezra Giterman, taped interview with author, December 3, 2002; Donna Whyte and Dianne McIntyre, taped interview with author, January 28, 2003.

46. "From Mrs. Phillip Indriola," [March 1961?], JKP; "From Mrs. Robert (Marjorie) Szanislzo," [March 1961?], JKP; Helen Frank to "Dear Sir," August 20, 1961, JKP; "From Shel-

ton Granger," [July–August 1961?], JKP; anonymous letter to "Dear Press Columnists," [ca. August 1961], JKP.

47. "Mount Pleasant Area Study," 10; Odelia Robinson, taped interview with author, August 6, 2001; Pamela Howell, letter to editor, *PD*, December 16, 2007; interview with A. B. Heard, July 20, 1961, MKP, container 6, folder 271.

48. Howard Whipple Green, *Jewish Families in Greater Cleveland* (Cleveland, 1939), 64; "From Mrs. and Mr. Robert A. Decatur," [1956], JKP; "From Mrs. Ruth (Harry) Selko," [1956], JKP. However, see *C&P*, February 7, 1959, for blockbusting on East 147th Street.

49. Mischa Kursh, taped interview with author, December 3, 2002; Joseph DeLuca, taped interview with author, January 10, 2003; Community Relations Board, "Report of the Executive Director," October 1957, AJC, container 1, folder 14; H. Jean Dorgham, taped interview with author, November 3, 2001; Munns interview. For a further mention of all-white apartments, see "Summary of Mt. Pleasant Human Relations Workshop," [ca. March 23, 1953], NAACP-CB, container 38, folder 3. On this phenomenon in Glenville, see *C&P*, October 2, 1954; *C&P*, September 22, 1956; and *C&P*, November 1, 1958.

50. "Mount Pleasant Area Study," 12, 14; Charles Lentini, taped interview with author, February 7, 2003; *CP*, June 24, 1954; *C&P*, September 25, 1954; "Union Square Incident," October 15, 1954, AJC, container 1, folder 7; Minutes, Community Relations Board, October 8, 1954, AJC, container 1, folder 11; Cleveland Community Relations Board, "Report for 1963."

51. "Study of the Recreational Needs of the Mt. Pleasant Area," April 14, 1952, p. 14, JCC, container 27, folder 119. A 1941 incident, in which five black boys were chased from the pool, was an aberration by that point. See Victoria W. Wolcott, *Race, Riots, and Roller Coasters: The Struggle over Segregated Recreation in America* (Philadelphia, 2012), 72; and *C&P*, August 2, 1941.

52. H. Jean Dorgham, taped interview with author, November 19, 2001; *CP*, July 19, 1955. As in many post-transitional neighborhoods, the city apparently relaxed maintenance at Woodland Hills; see *CN*, June 1, 1949. For a similar outcome, see Kevin M. Kruse, *White Flight: Atlanta and the Making of Modern Conservatism* (Princeton, N.J., 2005), 75–76.

53. For background on racial contention at Garfield Park, see *C&P*, June 6, 1942; on Baltimore's similar dynamic, see Kenneth D. Durr, *Behind the Backlash: White Working-Class Politics in Baltimore, 1940–1980* (Chapel Hill, N.C., 2003), 114–15.

54. "Garfield Pool Incident," [ca. July 7, 1950], USR, Series II, container 1, folder 17; Community Relations Board, "Report of the Executive Director, June–July 1950," CMP, container 1, folder 22.

55. "The Boy[']s Side of the Story," [ca. July 7, 1950], USR, Series II, container 1, folder 17. The pool also experienced a 1952 controversy, in which NAACP picnic-goers became entangled in a Communist Party–affiliated protest. See NAACP-CB, container 36, folder 2; and ULC, container 41, folder 3.

56. Minutes, City-Wide Recreation Committee, Mt. Pleasant Community Council, May 17, 1955, GCNCA, container 4, folder 56; "Request to Cleveland Foundation from Mount Pleasant Community Centers," December 1956, in ibid.; Henry Ollendorff to David Warshawsky, January 30, 1958, in ibid.

57. Minutes, Membership Meeting and Election, Sokol Tyrš Hall, December 11, 1963, Victor B. Ptak Family Papers, WRHS, container 3, folder 31; *CP*, October 28, 1960; *Catholic Universe Bulletin*, September 7, 1962; *CP*, October 5, 1964. On tolerance efforts and racial integration at Saint Cecelia's, see Dorothy Ann Blatnica, *"At the Altar of Their God": African American Catholics in Cleveland, 1922–1961* (New York, 1995), 151, 158, 162–64, 185.

58. *PD*, March 25, 2001; Community Relations Board, "Report of the Executive Director, June-July-August 1954," AJC, container 1, folder 11. The Community Relations Board noted that, like many white property owners elsewhere, some Lee-Harvard residents declined to sign for fear of "restraints" on their ability to sell. Minutes, Community Relations Board, May 7, 1954, AJC, container 1, folder 11.

59. *PD*, March 25, 2001; *C&P*, July 9, 1955; Community Relations Board, "Report of the Executive Director, June-July-August 1955," AJC, container 1, folder 12; Minutes, Cleveland Clearinghouse on Civil Liberties, September 1955, NAACP-CB, container 32, folder 6.

60. Minutes, Intercultural and Interracial Relations Committee, Group Work Council, December 5, 1957, FCP, container 36, folder 877; *PD*, May 12, 1960; "Jewish Community Centers of Cleveland: Report on the Branches," April 1958, JCC, Series II, container 5, folder 105; "Report on Community Relations in the Lee-Harvard Area," [January 15, 1959], National Association of Human Rights Workers Records, ARC, container 11, folder 13. A personal recollection of banks refusing blacks loans is "Neighborhood Movement, O.H. 53," Rubie J. McCullough interviewed by Edward Miggins, Cuyahoga Community College Oral History Program, March 20, 1984, in author's possession.

61. Minutes, Community Relations Board, June 5, 1958, AJC, container 1, folder 15; Minutes, Community Relations Board, September 18, 1958, in ibid.; *CP*, September 20, 1962; "To City Desk," August 13, [1961], JKP; "From K. C. Jones"; "Memo to Tanner," June 30, [1961], JKP; *PD*, May 20, 1961; "Memo to Krawcheck," June 28, 1961, JKP; "From Joseph Novak," [ca. August 1962], JKP.

62. *CP*, August 15, 1961; *C&P*, May 20, 1961; "From Mrs. Joseph Novak," July 1961, JKP; "From Mr. and Mrs. Thomas J. (Wilma) Fitzgibbons," July 1961, JKP; "From Mrs. Paul Mamolen," [ca. August 1962], JKP; "Harvard Comment"; "Mrs. Anthony DelGarbino," [ca. August 1962], JKP; "Mrs. Klima," [ca. August 1962], JKP. For harassment of white sellers in Atlanta, see Kruse, *White Flight*, 90, 96.

63. *CP*, September 20, 1962; "From Ray Kraft," July 1961, JKP; "Some Considerations in Dealing with Housing Problems," January 1958, Temple Emanu El Records, WRHS, container 41, folder 1058; "From Mr. and Mrs. Thomas J. (Wilma) Fitzgbbons"; "From Rev. Charles Rawlings," [ca. August 1962], JKP.

64. "Neighbors, Awaken!" [ca. June 1961], JKP; "History of Harvard-Scott-Lee Home Owners Assn.," August 1961, JKP; "From Walter Horn," June 1961, JKP; "From Joseph Novak, Bernard T. Stites, and Werner Kiessling," August 1961, JKP; Cleveland Community Relations Board, "Report for 1960–1961," February 23, 1962, Arthur J. Lelyveld Papers, WRHS, container 14, folder 293; *PD*, February 28, 1962; *PD*, March 2, 1962.

65. "From Ray Kraft"; Mrs. Martin Duffy to "Gentlemen," August 18, 1961, JKP; "From Mrs. Joseph Novak"; "From Mrs. James Keefe," July 1961, JKP; "From Mrs. Walter (Norma)

Jeschenig," July 1961, JKP. For similar rumors of black organizations bankrolling racial transition, see Arnold R. Hirsch, *Making the Second Ghetto: Race and Housing in Chicago, 1940–1960*, reprint ed. (Chicago, 1998), 199.

66. "From Mrs. Burt Siebert," [ca. August 1962], JKP; "Memo to CLF," August 27, [1962], JKP; "Memo on Block Bust—Tanner," July 27, [1961], JKP; undated clipping, "Schools Chief Factor," *CP*, [1961?], JKP; "From Mrs. Martin (Evelyn) Birnbaum," [ca. August 1962], JKP; "From Miss Dorothy Warner," [ca. August 1962], JKP.

67. "From Mrs. Burt Siebert"; "From Rev. Charles Rawlings"; "From Mrs. Frank Slaby," [ca. August 1962], JKP; "From Mrs. Arthur M. Litt," July 1961, JKP; "From Mrs. Werner Gottlieb," [ca. August 1962], JKP; "From Joseph Novak."

68. "From Mrs. Robert (Marjorie) Szanislzo," [March 1961], JKP; "From Mrs. Werner Gottlieb"; "From Mrs. William Schlessman," [ca. August 1962], JKP; "From Mrs. Bobby (Gwenn) Mitchell," August 1961, JKP; "From Mrs. Junius (Louise) Usher," July 1961, JKP; "From Mrs. Cecil (Wilhelmina) Lewis, [ca. August 1962], JKP; "From Mrs. Martin (Evelyn) Birnbaum"; Anita Duffy to "Dear Mr. Krawcheck," September 17, 1962, JKP; "From Mrs. Paul Mamolen." For other findings of white tolerance, see Clifton Jones, "Invasion and Racial Attitudes," *Social Forces* 27 (March 1949): 285–90; and Charles Bird, Eliot D. Monachesi, and Harvey Burdick, "Infiltration and the Attitudes of White and Negro Parents and Children," *Journal of Abnormal and Social Psychology* 47 (July 1952): 688–99.

69. "From Mrs. James Keefe"; "The White Elephant: Cleveland's Housing Dilemma," *Stride* (March 1961): 3, ULC, container 22, folder 4; "From Mrs. Frank Slaby"; "From Gerson Perlman," August 1961, JKP; Duffy to "Dear Mr. Krawcheck."

70. "From Ray Kraft"; "Blockbust Memo from Tanner," July 17, [1961], JKP; "From Mrs. Junius (Louise) Usher"; *CP*, August 17, 1961; anonymous letter, "Dear Mr. Krawcheck," [ca. September 1962], JKP.

71. Anonymous letter, "Dear Mr. Krawcheck," [ca. September 1962], JKP; "Memo on Block Bust—Tanner."

72. Eleanor P. Wolf, "The Invasion-Succession Sequence as a Self-Fulfilling Prophecy," *Journal of Social Issues* 13, no. 4 (1957): 7–20 (quote from 16).

73. "Area Descriptions—Security Map of Cuyahoga County," Cleveland, Area C-49, September 13, 1939, HOLC City Survey File, FHLBB, box 87, "Greater Cleveland, OH" folder; "General Description of [Southeast] Area," ca. 1967–68, ULC, container 21, folder 5; U.S. Bureau of the Census, *Housing—Analytical Maps: Cleveland, Ohio Block Statistics*, prep. Leon E. Truesdell (New York, 1942), 68–69; *The Church on Lee Road*, Regional Church Planning Office Report No. 21 (January 1964), WRHS.

74. [Eleanor] Ledbetter, "Cleveland Czechs," n.d., Theodore Andrica Papers, WRHS, container 1, folder 1; Winston Chrislock, "Cleveland Czechs," in *Identity, Conflict, and Cooperation: Central Europeans in Cleveland, 1850–1930*, ed. David C. Hammack, Diane L. Grabowski, and John J. Grabowski (Cleveland, 2002), 88–89; John J. Grabowski et al., *Polish Americans and Their Communities of Cleveland* (Cleveland, 1976), 138–42, 195; Casimir F. Bielen, "The Social Studies Teacher and the School Community," ca. 1950, CBP,

container 1, folder 1; "Historical Report of the Parish of Epiphany, Cleveland, Ohio," [ca. December 1945], Epiphany Parish correspondence, ADC.

75. U.S. Bureau of the Census, *Housing—Analytical Maps*, 90; U.S. Bureau of the Census, *Housing . . . Cleveland Block Statistics* (Washington, D.C., 1942), 59–60; *CP*, September 7, 1956; *CP*, September 8, 1956; Perry Jackson to Julian Krawcheck, March 16, 1956, JKP; "From Mrs. Harry L. Stewart," [1956], JKP; "From Edward Shafranek," [1956], JKP; *CP*, September 4, 1956. For more on individual black families in otherwise white neighborhoods, see Arnold M. Rose, Frank J. Atelsek, and Lawrence R. McDonald, "Neighborhood Reactions to Isolated Negro Residents: An Alternative to Invasion and Succession," *American Sociological Review* 18 (October 1953): 497–507; and Eleanor Leacock, Martin Deutsch, and Joshua A. Fishman, "The Bridgeview Study: A Preliminary Report," *Journal of Social Issues* 15 (December 1959): 30–37.

76. *CP*, October 19, 1964; Real Property Inventory of Metropolitan Cleveland, *A Sheet-a-Week* (December 3, 1965); Joseph LoGalbo, taped interview with author, August 7, 2003.

77. Memo, [United Neighborhood Centers] to Budget Committee, Group Work Council, "Budget Request for 1963," FCP, container 11, folder 250; Frank Gagliardi, taped interview with author, September 17, 2003; Frank DePaolo, taped interview with author, December 18, 2002; *C&P*, July 25, 1953 ("People's Forum"); *C&P*, November 12, 1955.

78. *CP*, April 14, 1958; *PD*, August 18, 1960; *C&P*, August 20, 1960; Lois Horn to Rev. Bishop Whalen, September 11, 1961, Holy Family Parish correspondence, ADC.

79. *CP*, October 10, 1960; *CP*, October 11, 1960; *CP*, October 17, 1960; *CP*, October 18, 1960; *CP*, October 24, 1960; *CP*, October 25, 1960; *CP*, November 10, 1960; *CP*, November 15, 1960.

80. "Memo to Krawcheck"; "From Leo Dombrowski," August 1961, JKP; "From K. C. Jones"; "Corlett Homeowners Improvement Association, Inc.," August 1961, JKP; United Neighborhood Centers, "First Annual Report," April 27, 1961, FCP, container 11, folder 250; Memo, [United Neighborhood Centers] to Budget Committee, "Budget Request for 1962," November 20, 1961, in ibid.; "NAACP Housing Committee Minutes," April 16, 1962, NAACP-CB, container 4, folder 4; "Attention Property Owners," n.d., JKP.

81. Cleveland Community Relations Board, "Report for 1963," 10; *PD*, May 10, 1963; *PD*, September 28, 1964; Johnnie Pros to "Dear Sir," April 12, 1964, Ralph S. Locher Papers, WRHS, container 19, folder 8.

Chapter 5

1. *Hearing before the United States Commission on Civil Rights: Hearing Held in Cleveland, Ohio, April 1–7, 1966* (Washington, D.C., 1966), 32–35, 37.

2. Ibid., 33, 38, 40–41.

3. Cleveland Urban League, Research Department, *The Negro in Cleveland, 1950–1963: An Analysis of the Social and Economic Characteristics of the Negro Population* (June 1964), 15–16.

4. "Facing Cleveland's Share of the Nation's Major Socio-Economic Problem," October 20, 1957, CDF, container 61, folder 3; *C&P*, June 14, 1958 (letter to the editor).

5. *PD*, May 11, 1945; *C&P*, June 30, 1945; *C&P*, December 1, 1951; *CP*, October 2, 1953; *C&P*, October 10, 1953. See also "Albert Cole, Housing Head, Conducts Public Hearing," *The Informer* (October 7, 1953), in FSH, container 47, folder 10.

6. "From Harry Templeton," [1956], in JKP; *CP*, September 8, 1956; "[K. C.] Jones—1a," July 8, 1958, p. 60, MKP, container 7, folder 331; "The Interview of Frank Baldau," [ca. 1957?], 47, MKP, container 1, folder 14.

7. *C&P*, November 29, 1952; *CP*, March 20, 1958; "The Negro in Cleveland—From CEI report," [1959], JKP; *C&P*, May 9, 1953; *C&P*, February 8, 1958; Quincy Savings & Loan Co., "Financial Statement," ca. December 31, 1959, Armond Robinson Papers, WRHS, container 1, folder 3.

8. "Charles V. Carr," April 3, 1958, MKP, container 2, folder 84; interview with A. B. Heard, July 20, 1961, pp. 2, 5–6, 22–24, 26, MKP, container 6, folder 271. Carr later estimated that Quincy financed half of Lee-Seville's new homes; see *C&P*, February 13, 1971. For confirmation, Quincy stimulated white-run banks to liberalize lending policies; see *C&P*, March 12, 1955; and *C&P*, December 24, 1955.

9. *CP*, November 17, 1976; *C&P*, January 25, 1941; *C&P*, December 6, 1947; *C&P*, August 13, 1949; *C&P*, January 29, 1955; *C&P*, April 20, 1957. For more on Dunbar Life, see Russell H. Davis, *Black Americans in Cleveland from George Peake to Carl B. Stokes* (Washington, D.C., 1972), 286–88. For a black Mount Pleasant resident who got financing through his insurance company, see Walter Burks obituary, *PD*, July 28, 2001.

10. The most extensive exploration to date of land contract abuses perpetrated against black buyers is Beryl Satter, *Family Properties: Race, Real Estate, and the Exploitation of Black Urban America* (New York, 2009). Another study found that African Americans, buying on land contract, paid, on average, a 69 percent markup; see Lynn Beyer Sagalyn, "Housing on the Installment Plan: An Economic and Institutional Analysis of Contract Buying in Chicago" (Ph.D. diss., Massachusetts Institute of Technology, 1980).

11. *C&P*, August 19, 1950; *C&P*, February 14, 1953; *CN*, April 27, 1954; *CN*, May 17, 1954; *CN*, July 1, 1954; *C&P*, July 3, 1954; *C&P*, May 14, 1955; *C&P*, November 6, 1954; *C&P*, January 15, 1955. For more on land contracts and speculators, see Albert J. Mayer, "Russell Woods: Change without Conflict," in *Studies in Housing and Minority Groups*, ed. Nathan Glazer and Davis McEntire (Berkeley, Calif., 1960), 208–9; and Arnold R. Hirsch, *Making the Second Ghetto: Race and Housing in Chicago, 1940–1960*, reprint ed. (Chicago, 1998), 31–33.

12. *C&P*, November 20, 1954; *C&P*, February 15, 1958; *C&P*, December 27, 1947. Second mortgages, "banished to a banking limbo in the Great Depression," were reportedly on the rise; *CP*, October 6, 1959.

13. *PD*, January 17, 1956; *CP*, April 2, 1959; *PD*, October 7, 1962; *CP*, October 16, 1963; *CP*, November 21, 1969. Despite federal reforms, black neighborhoods remained disadvantaged; see Harriet T. Taggart and Kevin W. Smith, "Redlining: An Assessment of the Evidence of Disinvestment in Metropolitan Boston," *Urban Affairs Quarterly* 17 (September 1981): 91–107.

14. *PD*, November 20, 1953. For contemporary research debunking assumptions about property value decline, see Robert C. Weaver, *The Negro Ghetto* (New York, 1948), 280–93; Charles Abrams, *Forbidden Neighbors: A Study of Prejudice in Housing* (New York, 1955),

287–89; and Luigi Laurenti, in *Property Values and Race: Studies in Seven Cities* (Berkeley, Calif., 1960).

15. Perry Jackson to Louis Seltzer, January 25, 1956, JKP; *CP*, September 3, 1956; *CP*, September 4, 1956; *CP*, September 5, 1956; *CP*, September 6, 1956; *CP*, September 7, 1956. The Cuyahoga County auditor affirmed that property values held steady amid demographic turnover; "From John Carney," [1956], JKP. For reactions to the series, see materials in the folder "Negro Neighbors," JKP.

16. See W. H. Brown Jr., "Access to Housing: The Role of the Real Estate Industry," *Economic Geography* 48 (January 1971): 66–78; and Raymond A. Mohl, "The Second Ghetto and the 'Infiltration Theory' in Urban Real Estate, 1940–1960," in *Urban Planning and the African American Community: In the Shadows*, ed. June Manning Thomas and Marsha Ritzdorf (Thousand Oaks, Calif., 1997), 23–42.

17. For notable examples, see *C&P*, April 4, 1942 (Thornton Real Estate Co.), October 20, 1951 (L. T. Huff Realty Co.), and March 20, 1954 (R. H. Riffe).

18. *C&P*, May 7, 1949; *C&P*, December 7, 1946; *C&P*, February 1, 1958; *C&P*, April 29, 1961; *C&P*, December 21, 1963; *C&P*, October 10, 1964; "From Councilman Leo Jackson," June 1961, JKP; "Memo to Tanner," June 30, [1961], JKP. Haggins's new branch in suburban Cleveland Heights was bombed in 1969, but even this did not slow the expansion of his business; see Ruth Zeager, "Haggins Realty Bombing," http://clevelandhistorical.org /items/show/640 (May 15, 2014).

19. *C&P*, October 26, 1963; *The Encyclopedia of Cleveland History*, ed. David D. Van Tassel and John J. Grabowski (Bloomington, Ind., 1987), 202. On the trademark, see Jeffrey M. Hornstein, *A Nation of Realtors*: *A Cultural History of the Twentieth-Century American Middle Class* (Durham, N.C., 2005), 75–79.

20. *C&P*, October 9, 1948; *C&P*, March 27, 1948; DeHart Hubbard to George A. Bremer, May 19, 1949, FSH, container 4, folder 7; *C&P*, January 29, 1955. For more details on the disagreements, see "Highlights of the 1955 Cleveland Urban League and Cleveland Association of Real Estate Brokers Real Estate Workshop," January 22–23, 1955, NUL, box I:C52, "Affiliates File, Cleveland, Ohio, 1952–1953" folder.

21. *C&P*, July 13, 1957; "11th Annual Banquet, Cleveland Association of Real Estate Brokers," June 13, 1958, NAACP-CB, container 24, folder 2; *CP*, October 17, 1960. Black real estate brokers made an earlier organizing attempt; see *C&P*, November 22, 1941.

22. "Cleveland Urban League Department of Housing Activities First Annual Report," September 25, 1957, CDF, container 61, folder 3; "Democratic Housing Means Better Living for All," [1957], NUL, box I:C52, "Affiliates File, Cleveland, Ohio, 1952–1953." For further context on the Three Year Project in Housing, see Todd M. Michney, "Changing Neighborhoods: Race and Upward Mobility in Southeast Cleveland, 1930–1980" (Ph.D. diss., University of Minnesota, 2004), 187–90.

23. "Initial Plan for the Cleveland Urban League Housing Activities," March 1, 1957, CDF, container 61, folder 2; K. C. Jones to "Dear Friend," March 29, 1957, CDF, container 60, folder 11; Urban League, Department of Housing Activities, "Progress Report 1959–1960," ca. 1961, EJB, General Files, container 10, folder 1.

24. *CP*, July 24, 1961; "From Albert Taborn," July 1961, JKP. On aggressive black and white Detroit real estate agents, see Thomas J. Sugrue, *The Origins of the Urban Crisis: Race and Inequality in Postwar Detroit* (Princeton, N.J., 1996), 194–97.

25. "From Mrs. John (Rita) Siple," August 1961, JKP; "Memo to Tanner"; "From Frank H. Pelton," July 1961, JKP; *CP*, August 16, 1961; *CP*, August 14, 1961; *CP*, August 17, 1961. On blockbusting tactics and responses, see Amanda I. Seligman, "'Apologies to Dracula, Werewolf, Frankenstein': White Homeowners and Blockbusters in Chicago," *Journal of the Illinois State Historical Society* 94 (Spring 2001): 70–95.

26. "From Mrs. Arthur M. Litt," July 1961, JKP; "From Mrs. James Keefe," July 1961, JKP; "From Isaac Haggins" [ca. July 1961] and attached "Haggins Addenda," JKP; "From Walter Gole," [ca. July 1961], JKP; *CP*, August 18, 1961; "From Albert Taborn"; *CP*, August 14, 1961; *CP*, August 16, 1961; "From Shelton Granger," [ca. July–August 1961], JKP.

27. *CP*, August 21, 1961; "Harvard Comment," [ca. August 1962], JKP; Anonymous to "Dear Press Columnists," [ca. August 1961], JKP; "Reaction Calls—from Tanner," [ca. August 1961], JKP; "Memo to City Desk," September 17, [1962], JKP; anonymous letter, "Hope Your [*sic*] Satisfied," [ca. September 1962], JKP; *C&P*, August 26, 1961.

28. *CP*, July 28, 1961; *CP*, August 1, 1961; *C&P*, August 12, 1961; *PD*, May 13, 1963; *C&P*, April 13, 1963; *PD*, September 28, 1964; *PD*, September 29, 1964; Memo, Urban League of Cleveland to Members of the Legislation Committee, October 7, 1964, ULC, container 19, folder 1; *CP*, October 8, 1964; *CP*, January 25, 1965; *PD*, May 6, 1965; *PD*, May 11, 1965.

29. Leonard N. Moore, "Class Conflicts over Residential Space in an African-American Community: Cleveland's Lee-Seville Public Housing Controversy," *Ohio History* 111 (Winter-Spring 2002): 1–19. This parallel has also been drawn with regard to elite black homeowners in Detroit; see Sugrue, *Origins of the Urban Crisis*, 41.

30. William Julius Wilson, *The Truly Disadvantaged: The Inner City, the Underclass, and Public Policy* (Chicago, 1987), esp. 56–57, 143–44; William Julius Wilson, *When Work Disappears: The World of the New Urban Poor* (New York, 1996), esp. 54, 64, 109. For critiques of Wilson's thesis, see Douglas S. Massey and Nancy A. Denton, *American Apartheid: Segregation and the Making of the Underclass* (Cambridge, Mass., 1993); and Michael B. Katz, ed., *The Underclass Debate: Views from History* (Princeton, N.J., 1993).

31. See Brigitte Mach Erbe, "Race and Socioeconomic Segregation," *American Sociological Review* 40 (December 1975): 801–12; Wayne J. Villemez, "Race, Class, and Neighborhood: Differences in the Residential Return on Individual Resources," *Social Forces* 59 (December 1980): 413–30; Douglas S. Massey, Gretchen A. Condran, and Nancy A. Denton, "The Effect of Residential Segregation on Black Social and Economic Well-Being," *Social Forces* 66 (September 1987): 29–56; Reynolds Farley, "Residential Segregation of Social and Economic Groups among Blacks, 1970–1980," in *The Urban Underclass*, ed. Christopher Jencks and Paul E. Peterson (Washington, D.C., 1991), 274–98; Scott J. South and Glenn D. Deane, "Race and Residential Mobility: Individual Determinants and Structural Constraints," *Social Forces* 72 (September 1993): 147–67; Norman Fainstein, "Black Ghettoization and Social Mobility," in *The Bubbling Cauldron: Race, Ethnicity, and the Urban Crisis*, ed. Michael P. Smith and Joe R. Feagin (Minneapolis, 1996), 123–41; and Norman

Fainstein and Susan Nesbitt, "Did the Black Ghetto Have a Golden Age? Class Structure and Class Segregation in New York City, 1949–1970, with Initial Evidence for 1990," *Journal of Urban History* 23 (November 1996): 3–28.

32. "From Mrs. Junius (Louise) Usher," [ca. August 1962], JKP; "From John Mapp," [1962], JKP; *C&P*, March 23, 1963; Odelia Robinson, taped interview with author, August 6, 2001; Barbara Danforth, taped interview with author, September 17, 2003. On African Americans associating mixed neighborhoods with better housing, schools, and services, see George C. Galster, "Black and White Preferences for Neighborhood Racial Composition," *American Real Estate and Urban Economics Association Journal* 10 (March 1982): 39–66; and Joe T. Darden, "Choosing Neighbors and Neighborhoods: The Role of Race in Housing Preference," in *Divided Neighborhoods: Changing Patterns of Racial Segregation*, ed. Gary A. Tobin (Newbury Park, Calif., 1987), 25–27.

33. *CP*, September 23, 1966; *PD*, January 25, 1966. In Chicago, Detroit, and Cleveland, middle-class blacks continued to live among relatively poorer whites; see Richard D. Alba, John R. Logan, and Brian J. Stults, "How Segregated Are Middle-Class African Americans?" *Social Problems* 47 (November 2000): 543–58.

34. "Broadway Y.M.C.A. Outpost," December 1958, YMCA, container 33, folder 7; "Broadway Y.M.C.A. Outpost Daily Log, Jan. 2–21, 1959," in ibid.; Fred Stashower to J. Kimball Johnson, June 25, 1959, TCF, container 6, folder 2; "Review Committee No. II Summary Review," June 1960, FCP, container 36, folder 890; *C&P*, May 15, 1965.

35. Donna Whyte, taped interview with author, January 28, 2003; Ronald Ferguson, taped telephone interview with author, August 29, 2003; Cherie McClain, taped interview with author, December 7, 2001; Anonymous, taped interview with author, October 21, 2003. On "marooned" or "nonconforming" whites remaining in post-transitional neighborhoods, see Paul Frederick Cressey, "Succession of Cultural Groups in the City of Chicago" (Ph.D. diss., University of Chicago, 1930), 300–308; and Richard Kerckhoff, "A Study of Racially Changing Neighborhoods," *Merrill-Palmer Quarterly* 4 (Fall 1957): 35–42.

36. "Where Will the Negro Live Tomorrow: A Report," ca. November 6, 1958, p. 12, CDF, container 60, folder 11; "Full Statement of the Urban League of Cleveland," May 25, 1960, CDF, container 61, folder 2; "Progress Report 1959–1960"; "Hamilton, Wm. J.," November 9, 1963, MKP, container 6, folder 266. On African Americans' reluctance to integrate neighborhoods, see Reynolds Farley et al., "Barriers to the Racial Integration of Neighborhoods: The Detroit Case," *Annals of the American Academy of Political and Social Science* 441 (January 1979): 97–113; and Maria Krysan and Reynolds Farley, "The Residential Preferences of Blacks: Do They Explain Persistent Segregation?" *Social Forces* 80 (March 2002): 937–80.

37. *CP*, December 3, 1965; "Stabilizing Property Values and Real Estate Demand," ca. 1965, ULC, Series II, container 4, folder 69; "Tentative Draft Proposal," 1966, TCF, Series II, container 31, folder 728.

38. "From Mrs. Junius (Louise) Usher," July 1961, JKP; "From Mrs. Bobby (Gwenn) Mitchell," August 1961, JKP; "From Mrs. Cecil (Wilhelmina) Lewis," [ca. August 1962], JKP; interview with A. B. Heard, July 20, 1961, MKP, container 6, folder 271, 38–39; "From Mrs.

James (Anthenette) Guilford," [ca. August 1962], JKP. For further evidence that upwardly mobile blacks move to white neighborhoods primarily for good amenities, see Donald L. Foley, "Institutional and Contextual Factors Affecting the Housing Choices of Minority Residents," in *Segregation in Residential Areas: Papers on Racial and Socioeconomic Factors in Choice of Housing*, ed. Amos H. Hawley and Vincent Rock (Washington, D.C., 1973), 85–147; and Wilhelmina A. Leigh and James D. McGhee, "A Minority Perspective on Residential Racial Integration," in *Housing Desegregation and Federal Policy*, ed. John M. Goering (Chapel Hill, N.C., 1986), 31–42.

39. On African Americans' continuing difficulties accessing federally backed financing, see Louis Hyman, *Debtor Nation: The History of America in Red Ink* (Princeton, N.J., 2011), 137–45.

40. *CP*, June 3, 1954; Leah Milkman Rich, "The Mount Pleasant Community Centers: Report of Consultant," February 1961, p. 25, TCF, Series II, container 48, folder 1191; *C&P*, November 14, 1953; *C&P*, October 23, 1954; Glenville Area Community Council, "Tenth Annual Report," May 1955, LAJ; *C&P*, December 22, 1956. On the same situation in Fort Worth, see William S. Hendon, "Discrimination against Negro Homeowners in Property Tax Assessment," *American Journal of Economics and Sociology* 27 (April 1968): 125–32.

41. H. Jean Dorgham, taped interviews with author, November 3, 2001, December 7, 2001; *C&P*, January 11, 1941; *C&P*, February 27, 1965. For Glenville as "Corn Flakes Blvd.," see *C&P*, September 6, 1941.

42. "A Look at the Negro Housing Picture"; *PD*, March 15, 1964; Gwendolyn Fuller to Greta Hampel, March 2, 1967, ULC, Series II, container 7, folder 139; Gary Fisher, "Abandonment Study," September 1971, ULC, Series II, container 1, folder 19; *C&P*, November 6, 1954; Memo, Gwendolyn Fuller to Urban League Housing Committee, July 14, 1967, CDF, container 61, folder 1; *C&P*, July 22, 1967; *C&P*, July 29, 1967; Memo, Gwendolyn Fuller to Urban League Housing Committee, September 10, 1967, CDF, container 61, folder 1; "Press Release," ca. January 5, 1968, ULC, container 22, folder 8. On post-1968 lending discrimination, see Taggart and Smith, "Redlining." On insurance access, see Gregory D. Squires and William Velez, "Insurance Redlining and the Transformation of an Urban Metropolis," *Urban Affairs Quarterly* 23 (September 1987): 63–83.

43. Henry Taylor, "Black Ohio in the Contemporary Era, 1950–Present: A Review of the Literature," n.d., Manuscript Vertical File, WRHS; "Area Characteristics: Mount Pleasant [1950]," FCP, container 9, folder 225; "Area Characteristics: Mount Pleasant [1960/1965]," in ibid.; "Preliminary Draft: Planning Settlement Service for the Mt. Pleasant Area," January 8, 1963, and attached "Selected Data Relating to the Mount Pleasant Social Planning Area," June 1962, Greater Cleveland Neighborhood Centers Association, WRHS, container 4, folder 58; Federation for Community Planning, "Harvard Community Services Center Plans for the Future," Spring 1977, RJM; *CP*, July 28, 1959; *CP*, March 6, 1964; Lee-Harvard Community Association, "Progress through a United Community," [1967], TCF, Series II, container 37, folder 884. On black buyers raising maintenance standards, see *PD*, January 25, 1966.

44. For a discussion of this dynamic, see Ronald M. Denowitz, "Racial Succession in New York City, 1960–1970," *Social Forces* 59 (December 1980): 440–55.

45. "Area Characteristics: Mount Pleasant [1950]"; "Area Characteristics: Mount Pleasant [1960/1965]"; Cleveland Business & Economic Development Corp., "A Combined Feasibility Study & Market Analysis of Businesses in Cleveland's Mt. Pleasant Area," June 1, 1969, TCF, Series II, container 46, folder 1151; Ad Hoc Staff Committee on Race Relations, "Reference Sheet," January 9, 1968, FCP, container 15, folder 352; "Median Income of Families and Unrelated Individuals: 1950, 1960, 1970," CBP, Series II, container 1, folder 4.

46. "Relative Income Shifts: 1959–1969," September 18, 1972, ULC, Series II, container 1, folder 19; "General Description of Area," ca. 1967–68, ULC, container 21, folder 5.

47. Rich, "Report of Consultant," 12; Memo, Robert Doggett to Eric Grubb, "Report of Survey on Existing Neighborhood Conditions in the Mt. Pleasant Community," March 7, 1963, GCNCA, container 4, folder 58; "From Mrs. Cecil (Wilhelmina) Lewis"; Greater Cleveland Neighborhood Centers Association, "Report of Long Range Planning Committee," December 21, 1965, ASS, container 4, folder 6; "Proposal for a Summer Youth Employment Program," April 23, 1969, CBS, container 40, folder 749; *PD*, February 25, 1985. On the importance of dual-income earning, see Bart Landry and Margaret Platt Jendrek, "The Employment of Wives in Middle-Class Black Families," *Journal of Marriage and the Family* 40 (November 1978): 787–97; and Bart Landry, *Black Working Wives: Pioneers of the American Family Revolution* (Berkeley, Calif., 2000).

48. Health and Welfare Department, Urban League of Cleveland, "What About Cleveland's Health and Welfare?" June 1963, CDF, container 61, folder 2; "Area Characteristics: Mount Pleasant [1960/1965]"; Ad Hoc Staff Committee on Race Relations, "Reference Sheet." See also U.S. Bureau of the Census, *Characteristics of Selected Neighborhoods in Cleveland, Ohio: April 1965*, Current Population Reports: Technical Studies, Series P-23, No. 21 (January 23, 1967).

49. On black Southerners' continuing departures after World War II, see Nicholas Lemann, *The Promised Land: The Great Black Migration and How It Changed America* (New York, 1991); James N. Gregory, "The Second Great Migration: A Historical Overview," in *African American Urban History since World War II*, ed. Kenneth L. Kusmer and Joe W. Trotter (Chicago, 2009), 19–38; and Leah Platt Boustan, *Competition in the Promised Land: Black Migrants in Northern Cities and Labor Markets* (Princeton, N.J., 2017).

50. Summary of Activities, Citizens Committee on Newcomers," January 24, 1958, NAACP-CB, container 23, folder 4; Crosby Ramey to "Dear Sir," April 30, 1957, in ibid.; Minutes, In-Migration Committee, February 28, 1956, NAACP-CB, container 7, folder 3; *CP*, January 23, 1957; *C&P*, December 13, 1958; "Area Characteristics: Mount Pleasant [1960/1965]"; "Interim Report, Glenville Community Study," [1961], KTNC, container 2, folder 8; Gene B. Petersen, Laurie M. Sharp, and Thomas F. Drury, *Southern Newcomers to Northern Cities: Work and Social Adjustment in Cleveland* (New York, 1977). For additional findings that Southern migrants were actually better adjusted, see Stewart E. Tolnay, "The Great Migration and Changes in the Northern Black Family, 1940 to 1990,"

Social Forces 75 (June 1997): 1213–38; and Townsand Price-Spratlen, "Urban Destination Selection among African Americans during the 1950s Great Migration," *Social Science History* 32 (Fall 2008): 437–69.

51. *PD*, December 31, 1958; Speech, "The Causes and Remedies for the High Rate of Crime among Negroes," November 11, 1958, McKinney Family Papers, WRHS, container 7, folder 6; *CP*, December 31, 1958; Leo Jackson, "Law Enforcement" (speech), 1961, Sol Kahn Papers, WRHS, container 1, folder 8; *CP*, December 16, 1966; Minutes, Urban League Housing Committee, March 10, 1967, CDF, container 61, folder 1. See also Councilman Jackson's remarks, in "Proceedings from the Urban Migration Workshop," April 27–29, 1961, Pamphlets, "Migrants 1," Mandel School of Applied Social Sciences Library, CWRU.

52. *C&P*, February 2, 1952; *C&P*, December 20, 1952; *CP*, February 13, 1957; *C&P*, December 17, 1955; "Review Committee No. II Summary Review"; Rich, "Report of Consultant," 11; Minutes, Mount Pleasant Planning Directions Committee, Group Work Council, August 2, 1962, GCNCA, container 4, folder 58. At least some Glenville residents considered a rehabilitation-based program for the neighborhood under the 1954 Housing Act; see *CP*, March 17, 1958. A never-implemented renewal map was drawn up for Glenville; see Cleveland City Planning Commission, *Planning in Cleveland 1964*, University Circle Inc. Records, WRHS, container 5, folder 80.

53. *PD*, October 2, 1963; "Stabilizing Property Values and Real Estate Demand"; *PD*, September 14, 1964; *CP*, January 10, 1967; "Relocation of Dike Area Families and Individuals as of September 16, 1966," ULC, container 20, folder 1; "Communities—Gladstone," [ca. 1965?], CDF, container 61, folder 5; "University-Euclid," [ca. 1965?], in ibid.; "East Woodland," [ca. 1965?], in ibid.; "St. Vincent Center Project—Ohio R-13," [ca. 1965?], in ibid.; "Erieview," [ca. 1965?], in ibid.

54. *CP*, October 5, 1964; "From Tom Dickey," [ca. August 1962], JKP; Philip Richards, "Coming of Age at Alexander Hamilton Junior High School," *Cleveland Magazine* (October 2006), 112; "Housing Improvement Program Proposal," ca. February 22, 1967, CDF, container 47, folder 7. For urban renewal's indirect impact on a Detroit neighborhood, see George Henderson, "Twelfth Street: An Analysis of a Changed Neighborhood," *Phylon* 25 (Spring 1964): 91–96.

55. *C&P*, October 3, 1964; *CP*, December 9, 1966; *CP*, January 19, 1967; Rubie McCullough to James Norton, November 29, 1967, TCF, Series II, container 37, folder 884; *CP*, January 21, 1967; Alvin Phillips to Carl Stokes, December 13, 1967, TCF, Series II, container 47, folder 1153; *CP*, March 26, 1968.

56. Murtis Taylor interview transcript, 49; "A Hard Look at Mt. Pleasant," [ca. 1968], TCF, Series II, container 47, folder 1153. For a sense of population movements between various sections of the city in 1971 and 1974, see Regional Planning Commission, "1974 Household Migration, Cuyahoga County," May 1976, at Special Collections, Michael Schwartz Library, Cleveland State University.

57. Dorgham interviews, November 3, 2001, December 7, 2001; Ferguson interview; Robinson interview; Whyte interview; Danforth interview. On African Americans assigning greater status to newer, further-outlying neighborhoods, see Leo F. Schnore, "Social

Class Segregation among Nonwhites in Metropolitan Centers," *Demography* 2 (1965): 126–33; and Wilfred G. Marston, "Socio-Economic Differentiation within Negro Areas of American Cities," *Social Forces* 48 (December 1969): 165–75.

58. John B. Turner, "A Study of the Block Club: An Instrument of Community Organization" (Ph.D. diss., Western Reserve University, 1959), 57; *C&P*, June 12, 1948; *C&P*, May 22, 1948; *C&P*, February 19, 1949; *C&P*, August 25, 1951; *C&P*, May 23, 1959; *C&P*, September 8, 1962.

59. The foregoing discussion is distilled mainly from Bart Landry, *The New Black Middle Class* (Berkeley, Calif., 1987), 13–65.

60. Minutes, Intergroup Relations Committee, Group Work Council, November 6, 1958, NSC, container 18, folder 4; Collins Munns, taped telephone interview with author, July 12, 2001; Paul Simpson, taped interview with author, November 26, 2002; Whtye interview.

61. "Request to Cleveland Foundation," December 1956, GCNCA, container 4, folder 56; Henry Ollendorff to J. Kimball Johnson, March 3, 1958, TCF, container 6, folder 1; Minutes, Board of Trustees, Mount Pleasant Community Centers, December 12, 1960, GCNCA, container 4, folder 56; Farntella Duncan to "Dear Sir," March 3, 1956, JKP.

62. "Mt. Pleasant Community Centers Present & Future—What Priorities," October 1960, GCNCA, container 4, folder 58; LHCA, "Progress Through a United Community."

63. "Preparation of the School Camp at Hiram House," ca. January 12–18, 1962, GCNCA, container 4, folder 58; "Motivating the Unemployed Youth and School Drop Outs," ca. November 1962–June 1963, in ibid.

64. H. B. Williams, "Mt. Pleasant Annual Meeting," January 26, 1961, NAACP-CB, container 38, folder 3; Rich, "The Mount Pleasant Community Centers," 12, 14, 17; Urban League Housing Committee, March 10, 1967, ULC, container 19, folder 2.

65. "Hard Look at Mt. Pleasant," 7, 9–10; "Housing Improvement Program Proposal"; Charlise Lyles, *Do I Dare Disturb the Universe? From the Projects to Prep School* (Boston, 1994), 3, 66; *CP*, March 28, 1967. For further confirmation that black families, regardless of income, seek good housing and education, see Elizabeth Huttman, "A Research Note on Dreams and Aspirations of Black Families," *Journal of Comparative Family Studies* 22 (Summer 1991): 147–58.

66. Whyte interview; Lewis Brightharp, taped interview with author, April 12, 2002; Munns interview; Richards, "Coming of Age," 113.

67. "Proposal[—]Cleveland Urban League Special Housing Program," 1956, TCF, container 6, folder 51; "Where Will the Negro Live Tomorrow"; *CP*, July 28, 1959.

Chapter 6

1. *PD*, December 14, 1972; *CP*, December 12, 1972; *CP*, October 20, 1971.

2. On "black capitalism," see William L. Van Deburg, *New Day in Babylon: The Black Power Movement and American Culture, 1965–1975* (Chicago, 1992), 117–20; and Robert E. Weems Jr. and Lewis A. Randolph, "The National Response to Richard M. Nixon's Black Capitalism Initiative: The Success of Domestic Detente," *Journal of Black Studies* 32 (September 2001): 66–83.

3. *CP*, June 4, 1973; *PD*, October 28, 1974; *CP*, March 13, 1975; *CP*, May 8, 1975; Mr. Fred X. (Arnett) to Robert McCall, June 2, 1975, RJM; *PD*, December 9, 1975; Urban League of Cleveland, Lee-Harvard Branch, Action Advisory Committee Meeting, January 22, 1975, ULC, Series II, container 1, folder 2.

4. *CP*, October 20, 1971; "Lee-Harvard Shopping Center Financial Statement," December 31, 1974, RJM; *CP*, June 4, 1973. Unbeknownst to McCall and others, Federal's Inc. was in financial trouble; the corporation filed for bankruptcy and shut down its remaining two Cleveland stores in 1972. See *CP*, September 7, 1972; and *PD*, August 18, 1972.

5. *CP*, November 25, 1976; *C&P*, May 12, 1973; *PD*, October 12, 1973; Urban League of Cleveland, Lee-Harvard Branch, Action Advisory Committee Meeting, September 18, 1974, ULC, Series II, container 1, folder 2; Federation for Community Planning, "Harvard Community Services Center Plans for the Future," Spring 1977, RJM; *CP*, February 1, 1978.

6. *CP*, February 1, 1978; Gary Fisher, "Abandonment Study," September 1971, ULC, Series II, container 1, folder 19; *CP*, April 13, 1971; Robert McCall to Carl Stokes, August 15, 1968, CBS, container 56, folder 1048; Urban League of Cleveland, Lee-Harvard Branch, Action Advisory Committee Meeting, September 19, 1974, August 21, 1974, and January 22, 1975, ULC, Series II, container 1, folder 2; "Harvard Community Services Center Plans for the Future."

7. Ronald H. Bayor, *Race and the Shaping of Twentieth-Century Atlanta* (Chapel Hill, N.C., 1996); Thomas J. Sugrue, *The Origins of the Urban Crisis: Race and Inequality in Postwar Detroit* (Princeton, N.J., 1996). See also Arnold R. Hirsch, *Making the Second Ghetto: Race and Housing in Chicago, 1940–1960* (Cambridge, 1983); and William Julius Wilson, *The Truly Disadvantaged: The Inner City, the Underclass, and Public Policy* (Chicago, 1987).

8. Note especially Jonathan Rieder, *Canarsie: The Jews and Italians of Brooklyn against Liberalism* (Cambridge, Mass., 1985); and Jonathan Rieder, "The Rise of the 'Silent Majority,'" in *The Rise and Fall of the New Deal Order, 1930–1980*, ed. Steve Fraser and Gary Gerstle (Princeton, N.J., 1989), 243–68.

9. Event program, "Working Together to Build Good Neighborhoods," ca. May 26, 1962, NAACP-CB, container 37, folder 5; *CP*, December 16, 1966; Lee-Harvard Community Association, "Progress through a United Community," [1967], TCF, Series II, container 37, folder 884; *CP*, February 22, 1968; *CP*, January 19, 1970; "Harvard Community Services Area: Description of the Area," CBS, container 11, folder 185; Greater Cleveland Neighborhood Centers Association, Long Range Planning Minutes, November 3, 1965, ASS, container 4, folder 6.

10. *CP*, February 1, 1978; *CP*, August 15, 1974; Urban League of Cleveland, Lee-Harvard Branch, Advisory Board Committee Meeting, October 15, 1975, ULC, Series II, container 1, folder 2.

11. In "Symposium on Thomas J. Sugrue: The Origins of the Urban Crisis," *Labor History* 39 (February 1998): 43–69: see Eric Arnesen, "History First: Putting Urban Poverty in Perspective," 46; Nancy Gabin, "Racial Boundaries and Class Designs in the Urban North," 49; Joe W. Trotter, "Race, Public Policy, and History: The Question of Priorities," 59–60; and Sugrue's rebuttal in "Responsibility to the Past, Engagement with the Present,"

66–67. In the symposium on the twenty-year anniversary of Arnold Hirsch's *Making the Second Ghetto*, in the *Journal of Urban History* 29 (March 2003): 233–309: see Amanda Irene Seligman, "What Is the Second Ghetto?" 275–77; Thomas J. Sugrue, "Revisiting the Second Ghetto," 283; Heather Ann Thompson, "Making a Second Urban History," 294; and Hirsch's rebuttal, "Second Thoughts on the Second Ghetto," 300, 301–3. For a recent study centering black agency as "facilitating and frustrating patterns of urban change," see Marcus Anthony Hunter, *Black Citymakers: How the Philadelphia Negro Changed Urban America* (New York, 2013) (quote from 8).

12. *CP*, September 3, 1956; Community Relations Board, "Report of the Executive Director, December 1957," AJC, container 1, folder 15; "Preliminary Draft: Planning Settlement Service for the Mt. Pleasant Area," January 8, 1963, GCNCA, container 4, folder 58; Minutes, Mt. Pleasant Urban Social Services Center Implementation Committee, Central Planning Board, Welfare Federation of Cleveland, November 7, 1963, FCP, container 15, folder 378; "Summary of Proposal to Develop an Urban Social Services Center in the Mt. Pleasant Community," April 19, 1965, TCF, Series II, container 37, folder 890; "Housing Improvement Program Proposal," ca. February 22, 1967, CDF, container 47, folder 7; "Glenville Multi-Purpose Corporation Proposal," August 27, 1969, Cleveland: NOW! Records, WRHS, container 3, folder 51.

13. "Survey of Social Problems in the Lee-Miles Social Planning Area," March 1971, p. 34, RJM; Craig Lewis to Rubie McCullough, February 6, 1973, TCF, Series II, container 37, folder 884.

14. Event program, GACC 13th Annual Meeting, May 29, 1958, FCP, container 28, folder 693; *Glenville Bulletin* (September 1958), in ibid.; *CP*, February 26, 1959; *Mt. Pleasant Community Council Bulletin* (April 1955), NAACP-CB, container 38, folder 3; *PD*, April 1, 1955; *CP*, April 3, 1958; *CP*, March 24, 1965; *CP*, March 30, 1965; *CP*, April 27, 1954; *Mt. Pleasant Community Council Bulletin* (October 1955), NAACP-CB, container 38, folder 3; *CP*, August 18, 1972; *CP*, July 13, 1959; *CP*, July 12, 1965; *CP*, October 24, 1957; *CP*, October 28, 1964; *CP*, September 23, 1969; *CP*, October 19, 1966; *CP*, November 1, 1966.

15. Lorenzo Spicer to Harold Williams, May 21, 1962, NAACP-CB, container 37, folder 5; *Lee-Harvard Community Association Newsletter* (May 1965), in ibid.; *CP*, November 22, 1965; *CP*, October 17, 1966; *CP*, October 12, 1967; *CP*, November 21, 1968; *CP*, September 18, 1969; *CP*, October 19, 1967; *CP*, June 11, 1968. McCullough thought the LHCA was organized around 1956–57; see "Neighborhood Movement, O.H. 53," Rubie J. McCullough interviewed by Edward Miggins, Cuyahoga Community College Oral History Program, March 20, 1984, in author's possession.

16. "Broadway Y.M.C.A. Outpost," December 1958, YMCA, container 33, folder 7; *CP*, January 17, 1961; *CP*, September 15, 1967; *CP*, July 12, 1968; *CP*, December 6, 1968; *CP*, May 14, 1969; *CP*, March 2, 1976.

17. *Mt. Pleasant Community Council Bulletin* (May 1954), NAACP-CB, container 38, folder 3; *CP*, September 6, 1956; *GACC Bulletin* (January 1957), JCC, container 28, folder 16; Dorothy Sims to N.A.A.C.P., [1956], NAACP-CB, container 34, folder 5; undated newspaper clipping, "Youngsters Carol for Shut-Ins," *CP* [ca. December 1958], in "Mount Pleas-

ant Community Services Center," CPC. For useful context, see Amanda I. Seligman, *Chicago's Block Clubs: How Neighbors Shape the City* (Chicago, 2016).

18. GACC, "Building a Better Community Together: 7th Annual Report," June 1952, FCP, container 28, folder 693; *CP*, January 23, 1959; Leah Milkman Rich, "The Mount Pleasant Community Centers: Report of Consultant," February 1961, p. 10, TCF, Series II, container 48, folder 1191; *CP*, November 6, 1962; "To the George Gund Foundation from the Mt. Pleasant Safety Committee," ca. 1978, GGF, container 14, folder 364; *Lee-Harvard Community Association Newsletter* (May 1965); *CP*, October 17, 1966; *CP*, November 17, 1966; *CP*, October 12, 1967; *Lee-Harvard Community Star* (February 12, 1970), TCF, Series II, container 37, folder 884; *CP*, June 3, 1966; *PD*, March 26, 1966; James Hereford, taped interview with author, September 17, 2003.

19. *Mt. Pleasant Community Council Bulletin* (September 1954), NAACP-CB, container 38, folder 3; *CP*, January 17, 1961; *CP*, November 19, 1968; *Lee-Harvard Community Star* (February 12, 1970); *Lee-Harvard Community Association Newsletter* (May 1965); *CP*, October 20, 1966; *CP*, October 17, 1967; LHCA, "Progress through a United Community," 12; *CP*, January 29, 1969; *CP*, July 26, 1965; *CP*, March 14, 1961; *PD*, July 15, 1968.

20. *C&P*, October 26, 1957; "Profile—for *The Clevelander* [/] *Voice against a House Divided*," [1971], LAJ; "This Petition Is Circulated by a Non-partisan Citizens Committee," [ca. October 1957], LAJ; *The 24th Ward Herald* (September 30, 1957), LAJ; *C&P*, November 9, 1957; "Remarks before Cleveland City Council," February 27, 1961, LAJ; *C&P*, April 21, 1962; "The Real Truth" (sheaf of photocopies), [1963], LAJ. See also Lerone Bennett Jr., "The Lawyer Who Turned Down a Judgeship," *Ebony* 16 (February 1961): 25–32; and Leonard N. Moore, *Carl B. Stokes and the Rise of Black Political Power* (Urbana, Ill., 2002), 23, 89, 156–57.

21. *C&P*, September 21, 1957; "NAACP Convention Housing Committee Assignments," [ca. 1957–62], NAACP (Cleveland Chapter) Records, container 4, folder 4; *C&P*, November 2, 1957; Carl B. Stokes, *Promises of Power: A Political Autobiography* (New York, 1973), 42; *C&P*, November 9, 1957; *C&P*, March 29, 1958; *C&P*, February 7, 1959. Jackson was also accused of using the GACC for political gain; see Leo Jackson to William Hamilton, August 14, 1957, LAJ. For an activist downplaying partisan politics in these organizations, see "Cook, Carriebell J. (Mrs.), Jan. 10, Febr. 8, March [1962]," 162–64ff, MKP, container 3, folder 108.

22. "Community Facts: The Lee-Harvard Community," April 1962, FCP, container 28, folder 680; *PD*, January 25, 1966; *Lee-Harvard Community Association Newsletter* (May 1965), NAACP-CB, container 37, folder 5; *CP*, May 22, 1969; "Harvard Community Services Center Plans for the Future."

23. Gwendolyn Fuller, "Tour of the Lee-Seville Area," June 28, 1966, ULC, container 20, folder 1; *CP*, December 5, 1969; *PD*, May 3, 1969.

24. *CP*, October 19, 1964; *PD*, March 26, 1966.

25. David Mayo Austin et al., "Community Council: Test Tube for Democracy; A Case Study of the Glenville Area Community Council" (M.S. thesis, School of Applied Social Sciences, Western Reserve University, 1948), 145, WRHS; *C&P*, June 17, 1950; *C&P*, June 6,

1953; Cleveland City Planning Commission, "Cleveland Today . . . Tomorrow: The General Plan of Cleveland," December 1950, pp. 18, 21, WRHS; Group Work Council, "Mt. Pleasant Area: A Study of Recreational Needs," April 9, 1952, p. 10, and attached "Table VII," GCNCA, container 4, folder 56; *C&P*, May 24, 1952.

26. *CP*, September 28, 1951; GACC, 8th Annual Report, May 1953, NAACP-CB, container 36, folder 4; *CP*, February 29, 1952; *PD*, February 27, 1953; *CP*, February 27, 1953; Helen Benes, "Glenville Area Community Council," [ca. April 1954], FCP, Field Service Advisory Committee, 1947–58, microfilm roll 10; *CP*, March 20, 1956; "Recommendation to the Executive Committee—Mt. Pleasant Community Council," [March 1954], FCP, container 29, folder 708; Minutes, Home Conservation Committee, Area Councils Association, June 17, 1954, EENH, container 27, folder 4.

27. *CP*, June 13, 1952; *PD*, June 13, 1952; *PD*, April 22, 1953; *PD*, January 19, 1955; *Mt. Pleasant Community Council Bulletin* (May 1958), GCCUC, container 1, folder 1.

28. "Mt. Pleasant Community Council" (typed responses to questionnaire), [ca. 1957?], FCP, container 28, folder 678; MPCC, "1959 Annual Report," 15, NAACP-CB, container 38, folder 3; *CP*, August 6, 1959; "Housing Improvement Program Proposal."

29. GACC, "1957–58 Committee Reports in Brief," FCP, container 28, folder 693; *CP*, March 12, 1958; *CP*, March 18, 1958; "Fact Sheet for Hearing Committee," [1958?], FCP, container 28, folder 694; *C&P*, February 1, 1958; "Statement of Leo A. Jackson, Councilman," [1958], LAJ; *C&P*, June 14, 1958; *Glenville Bulletin* (September 1958), FCP, container 28, folder 693; "Second Report—Community Cancer of Ward 24," [ca. March 1959], LAJ; Minutes, Glenville Rehabilitation-Conservation Steering Committee, December 9, 1959, LAJ; Minutes, Glenville Area Urban Conservation Steering Committee Meeting, October 31, 1961, LAJ.

30. *PD*, March 12, 1961; *CP*, February 26, 1965; "Housing Improvement Program Proposal"; *CP*, May 18, 1965. On the Businessmen's Interracial Committee, see Kenneth Wayne Rose, "The Politics of Social Reform in Cleveland, 1945–1967: Civil Rights, Welfare Rights, and the Response of Civic Leaders" (Ph.D. diss., Case Western Reserve University, 1988), 245–59.

31. "Housing Improvement Program Proposal"; Minutes, Advisory Committee, Housing Improvement Program, August 9, 1965, ULC, container 18, folder 1; Minutes, Advisory Committee, Housing Improvement Program, September 13, 1965, in ibid.; *CP*, September 17, 1965; *CP*, October 15, 1965; Minutes, Special Advisory Committee Meeting, Housing Improvement Program, October 19, 1965, ULC, container 18, folder 1; "The Housing Improvement Program: An Evaluation of Progress to Date," February 15, 1966, TCF, Series II, container 60, folder 1513; *CP*, April 12, 1966.

32. *CP*, March 2, 1966; *CP*, July 7, 1966; Memo, Gwendolyn Fuller to James Ethridge, July 5, 1966, ULC, container 20, folder 1; *CP*, October 11, 1966; "Housing Improvement Program Proposal"; *CP*, March 29, 1967; *CP*, August 23, 1966; *CP*, January 12, 1967.

33. "Housing Improvement Program Proposal"; "Report for Periodical Review Committee," October 1967, FCP, container 9, folder 225; "Co-Op Training Program," June 13, 1968, CBS, container 40, folder 750; *CP*, September 17, 1965; "Straight from the HIP:

Housing Improvement Program," n.d., American Civil Liberties Union of Ohio Records, OHS, container 18, folder 2; "The Housing Improvement Program."

34. Minutes, Advisory Committee, Housing Improvement Program, June 18, 1965, ULC, container 18, folder 1; Melvin Crouther to Richard Rangoon, December 13, 1966, ULC, Series II, container 7, folder 139; *CP*, March 29, 1967; "Housing Improvement Fund: Questions and Answers," ca. April 13, 1967, CDF, container 47, folder 7; *CP*, August 10, 1967; Businessmen's Interracial Committee on Community Affairs, "Report for 1967," CHR, container 3, folder 47.

35. "Report for Periodic Review Committee," October 1967, FCP, container 9, folder 225; Jane Hughes, "Summary of 'The Pilot Rehabilitation Project,'" June 30, 1967, TCF, Series II, container 47, folder 1154; Jane Hughes, "The Pilot Rehabilitation Project in Mount Pleasant," June 30, 1967, in ibid.; *CP*, October 2, 1967; *CP*, December 20, 1967; *PD*, December 27, 1967; *CP*, December 20, 1967. For profiles of the families helped, see "Appendix D: Case Histories from the Files of HIP," attached to "Request for Grant," [ca. 1969], TCF, Series II, container 46, folder 1152.

36. Carl Stokes to James Norton, December 14, 1967, CBS, container 38, folder 707; Madeline Bailey to James Norton, December 12, 1967, TCF, Series II, container 47, folder 1153; William Taylor to James Norton, December 12, 1967, in ibid.; *CP*, February 1, 1968; *CP*, March 28, 1968; *CP*, July 17, 1968; "Report for Periodic Review Committee"; *CP*, September 5, 1968; Stafford Williams, "Report," September 19, 1968, CBS, container 32, folder 593; Hughes, "The Pilot Rehabilitation Project."

37. *PD*, February 9, 1969; *PD*, June 21, 1969; *CP*, July 5, 1969; Stafford Williams to James Norton, July 17, 1969, TCF, Series II, container 46, folder 1151. On the project to move houses from Shaker Heights, see *CP*, June 24, 1969; *PD*, August 14, 1969; and "Relocated Shaker Homes Now Being Purchased," *CHC Report* (July 1970), CBS, container 30, folder 544.

38. Evelyn Solomon to James Norton, July 15, 1969, TCF, Series II, container 46, folder 1151; Ollie McKinney to James Norton, July 17, 1969, in ibid.; Evelyn Mickens to "Dear Sirs," ca. July 17, 1969, in ibid.; Jean Cassie to James Norton, July 23, 1969, in ibid.; Richard Green to James Norton, July 29, 1969, in ibid.; "Cleveland: NOW! Funding of Multi-Service Centers," September 1970, p. 24, CBS, container 11, folder 185; *CP*, November 20, 1969; *PD*, May 3, 1969.

39. Mount Pleasant Youth Action Council, "Proposal for a Program of Summer Outings," June 1971, GGF, container 29, folder 735; "To the George Gund Foundation."

40. See Sylvia Hood Washington, *Packing Them In: An Archaeology of Environmental Racism in Chicago, 1865–1954* (Lanham, Md., 2005), 158–92; Steven Gregory, *Black Corona: Race and the Politics of Race in an Urban Community* (Princeton, N.J., 1998), esp. 146–56; Steven Gregory, "The Changing Significance of Race and Class in an African-American Community," *American Ethnologist* 19 (May 1992): 225–74; and Charles E. Connerly, *"The Most Segregated City in America": City Planning and Civil Rights in Birmingham, 1920–1980* (Charlottesville, Va., 2005), 217–30.

41. Middle-class African American neighborhood organizing has gone practically un-

acknowledged. Robert Fisher's overview, *Let the People Decide: Neighborhood Organizing in America*, updated ed. (New York, 1994), generalizes 1950s efforts as conservative and white and 1960s efforts as poor and black. Robert Halpern, *Rebuilding the Inner City: A History of Neighborhood Initiatives to Address Poverty in the United States* (New York, 1995), focuses on low-income African American neighborhoods. On 1970s grassroots organizing, see Harry C. Boyte, *The Backyard Revolution: Understanding the New Citizen Movement* (Philadelphia, 1980).

42. *C&P*, May 6, 1950; GACC, "Building a Better Community Together"; *C&P*, November 19, 1955; *CP*, May 2, 1956; *CP*, April 29, 1965; *CP*, May 26, 1965; *CP*, June 16, 1965; *CP*, February 24, 1966.

43. *Mt. Pleasant Community Council Bulletin* (May 1956), NAACP-CB, container 38, folder 3; *Mt. Pleasant Community Council Bulletin* (April 1955), in ibid.; *CP*, August 17, 1961; *CP*, July 12, 1960; *CP*, November 3, 1966; *CP*, April 12, 1967; *CP*, June 13, 1967; "Proposal for a Summer Youth Employment Program," April 23, 1969, CBS, container 40, folder 749; *CP*, September 3, 1969; Sylvia Hood Washington, "Packing Them In: A Twentieth Century Working Class Environmental History" (Ph.D. diss., Case Western Reserve University, 2003), 286–87; "Harvard Community Services Center Plans for the Future."

44. *Mt. Pleasant Community Council Bulletin* (April 1955); undated newspaper clippings, "Mt. Pleasant Seeks Top Yule Lights" and "Mt. Pleasant Area Sells Lights for Fund," *CP* [ca. December 1958], both in "Mount Pleasant Community Council," CPC; *C&P*, January 5, 1963; *CP*, December 9, 1966; *CP*, December 11, 1967; *CP*, December 30, 1969; Minutes, GACC, Executive Board, October 1, 1945, JCC, Series II, container 5, folder 103; GACC, Annual Report, June 1948, FCP, container 28, folder 693; GACC, "Building a Better Community Together," 2; *CP*, December 17, 1965.

45. GACC, "Toward a Better Glenville—4th Annual Report," June 1949, FCP, container 28, folder 693; Minutes, Area Councils Committee, November 3, 1950, FCP, container 28, folder 674; *CP*, September 19, 1950; *CP*, September 28, 1951; *CN*, April 3, 1952; Petition, "Public Safety Committee, Glenville Area Community Council," January 12, 1955, LAJ; *CP*, February 11, 1959; MPCC, "1959 Annual Report," 11, NAACP-CB, container 38, folder 3; *C&P*, July 28, 1956; *C&P*, July 27, 1957; "Broadway Y.M.C.A. Outpost Daily Log, Jan. 2–21, 1959," and "Daily Log, Broadway YMCA Outpost," [February 1959], both in YMCA, container 33, folder 7; *C&P*, February 15, 1964.

46. *Lee-Harvard Community Association Newsletter* (May 1965); Rubie McCullough to James Norton, November 29, 1967, TCF, Series II, container 37, folder 884; *CP*, January 12, 1968; *C&P*, January 13, 1968; *CP*, January 16, 1968; *CP*, January 17, 1968; *CP*, January 18, 1968; *C&P*, January 27, 1968; *PD*, January 19, 1968.

47. *C&P*, January 27, 1968; *PD*, February 22, 1968; *CP*, April 11, 1968; *CP*, April 18, 1968; *CP*, June 4, 1968; *CP*, November 11, 1968; *PD*, November 8, 1968. The Corlett Area Council also looked into local option restrictions. See *CP*, May 5, 1969; *CP*, May 7, 1969; and *CP*, June 5, 1969.

48. *C&P*, June 7, 1958; *PD*, April 7, 1962; *CP*, May 2, 1962; Flyer, "The Value of Your Home

Is Being Threatened . . . ," n.d., LAJ; *C&P*, May 20, 1961; *C&P*, May 27, 1961; *CP*, December 21, 1967; *PD*, December 25, 1967; *C&P*, January 6, 1968; Minutes, "Brainstorming Group," February 10, 1973, RJM.

49. *CP*, March 22, 1967; *CP*, March 29, 1968; *CP*, May 12, 1948; *CP*, December 7, 1948; GACC, "Building a Better Community Together"; *CP*, December 6, 1957; *CP*, June 12, 1965; *CP*, September 17, 1951; *C&P*, December 11, 1954; *C&P*, May 8, 1954; Albert Mitchell to John McCormick, July 1, 1957, LAJ; *Glenville Bulletin* (September 1958), FCP, container 28, folder 693.

50. *CP*, March 24, 1961; *CP*, March 27, 1961; *CP*, April 24, 1961; *C&P*, April 29, 1961; *CP*, May 11, 1961; *CP*, October 1, 1964; *CP*, June 13, 1968; *CP*, August 22, 1968.

51. See Jon C. Teaford, *Cities of the Heartland: The Rise and Fall of the Industrial Midwest* (Bloomington, Ind., 1994); and Jefferson Cowie and Joseph Heathcott, eds., *Beyond the Ruins: The Meanings of Deindustrialization* (Ithaca, N.Y., 2003).

52. On education reform efforts in Mount Pleasant, Lee-Harvard, Lee-Seville, and Corlett, see Todd M. Michney, "Changing Neighborhoods: Race and Upward Mobility in Southeast Cleveland, 1930-1980" (Ph.D. diss., University of Minnesota, 2004), 342–46. Quality public education was also a concern in Glenville; see, for example, *CP*, October 21, 1959.

53. See especially Howard Aldrich and Albert J. Reiss Jr., "Continuities in the Study of Ecological Succession: Changes in the Race Composition of Neighborhoods and Their Businesses," *American Journal of Sociology* 81 (January 1976): 846–66, which found that white business turnover rates were unaffected by racial residential transition.

54. GACC, "5th Annual Report," May 1950, FCP, container 28, folder 693; GACC, 6th Annual Report (1951), in ibid.; GACC, "Building a Better Community Together," 2; GACC, "Tenth Annual Report," May 1955, LAJ; *GACC Bulletin* (February 1958), JCC, container 28, folder 16; *CP*, May 8, 1959; *CP*, July 26, 1960; "Glenville Area Analysis," [ca. 1960?], FCP, container 28, folder 694; *CP*, September 14, 1961; *CP*, August 7, 1961; *CP*, July 9, 1962; *CP*, April 11, 1963.

55. *PD*, April 22, 1950; *The Clean Sweep* (April 24, 1958), GCCUC, container 1, folder 1; *Mt. Pleasant Community Council Bulletin* (May 1958), in ibid.; *PD*, May 4, 1958; *CP*, November 13, 1958; *CP*, December 1, 1958; *CP*, December 4, 1958; *CP*, February 5, 1959; *CP*, February 12, 1959; *PD*, May 3, 1959; *CP*, May 2, 1959; *C&P*, December 6, 1958; *CP*, January 8, 1960; *CP*, January 12, 1960.

56. *CP*, May 12, 1960; Rich, "Report of Consultant," 14; *CP*, June 30, 1961; *CP*, August 7, 1961; *CP*, August 21, 1961; *CP*, September 18, 1961; *CP*, November 24, 1961; *CP*, November 28, 1961; "Preliminary Draft: Planning Settlement Service."

57. *CP*, October 18, 1963; *CP*, July 12, 1963; Cleveland Community Relations Board, "Report for 1963," CHR, container 3, folder 64.

58. *CP*, December 7, 1964; *CP*, December 1, 1964. For a black reminiscence on Jewish-owned businesses in Lee-Harvard, see John Baden, "Residual Neighbors: Jewish–African American Interactions in Cleveland from 1900 to 1970" (M.A. thesis, Case Western Reserve University, 2011), 66.

59. Cleveland Business & Economic Development Corp., "A Combined Feasibility Study & Market Analysis of Businesses in Cleveland's Mt. Pleasant Area," June 1, 1969, pp. 22, 29–30, 37, TCF, Series II, container 46, folder 1151; Memo, James Campbell to Urban League Board of Trustees, October 14, 1971, RJP, container 3, folder 48; "To the George Gund Foundation."

60. "Working Together to Build Good Neighborhoods"; *CP*, May 11, 1967; "Harvard Community Services Area: Description"; *Lee-Harvard Community Star* (February 12, 1970); Fisher, "Abandonment Study," 2, 9–12; "Harvard Community Center Plans for the Future."

61. Fisher, "Abandonment Study," 11; *CP*, February 4, 1970; *CP*, January 2, 1975; *CP*, January 18, 1972; *PD*, March 30, 1973.

62. For findings that residents interpret crime's significance selectively, with no clear correlation to out-migration, see Martin T. Katzman, "The Contribution of Crime to Urban Decline," *Urban Studies* 17 (October 1980): 277–86; and Richard P. Taub, D. Garth Taylor, and Jan D. Dunham, *Paths of Neighborhood Change: Race and Crime in Urban America* (Chicago, 1984). For evidence that homicide, at least, may link directly to population change, see Jeffrey P. Morenoff and Robert J. Sampson, "Violent Crime and the Spatial Dynamics of Neighborhood Transition: Chicago, 1970–1990," *Social Forces* 76 (September 1997): 31–64.

63. *C&P*, September 13, 1952; Memo, "To: Member Organizations," November 5, 1953, LAJ; *C&P*, December 15, 1951; *CP*, January 15, 1953; "Members, Public Safety Committee," December 1, 1954, LAJ; "How Safe Is Glenville?" January 1955, FCP, container 28, folder 693; *CP*, January 27, 1955; "Report of the Public Safety Committee, 1955–1956," LAJ; Memo, Leo Jackson to Deputy Inspector Mel Massey, February 27, 1956, LAJ; *CN*, March 31, 1955. For an illegal "basement bar" shut down in Glenville, see *C&P*, December 6, 1952.

64. Stanley Tolliver and William Hamilton to John McCormick, December 4, 1957, copy in LAJ; *CP*, August 21, 1958; *Glenville Bulletin* (September 1958), FCP, container 28, folder 69; *CP*, October 20, 1960; "Here and There," *Glenville Bulletin* (October 1960), TCF, container 4, folder 23; *CP*, July 6, 1966; "Meeting of the Board of Directors, Glenville Neighborhood and Community Centers," February 1968, KTNC, container 1, folder 4; *CP*, May 24, 1969; *C&P*, July 9, 1969. On the Glenville shoot-out, see especially Daniel R. Kerr, *Derelict Paradise: Homelessness and Urban Development in Cleveland* (Amherst, Mass., 2011), 171–80.

65. Minutes, Area Councils Committee, April 12, 1950, FCP, container 28, folder 674; "The Mount Pleasant Area Study," May 16, 1950, p. 14, FCP, container 49, folder 1175; Rich, "Report of Consultant," 13; Mount Pleasant Youth Action Council, "Proposal for a Program of Summer Outings," 2; *CP*, September 24, 1968; *CP*, July 3, 1969; *PD*, February 1, 1972; *CP*, August 11, 1972; *CP*, August 7, 1975.

66. *Lee-Harvard Community Association Newsletter* (May 1965); *CP*, May 11, 1967; *PD*, January 17, 1971; Rubie McCullough to Robert Bauerlein, May 3, 1971, CBS, container 12, folder 192; Harvard Community Services Center, "Program Development and Evaluation,"

August 31, 1972, TCF, Series II, container 37, folder 884; *CP*, January 20, 1972; "Harvard Community Services Center Proposal," May 31, 1977, RJP, container 82, folder 1277.

67. *CP*, November 26, 1969; *CP*, November 18, 1971; *CP*, November 11, 1971; *CP*, February 22, 1972; *PD*, January 17, 1971; *CP*, August 15, 1974; Lee-Harvard Urban League, Action Advisory Board Sub-Committee Meeting, February 27, 1975, ULC, Series II, container 1, folder 2; Urban League of Cleveland, Lee-Harvard Branch, Advisory Board Committee Meeting, October 15, 1975; *C&P*, May 31, 1975.

68. Early on, Richard A. Cloward and Lloyd E. Ohlin, in *Delinquency and Opportunity: A Theory of Delinquent Gangs* (Glencoe, Ill., 1960), discussed different motivations among various types of gangs, as well as cultural bias and problems of definition.

69. *CP*, November 20, 1952; *CP*, November 21, 1952; *CP*, February 5, 1953; *CP*, April 6, 1953; *CP*, April 23, 1953; GACC, 8th Annual Report; Benes, "Glenville Area Community Council"; *CP*, May 24, 1955; "Glenville Area Community Council's Current Program," [1959], FCP, container 28, folder 694; *CP*, June 17, 1963; "Excerpts from Two Meetings with Representatives of Teen-Aged Boys Clubs in Glenville—February 14 and 16, 1967," KTNC, container 2, folder 7; Minutes, Advisory Committee Meeting, United Youth Program, December 12, 1966, FCP, container 11, folder 264; Minutes, Advisory-Allocation Committee Meeting, United Youth Program, February 13, 1967, in ibid.

70. *PD*, January 26, 1954; *C&P*, February 20, 1954; *CP*, May 24, 1957; *CP*, February 5, 1958; *CP*, May 26, 1958; Minutes, Advisory Committee, United Youth Program, December 14, 1959, FCP, container 4, folder 91.

71. Henry Ollendorff to Wilson Clark, September 21, 1961, FCP, container 11, folder 250; Research Department, Welfare Federation of Cleveland, "Cleveland Police Department Juvenile Unit, Total Cases, 1962," October 1963, FCP, container 33, folder 820; Charles Vance and Ronald Glosser to James Norton, May 7, 1969, TCF, Series II, container 37, folder 888; *CP*, August 13, 1965; *CP*, September 14, 1965; *PD*, March 28, 1971.

72. Memo, Lee-Harvard Area Council Recreation Committee to Mt. Pleasant Community Center, [ca. 1963], GCNCA, container 4, folder 58; *PD*, February 10, 1967; *CP*, January 15, 1965; *PD*, December 13, 1968; *CP*, June 11, 1968; "One Year Review of the Harvard Community Services Center," ca. July 20, 1970, and the attached "Notes: Discussion Group No. 1" and "Harvard Community Services Review Committee: Discussion Group #2," both dated April 29, 1970, GCNCA, container 3, folder 53; "Harvard Review Committee: Discussion Group #3," April 29, 1970, in ibid.

73. *C&P*, September 18, 1965; Urban League of Cleveland, Lee-Harvard Branch, Action Advisory Committee Meeting, February 19, 1975, ULC, Series II, container 1, folder 2; *CP*, February 6, 1970; *CP*, October 30, 1973; *CP*, January 23, 1974; *PD*, January 29, 1974.

74. *PD*, February 4, 1974; *CP*, March 26, 1974; *CP*, February 27, 1970; *CP*, March 17, 1970; *CP*, October 7, 1970; *PD*, October 15, 1975.

75. *CP*, December 9, 1966; Minutes, Urban League of Cleveland, Lee-Harvard Branch, Action Advisory Committee Meeting, November 28, 1973, ULC, Series II, container 1, folder 2; *CP*, August 15, 1974; *CP*, September 10, 1981.

76. *PD*, February 25, 1985; "Newsletter, East 111th Street Club," July 7, 1981, Dovie Sweet Papers, WRHS, container 2, folder 31; *PD*, July 10, 1985; *CP*, September 7, 1979.

77. *PD*, February 25, 1985. For neighborhoods following trajectories similar to Lee-Harvard's, see Mary Pattillo-McCoy, *Black Picket Fences: Privilege and Peril among the Black Middle Class* (Chicago, 1999); and Rachel A. Woldoff, *White Flight/Black Flight: The Dynamics of Racial Change in an American Neighborhood* (Ithaca, N.Y., 2011).

Epilogue

1. See "Cleveland's Ward 1 Learns More about Its Roots from the Cleveland Restoration Society," http://www.cleveland.com/opinion/index.ssf/2016/01/clevelands_ward_1_learns_more.html (January 2, 2016).

2. For details, see W. Dennis Keating, *The Suburban Racial Dilemma: Housing and Neighborhoods* (Philadelphia, 1994); Andrew Wiese, *Places of Their Own: African American Suburbanization in the Twentieth Century* (Chicago, 2004), 70–91, 249–54; and Todd M. Michney, "Changing Neighborhoods: Race and Upward Mobility in Southeast Cleveland, 1930–1980" (Ph.D. diss., University of Minnesota, 2004), 384–93.

3. See the map, "Percent African American Population, 2010, Cuyahoga County," http://cua6.urban.csuohio.edu/nodis/gis_CBMaps.html (March 23, 2016). Cleveland was the fifth-most-segregated SMSA in that year, after Milwaukee, New York, Chicago, and Detroit (and narrowly trailing the latter two); see the spreadsheet at http://www.psc.isr.umich.edu/dis/census/segregation2010.html (March 23, 2016).

4. Kermit J. Lind, "The Perfect Storm: An Eyewitness Report from Ground Zero in Cleveland's Neighborhoods," *Journal of Affordable Housing and Community Development Law* 17 (Spring 2008): 237–58; Yanmei Li and Hazel A. Morrow-Jones, "The Impact of Residential Mortgage Foreclosure on Neighborhood Change and Succession," *Journal of Planning Education and Research* 30 (September 2010): 22–39; Jeffrey D. Dillman, "Subprime Lending in the City of Cleveland and Cuyahoga County," in *Where Credit Is Due: Bringing Equity to Credit and Housing after the Market Meltdown*, ed. Christy Rogers and john a. powell (Lanham, Md., 2013), 140–62.

5. See Table 2 in Dan Immergluck, "The Accumulation of Lender-Owned Homes during the U.S. Mortgage Crisis: Examining Metropolitan REO Inventories," *Housing Policy Debate* 20 (September 2010): 627.

6. Elvin Wyly et al., "Cartographies of Race and Class: Mapping the Class-Monopoly Rents of American Subprime Mortgage Capital," *International Journal of Urban and Regional Research* 33 (June 2009): 332–54; Jacob S. Rugh and Douglas S. Massey, "Racial Segregation and the American Foreclosure Crisis," *American Sociological Review* 75 (October 2010): 629–51; Meghan Kuebler and Jacob S. Rugh, "New Evidence on Racial and Ethnic Disparities in Homeownership in the United States from 2001 to 2010," *Social Science Research* 42 (September 2013): 1357–74. For context, see Melvin L. Oliver and Thomas M. Shapiro, *Black Wealth/White Wealth: A New Perspective on Racial Inequality*, 2nd ed. (New York, 2006).

7. See Figure 7 in Claudia Colton et al., "Facing the Foreclosure Crisis in Greater Cleveland: What Happened and How Communities Are Responding," *Urban Publications*, Paper 374 (2010), http://engagedscholarship.csuohio.edu/urban_facpub/374/ (March 23, 2016). The researchers also found that African American borrowers were saddled with subprime loans at two to four times the rate of whites, regardless of income.

8. See W. Dennis Keating and Thomas Bier, "Greater Cleveland's First Suburbs Consortium: Fighting Sprawl and Suburban Decline," *Housing Policy Debate* 19 (January 2008): 457–77.

9. See the map, "Change in African American Population per Square Mile, 2000 to 2010," http://cua6.urban.csuohio.edu/nodis/gis_CBMaps.html (March 23, 2016); and Robert L. Smith, "Census Data Reveals New Migration Pattern as Black Families Leave Cleveland," http://blog.cleveland.com/metro/2011/03/census_data_reveals_new_migrat .html (March 28, 2011).

10. As a point of departure, see Robert D. Bullard, ed., *The Black Metropolis in the Twenty-first Century: Race, Power, and the Politics of Place* (Lanham, Md., 2007).

Index

Page numbers in italics indicate illustrations.

market in, 6, 99, 108, 171–72, 191, 196, 212, 257; foreclosure crisis in, 258; Jewish population of, 11; land contract business in, 184–85; other cities compared to, 8, 9–10, 35, 52, 134, 135; population of, 5; public housing controversy in, 97, 98–100, 101–3, 108–15; reputation for good race relations, 10, 70, 134, 265n21; riot of 1966 in, 10, 178; urban renewal program in, 201–2; urban sprawl in, 258–59. *See also* Community Relations Board; Corlett; Glenville; Lee-Harvard; Lee-Seville; Mount Pleasant

Cleveland Area Church Federation, 70, 72, 75, 110, 147, 198

Cleveland Association of Real Estate Brokers (CAREB), 116, 121, 175, 187, 188

Cleveland Baptist Association, 166

Cleveland Board of Education, 76, 79

Cleveland Citizens' Committee on Newcomers, 200

Cleveland City Council, 123, 134, 183, 197, 248; and blockbusting, 176, 190–91; Leo Jackson as member of, 197, 202, 204, 223, 228, 247; and public housing controversy, 101, 107, 108, 111, 114; racial polarization in, 135–36

Cleveland Clearinghouse on Civil Liberties, 106, 107, 108, 113, 132, 133

Cleveland Development Foundation, 124, 232

Cleveland Federation of Labor, 110

Cleveland Federation of Settlements, 70

Cleveland Heights, Ohio, 66, 155, 257, 303n18

Cleveland Herald, 66

Cleveland Home Builders Association, 110, 118, 121

Cleveland Labor Committee for Human Rights, 181

Cleveland Metropolitan Housing Authority (CMHA), 64, 101, 108–9

Cleveland News, 102

Cleveland: NOW! development program, 233

Cleveland Plain Dealer, 127, 152, 165

Cleveland Press, 63, 152–53, 173, 218–19; Krawcheck blockbusting series in, 151, 160–61, 166–71, 175, 186, 189–90; Krawcheck "Negro Neighbors" series in, 66, 141, 148–49, 150, 162, 173, 181, 185–86, 189–90, 208–9

Cleveland Public Library, 21, 143, 158–59

Cleveland Real Estate Board, 101, 186

Cleveland Trust Co., 20, 29, 82, 84, 127, 180–81, 182, 213

Cobo, Albert, 10

Cole, Albert M., 180

Collins, Elmer E., 84

Collinwood, *14*, 81, *83*, 263n9

"Colorblind racism," 108, 136

Committee on Democratic Practices, 70

Committee on Negro-Jewish Relations, 73–74

Communist Party, 7, 11, 36, 47–48, 49, 51, 74–75, 275n78, 298n55

Community and neighborhood activism, 69–81, 220–21, 234–53; around businesses and storefronts, 244–46; around clean-up, 234–35; around crime control and vigilance, 217–18, 248, 249; around liquor availability and control, 237–38; around shopping centers, 241–43; around traffic safety, 239–40; left-wing, 74–75; as springboard into politics, 222–23. *See also* Glenville Area Community Council; Lee-Harvard Community Association; Mount Pleasant Community Council; Protest movements; Street and block clubs

Community Relations Board (CRB), 63, 87, 102, 107, 116, 122–23, 148, 219, 243; and blockbusting practices, 149, 168, 176, 187, 190–91; establishment of, 71; intergroup relations promoted by, 73, 77; and Stewart case, 10, 127, 133; on violence, vandalism, and intimidation, 134, 135, 144, 145–46, 147, 152, 160, 163, 165

Congress of Racial Equality, 75

Congress of Urban Men, 245

Construction companies: black-owned, 118, 119–22, 134, 159; white-owned, 122–25, 290n54

Cooper, Ernest, 203–4

Corlett, *14, 24,* 126, 139, *154,* 172–76, 199, 202, 225, 249; anti-blockbusting efforts in, 168, 174–75, 176; history of blacks living in, 46, 173; racial tensions in, 175–76, 253; street clubs in, 222

Corlett Area Community Council, 221, 235, 245, 249, 315n47

Corlett Homeowners Improvement Association (CHIA), 174–75

Cory Methodist Church, 75, 77, 85, 186, 247, 250

Council Educational Alliance (CEA), 28, 59, 62, 67, 71, 89, 155; efforts for racial tolerance by, 92–94

Council on Human Relations, 159

Cranbrook Builders, 123

Crime, 89, 242, 243, 244, 246–49; fear of, 79, 80, 92, 142, 174, 217, 241, 246, 248, 257; increase in rate of, 63, 89–90, 201, 240, 246, 248–49; and juvenile delinquency, 248, 249–50; neighborhood fight against, 246–49; stereotypes about, 216

Davis, Harry E., 32, 68

Davis, Harry L., 47, 48

Davis, Russell H., 51–52, 62, 63, 68

Deed restrictions, 6, 9, 13, 58, 101, 126, 129, 150; *Shelley v. Kraemer* invalidation of, 2, 60, 125, 127, 133

Deex, Oliver J., 87–88, 152

Demographic transition: and changes to income and educational levels, 197, 198–99; and class structure, 191, 197–98; in Corlett, 139; in Glenville, 81, 95–96, 139, 142–43, 150–51, 153, 176–77; in Lee-Harvard, 139, 165–72, 177, 193, 203; in Mount Pleasant, 54–55, 80, 81–82, 95–96, 139, 153–65, 176–77, 193; and neighborhood "decline," 185, 258; "tipping point" hypothesis, 139, 293n5; urban renewal as factor in, 202–3;

whites remaining during, 61–62, 153, 156, 158, 162, 164, 170, 186, 192–94, 198

Detroit, Mich., 172, 279n26, 288n33; hands-off approach to racial conflict, 10, 130; race riot of 1943 in, 70; white violence toward blacks, 8–9, 39, 99, 133, 146, 216

Dickerson, Ralph H., 117

Dillard, Roger N., 45–46

Dobbins, H. D., 135

Dombrowski, Leo, 114, 115, 174, 175

Domestic employment, 26–27, 33, 43, 53, 207

"Don't Buy Where You Can't Work" boycott movement, 48, 64

"Dual" housing market, 6, 99, 108, 171–72, 189, 191, 196, 212, 257

Dual-income families, 12, 18, 27, 33, 178, 199–200, 207–8, 217, 231–32, 249, 251, 254

Dubin, George L., *105,* 123–24, 199, 290n58

Du Bois, W. E. B., 6, 75

Dumping, 225, 235

Dunbar Life Insurance Co., 182–83

East Boulevard, 65, 150, 182, 225, 238, 256

East Cleveland, Ohio, 8, 92, 139, 179, 241, 256–57

Eastern Glenville, 28, 94, 95, 139–53

Educational levels, 197, 215

Electric Controller & Manufacturing Co., 103, 106–8, 114

Empire Savings & Loan Co., 20, 32, 53

Ephraim, Leslie, 119, 120

Episcopal Church of the Incarnation, 153

Ethnic diversity, 128; in Corlett, 172; Czechs, 13, 125, 127, 164, 172, 174, 181, 225; Hungarians, 21, 40–41, 46, 47, 125, 165; in Lee-Harvard, 125, 167–68, 291n67; in Mount Pleasant, 21–22, 36, 155; Poles, 41, 63, 103, 164, 172, 174, 175, 176, 179, 225. *See also* Italians; Jews; Southern and Eastern Europeans

Euclid, Ohio, 256, 257, 258

Evans, Fred (Ahmed), *140,* 247

Fagan, George W., 117, 121
Fair Housing Council, 195
Fair housing legislation, 182, 187, 188, 191, 194, 195
Feagler, Dick, 165
Federal Homes, Inc., 124–25
Federal Housing Administration (FHA), 118, 121, 122, 124, 182, 183, 185, 197; discriminatory policies of, 54, 82, 107
Federal National Mortgage Association (Fannie Mae), 123, 124
Federation for Community Planning, 153
Fellowship Lutheran Church, 153
First Mount Olive Baptist Church, 34
Fishman, Maurice, 122
Fleming, Thomas W., 46
Forbidden Neighbors (Abrams), 185
Foreclosures, 55, 183, 258
Foster, William Z., 75
Fowler, Joseph, 237
Franklin, William, 248
Fuldheim, Dorothy, 77
Future Outlook League, 2, 48, 50, 64, 74, 75, 131

Gambling, 76, 88, 89–90, 145, 207, 217, 246, 251
Gangs, 46, 63, 89, 143, 250, 251, 253, 254
Garb, Margaret, 13
Garfield Heights, Ohio, 101, 102, 108, 109, 256, 257, 258
Garfield Park, 52, 163–64, 298n53
Garvin, Charles, 39, 40, 144
Gassaway, Harold T., 106
Gas stations, opposition to, 115, 239
Geographic mobility, 3, 67; black, 2, 6, 7, 17, 35, 55–56, 256–257
George, Clayborne E., 48, 50, 129
"Ghetto" (term), 1, 2, 3, 13, 21, 46, 54, 84, 169, 178, 192, 203, 209, 215, 219, 262n4. *See also* "Second ghetto" concept
Gillespie, Chester K., 48, 50, 54, 59–60
Glenn, Alonzo L., 32
Glenn, Selmo C., 32, 38
Glen-Lee Civic Club, 103, 132

Glenville: after 1980, 256, 258; beach access struggle in, 45, 47, 48, 49; becoming slum ghetto, 3, 203; black homeownership in, 29, 55, 56, 58, 82, 84, 181, 182, 196, 197; black landlords in, 86–87; black-owned businesses in, 66, 84–85; blockbusting in, 68, 148–49; churches in, 34, 85; crime in, 89–90, 246–47; demographic transition in, 66, 81, 90–92, 95–96, 139, 142–43, 150–51, 153, 176–77; eastern, 28, 94, 95, 139–53; as "Gold Coast," 65, 66, 82, 87, 96, 225; growing poverty in, 200; homeowners' associations in, 59–60, 61, 62, 68, 71, 147–48; housing conversion in, 69, 85; housing prices in, 65–66; housing stock in, 68–69, 225; interracial frictions in, 63, 87, 95, 152–53; Jews in, 28, 61, 66–67, 81, 93, 139, 141–43; juvenile delinquency in, 88–89; as middle-class community, 13, 15, 33, 58, 106, 256; migration of blacks to, 65–67, 201, 203; Miles Standish section, 229; neighborhood activism in, 61, 62–63, 238–39, 254; neighborhood organizations and clubs in, 34, 207, 219, 235, 247, 254; occupations of residents in, 29, 31–33, 82; police shootout and riot of 1968 in, 247; population of, 55, 61, 66, 81, 139–41; prior to 1940, 28–33; swimming pool access struggle in, 51, 151–52; and urban renewal, 202, 308n52; violence, vandalism, and intimidation in, 51, 65, 144–47, 149–50; white responses to blacks in, 39–40, 67, 68, 150–51
Glenville Area Community Council (GACC): activities of, 74–79, 220, 235, 236, 239, 241–42; Community Relations Committee of, 143–44; formation of, 62–63, 69, 71; Home and Neighborhood Conservation Committee of, 77, 84, 226, 228; and housing conversions, 226, 228–29; interracial strategies of, 63, 76–77; Jewish participation in, 71, 78, 90, 144; and juvenile delinquency, 88–89, 250; Law Enforcement Commit-

Ludlow Area, 135, 168, 186, 212, 292n79
Ludlow Community Association, 135
Lysowski, Anthony P., 110–11, 113, 114, 123;
   and Stewart case, 128, 129, 131, 132

Maple Heights, Ohio, 97, 102, 109, 256, 258;
   early black enclave in, 124, 257
Maple Heights Home Owners Association,
   109, 111
Marshall, Harry T., 59, 223
Mayo, Leonard W., 62, 71
McCall, Robert C., 214, 215, 252
McCullough, Rubie J., 200, 201, 203, 217,
   219, 238, 251, 254
McGee, Willie (case), 75
McKinney, Wade Hampton, 117, 122, 129–
   30, 180, 201, 202
Meade, Emmett, 23, 26, 45
Merida, James, 39
Middle class, black, 6, 19–20, 58, 194, 256;
   and African American class structure, 6,
   12, 197–98, 207–12; and behavior socialization, 209–10, 218–19, 230–31; as category, 12, 82, 191; challenges facing, 179,
   225–26; downward mobility during
   Great Depression, 52, 54, 55–56; dual
   family incomes of, 7, 12, 18, 27, 33, 170,
   199–200, 207–8, 254; expanding housing
   options, 114, 185, 194–95, 212; homeownership as marker of, 12–13; insecurity of, 191–212; indifference on integration, 91, 148, 194, 196, 219; investment
   property, 15, 85, 86, 184; maintaining
   and improving houses, 69, 150, 161–62,
   186, 198, *204*; overcharged for houses,
   171, 176, 202, 227; overextended financially, 92, 196, 198, 199, 232, 254, 306n41;
   securing of loans by, 5, 123–24; status
   distinctions among, 206–9; and suburbanization, 8, 256; views and concerns of, 7–8, 62, 75, 79, 92, 114, 177,
   191–92, 234–35, 236
Miles Ahead, Inc., 246
Miles Heights, Ohio, *14*, 22, 53, 54, 58, 74,
   100–101, 103, 225, 263n9

Miles Heights Improvement Club, 222
Miles Heights Progressive League, 103,
   106, 107, 110, 112
Miles Island Homeowners Association,
   235, 239–40
Miles-Lee Civic Club, 103, 109
Miles Standish Conservation Associa-
   tion, 86
Mills, George E., 252
Moon, Roddy K., 28, 32
Montgomery Bus Boycott, 221
Moore, Albert, 217
Moore, Arthur, 119
Morgan, Robert P., 117
Mortgages, 5, 20, 29, 37, 123–24, 183; discrimination in obtaining, 29, 54, 65,
   82, 84, 180, 197; insurance for, 123, 182;
   lending by individuals, 6, 37–38, 273n52;
   second, 184, 196, 302n12; "sub-rosa," 173.
   See also Banks; Loans and lending
Mount Pleasant: after 1980, 258; black
   homeownership in, 18–21, 27–28, 36, 56,
   58, 65, 181, 197; black migration to, 22,
   67, 200, 201, 203, 204–7; blockbusting
   in, 160–61; business establishments in,
   42–43, 243–44; churches in, 33–34; community activism in, 74, 235, 237; crime
   in, 89, 248; demographic transition in,
   54–55, 67, 80, 81, 95–96, 139, 153–65,
   176–77; dual housing market in, 196;
   ethnic composition of, 21–22, 36, 155;
   history of, 21; housing conversion in,
   85–86; housing rehabilitation in, 233–
   34; housing stock in, 22–23, 225–26, 254;
   interracial relations in, 41, 87, 93, 137–38,
   158–59, 209–10; intraclass tensions in,
   208; Jews in, 21–22, 40, 42, 67, 80, 81, 93,
   94, 155–56; juvenile delinquency in, 89,
   250; Kinsman Heights section, 23, *24*,
   27, 36, 37, 39, 41, 55, 56, 81, 122, 153, 160,
   173, 174, 196; median income in, 198;
   occupational structure of, 25–27, 197;
   original black enclave in, 22–23, *24*, 34,
   36, 56, 153, 227; overcrowding in, 69;
   population of, 21, 67, 81, 153–55; poverty